TOWARDS THE
TWENTIETH CENTURY

THE MACMILLAN COMPANY
NEW YORK · BOSTON · CHICAGO · DALLAS
ATLANTA · SAN FRANCISCO

TOWARDS THE TWENTIETH CENTURY

ESSAYS IN
THE SPIRITUAL HISTORY OF
THE NINETEENTH

by

H. V. ROUTH, M.A., D.Lᴛ.

*Byron Professor of English Literature and Institutions
at the University of Athens*

NEW YORK: THE MACMILLAN COMPANY

CAMBRIDGE, ENGLAND: AT THE UNIVERSITY PRESS

1937

PRINTED IN THE UNITED STATES OF AMERICA
BY THE POLYGRAPHIC COMPANY OF AMERICA, N.Y.

CONTENTS

FOREWORD

It is hoped that this book may be of use to serious students of the nineteenth century, in that it presents the literature of that period in an aspect not often discussed, and, moreover, traces the survival of Victorianism in the minds of the last two generations. But the work is intended to be more than a treatise. It is an inquiry into ourselves as tested by our predecessors. *purpose*

When studied for this purpose, I have found that the great authors of the last century could not be explained by generalisations—streams of tendency, periods of transition, spirit of the age—such as text-books are bound to use. At least, not to any great extent. Now and then, under the lead of certain doctrines and discoveries, groups of individuals agreed to think alike. But the true sign of the times was spiritual isolation, not intellectual fellowship. Despite appearances, culture had become a personal problem, intimate and fundamental, both for the writer and the reader, and on both sides obscured by touches of disingenuousness. So it was necessary to concentrate on individualities, the most prominent, because the most representative. At the same time, it was necessary to penetrate deep below the surface in order to discover what their thoughts really meant to them and should mean to us.

It has also proved advisable to discuss some writers of other countries and ages. Our supposedly insular genius is astonishingly sensitive to foreign thought, and it is often difficult to see British culture in its proper perspective without reference to French, German, Greek or Latin influences. There is another reason. England may have absorbed all the ideas and ideals of Europe but (like any other country) she has not bestowed equal honours of recognition upon all. Some persuasions float vaguely through our land, influencing culture, but not adequately asserted by an

English spokesman. So in order to appreciate the value of this or that tendency, and to understand what it could produce, we must sometimes refer to a master-mind, who did not happen to be born in this island. But in any case no apology is needed for these inclusions. It must already be recognised that the study of English literature is more than the study of English books.

This book has not been produced without the help of others who are in no way responsible for its defects. I am under a great obligation to Dr W. Rose for allowing me to consult his two unpublished articles on Goethe's reputation in England; to Professor A. Wolf the philosopher who has listened to my most extravagant questions with more than philosophical patience; to Dr W. P. Barrett who has had the heroism as well as the generosity to revise the whole set of my proofs. I am especially grateful to Professor O. Elton. Under what particular circumstances he came to read the MS. and to make invaluable suggestions need not here be explained, but for that as for many other services I herewith render him my heartiest thanks, *scienti sciolus*.

H. V. ROUTH

"STARKES"
7 *March* 1937

CHAPTER I

The purpose of this spiritual history—Meaning of the word "spirit"—The nineteenth century contains the explanation of the twentieth—Mill's On Liberty *the turning point.*

It is not the purpose of this book to present a complete history of Victorian and Edwardian literature. Several excellent surveys of these periods have already appeared, and many more must surely be in preparation. My object is to select and discuss the prose and poetry which should contribute towards our present enlightenment and guidance, as a stimulant to thought and as an inspiration for conduct. Assuredly we are in need of both. The more one examines oneself and talks to other people, the more it becomes evident that what the twentieth century lacks is spiritual certainty. Other generations have passed through times of trouble and perplexity as formidable as ours without losing their self-possession. Our forbears have often had occasion to doubt each other, but without doubting themselves. In fact the human spirit often thrives on dangers and difficulties. What really ought to arrest our attention is the anomaly that dangers and difficulties are here, as ever, but the human spirit is not thriving at all. There is no undercurrent of intellectual and emotional earnestness in the varied activities of our age. No unity of mood amid all the diversities of opinion.

Perhaps it will in the end be proved that we have little to regret in this period of uncertainty and indifference through which we are passing. We may, perchance, be groping our way towards a more creative and spiritual existence, and our hesitancy and indecision may be due to impatience with anything less than the best. Be that as it may, the intervening phase, in which we are now labouring, is deadened by the worst of all spiritual poisons, the blight of aimlessness. The human being, who has the time and the disposition to think over these things, cannot reconcile himself to such a life and wait passively till his contemporaries drift with him into port. It is a spiritual necessity to know something of the course we are steering. Nor need we remain in complete ignorance. If we cannot any more visualise our goal, we can at least examine the tracks by which we entered these uncharted seas and so perhaps

real purpose

get our bearings. We may win to a glimpse of the future by looking towards the past. Such is the real purpose of this book. It aims at examining the atmosphere in which the human spirit has lived during the last eighty years or so, the influences which have shaped our motives, sentiments and imagination. Thus we may get some notion of the transformation, not in man's outward circumstances, but in his intimate self.

But where exactly are we to look for the data from which so much is expected? For answer, let the reader recall the attitude of the twentieth century to the nineteenth. It was over thirty years ago, at the end of the Boer War, that the British public came to the conclusion that Victorianism was dead, and the younger generation began to range forward as if it had just left this last enemy slain with the others on the veldt. Since then, as was natural, the progressives have begun to reconsider their hastiness and they have returned again and again to look at the corpse. There it still lies, but the more closely it is inspected the less substantial it appears to be. It begins to look more like a figment of our imagination. In the following pages we shall have ample opportunity for convincing ourselves that the nineteenth century does not stand for any established and widely accepted set of doctrines and principles, or even of ideals, as did the thirteenth, sixteenth, or eighteenth centuries. Spencer was a contemporary of Newman, Trollope of George Eliot, Hardy of Wilde, John Mill of Matthew Arnold, Browning of Tennyson. When we look on to the following generation we shall find that neither their knowledge, nor their beliefs, nor yet their outlook was unified. The ages of Ruskin, Darwin, Meredith, Butler and Kipling were intellectually more unstable than our own, and to that extent no less discursive, adaptable, open-minded and tolerant than the age which has produced Lytton Strachey, Galsworthy, H. G. Wells, D. H. Lawrence, Aldous Huxley, and encouraged Bernard Shaw in the dogmatism of his old age. So the Victorians were really in sympathy with the iconoclasm of our age. And it is now being discovered that they were something more. They may have left us many images which we find pleasure in breaking, but they have also provided the weapon with which to set about the work of demolition. Here again, the dissatisfied reader must wait for the evidence till he has read the pages which follow. At this stage it can only be affirmed that nearly all our most daring and destructive ideas were freely mooted among our fathers and grandfathers, and that we are living on the thoughts which they originated (or in their turn borrowed from their predecessors), especially when we condemn them as unprogressive.

So, for all these reasons, which will be justified later, it looks as if the passing of Victorianism was an illusion—as if we were merely continuing the culture which we claim to have cast behind us. And yet the twentieth century certainly dawned with the conviction that we had been born anew. There was a feeling of release and hopefulness with which young people entered on life and some older ones renewed their contact. It really seemed as if some burden, or at least restraint, had fallen away from the human spirit. New interests and enthusiasms sprang up; existence once more began as an adventure; and it was only natural, if unjustified, that "Victorian" became an expression of contempt. So something must have happened. Of course there were new theories and doctrines, but new impulses must have been liberated. It is the object of this book to trace the chain of causes which led up to that short-lived efflorescence and then again darkened us with doubts and denials, like travellers in a mist.

Where are we to look for these influences? It is usual and natural to answer that we should refer to the history of society, politics and industry; that the aggregate is always passing through a series of metamorphoses, moving on its myriad feet in a certain direction, and that the individuals submit to this process, not realising all that it implies. The inner man changes in adaptation to the changes outside. Such is undoubtedly the case to a very considerable extent. But in this book it is suggested that the deciding factor in our reactions will be found not so much in our environment, as in the tone and temper with which the individual faces it, in the content of his mind, his motives and impulses, his sense of values. As Spinoza has said, "unumquemque pro dispositione cerebri de rebus judicasse".[1] That is to say that the course of culture depends less on the sequence of events than on the sequence of ideas, and that if we are to understand ourselves, we must understand those forms and formulas by which our intellects have revealed or concealed our innermost feelings. In other words, we must look for an explanation of the present in the spiritual history of the immediate past.

As a first step we must explain what is meant by spirit and

[1] "Everyone judges his circumstances according to the complexion of his brain." *Ethics*, Pt I, Append.

spiritual. Both words will recur a thousand times in this volume for the simple reason that both are used again and again by the authors whose testimony we are going to examine. None of them has explained what he means by the expression, but all use it as frequently and consistently as if they had privately agreed on its significance. According to this agreement the word seems to contain a double implication. It implies, in the first place, that the speaker has cultivated a system of principles, an edifice of ideas, an ideology, which gives shape and direction to his plexus and nexus of thought. This framework, partly inherited, is cherished because it is congenial to the individual's aspirations; it helps him to contemplate humanity as a force capable of growth even to perfection; it suggests forms in which his own vitality can find imaginative self-expression. It differs according to different ages and temperaments: for instance, Dante could find the peace of self-fulfilment in the Will of God, Shelley in cultivating Beauty as a cosmic force. But in any case this comforting religion or philosophy, this reassuring theory of existence is the soil in which the spirit germinates. Such is the first implication. But before the nascent spirit can spring into full life, the dream must come true. The humanist must not only believe in his vision but be able to prove it in daily experience—be able to find his heart's desire reflected in the sights, sounds and eventualities of the world around him. This environment may at first seem to be as black as night, but when he becomes accustomed to the darkness, his spirit opens its eyes and discerns in outline the realities it seeks. It is in this adjustment of ideal to actual that the spirit finds its strength. One might almost say that it comes to life through an effort of self-recognition.

Such an explanation does not exclude the idea of religion, but it does exclude the specially doctrinal and pneumatological associations which once adhered to the word. In this secular, nineteenth-century sense, "spirit" might rise to the lips of any humanist (an agnostic, or a pagan, no less than a saint) and would connote an impulse towards intellectual or imaginative creativeness; not necessarily to the writing of poetry or the painting of pictures; but to the identification of one's best self with the best things. The human who succeeds in this adjustment will constantly be multiplying himself in his experiences, and even in the most platitudinous existence will create hill-tops from which to glimpse something rare and strange. Thus men go through life, trying to substantiate their ideas in their environment, in order to give their spirit scope. Even at the most favoured epochs the adjustment is seldom perfect, and at some other periods there seems to be no accord whatever between the man's spiritual needs and the life which he has to lead and to witness around him. At such times he relapses into the activities of a very highly organised animal, his thoughts mainly concerned with the welfare of himself and his associates, exercising his intellect as a defence against religious fear or self-contempt.

It need hardly be added that these spiritual adventures and experiments are at once the chief inspiration and material of literature. Their history is written in the sequence of poems, plays, novels, histories, sermons, essays and treatises which carry the culture of the nineteenth century on into the twentieth. As soon as these urges and enthusiasms take an artistic form, such as appeals to the intellect and fires the imagination, they bring to the surface another human aptitude which is of importance to our inquiry. This aptitude comes from what, for want of a better expression, might be called the obligation to service, which seems somehow to be rooted in our nature. Whether this sense is an inspiration from heaven, or a development of the social instinct, or whether it be that the more human beings are conscious of their powers, the more they realise their weakness, nevertheless it is true that no men or women are known to us who have not recognised some powers above them, accessible only through certain immaterial channels, powers which curb and control their existence. Equally true is it, that up to the present all human beings of all ages and countries have found their fullest felicity and development not merely in conforming to these powers, real or imaginary, but in thinking of them as something higher and nobler than their ordinary selves. This supernaturalism need not be anthropomorphic, nor even anthropopsychic; there is the widest diversity in the forms by which it expresses itself in the imagination. As extreme examples we can take on the one hand Coleridge's definition of religion as the binding (*religio-religatio*) of man's will to a Will which is greater than itself;[1] on the other hand Keats's assertion: "I have not the slightest feel of humility towards the Public—or to anything in existence—but the eternal Being, the Principle of Beauty, and the Memory of great men."[2] As we shall see, human

[1] See J. H. Muirhead, *Coleridge a Philosopher*, 1930, chap. I, § 1.
[2] To J. H. Reynolds, 9 April 1818.

beings may even go so far as to look in themselves for a God worthy to be served. They may even claim to be true to nothing but their own powers of thought. But whatever the authorisation, literature at its best is the commentary to this allegiance. You cannot render even a flower poetical unless you think of it as something more than a flower, as a type of beauty, an expression of Nature, or a creation of God. Did not Arnold in 1873 copy in his note-book "Das schöne (*sic*) ist eine Manifestation geheimer Naturgesetze, die uns ohne dessen Erscheinung ewig wären verborgen geblieben?"[1]

To sum up. We may conclude that literature expresses, amongst other things, the human instinct to justify our personal religion or philosophy in experience, thus giving expression to the spirit through art; and that as soon as these illustrations reach our intellect we become aware that we belong to something more than to ourselves. We wish to discover (or invent) a higher order of things, a supernatural or super-egoistic system in which we can play a more inspiring part than is possible in the otherwise un-illumined battle of life. We want an allegiance for the developing of the best in ourselves. So it results that literature helps to inspire us with motives; not by indoctrination; but by demonstrating that there is a significance in things worthy of our spiritual ambitions.

So in every age we find that the epics, allegories, dramas, essays, novels or lyrics are bound up with the particular ideas which at that particular time make life worth living. They smack of our religious, aesthetic, social, humanitarian or humanistic dreams. Sometimes they preach this idealism as a serious conviction, but their proper function is rather to live in its spirit, to raise common or even sordid things to the level of its pure, inspiring atmosphere. They teach the tone and tendency of our life-philosophy rather than its formulae.

And now, after this elaborate introduction, what does literature teach us about the spirit of the Victorian age and its subsequent dissolution? This also is a question which cannot be satisfactorily answered without full discussion and impartial evidence, as the following pages will testify. But it will help the reader if those conclusions are anticipated, and the problem to be discussed is

---

[1] "Beauty is a manifestation of the secret laws of Nature, which would have been forever hidden from us, but for this revelation." Emerson also quotes the passage in his essay on *Beauty*.

clearly stated at the outset. So let us begin by claiming that what
most impresses the student of this period is the show of confidence,
even the insistence with which the writers asserted each his own
adjustment, and his claim to have won to truth; the more ardent
and imaginative spirits wrote as if they were sure of themselves,
however much irritated by the uncongenial atmosphere around
them. They were at one with life. Not, of course, with the actual
circumstances in which they lived, nor with the opinions to which
they had to listen, nor generally with the government to which
they had to conform, nor even with the landscape they wished to
enjoy. But with something which these and such like things could
promise to become. No man of culture, they might say, ought to
be content with his environment, but luckily that environment is
transparent. Through and beyond it he sees another world. If he
can discern therein the things that he wants to do, to think, and
especially to feel, if the intervening curtain of real life seems in
moments of insight or inspiration to be diaphanous and yielding to
the touch, he is at one with life. So one does not think of adjustment to circumstances—to appearances—but to their fuller, more
perfect development which can be glimpsed beyond.

But of course this union of spirit with environment depends on
two conditions. In the first place the humanist must know what
he wants to see. The illusive yet intractable mechanism of this
world encircles him like a wall; it will not give place to his insight
unless he has thoughts to project. And, in the next place, the
humanist must be confident that the veil can be pierced. It is not
enough to be conscious of the world within, he must also be convinced that the world without will yield to its visions. Now the
Victorians amply fulfilled the first of these two conditions. They
started on the period of post-Napoleonic reconstruction and expansion, with three centuries of culture and hard thinking to
guide them. They were the culmination of a great movement
inaugurated by Erasmus, Luther, Descartes, Bacon and Shakespeare. What does it matter that these streams seem to diverge
into different channels? If they divided men according to their
temperaments and training, they united them in the activity of
the spirit. They all gave human beings something to live by. But
such hopes of self-fulfilment and self-expression were not realised
by the next two generations. Between the 'forties and the 'fifties,
though this adjustment was insisted on more vigorously than ever,
yet the adjustment was lost. It could not be otherwise, since the

second condition was no longer fulfilled. Life no longer gave scope to the activities of the spirit.

It will readily be understood that this disharmony did not arise from any changes in the political or economic situation; nor was it due to any purely educational or academic developments. The soul of man, as has been said, thrives on opposition and disappointments. Besides, the history of the mid-century presents us with no discords and failures except those which seem to be inseparable from the progress of a great modern nation. The explanation is rather that even at the height of social, political and commercial prosperity life-experience became indued with a quality which resisted spiritual penetration. The individual's better nature did not seem able to expand amid the exigencies and contradictions of this triumphant civilisation. The man of letters seemed to feel that his soul could no longer work for the same spiritual masters. He might still be convinced that there are supernatural influences, but they did not inspire the same spirit, much less move in the old directions. He had learnt or unlearnt so many things about them that they had ceased to call to his impulses with the same voice of friendly authority. Thus while engineers, economists, politicians, men of science and humanitarians were busy improving and facilitating the machinery of our corporate life and organising reforms, for which it is impossible to be too grateful, another set of thinkers were wondering how to preserve their spiritual identity in this world of changing experiences.

As the century advanced, new and ever newer ideas crowded jostling into one's thoughts, confusing the individual's consciousness of his own nature; and at the same time the world without became less and less congenial to his search for self-reflection. So it became increasingly difficult to find scope for the emotional and imaginative reactions of the individual—to live the life which civilisation imposed without sacrificing one's sense of human grandeur, integrity and permanence. The humanists of the mid-century had first to feel within themselves that the spirit of man had retained the possibilities, of which their fathers and grandfathers had no doubt, and then they had to justify this assurance. How was the old-fashioned serenity and self-confidence to be recovered? The choice lay between seeking help from the past or surrendering wholeheartedly to the present. On the one hand, both poets and prose-writers could continue to cultivate the older well-proven humanism which had for so long satisfied the aesthetic and moral senses, giving to this treasured inheritance just a touch of modernity, a flavour of social and scientific interest, so as to impose it on the changing surface of experience. On the other hand, they could embrace the flux and metamorphosis of their time with both arms, and create something for their thoughts as unprecedented as their daily lives—something as fundamentally independent, expansive and adventurous—a reflection of the uncertainties around them.

It was, perhaps, inevitable that the Victorians should choose the former alternative. From about 1830 to about 1880 we find that humanists, humourists, moralists and poets still for the most part looked back to the older culture as their source of spiritual strength and clung to its well-tried wisdom as a guiding-light in their perplexities and as an inspiration to compensate for their disillusionments. The more difficult their task became, the more earnestly they pursued it. They insisted on interpreting the complex and enigmatical present by the light of the past. They poured new wine into old bottles, not because they were afraid of the wine, but because the bottles were too good to be lost. Even Swinburne convinced himself that the happiness and self-fulfilment denied to nineteenth-century Christians was really here, all around us, easily enjoyed; you had only to acquire nineteenth-century hellenism at Oxford. That is why Victorian literature, though full of conflicting creeds, and incompatible ideals, has preserved, at its most characteristic period, this one common quality—the affectation of adjustment. The writers were all quite clear-headed and purposeful about the questions which they put to life; they were even more persistent in exacting suitable answers; and they ransacked the literary expressiveness of the past, exhausted every artistic resource, to render those responses persuasive and convincing. So it looked as if they had solved their problem and were at one with life. Yet in reality they were hastening the reaction and intensifying its effects. To begin with, their inspiration was not wholly spontaneous; they were over-anxious to convince themselves and their readers; they were not, like Keats, content with "gusto".[1] This advocacy was bound to weaken their influence, because literature at its best leaves half to the goodwill and imagination of the reader. For instance, Wordsworth's immortality is partly due to the tact with which he introduces a simple situation, inspires a pensive mood,

[1] To R. Woodhouse, 27 Oct. 1818. Letter 88. M. B. Forman, *The Letters of John Keats*, vol. I, 1931.

and then leaves the reader free to follow his own contemplation. But the Victorians sacrificed fascination to eloquence; and in cultivating persuasiveness they lost the power to persuade. And in the next place, they unwittingly prepared the way for their critics, and made their opponents' task easier, because, through their very earnestness, they allowed themselves to become specious. However sincere they believed themselves to be, there is something disingenuous in the way they over-emphasised their arguments, and even falsified their illustrations. And lastly, by their mere insistence on the wisdom and artistry of the past, the Victorians helped to intensify a desire for change. So the younger writers, always eager for innovation, made too much of their opportunities. They set themselves to capture the sympathy and the understanding of their generation by a literature which should be as new and un-expected as life, and then found that they had unlearnt how to live.

When did this change of attitude really begin to take place? It is extremely difficult to say. The reaction had become an established fact (as has been said) after the Boer War, but signs of impatience and two-mindedness are easily recognised (as will be shown) as early as the 'seventies or even the 'sixties. Whereas the ideas which disintegrated Victorianism begin to germinate much earlier still, almost before Victorianism was established. But it often happens that some independent and self-assertive character catches these subterranean influences and gives them prominence by his words or acts. Can some such event be found, in order to give precision to our thought?

Various dates have been suggested: 1847, when Helmholtz read his paper to the Physical Society of Berlin on *The Conservation of Energy*; 1859, the year in which *The Origin of Species*, *The Ordeal of Richard Feverel* and *Adam Bede* were published; 1860, when Gari-baldi founded modern Italy and gave to Europe a new ideal by winning the battle of Calatafimi; 1861-5, the years of the American Civil War; 1866, the date of the Treaty of Prague, which founded the German Empire and thus gave a new direction to the politics and civilisation of all Europe; 1870, the year of the Elementary Education Act. One might even be tempted to add to the list the "Act for Regulating the Gauge of Railways" of 1846, for this interconnection of separate systems rendered the population un-stable and created internal trade; two conditions which have never ceased to react on our habits and thoughts. But it will be noticed that none of these events necessarily contained the germ of the

new spirit. Each might have proved an occasion for strengthening
the Victorian ideal of adjustment. Each might have helped to
confirm the humanists in their search for certainties. All depended
on the use which was to be made of such ventures, and the spirit
in which they were approached. Even the ideas put forward by
George Eliot, Darwin and Meredith could have been interpreted
and applied in a conservative spirit. None of these events need
necessarily have unsettled men's motives or have sent the next
generation looking for new ideas on happiness, duty, God, pleasure,
destiny and themselves. The impulse must have come from elsewhere; they only gave it so many opportunities.

If that be so, it would be better to look for some manifestation
which is less specialised and more explicit; which reveals a change
of mood rather than of habits, and we shall find what we seek in
another book which appeared in this same year, 1859, J. S. Mill's
On Liberty. To understand the significance of this work, it should
be remembered that many of the most typical Victorians, including
Newman, Tennyson, Carlyle, Froude, Gladstone, Arnold and
MacCall, repudiated his challenge with indignation. At first sight
their criticisms seem indefensible—mere confessions of middle-
aged prejudice. J. S. Mill demanded complete liberty for "that
portion of a person's life and conduct which affects only himself",
extending his claim to "absolute freedom of opinion and sentiment
on all subjects",[1] and this assertion of independence was not very
subversive nor indeed very new. The right to be wrong had often
been claimed before. Lessing is said to have asserted that if God
Almighty were to offer him the truth, he would refuse, preferring
the labour of finding it out for himself.[2] Helvetius insisted that "Il
est utile de tout penser et de tout dire" and declared that men can
never reach a reasonable conclusion till they have exhausted all
possible errors on the way.[3] Towards the end of the eighteenth
century G. C. Lichtenberg wrote in his note-book: "Die Wahrheit
finden wollen ist Verdienst, wenn man auch auf dem Wege irrt."[4]
Coleridge influenced Mill by "his theory and practice of enlightened tolerance in matters of opinion",[5] maintaining "we have
imprisoned our own conceptions by the lines which we have drawn

---

[1] Chap. I.   [2] Eckermann, *Gespräche mit Goethe*, 11 April 1827.

[3] *Livre de l'Esprit. Catechisme*, Première Partie.

[4] *G. C. Lichtenbergs Aphorismen, nach den Handschriften* herausgegeben von A.
Leitzmann, 1902: "It is profitable to wish to find the truth, even if one goes
astray.   [5] *London and Westminster Review*, March 1840.

in order to exclude the conceptions of others".[1] Keats felt that "the only means of strengthening one's intellect is to make up one's mind about nothing—to let the mind be a thoroughfare for all thoughts. Not a select party."[2] Emerson advanced the same kind of protest in his essay on *Self-reliance*, especially "Society everywhere is in a conspiracy against the manhood of everyone of its members" and "What have I to do with the sacredness of traditions if I live wholly from within?" All these quotations contain or imply contentions such as Mill advanced. In fact he was reasserting what the more progressive minority of the previous generations had often dared to claim. But he argued more aggressively and in this aggressiveness we can perceive the originality and significance of the essay. It is addressed to a generation which knows all about free thought and free speech and thinks that it now knows something better.

For what did the humanists of the nineteenth century believe? They believed in the fellowship of the human spirit; men and women must be agreed on certain truths or they would never be worthy of themselves, nor even hold together in this changing deceptive materialistic life. Certain convictions and observances unite them amidst all the egoism and competition necessitated by modern civilisation. Thus they were often ready to conform to ritual, traditions and conventionalities, which might in themselves be inadequate. What did inadequacy matter, since they somehow felt that they were celebrating their common allegiance to the higher powers? They were joining in an act or thought which involved them in something more universal than their private considerations. An idea or an ideal was ten times more valuable if it could be *shared*. So they tried to reserve an area on which their religious and philosophical differences might be forgotten in the claims of humanity and spiritual kinship. After such mutual confirmation they could pass on more hopefully to the service of progress. For the same reason they were bound to resent the intrusion of heresies, if openly professed. A thinker might feel it his duty to expose some fallacy, but he must beware; he might weaken the bond which held society together. Some creeds and causes were too sacred to be tampered with; they were the passwords to spiritual fellowship.

Such was the creed which Mill attacked when he tried in this book to release the human mind from every other influence except

---

[1] *Biographia Literaria*, chap. XII.
[2] To George and Georgiana Keats, 17 Sept. 1819.

logic. *On Liberty* looks forward to a time when educated people will have no allegiances, and no convictions which are too precious to be disproved or too profoundly intimate to be capable of disproof. We shall have only opinions which are so far valuable to each as they provide material for discussion. So it then appeared to many. We of this present age can see that their apprehensions were not without some measure of justification, but yet Mill's essay was much more than the product of a "logic-chopping machine". Man was not to be a mere will-o'-the-wisp, the sport of every wind of vain doctrine. The generations of the future were to have their own fraternity, which should ennoble them and give them peace. But it was to be a fellowship, not of creeds, but of self-reliant inquiry. Mill recognised the infinite variety of men, even in conventional England, but pictured them united in one common privilege: the right to use their brains. All fellow-creatures, however different, even his own opponents, were to be one with him in intellectual restlessness, in the resources of the mind. So they would attain to their full stature as human beings. So, also, they would recognise in each other the tokens and passwords, which lead to the highest freemasonry. Renan was cherishing much the same idea when he wrote "L'Esprit Moderne, c'est l'intelligence réfléchie".[1]

These far-reaching presumptions are only implicit in Mill's essay. He was, himself, too embarrassed with the actual disabilities and inconsequences of his own time to give himself freely to such speculations. Yet nevertheless such is the significance of his book, at this stage of our inquiry.

Such is also the reason why the younger generation was as ready to applaud as their elders were ready to condemn. If we are to believe Thomas Hardy,[2] the students of about 1865 knew the book almost by heart, and Kingsley declared that it made him "a clearer-headed and braver-minded man on the spot".[3] Yet what attracted them was not merely the incitement to iconoclasm. Having now been encouraged to shake off what Humboldt called "the deep slumber of a decided opinion", they were beginning to appreciate an unexpected advantage in being awake. It brought them a new kind of self-knowledge. As they sat in judgment on the gods outside, they discovered the god within—the unlimited power to reshape their own minds, to create, destroy and recreate

---

[1] *L'Avenir de la Science*, chap. III: "The Modern Spirit is simply intelligence steadied by thought." [2] To *The Times*, 21 May 1906.

[3] *Life of Kingsley*, vol. II, p. 88. Quoted by E. Neff in *Carlyle and Mill*, 1926.

the world of thought; for such people the only world which really exists. Those who were not so metaphysically minded could yet derive encouragement and worldly wisdom from the book. It convinced them that to be free a man need not be a bohemian, an eccentric, a strayer from the drove, a Richard Horne, a Mr Cypress or a Mr Scythrop.[1] In his daily habits he ought to be, and perhaps must be, the slave of society, but in his daily thoughts and sentiments he can and should keep himself untamed by the world.

Even when full allowance has been made for all these consequences, Mill's protest cannot be hailed as a daringly original stroke for intellectual freedom; and the spirit which he kindled would have been less worth studying, if he had raised his voice in the Athens of Socrates, the Florence of the Medici, the Paris of Mme de Rambouillet, or even in Lord Chesterfield's drawing-rooms. But it was heard in the London of Queen Victoria, provoked by a new kind of compulsion, and nourished by a new kind of restlessness. On this background, the book assumes an unexpected significance. It implies a half-unconscious protest against an inheritance which had become unmanageable. Culture had gradually accumulated so many ideas, notions and doctrines and had devised so much machinery for disseminating them, that nearly everyone could hold and propagate opinions without taking the trouble to think them out. They did not possess their beliefs; they merely owned them at second hand; but they claimed the same authority as the originators were entitled to claim. In de Gaultier's[2] phrase, they were like men who use a currency so freely that they believe it to be stamped with their own image. So they lost in self-possession what they gained in facility. This education by hearsay was to become one of the great difficulties of the age, and that is why Matthew Arnold so often complained of the intellectual superficiality of his time, and why Samuel Butler, Nietzsche, Bergson and even Hardy, distrusted ideas. *On Liberty* insisted that we need not add to our culture, but that we must sort it out for ourselves.

Thus there are many reasons why Mill's essay helps us to understand the issues which were being brought to a head. We may take his carefully argued thesis to be the chief clue to the dissolution which would have ensued without his agency.

[1] Names under which Byron's and Shelley's unconventionality is caricatured in T. L. Peacock, *Nightmare Abbey*, 1819.

[2] J. de Gaultier, *Le Bovarysme*, 1902, chap. i, §4.

CHAPTER II

The nineteenth century dawns in hope—The inspiration of romanticism and transcendental philosophy—Will succeeding generations be able to honour these ideals?

So it may be assumed that Mill's essay *On Liberty* was more than a protest against the drift and tendency of mid-Victorian culture. It was an assertion of something which that culture could no longer satisfy. The book justified spiritual wilfulness; it argued that free-thought was its own reward. In fact, the doctrines would have spread more rapidly and would, perhaps, have hastened the crisis, if they had not been so exclusively addressed to the reasoning faculty. Mill championed the freedom of the intellect too intellectually. If only he had not argued his case with such austere self-effacement, but had invested his attitude with the life and picturesqueness of personality, as Montaigne, Addison, or De Quincey would have done, he might have moulded these inclinations into a type or symbol or figure-head which appeals to the imagination, and have given to his age what Keyserling afterwards called a *Lebensform*.[1] That is to say, he might have hung a pattern in each reader's head by which to shape his aims and habits. As it was, the utilitarian confined himself to proving that one's own way was the most advantageous way. He exhausted every resource of logic to convince others of the wisdom of thinking for themselves.

But why did Mill need to labour his case so carefully? Why elaborate such delicately balanced arguments, addressed to the most thoughtful and serious-minded intellects of his time? Why single out the trustees of posterity as his special audience and appeal to their sense of justice and social responsibility? Because, at that time, the issue was not clear. Much more than bigotry and intolerance were involved. Social, political, religious, industrial and domestic life had developed unexpectedly, dividing and diversifying the judgments of mankind, even where men of goodwill might otherwise have held together; and with each successive crisis the highest as well as the lowest elements in human nature

---

[1] *Die Neuentstehende Welt*, 1926. [Defines culture as *Lebensform als unmittelbarer Geistesausdruck*: "A mode of life so conceived as to express the spiritual values."]

had come to the surface, often ranged on the same side. Thus the movement towards spiritual independence was to assume a peculiar character and direction because of the many-sided and inconsistent opposition which it encountered. In fact we cannot understand the new spirit without understanding the wealth and depth of sentiment which stood in its way and deflected or diversified its course. Mill is only one influence out of many, but one of the first; and in order to see how his idea was manœuvred into victory we must understand what his supporters and opponents expected from life. For this purpose it is necessary to take a glance backward at the train of ideas which began with the beginning of the century.

The first two or three decades ought to be reckoned among the most fateful in the history of nineteenth-century culture. We have to thank them for some of our most sacred enthusiasms and most disconcerting perversities. But the writers of that time were quite unconscious of what they were preparing for their descendants. At any rate the young men seem to have entered upon life as if it were a newly discovered country illuminated by a dawn of boundless possibilities. Their enthusiasm was not due to the political situation, nor to the social conditions under which they soon realised that they would be forced to live, much less to any expectation of worldly comfort or plenty. No one with a spark of idealism could congratulate himself that the world was being refashioned to suit his visions. Perhaps it was just as well. Poets and men of letters do not really want a perfect world; they want a world which is always challenging their own unworldly sense of perfection. So it was with the moralists and visionaries of this time. They were not paralysed by the weakness and wickedness outside, because they had discovered an inexhaustible source of strength and goodness within. What was the mainstay of this group of writers who had nothing to hope from their own limited and often disease-stricken existences, nor from the social order to which they seemed to be condemned, who despaired of *men* without despairing of *man*, and between them created the romantic movement? They were convinced that nothing earthly could now conquer the human soul, because it was *proved* to be of more than earthly temper. They were upheld and encouraged by the philosophical doctrines so eagerly discussed in Germany. The new country of the dawn which they were entering was the world of metaphysical thought.

Poets and humanists do not often seek help from philosophy.

They abhor the Euclidean subtlety and the most un-Euclidean obscurity in which these speculators, except Plato and Pascal, generally involve their researches. Besides, they were disconcerted by the trend of eighteenth-century thought. So we should not have expected nineteenth-century culture to begin by embracing abstract theories. Yet such was the chief inspiration of the age, and it came about in this wise. Reasoners from Locke to Hume had tried to convince their contemporaries that we know nothing of life except through the five senses, or rather, through the six senses, including hunger. Our finest and most spiritual perceptions were limited to these unreliable and incomplete channels. Thus each human being lives, as it were, a sort of dream-ridden sleep. Ideas, according to Berkeley, were the copies of impressions; the soul, according to Hume's *Treatise of Human Nature*, was "a bundle of perceptions that succeed each other with inconceivable rapidity, and are in a perpetual flux". There had, of course, always been thinkers who insisted on the sacredness of intuition, and the possibilities of spiritual contact with the realities beyond sense-experience—for instance, Plato, the Neoplatonists, Bruno, Boehme, Shaftesbury and Hamann. Idealists could keep to these older teachers, but if they trusted themselves to think in the modern spirit, in the light of their own time and country, they found that their reason had become the enemy of their souls. So before the end of the eighteenth century humanists were well aware of a rift in their culture. You had to risk your inward convictions on which your spirit thrives, or content yourself with a *Glaubensphilosophie*— a philosophy of faith. Beattie, a theologian and poet, tried to reconcile the two attitudes in *An Essay on the Nature and Immutability of Truth* (1770), arguing that even when you follow your own logic to its conclusion you have in the end to rely on an "internal sense" of truth. At long last, even when accepting one of Euclid's deductions, it is the instinctive act of thinking, not the manufactured piece of evidence, which decides. An axiom cannot be proved but only recognised. So there must be behind the brain some spiritual power bound up with the intellect. "Nihil est in intellectu quod non fuerit in sensu, nisi intellectus ipse",[1] said Leibnitz, correcting Locke. Beattie pushed that principle to its logical conclusion, and forty years later Mme de Staël was able to declare that it made the new philosophy possible.[2]

[1] "There is nothing in the intellect which cannot be traced back to the senses, except the intellect itself."   [2] *De l'Allemagne*, Troisième Partie, chap. 5.

All through the nineteenth century imaginative thinkers clung to this assurance of their inborn personality. But it is doubtful whether even the most confirmed visionary could long have maintained that attitude, if left to the resources of eighteenth-century culture—especially as the new learning was to bring overwhelming arguments against the old idea of human dignity. But just when the humanist was most tempted to regard himself as a spiritualised thinking machine, a group of German philosophers gave new life to metaphysics, and a group of English poets showed how any educated man could apply their doctrines to his mode of life.

This school of thinkers demonstrated that the most intensified exercise of the intellect need not leave the spirit unsatisfied. The reason did not close up the outlets of the imagination, nor stultify the yearnings of our innermost being. The seventeenth and eighteenth centuries were mistaken in so far as they taught that all we know of ourselves and of God originates in the evidence of our senses. They were wrong when they argued that an impression comes from nothing real, being itself the only reality; that man by his very nature is excluded from contact with the boundless spirit world, of which he once believed himself to be a part. On the contrary, the more we give the rein to our aspirations and idealisms, the more surely we penetrate to the realities within us and without. We might have to resign the old systems to which our forefathers were proud to belong, but in exchange we were offered another superterrestrial world which we could explore by exploring ourselves. This revelation gained in power because it came as a counterblast to the age of reason. It filled its believers with a sense of release and exhilaration, such as a mountaineer experiences. He leaves the picturesque village in the green valley with all its varied and narrow homeliness, for the mountains which overshadow it, and after a toilsome climb, he finds himself in a land of far-flung, pure outlines, and towering peaks. He loves the wild crags and stretches of glacier all the more because he feels that he can conquer them.

These were not dreams; they were founded on arguments—or at least so it seemed. The man who contributed most to this possibility was Kant. He subjected the operations of the mind to a searching examination, and concluded that it was not solely receptive in its attitude, much less confined to the evidence of the senses. It does not merely construct itself and take shape out of contacts with the outside world. It has ideas of its own, independent of external impressions, precontained in the intelligence, and it brings these to bear on experience. Having found, according to its own lights, that certain impressions occur and always recur, that, in fact, it is impossible to conceive of anything contrary to these impressions, it frames these notions into laws and imposes them on nature. Thus the mind takes up a creative attitude, expressing itself, for instance, in such ideas as relationship, existence, causality, unity, plurality. These were Kant's famous categories, and at first it would appear that they were not enough to inspire poets and humanists with the hope of finding a new world. They represent life as only a piece of sealing-wax on which the human mind stamps its own impress; and Kant would be forced to admit that we can know no more for certain. But whence comes the design on the seal, and the impulse to impose on the wax a regularity and grace of outline, quite alien to its natural composition? In answering that question the philosopher demonstrated that this spontaneity is the proof of superterrestrial urges and affinities. If we mentally refashion matter it is because our minds are framed on an immaterial plan; we have an inkling of something wider and deeper than experience. This creativeness works by means of the senses, but through their aid it tends towards ultimate reality, the *Ding-an-Sich.*

Encouraged by these convictions, Schelling showed how the mind could arrange itself so as to bring the Absolute within the reach of our intellect. Reality in its simple purity was beyond our ken. But we can recognise, not indeed its essence, but its influence and presence in ourselves, and in the world outside us. We do so in the different branches of learning. The sciences are, of course, the fruit of our observation and of our thought; they are shaped into systems by our powers of reasoning; to that extent, and in that sense, they are subjective. But they do not turn the eyes inward, they aim at making us conscious of something outside ourselves—of forces and conditions quite independent of our mentality—each is an aspect of what is absolute and universal. We enter into their meaning so far as we can forget our earthly selves and understand this or that manifestation of God. To that extent the sciences are objective. Each is a picture of the soul of the world. If we can gain insight into these secrets; then each step in knowledge must be an awakening of some other-worldly strain in our nature. The spirit within is reaching to the spirit without. Thus Schelling demonstrated that there was something mystic and sacred in learning. Our modern pedestrian culture should lead to a vision more cosmic than those which were vouchsafed to Dante in Paradise. Only, of course, our sciences must no longer be pedestrian. Up till then, the investigator had trusted to the mechanism of the human brain, a fallible and defective interpreter. But the eyes of the soul can see further than the eyes of the mind, so the spirit must join in the search. It must bring to bear its imagination, its sense of beauty and order, its yearning for the infinite, since these are the qualities through which man transcends himself and approximates to the Absolute. If human knowledge is to touch heavenly wisdom, the spirit must enlarge the intellect, that is to say, poetry becomes the sum and crown of all knowledge. Thus Schiller could exemplify the divinity of human nature out of history which Gibbon described as a record of "the crimes, follies and misfortunes of mankind"; thus Wordsworth could detect spiritual presences in nature which d'Holbach dismissed as "dépourvue de bonté comme de malice...en produisant et détruisant des êtres".

But poetry implies self-discovery. Those who write or read verse, do not take things as they find them; they become responsive, they give the rein to their emotions, they consult their own reactions. They are guided by their inborn sense for spiritual things. If, then, the inquirer must trust to his own orientations, he must study himself. So it was interesting to hear that a certain J. G. Fichte was appearing as the prophet of individualism, and could prove that each man's complex and inexplicable *ego* was his chief title to Truth. Our spontaneous urges and appetencies guide us towards Reality. When we are most our own peculiar selves, we are nearest to mastering the Absolute. Thus Kant's *Ding-an-Sich* became *Ich-an-Sich*. We can never reach the Infinite because we are finite, but these individual gropings are not wasted; they are the truest expressions of our kinship with the divine; the only efforts by which humanity can transcend itself. So an immense importance should be attached to the indulgence of personality.

Hegel had something even more elevating to teach. He was supposed to argue that the individual spirit is not merely an approximation to the Absolute; it is the Absolute itself, made real in experience, through the power of thought. If so, the changes, chances and conflicts which take place in our minds and make up our emotional and intellectual being are of the greatest significance. They are nothing less than moments in the self-expression of Reality. Thus what Beattie termed "the internal sense" could now be understood in Coleridge's phrases as "the philosophic imagination, the sacred power of intuition", or, "the vision and the faculty divine".[1]

These speculations were only half understood. Some, perhaps, would not bear close inspection. But they aroused enthusiasm. And now the intellectually minded began to recall Spinoza the pantheist who taught that the Infinite God was gradually finding expression through finite man. His doctrines seemed to agree with Schleiermacher, who asserted that religion was no self-dedication to the God of Israel but the perception of the Universe. When we acquire an inkling of the Divine Presence around and beyond us, we are fitting our own divine urges into an idea which our intellect can grasp. The human being who is conscious of this adjustment has found religion. Hence it is everyone's most sacred duty to win free play for his own self-consciousness. We become aware of God when we become aware of ourselves.

We need not wonder that these theories stimulated a new phase of culture. In the first place, they seemed to give equal scope to our reason and to our intuition. To grasp the scheme of the universe was a task for the intellect, yet it brought into play the aspirations of the spirit. In the next place, thinkers were delighted to learn that the human mind was so great. However distant and transcendent the principle of life might be, it was to be visualised through the brain. You turned your eyes inward for enlightenment, the secrets of space and time were to be learnt from your own spirit which created those ideas. And thirdly, this age was particularly happy in the revival of wonder and mystery. Truth was still like some lonely peak, "pinnacled deep in the intense inane", and this profound expanse might in one sense be for ever beyond our comprehension; and yet, in another sense, we could divine something new about its profundity, every time we looked into our own hearts. It mattered little that this school propounded its doctrines in complicated and abstract arguments which imaginative thinkers found difficult to follow. When great ideas are abroad they have the quality of permeating the minds of humanists who have not studied them at first hand; and so it came about that Kant, the most unsympathetically abstruse of them all, has exercised the most influence, as Goethe observed to Eckermann.[2]

If Kant and the Kant-inspired played so large a part in the redirection of culture, they did so because their teaching was

[1] *Biographia Literaria*, chap. XII.   [2] *Gespräche*, 11 April 1827.

congenial to literature. They encouraged poets and essayists to contemplate themselves, to experiment with their feelings, to culti-vate the so-called *romantic irony* in which the writer observes his own spiritual vagaries in a detached and critical mood. Without knowing it they brought back into favour Sir Philip Sidney's prin-ciple:

> Fool, said my muse, look in thy heart and write.

But their expectations and anticipations were not those of the Renaissance. German metaphysicians promised the nineteenth century not only the discovery of themselves but also thereby a truer contact with the cosmic intelligences; and unfortunately these promises proved to be fallacious. Their disciples looked in their hearts in order to trace the pure outlines of the spirit, but what they generally found was a microcosm all too full of things which an idealist would gladly forget. Gazing into that crystal, they would indeed discern their own thoughts—all too fully—and amongst them their animal impulses, their egoistic resentments and that overwhelming sense of impotence, which is the death of the spirit. Many, like Werther, must have found that their vision was riveted by the bitterness of thwarted love and wounded vanity. So the philosophy of the romantic movement created the wish rather than the means towards revelation, and its influence was to continue all through the century more as a baffled quest or an obligation than as a clue to certainty. Shelley has often confessed to this disillu-sionment, as when the Spirit of Earth[1] warns us:

> Leave man, who was a many-sided mirror,
> Which could distort to many a shape of error,
> This true fair world of things, a sea reflecting love.

How were poets to keep their eyes on "this true fair world"? Clearly it was not enough to have the literary temperament. The inquirer needed the powers of literary adaptability. So, as the ideal was too good to be lost, the man gifted with the necessity for self-expression experimented with all the artistic methods and processes which were likely to turn experience into insight and prudence into wisdom. They revived or invented the kind of prosody, diction, imagery and rhythm which lend themselves to fantasy or aspiration and often impose some such mood on the writer, by their form and tone. They invoked any study or interest which promised to lead their thoughts in the desired direction.

---

[1] *Prometheus Unbound*, IV, 4.

Above all, they called in the help of writers who seemed to have made a success of a similar problem, using past literature as so many manuals of the art of spiritual selection. By such creative self-discipline they eliminated their lower feelings and gave their better impersonal selves their chance of achieving self-expression. They succeeded so well that their felicitous phraseology still charms and convinces us, though civilisation now imposes a different attitude of mind.

For the nineteenth century has not proved itself to be a friend to this metaphysical and idealistic culture. It has filled the Victorian generations with ideas and impressions very different from those which the romantics were skilled to etherialise. Shelley, Keats, Byron, Coleridge were hardly dead and Wordsworth had hardly lost his genius, before the need for a new conception of human destiny was beginning to be felt. Never, perhaps, has a phase of human self-confidence been so inspiringly created and so quickly lost. The rift in eighteenth-century culture was only just healed, when another rift began to appear. Yet this review of pre-Victorian thought will be found to be an indispensable introduction to our inquiry, because the succeeding generations clung to the tradition. The more impracticable conditions became, the more earnestly the creative writers worshipped the older prophets; some are worshipping them still. Only the future can disclose whether this succession of reactionaries will prove to be the true seers, but in the meantime they have contributed towards a sort of double-faced and over-emphasised culture, which was bound to lapse, if only temporarily, into the aimlessness of the present time.

This conclusion, however unexpected and unpalatable at first sight, seems to be inevitable when one considers what nineteenth-century humanists taught and might have taught. We shall watch an unusually brilliant and industrious fraternity combining and remodelling the old culture into new forms which ought to be equal to the new civilisation, and when their adaptations prove futile, they lose their hold on their generations. We shall see other more adventurous spirits endeavouring to interpret the new knowledge and adjust themselves to the morality of the new life, but not penetrating to the core of their problem, because either they or their readers could not escape from the spell of the older masters. The explanation is that the early nineteenth century in its enthusiasm established certain cults so effectively and persuasively that, rightly or wrongly, they seemed too good to be discarded.

In the first place, the romantic school taught their admirers to make the most of the occasional poem. This influence is just what one would not have expected. Transcendental philosophy seemed to be based on reason. Its arguments were addressed to the understanding; so it encouraged the disciple to carve out his own faith and build it up by the might of his intelligence. Once the structure was reared, the man of intuition then found himself on a tower, from which (to use Coleridge's[1] simile) he could overlook the encircling hills, and catch glimpses of the mysterious realms beyond the ridge. Ought not these poets to have embodied their meditations in long philosophical poems? So indeed they tried to do, much after the manner of the Classics and of the seventeenth century. But none of them succeeded. It was soon found that the spirits of the world could be studied only in human beings—chiefly in oneself. So the research became personal and impressionistic. In fact the simpler the experience, the easier to perceive and suggest its inward significance. A transitory encounter, an accidental episode, a fleeting glimpse of beauty meant more to the thoughtful observer than could a system of ethics or metaphysics. Besides, an incident appealed more directly to the imagination. So the romantics cultivated the art of enduing a fugitive impression with the immanence of the spirit. Some of these occasional verses are sublime, thanks to their sincerity and technical skill, and they have left behind them some inspiring examples of what poetic creativeness should be. But such masterpieces laid a heavy obligation on their successors, and henceforth a poet often felt himself bound to create a like sense of inward vision and exaltation, although the conviction had also to be created.

Blake, Byron, Coleridge, Wordsworth, Shelley and Keats taught their countrymen to look for light within themselves. But, as has been mentioned, they invoked as allies any cult or study which promised the same sort of opportunities, and the prose-writers of their age collaborated in this quest. So between them they stamped the impress of their own spirituality on some of the older elements of British culture.

That is how classical literature acquired a new significance. Of course it was to be expected that these two dead languages would live. Of the less utilitarian and the more difficult Johnson had said, "Greek, Sir, is like lace; every man gets as much of it as he can".[2] So we are not surprised that the literatures of Athens and

[1] *Biographia Literaria*, chap. XII.   [2] *Boswell's Life of Johnson*, chap. LXX.

Rome continued to be the resource of culture. But it is not so obvious why Greek should have become one of the chief sources of inspiration. The eighteenth century had been for literary men an age of classical study and the reaction was long overdue. Yet we find that the romantic movement was not only allied to Greek philosophy, it embraced Greek expressiveness and one of its most precious gifts to the nineteenth century was neohellenism.

This revival became possible because Athens enjoyed another renaissance and drew Rome along in her train. The first renaissance had been the discovery of the classical character and of the theory and practice of classical composition. The second renaissance was inaugurated by Winckelmann and arose out of the study of Greek art and the cultivation of Greek estheticism. Winckelmann taught the world the Hellenic principle of concentrated significance, what he called *das Viele im Wenigen*, the art of symbolising, merely suggesting the deepest truths, or the finest sentiments, by touches of apparently artless simplicity. The nostrils of the Apollo Belvedere reveal his spirit, a single word in Homer contains a picture, if only you have the insight to perceive it. This doctrine in itself suited the romantics. But they were captivated twice over when Winckelmann revealed to them some of the secrets which this symbolism suggested. In the first place he showed them that Greek art did more than portray the beauty we find in nature; it portrays the beauty we cannot find, but only imagine, according to Aristotle the type which nature willed and could not achieve; according to the transcendentalists the unrealised ideal, the dream of the soul, that inner vision which makes itself felt in the intelligence and comes from God. They learnt yet more; they gathered some hint of what to look for. This idealism, the sign of the masterpiece, was to be recognised in "eine edele Einfalt und eine stille Grösse, sowohl in der Stellung als im Ausdruck" (a noble simplicity and a calm grandeur, both in pose and expression). That is to say, the Greek sculptors not only understood but knew how to exemplify a spirit at one with the universe. A classical figure could be valued as suggesting this ideal all the more because its statuesque nudity betokened one who had shed the material accessories of life, and lived in the purified upper sphere. It had the strangeness of romance and a romantic significance. It appealed to a sense of form and yet had the pregnancy of an allegory. Besides, classical mythology could be interpreted so as to typify some of human nature's most godlike qualities, or noble desires. For instance, the world awoke to a new vision when they read Lessing's *Wie die Alten den Tod gebildet* (1769), and learnt that the ancients depicted death not as a grisly skeleton but as a beautiful youth with an inverted torch.

It is impossible to decide what humanists had read Winckelmann. Nor is it necessary. As we have said, ideas have a way of spreading further than the books which contain them. However conveyed, the hellenist's influence is unmistakable; at any rate through his disciples the classics were to be one of the most powerful influences which shaped the spiritual and intellectual life of the nineteenth century. In fact Greek and Latin were to rise to yet a third renaissance in which the ancients and especially the Athenians stood forth as the practitioners of an existence simplified into bodily perfection and lucidity of thought. So another obligation was imposed on the nineteenth century. Hellenism became almost a religious cult. Despite the evidence of Hesiod, Herodotus, Aristophanes and Theophrastus, scholars and humanists felt that they must worship the Greeks as a nation of geniuses as glorious as their climate, for which we yearned over our coal fires. The nineteenth century, thanks to these studies, has been able to keep before its eyes some of the best qualities of human nature. Nay more, while continuing the romantic tradition, some writers have learnt from Greek literature how to avoid the characteristic blemishes of romanticism—redundancy, formlessness, and egocentricity. But so intensive and enthusiastic a cult was bound to lead to preciousness, adulation, almost insincerity, and led (as we shall see) to a reaction in which students sacrificed all too willingly their classical ideals, in order to dissect classical civilisation under the cold light of archaeology and folk-lore.

The tendencies which found their scope in hellenism, also led students to pursue what is generally regarded as its antithesis—medievalism. After all, the Rhine, the Border, the Marches, and the hill-towns of Italy were more familiar to English poets than Attica or the Ionian Sea. Besides, antiquarians and folklorists were preparing the way. So it was natural for imaginative and sentimental writers to celebrate the supposed age of faith, the culmination of old-world virtues and heroism; to meditate on the fellowships and obligations of feudalism, the brotherhood and internationalism of the religious orders; to let their fancy loose among the perspective of medieval streets, the profiles of rocks crowned with castles, and all the colour and picturesque irregularity of Gothic civilisation. These interests are too well known to need explaining. Nor need we linger over the supposed pageantry of the Renaissance, which fascinated so many imaginations, as exemplified in Spenser, Shakespeare and Milton. It is enough to remember that people who insistently search through the broken shell of a vanished age for what they lack in their own, will at any rate end by understanding that they have deceived themselves.

The romantic schools were, perhaps, bound to be attracted by the history of civilisation, because it offers a human interest, such as poets can rarely resist. But it is not so obvious that these lovers of sunsets, spring-time, mountains and animals, should also find something congenial in the impersonal and impartial researches of experimental science. Yet at this period, about the turn of the century, such an upshot was almost inevitable. The beginnings of modern science have been so often recorded[1] and are now so familiar that it is enough to remind the reader that the theories and discoveries of chemists, physicists, electricians and astronomers had gone just far enough to imply that all phenomena are pervaded by forces like those which we feel moving within ourselves. About 1800 Haller of Bern was able to disprove the old conception of nature as a machine, and to establish the idea of a system both organic and vitalistic, the growth and co-operation of cosmic tendencies. So it was permitted to believe that there were mystic bonds between nature and the human soul; that the same spiritual life ran through both. Such was the deduction authorised by the experts. No wonder idealists felt at home with such knowledge; that men otherwise so different as Shelley and Newman were fond of chemistry; that Goethe gave up nearly half his life to the study of biology; that Wordsworth was attracted by Euclid; that Emerson saw his way through the mysteries of human nature, when he studied the aquarium in the Jardin des Plantes.[2] The influence of these theories—however indirect—on romantic poetry is self-evident, and often amounted to a noble inspiration. But it must not be forgotten that at this period they could be construed into a confirmation of religious convictions, almost of orthodoxy, and that in the succeeding period humanists clung to this persuasion (generally at second hand), and bitterly resented the surrender of their hope, until that same study which had once been the idealist's best counsellor became his worst enemy.

[1] E.g. O. Walzel, *German Romanticism*, Pt I, chap. II, esp. §2. (Transl. A. E. Lussky, 1932.)

[2] Bliss Perry, *Emerson To-day*, 1931, chap. II, §3.

We have now seen that a century or more ago it was possible for the most sincere and introspective thinkers to conceive of man not only as the crown and climax of creation, but as a spirit more than earthly, created to transcend human limits, and in the meantime, by the sacred force of intuition, they were enabled to recognise a kindred divinity in all they saw, heard and touched. How was it that the poet could impose his spiritual personality on all that he experienced? Take the theme of nature—merely hundreds of scattered observations and impressions recorded in the memory. How is it that the mind sees in this jungle of low-life and no-life a scheme, a design, even a parable of human aspiration? It is not so much an act of self-conviction as of self-recognition. But how comes it that our spirit looks so deeply and expects so much? We know only too well that our own daily conduct is not so motivated. We live from hand to mouth, and give way to the impulse of the moment. The romantics would reply that this assertion of our better self must either be the result of some heavenly influence or the expression of a second self within us, some exalted and pur-posive strain always struggling to realise itself, among these other influences which we call experience. It is (or is thought to be) the binding spell which permeates and unifies our consciousness, just as the most elaborate cathedral needs its own centre of gravity to hold its manifold and complex parts together and to ensure its identity. But we, who are thinking beings, cannot merely enjoy our identity; we must be convinced of it; we must feel it through our intelligence. So each educated person has to cultivate the sense of his own intellectual personality, that is to say, a method and mood by which to fit all his experiences into their proper place in his scheme. Of course we are not now thinking of philosophies or religious principles such as a man may borrow from someone else, and may profess without expressing his own identity. You can be an utilitarian or an unitarian without being yourself. We are concerned with the temper by which a humanist harmonises all he feels that he is with all he wishes to be, and derives from a changing world ideas which attest his own continuity.

We shall find that this quest of spiritual permanence and in-tellectual self-possession, this conquest and cult of what the French call *l'âme*, becomes one of the chief pre-occupations of the nine-teenth century. For instance, in 1810 Mme de Staël writes: "La sensibilité, l'imagination, la raison servent l'une à l'autre. Chacune de ces facultés ne serait qu'une maladie, qu'une faiblesse au lieu d'une force, si elle n'etait pas modifiée ou complétée par la totalité de notre être."[1] In 1935 J. S. Haldane wrote: "It is concrete personality, and not the mere abstract and shadowy unity called 'mind', which is embodied in conscious experience."[2] But we shall also find that, as the years advanced, the poets, romancers, essayists and thinkers began to fear that their personality would slip away from them. The soul seemed in danger of losing its identity. The intellect could observe—only too clearly—the *ego* continually changing in contact with changing experiences; but was not so confidently conscious of that other *ego*, which should remain always the same, the judge and director of one's more superficial self.

The more one was threatened with spiritual *aphasia*, the more one clung to the romantic sentiments and aspirations which seemed to ensure the unity of the soul. So far we have discussed these influences as enthusiasms which prevailed by their own persuasiveness; and so at first they may have spread, like the breath of the spirit. But ideas which circulate freely, as if by magic, do not generally preserve their power for more than one generation, they tend to lose themselves in quotations, references, and obscure controversies. If they are to be preserved for posterity, they must be concentrated and exemplified in some commanding figure. Besides, in the history of literature it is the human being which gives power to a tendency. So at this stage we must inquire whether the idealism of the romantic movement was worthily enshrined in the life and work of one pre-eminently great man. By such an example, we shall see all that the first generation gained by romanticism and their successors lost; by the rise and fall of his reputation we shall be able to measure the vitality of the movement.

Who will serve us best as an example? One would like to have instanced Coleridge. But Coleridge, as is only too well known, rarely finished anything which he began and seldom achieved the art of confirming his theories by poetry. Then one would like to turn to Wordsworth who, at any rate, learnt much from Coleridge. *The Prelude* explains how its author was initiated into the mystery of the World-spirit, first in creation and then in his soul. Feeling

[1] *De l'Allemagne*, Troisième Partie, chap. 2: "The power to feel, to imagine and to reason serve one another. Each faculty would be no more than a perversion or a weakness, instead of a force, if it were not modified or completed by the co-operation of our whole being."

[2] *The Philosophy of a Biologist*, chap. III.

himself to be in touch with the wonders of earth and sky, he taught himself to look for these "Presences of Nature" in the human life around him, and after many false starts and disappointments he found what he sought. The effort made him a great poet. His best verses, which seem to be so artless and spontaneous, are a highly technical achievement. They show how one can enjoy self-fulfil-ment in the contemplation of other people and things.

But the poet labours under one defect. His attitude to a cloud or a flower is Olympian; not so his attitude to the bigger aspects of life. He remained to the last an irreconcilable, who would not risk his peace of mind amid the adventures of modern society. This aloofness has been imputed to him for righteousness—he kept himself untamed, unsullied. But, on the other hand, he never accomplished all that one might hope and expect from his cult of wild nature and the simple life. He could not confirm and attest his philosophy by contemplating the creative ideas of his time. Nowadays such comprehensive self-fulfilment is questionable—perhaps out of the question. Then it was possible; and we can learn the secret if we go outside our own country and take Goethe as our example.

CHAPTER III

Goethe and Emerson illustrate the strength and weakness of the epoch which they close.

There is no need to apologise for introducing a German humanist into the consideration of English literature. In studying the nineteenth century we cannot remain insular. During that period culture gradually became so cosmopolitan (either by instinct or imitation) that any author may be regarded as English who illustrates or influences English literature. Though we cross the German Ocean we need not be severed from British culture. For just as Goethe was always ready to recognise the greatness of English civilisation and admired our eighteenth-century poetry[1] no less than he admired Byron, Scott and even the earlier efforts of Carlyle, so we have been ready to discuss his ideas as if they had special significance for ourselves. Not without reason. Goethe had the good fortune to explore the cross-currents which combined in conflict first to produce and then to complicate the progress of nineteenth-century culture. Moreover, he mastered and interpreted these influences in so whimsical and unexpected a fashion that he was bound to antagonise as well as to convince.

To begin with, he lived a very long life (1749–1832). He first began to observe and to ponder in the light of the *Aufklärung*, when Germans were learning from the French rationalists to think for themselves. His youth and early manhood were passed amid the enthusiasms of the *Sturm und Drang* period, the interlude of storm and stress when the rising generation argued their traditions and beliefs out of sight, in order to develop and enjoy their emotions with freedom. In his maturer manhood he watched the French Revolution and its consequences, not always at a distance, since he saw and heard the French artillery firing at Valmy in 1792, and talked with Napoleon when Germany was invaded and Weimar occupied in 1808. As he did not die till 1832, he had time to play his part in the rise and fall of romanticism, but without sacrificing his genius to its extravagancies and eccentricities. In fact, though he began his career with a youthful burst of passionate sentimentalism, and later in life joined Schiller in writing some of Germany's

---

[1] *Dichtung und Wahrheit*, 3er Thl. 13es Buch.

best ballads, yet he dissented from his friend's idealism, and as for the later development of the romantic school, he described their verse in his old age as poetry which must have come from a hospital (*Lazarett-Poesie*).[1]

His own idea of the poet's function was quite clear and did not vary throughout his long life. In 1774 he declared the true virtue of creativeness (*Dichtkunst*) to be "dass man das Vortreffliche erkenne und es auszusprechen wage";[2] in 1825 he defined it as "lebendiges Gefühl der Zustände und Fähigkeit es auszudrücken".[3] This cult of poetry out of experience was, of course, pure romanticism at its best, purged of ecstasy and religious enthusiasm but refined by the most conscientious study of artistic expressiveness, and was besides particularly congenial (as we shall see) to the practices of Victorian poets. Goethe himself considered his art to be a kind of inspired empiricism. He even denied in old age that there was, properly speaking, any theory embodied in *Faust*. There were only, he explained to Eckermann,[4] vivid impressions of what was beautiful, sensuous, lovable, elevating. He had simply built up and rounded off his experiences in dramatic form, so that others could feel them in the same spirit. This principle involved a challenge. For instance, Heine had to admit his artistic perfection ("die Vollendung alles Dessen, was er darstellt") but compared his masterpieces to statues which adorn a garden; nothing more than statues; "die Goethe'schen Dichtungen bringen nicht die That hervor wie die Schiller'schen. Die That ist das Kind des Wortes, und die Goethe'schen schönen Worte sind kinderlos."[5] That is to say that Heine expected a definite morality, an exemplification of the highest conduct, had set his heart on perfect characters, and English writers of his generation were to aim at the same ideal. We shall see later whether the realistic Goethe was not more in accord with the trend of culture, especially as his principle involved another different kind of activity, the intensive cult of oneself.

In order to recognise and recreate *the excellent* as found in the

[1] Eckermann, 24 Sept. 1827.

[2] *Werther*, 30 May: "Recognition of the excellent and the heart to give it expression."

[3] Eckermann, 11 June 1825: "A vital sense of one's surroundings and ability to express that sense." [4] *Ibid.* 6 May 1827.

[5] *Die Romantische Schule*, 1833. 1es Buch: "Goethe's poetry does not give birth to the deed as Schiller's poetry does. The deed is the child of the word, and Goethe's fine words are childless."

day's experience, it is necessary to be oneself stronger and nobler than circumstances; to acquire and perfect in the intelligence a sense of beauty and fitness which can be imposed on life; to originate and apply in the realm of art one's spiritual preconceptions as effectively as Kant[1] had established his categories in the realm of psychology. In a word, Goethe showed the man of culture how to conserve and assert his intellectual personality; how to be essentially and supremely himself, while assimilating his environment. Once more, we find in this attitude that he stood between two divergent streams of tendency. His passion for self-culture was to be condemned as selfishness and isolation all the more dangerous because the rise of democracy and industrialism made it necessary for idealists and humanitarians to think more and more of their fellow-creatures. Some people wondered how he could work at *West-Östlicher Divan* while the fate of his country hung in the balance at Jena; or could attach more importance to the controversy between Cuvier and St Hilaire than to the French Revolution of 1830. Tennyson even composed *The Palace of Art* to show whither such isolation would lead the man who thus misused his supreme gifts. On the other hand, Goethe gave effect to one of the most essential principles of the romantic movement and thereby taught the post-romantics a lesson which the best were not too good to learn—how to preserve one's spiritual identity amidst a flux of impressions, how to extract a sense of reality out of the changing surface of appearances; how to maintain the principle of *Dauer in Wechsel*. This principle first found expression in his theory of art. He believed that the artist had secret intimations of how things and people ought to grow and develop, could see the perfect design in the imperfect realisation and, by the light of this inward conception, could complete the unfulfilled plan in his pictures, poems and statues. The wisdom, which Goethe learnt from the past, was to be immensely significant for the future. It was to reappear (with many readaptations) in the aesthetic theories of Ruskin, Pater, and even of Oscar Wilde; it was to offer one corrective to the deadness of later nineteenth-century materialism, supplying that strain of imaginative inventiveness and interest which Nietzsche[2] lamented as the need of his age.

It is also particularly to be noted that in the romantic era it was possible to be an aesthete and an intellectual without being a recluse, much less a pessimist. Goethe, despite what his critics have said,

---

[1] *Ante*, p. 18. [2] *Wille zur Macht.* See *post*, chap. XXII.

ended with a full measure of the optimism which the nineteenth
century first misapplied and then lost. Thanks to his poetic perceptiveness, he could see values outside himself. He could believe
in the goodness of man even though the world were evil, and could
believe in imperfect men, because man aims at perfection. He
believed that the human spirit could ennoble experience, so that
the Godlike and the Helpful should enter into all our difficulties
and disappointments. In this mood he invented or rather established Winckelmann's hellenism, because the Greeks did not
imitate this dreary, inadequate world, but recreated it according
to their idea of harmonious and simplified perfection and raised
us to the height of their point of view. And among the moderns,
that was why he particularly loved Claude Lorrain and above all
Molière and Shakespeare.[1]

So it was quite unjust to accuse Goethe of aloofness and egocentricity, and to imply that his writings voiced no call to action.
On the contrary, he was so inspired by his artistic and constructive
ideals, that he could look beyond the purely aesthetic development
of his own powers, towards the possibilities of making human
existence more efficient and vigorous. Although so much an in-
dividualist, he understood that man lived a *kollektive Wesen*, and
could not be truly himself unless his welfare depended on that of
his fellow-creatures, and part of his energy was devoted to serving
them. So he retained an interest in those material activities which
are the readiest means for mutual help and advancement. Among
his favourite dreams was the cutting of the Panama and Suez
Canals;[2] and he rejoiced that in his epoch Franklin's discovery of
electricity had been followed by the achievements of Carus, Dalton
and Meyer.

This in itself was no small achievement. It meant that the older
and more exquisite paths of culture could lead some adventurers
to humanitarianism and the study of materialistic progress. But
the marvel was that Goethe did not confine himself to the older
streams of inspiration. He embraced the new and almost revolutionary science of his age. This man of imagination, who once
wrote medieval ballads and looked to the moon to shed her soft
beams of sentiment over his spirit, or wept for the sake of weeping,
now turned to the researches of these experimentalists, these so-
called enemies of religion and classical learning, in his quest for

[1] Eckermann, 10 April 1829. *Ibid.* 8 Nov. 1826.
[2] *Ibid.* 21 Feb. 1827.

the realities of life. He even joined them in their researches and explorations.

His achievements are well known and there is no need to discuss his theory of colour, or the genuine discoveries which he made in the morphology of plants, in the law of development according to type, in the traces of the inter-maxillary bone which man shared with animals, and of the vertebral structure of the skull. But it is important to notice that these researches accompanied and expressed a new habit of mind for a humanist, a development and discipline of the cultured intelligence, such as the later nineteenth century was to need and to acquire with much travail and disillusionment. In the first place he appreciated the disadvantage under which a pure man of letters must labour, because, as he noted in 1792, it is natural for a human being to contemplate his surroundings with reference only to himself. "Denn es hängt sein ganzes Schicksal davon ab, ob sie ihm gefallen oder missfallen, ob sie ihn anziehen oder abstossen, ob sie ihm nutzen oder schaden."[1] So far the older culture will still help him. But it is also a part of our nature to generalise, to form deductions; we have a leaning towards hypotheses and theories, if only for our spiritual satisfaction. The wisdom and learning of other days can no longer satisfy this function, because a new culture has sprung up under our eyes, for which our traditional authorities were unprepared. Unless we are to lose our inborn talent for constructive speculation, we must set ourselves to collect the new facts which have no literary history behind them. Nay more, though the inquirer will be seeking for some comprehensive idea, yet he must be prepared to confine himself to a narrow line of research, and share his discoveries and deductions with his fellow-workers, for it is the habit of science to realise her truths through the slow progress of many collaborators, not by sudden inspiration. It is only thus, by the help of time, that the inquirer can penetrate below the facts to the ideas.[2]

It would seem that the experimental philosopher must be prepared to exercise his reason on subjects which promised little exhilaration of spirit. Yet he would meet with an unexpectedly ample compensation. The study of nature conferred a certain sense of inward purity and peace.[3] The spirit of contradiction and

---

[1] Written in MS. 1792. Printed *Zur Naturwissenschaft Überhaupt*. 2. Band, 1. Heft: "For all his fate depends on whether his surroundings please or displease, attract or repel, profit or harm."   [2] *Ibid.*

[3] Eckermann, 18 May 1824: "Eine gewisse ruhige Reinheit des Inners."

controversy (*das Wesen der Dialektik*) was hushed, for no man could keep his gaze fixed on these infinite and everlasting perspectives, unless his spirit was untroubled and free from guile. Goethe once suggested that a course of scientific study should be prescribed for any patient suffering from academic contentiousness.[1] So he developed the Olympian attitude, aloof from human and egoistic prepossessions, which Meredith and Huxley were to preach rather than practise, and which the English of the later nineteenth century were to find so hard to cultivate.

In Goethe's day the reward for this sincerity and detachment seems to have come more quickly than it did two generations later, though perhaps not more easily. The student of nature realised only too clearly that he was tracking an endless maze far too intricate for his single intellect, but he also understood that if he persevered in the new methods and compared his few poor results with those of other fellow-workers, he would find that these truths were interlinked, that phenomena reacted on each other, that the multitudinous world was made up of interconnections, and was more like a network than a chaos. *Mannigfaltigkeit* assumed the character of an *Einheit*. Leibnitz[2] had taught that all things in God's world are interrelated and nothing can be abolished without deranging the whole scheme, just as in a row of mathematical figures you could not alter the smallest number without altering the aggregate sum (*individualitas numerica*). This comforting theory assumed a more enlightening significance under the authority of the new knowledge. It could even be said that each single phenomenon was bound up with so many others that it could be compared to a free swinging light which sends out rays in every direction.[3] In moments of enlightenment it was possible to recognise the underlying structure, the *Urphänomen*, and get some glimpse of the principle on which nature worked. When once the mind was fired by this revelation, the more human sympathies rekindled and the inquirer could work backward from his abstract conclusions to the surface phenomena, could reflect on these manifestations and understand how the world of experience, rightly understood, affected the destiny of man. Long ago, when a student at Strasbourg, he had noted that "separatim de Deo et rerum Natura disserere difficile et periculosum est, eodem modo quam si

---

[1] Eckermann, 18 Oct. 1827.
[2] *Théodicée*, Pt I, §§ 9, 10.
[3] *Zur Naturwissenschaft Überhaupt.* 2. Band; 1. Heft.

de corpore et anima sejunctim cogitamus".[1] In mature manhood
the learning of his time enabled him to verify this conviction of the
unity of nature, the comprehensiveness of her plan. In his own
phrase, "so führt uns das Besondere immer zum Allgemeinen, das
Allgemeine zum Besondern".[2]

These conclusions were the fruit of close observation and accurate
thought, what Goethe called *gegenständliches Denken* and *anschauende
Urteilskraft*, but they gave full scope to the "rebirth of wonder".
The scientist of that time could not stop admiring the resourcefulness and productivity of nature, the way a few leading principles
(*Grundmaximen*) could multiply into an endless diversity of phenomena. At times one could even intuit the primordial cause: a
constructive intelligence at work vivifying a system of which we
can see only the past around us, just as a great artist can conceive
a picture in its entirety—its composition—while the *tiro* can understand only the contributory details.[3] It was already possible to
divine that man is not the centre of the universe but only one
among a million other products, a struggling creature, privileged
to make his way by fitful glimpses of the design. We shall see in a
later chapter that the pursuit of science was to impose the surrender of much that human beings once held dear; especially the
consciousness of allegiance to a supernatural power. So it is important to notice that Goethe was still able to feel contact with
what was more ethereal than himself, fearlessly to pursue the truth,
without risking the spiritual satisfaction which culture or God had
made necessary. To the last he believed in the deity as an august
mystery whom we should understand more clearly as we rose in
the scale of intelligence. In fact he was so far a mystic that he
believed, like Tennyson, "dass in besonderen Zuständen die
Fühlfaden unserer Seele über ihre körperlichen Grenzen hinaus-
reichen können".[4] He believed in a power, inexplicable and
incomprehensible to our intelligence, which he named *das Dämo-
nische*. It seemed to assert itself in the shuffling of events, or even
to enter the spirit of certain human beings, so that they were
possessed by a godlike or at least superhuman energy, either for

[1] "To discuss God apart from nature is as difficult and dangerous as thinking
separately of the body and soul."
[2] "Thus the Special leads us ever to the Universal, the Universal to the
Special." [3] Eckermann, 28 Feb. 1831.
[4] *Ibid.* 28 Feb. 1831: "That under unusual conditions the antennae of our
soul can reach out beyond our bodily limitations."

action or thought—a sort of half-personified *Entelechia*,[1] which originated, or recombined, human vitality according to its own inscrutable urges. Carlyle was to say more on the subject.

It is easy to see that Goethe's imagination was not antagonised by his reason, as was to prove to be the misfortune with some younger poets, for instance, Matthew Arnold. He has said that "der innere Gehalt des bearbeiteten Gegenstandes ist der Anfang und das Ende der Kunst",[2] and what science taught him of reality did not shock his artistic impulse to create. He professed a dislike for metaphysics, as did the mid-Victorians, but like them he was really condemning, not the vision but the nebulosity. He could not bear with abstractions till they were established by scientific observation, or by artistic expression. He was even more significant for the nineteenth century because he went further and embodied all this learning and speculation in studies of conduct. He was able to trace the workings of nature, as he understood it, in the varied problems and ventures of human life, showing how the same principle of growth, expansion, and seeming conflict prevails; how goodness and badness, happiness and sorrow, truth and error, light and darkness, birth and death, are all alike manifestations of one universal power. Those who were interested in the restrictions of society, the limitations of the ordinary character, the problems of self-culture which must end in self-education and devotion to others, found his most persuasive exposition to be the *Wilhelm Meister* series, *Dichtung und Wahrheit* and *Hermann und Dorothea*. Those who were principally concerned with the dualism of human nature, the problem of self-adjustment, the historical development of man and the emergence of modernism out of the Renaissance, found that the two parts of *Faust* were the most convincing demonstration. In these, as in all his imaginative works, he dwells on the thrusting, restless, aspiring, acquisitive nature of the modern, northern European, his romantic ambitiousness, his passion for self-fulfilment beyond his powers. At the same time he dwells on the imperious necessity for *Entsagung*, for self-denial. First because it is the nature of man to aim at more than he is destined to achieve, and to be betrayed into a futile titanism, if he yields to this wilful impulse; secondly, because there is another avenue of

[1] *Dichtung und Wahrheit.* 4er Thl. 2es Buch. Eckermann, 11 March 1828. 28 Feb. and 2 March 1831.

[2] *Dichtung und Wahrheit.* 2er Thl. 7es Buch; "The inner content of the subject under treatment is the beginning and end of art."

expansion awaiting him as a compensation, what one might call social adaptation, the reshaping (not repressing) of one's egoism, so that it will find its scope within the mould of society, assimilated to the thoughts and aspirations of our fellow-creatures. Browning, as we shall see, was to develop the idea.

Thus, with the exception of a few farces, comedies, and drinking songs, Goethe wrote with a "high seriousness", generally combining imagination with a moral intent. Yet his most thoughtful and far-seeing creations are pervaded by a singular streak of realism. He loves to keep his idealists and visionaries in contact with ordinary people and circumstances, and these pedestrian, sometimes banausic, conditions are portrayed with unmistakable insight and enjoyment. This play of contrast is of course most salutary; it helps the reader to remember that the portraiture of fiery and profound personalities is not so much the portraiture of life, as of what life ought but is rarely able to be; and that literature is therefore in danger of missing all that is not exceptional. Goethe was no doubt reacting against this tendency, and many writers were to follow in his steps; and we shall see how few were able to copy his impartiality and to balance the claims of the actual with those of the ideal. So once again, he will serve us as a standard of judgment. But in the meanwhile he was not serving his own reputation quite so well. Viewed from the later nineteenth-century standpoint, he had not the equipment to be a realist. This man who had a heart for all the mysteries of life, knew no more of its surface than could be found within the scholarly and courtly circles of a small government town. If his vision was cosmic his tastes were far from cosmopolitan. The later nineteenth century was to discover the fascination of great million-peopled cities, and was to learn from the big outside world the art of multiplying human nature, and turning every experience into an adventure. After these many-sided contacts, readers were often to yawn over the banalities of Wilhelm Meister's existence, or the petty and commonplace inducements by which Mephisto tempted Faust to stay the passing hour. There were many more subtle and searching tests awaiting the soul of man.

Nevertheless, a study of the English nineteenth century should begin with a study of Goethe. He represents the best that his generation had achieved and much that the following generations were to resign. On the whole it may be said that he stands for a phase of culture which was gradually to be effaced. This phase began with the Renaissance. Bacon had asserted "that a little philosophy inclineth man's mind to atheism: but depth in philosophy bringeth men's minds about to religion".[1] Goethe still belonged to that school. Like Bacon, he understood that life is more worth living the more it is organised and self-directed; that intelligence is the secret of human excellence; and he expected the same from the universe. This lesson had originally been learnt from ancient Athens, and at the beginning of the nineteenth century it could still be confirmed. The toiling, aspiring intelligence of man could find its goal in the serene and universal intelligence of God. While this conviction prevailed one could believe that the world really was as wonderful, as inspiring, as the poet would like to imagine.

The romantic movement inherited this tradition. Their revolt against classicism was only superficial, confined to points of technique; they really reinforced its doctrines. They applied all the old idealism of the Renaissance and added thereto the new idealism of the transcendentalists in order to hold up as it were a vast mirror in which we saw man's spirit soar up into the skies, like Shelley's skylark.

Goethe becomes one of the tests of nineteenth-century culture, because he pursued these visions on foot, feeling his way. If (he might say) it concerns us to know what God is, we must look for Him not only in our hearts but in the activities of the world. He trusted less to revelation than to research; and was prepared to abide by the results. Consequently, his influence on Englishmen depended on their readiness to accept his principle. In the eighteenth century, he was chiefly known as the author of *The Sorrows of Werther; A German Story* (first translated in 1779) or as the poet of romance and medievalism, admired by "Monk" Lewis and Sir Walter Scott, who translated *Goetz* in 1799; or perhaps as the scholarly and dignified author of *Iphigenie in Tauris*, which William Taylor of Norwich translated in the same year. The great romantic poets did not care to penetrate more deeply, because they had already found their ideals and did not wish their gaze to be diverted. From 1800 onwards Crabb Robinson began to tell his circle what a wonderful lyrical genius he had found, but Wordsworth was not interested in "these poetical sensualists"; Lamb considered *Faust* to be "a disagreeable canting tale of seduction", and like Hazlitt preferred Marlowe; Coleridge was so disgusted

[1] *Of Atheism.*

with the immorality of the drama that in 1814 he refused Murray's offer of £100 for a translation.

It was rather the Byronic mood of disillusionment and discontent which inclined the younger generation to look more deeply into this outspoken and unconventional foreigner. *The Quarterly* and *The Edinburgh* might protest, but the popularity of *Manfred* (1817), *Cain* (1821) and *The Deformed Transformed* (1824) proves that the age was ripe for Goethe's view of life, especially as Mme de Staël's *De l'Allemagne* (translated in 1813) had praised the German's universality, and *Blackwood* in 1818 and again in 1819 published appreciative and enlightening essays on his genius. Nor was it overlooked that Byron figures in Pt II as Euphorion.

So in the 'twenties, translations, both fragmentary and complete, begin to multiply; Shelley, G. Soane, and Lord Gower, amongst the translators. In 1824 *Dichtung und Wahrheit* appeared as *Memoirs of Goethe*. In the same year Carlyle completed *Wilhelm Meister* and as soon as this advocate had raised his voice, Goethe begins to be one of the leaders of English thought. By the time that G. H. Lewes had completed his *Life* in 1855, the German's name was a commonplace of culture.

His prominence was due to his steadiness and thus he helped others to see what was fading out of sight.

Goethe was hardly dead when the most brilliant cosmopolitan author of the next generation was lamenting the rift which had been sprung across the culture of Europe,[1] and was widening between the old intelligible world which Goethe was able to interpret with such comforting assurances, and the developments of the mid-century—all those practices, observances and even convictions which no longer conformed to man's higher spiritual will, much less to the religion, literature and philosophy in which that will was symbolised with artificial clearness and consistency.

So much by way of introduction. But a history of literature must not confine itself to generalisations; it must demonstrate and illustrate. The following pages will investigate the expedients by which Victorians tried to bridge the gulf, and for the most part failed. It remains, in this chapter, to give an example of the kind of difficulties which they had to face. We shall find an indication in Emerson's career.

He was of pure English stock, born in 1803 into the austere religious atmosphere of eastern Massachusetts. Ralph Waldo's

[1] Heine, *Die Bäder von Lucca*, Kap. IV. See *post*, p. 136.

father was the eloquent and public-spirited pastor of the First Church in Boston. The son was called in 1829 to be associate pastor to the old Second Church of Boston. He soon became sole pastor and seems to have served his church with the uttermost devotion. Gradually he found that he could not as a minister think for himself with sincerity and independence. The actual grounds of his severance was his unwillingness to celebrate Holy Communion. So he took leave of his congregation and sailed for Europe, in order to learn the secrets of life from the older civilisations. Bliss Perry[1] retells the story how he visited the *Jardin des Plantes* one July day in 1833, and gazing into the Aquarium caught some inkling of the affinities between human nature and the rest of creation. "Whilst I stood there, I yielded to a singular conviction, that in all these rich groups of natural productions which surrounded me, and in all the vast system which they represented, not a form so grotesque, so savage, so beautiful, but is an expression of some property in man the observer."[2] Thus enlightened, he aspired to become a "naturalist of souls". In fact, in 1837, he formed the resolution "to write the natural history of reason".[3] This work was never achieved, but Emerson returned to his own country convinced that there was an occult relation between the most fantastic forms of nature and the human spirit; that "the laws of moral nature answer to those of matter as face to face in a glass";[4] and that consequently the secret of human progressiveness is hinted, if not mirrored, in all the lower stages of creation. Eighteenth-century philosophers might argue against such conclusions, but their logic was not so convincing as the observers' own intimations. Moreover, these guesses and intuitions were elucidated or at least sanctioned by Plato (especially *Symposium*), Neoplatonism (especially Plotinus), the seventeenth-century divines, the metaphysical poets, Swedenborg, Goethe, the transcendental philosophers and eventually by Carlyle. At least, Emerson found encouragement in all these thinkers. Thus he convinced himself that the soul can come into contact with reality even against the report of the senses, and that to the eyes of the mystic the will of God is discernible amid all the perplexing phenomena by which experience obscures thought. In

[1] *Emerson To-day*, 1931, chap. II.

[2] A later account, contributed to the *Gift* in 1844 (see Bliss Perry, *op. cit.*).

[3] J. E. Cabot, *A Memoir of Ralph Waldo Emerson*, 2 vols. Boston, 1887, vol. II, p. 633.

[4] *The Uses of Natural History*. Lecture delivered before the Boston Society of Natural History, 4 Nov. 1833.

a word, he had acquired the best culture of his age, and the vision
to recreate that learning into a religion such as his age might need.
For the rest of his long life, he meditated on these doctrines,
working them out for his own purposes in his voluminous journals,
then expounding them in the addresses and speeches which he
delivered as an itinerant lecturer; and then again elaborating the
spoken word into essays and books.

And what is the special import of this religion? It aims at
restoring man to his old supremacy in the scheme of creation; it
entitles him to participate in the divine plan hidden beneath
appearances; to share its mysteries, to further its purposes, to
assimilate its infinitude—to be the confidant of God. This insight
ought (one would think) to involve not only the understanding of
God, but of oneself, for it was acquired by a sense of identity with
the "Over-Soul". Such a revelation could not be won unless the
initiate also realised the depth and mystery of his own perceptiveness, since these convictions could not be established by logic.
They were founded on inward consciousness, on analogies between
the visible and invisible worlds. So in the first place the imagination was always at work inventing flashes of poetic insight, which
continually opened new vistas—glimpse linked to glimpse of what
he might be—till he persuaded himself that "man is a god in
ruins", that "whilst the world is a spectacle something in himself
is stable".[1] This creativeness served a yet more vital purpose. It
led on to an intense self-realisation. Emerson has himself announced "the definition of *spiritual* should be: that which is its own
evidence", and the more his disciples recognised their best selves
in God's world, the more they were strengthened to trust each to
his own personality. So in the third place, Emerson's teaching
culminated in the doctrine of self-reliance. He even went so far as
to say that he had nothing to do with the sacredness of traditions,
since he lived wholly from within, and affirmed that "no law can
be sacred to me but that of my nature".[2]

Surely a message of great value to his own age and to ours. Yet
his influence falls far short of his reputation; it never reached much
further than the assemblies of simple, middle-class folk who admired him without understanding what he said. During his own
lifetime his reputation was no doubt impaired by the fragmentary,
unsystematic and often inconsistent way in which his doctrines
were propounded in occasional lectures and disconnected publica-

[1] *Nature*, chaps. IV, V. [2] *Self-Reliance.*

tions. But all such disadvantages have now been amply rectified. His fame is established as America's foremost writer, and in this age of collected works and academic monographs the system and development of his thought can easily be studied as a whole. Yet despite Matthew Arnold, H. W. Garrod and his other academic admirers in New England, Emerson is not often read as a guide and a counsellor, much less as a seer. He is read very little and generally with impatience. A few connoisseurs enjoy his masterly phrases, his eloquence, and the serenity and poise of his mind. He is valued not for his teaching but merely for his style and personality.

Is it then still a case of the "monstrous, dead, unprofitable world"? Not altogether. The most natural explanation of his neglect will be found in the circumstances of his birth, breeding and career. This immensely effective writer is ineffective because he could never to the end of his days escape the limitations of the preacher. Though he resigned the Second Church of Boston, he never resigned the atmosphere of the chapel. There is about a pulpit a certain mood of aloofness and exhortation. A congregation assembles in a church or a conventicle in order to escape from their profane lives. Even if they review the deeds of the past week it is not in the weekday spirit. Such is Emerson's attitude. He has thought out the problems of his soul, and he displays an astonishing grasp of the religions and philosophies of the past. No one can explain the systems of Buddha, Swedenborg or Kant as he can. No one can so easily and so confidently make his readers or listeners masters of the wisdom and piety of the past. He exhorts you to meditate on their teaching, to acquire their powers of second sight, to understand their interpretations. "The human mind", he declares, "stands ever in perplexity, demanding intellect, demanding sanctity, impatient equally of each without the other."[1] But he can achieve this combination only in aloofness, as if he and we were still in his chapel. That is why he is one of those moralists chiefly appreciated by the middle-aged. We do not value him till the climacteric of life is reached, because he gives us a distaste for this world.

Such a view is not taken by his apologists. They emphasise the duality of his mind—his eye for progress, his sense of the practical advantages of life; his interest, for instance, in English civilisation. *English Traits* is certainly a remarkable book, full of quiet irony.

[1] *Representative Men. Swedenborg or The Mystic.*

He describes Victorian civilisation, at which English humanists were raving, as if he admired the stalwart race, manly rather than warlike, too sincere to be pretentious, who had gained the leadership of the world by coupling means to ends and had acquired something of the power and precision of the machines they minded. But in reality he lets the modern world go on its own way, he contemplates its superficial bustling progress with tolerance and half-concealed disapproval, because he has built up this other spiritual existence into which every *thinker* can train himself to retire. "Every material thing", he insists, "has its celestial side; has its translation, through humanity, into the spiritual and necessary sphere, where it plays a part as indestructible as any other."[1]

He may have been well counselled in forming his idea of human nature on the older ideas; his mistake was in calling on his contemporaries to do the same and then, as soon as they came to face the experiences of the nineteenth century, to think in analogies. That is to say, he invites us to persuade ourselves that our life is worth while only so long as it interprets, symbolises and exemplifies the principles of the older philosophers all innocent of railroads and division of labour. We ought to *will to live* in their way, and countenance our own civilisation only so far as we could imagine that it expressed their dreams.

So in this age, when men and women were called upon to make an heroic effort at adaptation, to readjust the spiritual heritage to the new situations, Emerson encouraged them to retire into the old world culture and to realise themselves in its atmosphere—"a state in which the mind has no other employment but to observe and regulate her own motions, to trace thought from thought, combine one image with another, raise systems of science, and form theories of virtue". So said Dr Johnson,[2] more modern than Emerson, who did not effectively exemplify this self-recovery and so encouraged that home-sickness for the past which became one of the maladies of Victorianism.

[1] *Uses of Great Men.*   [2] *The Idler*, No. 19.

CHAPTER IV

The influences of romanticism reach the Church—The Oxford Movement—Tractarianism founded on theological scholarship and the voice of conscience—Newman has the intellect of a rationalist and the temperament of a saint—He takes the lead.

We have seen that the humanists of the early nineteenth century believed the Deity to be within them and without; but being educated people they had to satisfy their intellect of this omnipresence. So culture became the quest of evidence by which to recognise God. We have also seen that learning had reached a stage which rendered such recognition possible. You looked on nature and you found the spirit of beauty and creativeness; you turned from contemplation of these sights and sounds to study their secrets—to ask what new insight the experimental sciences offered—and you discerned evidence not only of a design, but of mysterious influences such as you felt to be within yourself. Or, like Herder and Schiller, you referred to history, and you learnt that human destiny exemplified moral laws and universal tendencies such as only a Higher Power could impose, and that progress was one continuous march towards a higher and fuller humanity. Best of all, you opened the great poets and moralists, and you found in their pages a succession of character-types so noble and heroic that they seemed to be superhuman, yet you knew intuitively that they were portraits, true to life.

All the activities of man promised fair to reflect our aspirations, yet the most promising of all had so far been overlooked—the Church. It was not so on the Continent. The French, and especially the German enthusiasts for medievalism, had come to regard the Roman Catholic Church as the culmination of the old world virtues—the one complete institution which seemed to enjoin the best that man could do in this world, and to symbolise the best that he could know of the world beyond.[1] The English were slower to realise the grandeur and significance of Christian worship. Their indifference was not, for the most part, due to infidelity. We hear much of agnosticism in the eighteenth century, especially of Hume

[1] See F. von Hardenberg, *Die Christenheit oder Europa* in *Schriften*, posth. 1805; F. Schlegel, *Geschichte der alten und neuen Literatur*, 1815.

and Gibbon, but it is sometimes forgotten that no thinking man of that age was intellectually constrained to be an agnostic.[1] There were plenty of good reasons for remaining orthodox. Moreover, the poets, essayists, playwrights and novelists, who represent the tendencies of educated opinion, for instance, Addison, Fielding, Johnson, Young, Gray, Cowper, Burke, do not write as if they or their readers cared anything for free thought. If some were luke-warm about the sacredness, grandeur and mystery of their ritual or doctrine, it was because they disbelieved in an infallible church and pinned their faith on an infallible book.

God had spoken to man in print; through the Hebrew idiom translated into Jacobean English. So as often as an earnest Pro-testant had doubts concerning his "Maker's" will, he was inclined to consult, not the parish priest, but the Sacred Book. In those pages he would find (he believed) an answer to his questions, but he also found that the oracle was often involved in symbolism, and exotic allegory, though not seldom illumined by touches of ex-quisite humanity. This other-worldliness might test and purify his latent sense of values, for at the long last a Christian had to rely on his individual responsiveness to an ancient literature. In a perfect world, such exercises would be a perfect training.

Unhappily, the world seemed to be further than ever from perfect, and such freedom threw too much responsibility on the individual temperament. There was a fatal inducement to fasten on to those texts and doctrines which could be accommodated to one's own objects in life. For instance, modern civilisation required energetic and enterprising men to do many things contrary to the Sermon on the Mount—to compete with their fellow-creatures, to lay up treasures on earth, to sell all they had not, and keep the profits. So it was dangerously easy to overlook the moral code of the New Testament, or to persuade oneself that belief in salvation was the one essential requisite; that justification could be worked by Faith. Had not our Lord said, "Believe, and ye shall be saved"?

This reliance on conformity enhanced the social importance of the Church, but impaired its spiritual influence. As religion was so much a matter of self-examination, frequently ending in self-approval, church attendance became merely an aid to the process. In many cases sabbatarianism had degenerated into a respectable habit, the outward expression of a regular orderly life. No wonder

[1] Cf. *Religious Thought in the Eighteenth Century. Illustrated from Writers of the Period.* By J. M. Creed and J. S. Boys Smith, 1934.

such avowed antiritualists as Carlyle and Froude complained that England's most sacred institution was now *petrified*.

In view of these insufficiencies, there was always a certain tendency to return to Rome—a tendency just sufficiently marked to keep Protestantism on its guard. Macaulay had declared that "the Papacy remains not in decay, not a mere antique, but full of life and youthful vigour",[1] and any Protestant still touched by romanticism must have regretted his own sectarianism and modernity when he let his imagination linger on this universal fraternity which began with the beginning of Christianity and had for so long ruled the civilised world. But during the first three decades of the century, the movement was not formidable. The epic of the Protestant martyrs was too well known; Englishmen still believed all they had read or were reading about Romish corruption and superstition; besides a Protestant hates to bow down. But there was nothing in England to take the place of Catholicism. The laymen relied chiefly on themselves and their Bible, and if they took pride in the pre-eminence of the Established Church, it was rather as a national institution, authorised by the universities, and endued with the prestige and dignity of the secular government. In fact, during the eighteenth century, the Church was expected to play a part in politics; preferment was often the reward for loyalty to the Hanoverian dynasty; bishops were, for the most part, regular attendants at the House of Lords. Even cathedral stalls, deaneries and chaplaincies were frequently party appointments. Sydney Smith, a pious if not unworldly wit, claimed as his due a living of seven hundred pounds a year and a prebend worth an annual £1000. More and more the Church was becoming a department of the State.[2]

For all these reasons, the romantic movement left ecclesiasticism and dogma untouched. And yet, for the same reasons, a reform of English worship was bound to be attempted. A new generation had succeeded; it had caught the enthusiasm and the spirituality of its predecessors; it could begin where they left off. The weakness of the romantics was their dreaminess. Though they claimed between them to bring all divine and human interests within their ken, yet such was not the effect of their writings. They recalled their disciples to the contemplation of self. A romantic might see the truth in moments of solitary enlightenment, but not feel its

---

[1] *Von Ranke's History of the Popes.*
[2] See N. Sykes, *Church and State in England in the Eighteenth Century*, 1935.

influence among the pursuits which made him one with his fellow-creatures. Contact with God might preclude contact with humanity. The younger generation wanted to make this idealism effective among the mazes of the world. That is why they cultivated Goethe, that is also why some of them looked to those practices and observances in which God and Man ought to meet—to the religion of their forefathers; and all but the very fortunate must have been conscious that the old apathy and maladjustment of the eighteenth century still weighed upon this the most important function of English life. So the more spiritually minded joined together to make their religion worthy of the new era and the Oxford Movement became a fact. Their course of action was, inevitably, controlled by the defects and abuses which they resolved to remedy.

As usually happens, an external event brought these feelings to a head. We are at the period of The Reform Bill of 1832. The Whigs had come into power, and their party urged the government to reorganise the administration of the Church and to redistribute her revenues. Three years later a Royal Commission actually did report on "The Revenues and Patronage of the Established Church" and public action was taken. Some of the more broad-minded and less spiritual churchmen, the continuators of the eighteenth-century latitudinarians, concurred. Dr Thomas Arnold, in *Principles of Church Reform* (1813), even proposed to identify the Church with the State, to obliterate dogmatic distinctions, and to admit all denominations into the fold. This governmental interference outraged the religious sentiment of the new school. It seemed to deny that the Christian had a soul which is immortal and therefore transcends the State; it seemed to imply that this man-made institution could control our relations with the supreme and final immortality of God. So Keble preached his famous assize sermon in July 1833, comparing the English nation to the Israelites who under Saul rejected the government of God, preferring the government of men. The Rev. H. J. Rose invited the group to meet at Hadleigh Rectory and resolve on action. In February 1834 the Archbishop of Canterbury received an address signed by seven thousand clergymen, and another signed by twenty-three thousand laymen. Besides their avowed convictions, there must have lurked in their hearts a subconscious resentment against the kind of domination familiar to us in the twentieth century as a dictatorship.[1]

[1] See R. B. Lloyd, *Christianity, History and Civilisation*, 1936.

Such protests would have amounted to no more than one of those agitations which continually trouble the Church, unless the leaders of the movement could prove the authority by which they acted. So, being experts in theology, their first step was to find out which school was really following the will of God and whether, in the course of the ages, man had made the best use of what Divine Wisdom had imparted to him. Accordingly the tractarians re-traced the course of Christian belief through the ages, back to the Fathers of the primitive Eastern Church, examining and comparing the channels through which the tradition had been passed, de-manding of each authority his credentials and, above all, studying the great theologians and controversialists, who seemed somehow by their fervour, their earnestness and insight, to have caught the true spirit of God. Thus the Tractarians were initiated into the new romance of history which Herder had discovered; not the old-fashioned wonder of the Past, but rather the sense of unity with bygone aspirations and endeavours. They might even be convinced of their own immortal spirits by sympathy with the spirits which had proved themselves immortal.

How was it possible to sift the truth among so much conflicting evidence and so many jarring creeds? Partly by scholarly acumen and the exhaustive study of that literature which ought most of all to concern human beings—in itself an inspiring task—but much more by exercising and refining a kind of inward perceptiveness which they generally called *conscience*. The word has been so often debased by subsequent cant and formalism that we do not easily realise the sense in which it was used by, for instance, W. G. Ward,[1] or Newman.[2] The leaders of the Oxford Movement claimed that they could discriminate and appropriate moral and religious truth wherever found, because they were conscious of a corresponding tone and touch in their own hearts. The spirit within recognised the spirit without. It was "the secret inexplicable spontaneous movement of the mind (however arising) towards the external word".[3] Often the saints threw their religious impressions into illusive shapes that perplexed the modern mind. Conscience enabled the Christian to discern the real objects of his faith amidst the indistinctness of their opinions and impressions. Scholarly penetration was not enough; it had to be guided by the

---

[1] *The Ideal of a Christian Church*, 1844, chap. IX, §3.
[2] *Passim*, and especially *Lectures on Justification*.
[3] Newman, *Lectures on Justification*.

insight which comes from sympathy and fellowship of mood. In the words of one of the tractarians: "You must search for yourself and God must teach you."[1]

In this union of argumentative subtlety and mysticism, the reformers bid fair to develop a new faculty or at least a faculty once starved and now restored to full life. The effort had been made before. It is sketched in the so-called *Glaubensphilosophie* with which F. H. Jakobi opposed the complacent rationalism of the German *Aufklärung*. He argued that the man who seeks truth through his intelligence (*Verstand*) falls a victim to atheism; he who relies on reason (*Vernunft*) ends in dreams; and that Divine Truth will only be found by fusing both illuminations into a single light. To the philosopher's mind this miracle could be accomplished only by what he called a *salto mortale*, a leaping forward of the mind which at a bound might attain to intuition, that is to say, to belief.

The Oxford reformers discovered, or seemed to discover, how the wonder could be worked. It was by asceticism. Lest the reader should conclude that such self-discipline was a mere revival of ancient practices, it must be remembered that the asceticism of the nineteenth century was no longer that of the second. It did indeed involve fasting, prayer, meditation; but merely as aids and incentives to a certain way of thinking. What the modern man hoped to conquer was not so much the lusts of the flesh—on the contrary these churchmen encouraged each other to study their health—but the lusts of the intellect: the habit of mind generally known to the world as liberalism. On 10 February 1827 R. Hurrell Froude wrote in his Journal: "Save me, O Lord, from the snares of a double mind, and make my way stable before thee."[2] He was praying against the mixture of worldly speculations with his innermost thoughts; the coarsening and materialising of his intellect. His ideal was a kind of mental chastity and singleness; a release from what Sir Francis Palgrave called "the harlotry of philosophy". They did not fear "neology" because it was new, but because it clogged their perceptiveness. Thus cleansed and enlightened their thoughts should be equal to the newest of truths—the realities immanent in formularies and ritual. This asceticism worked so effectively on the mind of Hurrell Froude, that after his death his friend and admirer, Newman, on examining his papers, could

[1] *Tracts for the Times*, No. 11.
[2] *Remains of the late Rev. Richard Hurrell Froude.* [Edited by J. H. Newman and J. Keble, 1838–9.]

write to Keble: "These 'Thoughts' present a remarkable instance of the temptation to Rationalism, self-speculation, etc., subdued. We see his mind only breaking out into more original and beautiful discoveries, from that very repression which at first sight seemed likely to be the utter prohibition to exercise his special powers."[1]

Trusting to this sense of divine fitness, almost of theistic intimacy, their brains seemed able to discern what those heavenly objects are on which the spiritual life of this or that saint was fed, or could appreciate "all the delicate shades of truth and falsehood, the unobtrusive indications of God's will, the low tones of the 'still small voice' in which Scripture abounds".[2] A rationalist, for them, was simply a man who could not think further than the evidence of his senses, while the faithful could venture beyond such limitations; could throw their minds forward, and embrace, maintain and use truths that were beyond their intelligence.[3] It was even argued that God punishes with blindness those who approach sacred truths in a worldly spirit;[4] and that consequently there should be a keeping back in reserve of the higher doctrines—a *disciplina arcani*—until the initiates were rendered fit to receive them.[5]

Thus these men claimed to have discovered the secret of converting emotional and intellectual activity into spiritual insight. And what did they see? In the first place an overwhelming responsibility. Since an eternal power permitted them to perceive the Truth, they must follow this guidance wherever it might lead. In the next place, they convinced themselves that God was not only to be found, as so many Protestants believed, in a "still small voice". The Divine Presence had made itself visible; not of course as a pure ethereal spirit, but through God's special manifestation of Himself—the Church. When Christ rose from the dead, His perfections rose with Him and continued as spiritual influences through the rites and traditions which He founded. The ceremonies and institutions of Christian worship are not mere aids to piety, they are literally the channels of grace. The votary sees, hears and feels the Divine Presence, he does not merely think it. "Mystical" does not mean "figurative". Outward forms were appointed "to serve as a kind of ladder between earth and Heaven, between our spirit and the Spirit of Holiness".[6] For instance, the rite of baptism

---

[1] 30 June 1837.
[2] *Tracts for the Times*, No. 45; cf. Nos. 4, 8, 19.
[3] Tract 73.   [4] Tract 80, Pt II, §6.
[5] Tract 87, Pt IV.   [6] Tract 32.

literally implies the washing away of original sin and the starting of a new life in the lineage of Christ, though the recipient is unconscious of it; at confirmation, the Spirit is actually conveyed by the laying on of hands; it is the action which speaks, not the words of the officiant.

Hence the vital importance of recognising the rites and mysteries which could be proved irrefutably to have been instituted by Jesus. Men could not run the risk of "prejudice in favour of a particular theory" or "take upon themselves to choose Christ".[1] Whichever was the authentic institution was a Divine Ordinance, the appointed means of spiritual blessings. A heretical church might cherish a holy spirit in its institutions, but could not impart it, since its channels were made by man.[2] Hence also the power of public worship. God made Himself known in the spiritual atmosphere of the society which He had ordained. Divine Service with its glimmering tapers, sacred music, earnest voices and inspired liturgy absorbs all individual weaknesses and treacheries in the cult of a common ideal, each participant contributing what is finest in his own character and sinking his own peculiar baseness.

These convictions were quite in the tradition of the romantic movement. There was something in them not uncongenial to the ethical doctrines of Kant, and to Hegel's theory that the individual's life is rooted in social relationships.[3] It is unlikely that many of the promoters had studied German philosophy or were versed in romantic poetry, but there is an intellectual telepathy between humanists whose brains move with their age. In fact Newman records in his *Chronological Notes*: "During this spring (1835) I for the *first time* read parts of Coleridge's works; and I am surprised how much I thought mine, is to be found there."

It must now be clear that the Oxford Movement was much more than a theological controversy. It played upon man's interests and enthusiasms, his instinct for progress and his sense of duty; and aimed at reconciling all that was most spontaneous and creative with the oldest and most sacred of English institutions. Newman described it as "the spiritual awakening of spiritual wants".[4] This movement was promulgated with all the resources of scholarly research, and the promoters thereby convinced themselves that the fundamental truth lay in the Apostolic Succession of the

---

[1] Tracts 49, 52. [2] Newman to Mrs J. Mozley, 22 Dec. 1844.
[3] C. C. J. Webb, *Religious Thought in the Oxford Movement*, 1928.
[4] *Prospects of the Anglican Church*, §2, *The British Critic*, April 1839.

Anglican priesthood. Christ promised that His apostles should be alive till He came again and must therefore have meant their representatives, the bishops, who maintain the continuity of His Church and transmit His power. So it was possible to ally oneself to the actual plan and system which originated in our Saviour. English worship, thus examined and authenticated, could be proved to be not a mere protestation against Rome, not Puritan, much less Wesleyan, but the one voice which Christianity had from the beginning, just as all good and holy men were possessed by the same spirit; Hooker and Taylor, Ridley and Laud, no less than St Bernard and St Chrysostom. To consider such a tradition to be a department of state, dependent on civil authority, was as criminal as foolish. In their moments of greatest enthusiasm these high churchmen must have hoped, like Sir James Stephen, that the Gospel would "have a kingly way and appropriate Truth everywhere, new and old";[1] that they would bring about the reunion of Christianity under one liturgy as well as one faith. In the meantime, it could be proved that the English were hardly less favoured than the Chosen People if only they had eyes to see.

How were their eyes to be opened? It was at first suggested that an association should be formed with prominent figures at the head and an influential committee. Then came the objection that mighty works are not accomplished by a system, whereas systems rise out of individual exertions. Besides, this movement was the expression of individual minds. The promoters agreed in their doctrine, but not always in the arguments by which it was established. On the other hand, a sporadic and casual output of sermons and treatises would conduce to that decentralisation which was the weakness of Protestantism. It was necessary to make educated people realise that the impulse came from a united body of opinion. It was decided to enforce this impression by the periodical issue of pamphlets, which could be controlled and edited, could bear the name of the movement and by reiteration would compel their readers to think for themselves. Thus *Tracts for the Times* (1833–41) became the burning question of the period.

It is, of course, neither possible nor desirable to trace the history of those ninety publications. But in order to learn the lesson of their success and of their failure, we must look into the mind that inspired tractarianism. Who is their leader, the representative of what was true and false in their position? At the time when the

[1] J. H. Newman to R. H. Froude, 17 Jan. 1836.

movement was at its height, there would have been many answers to that question. It might have been Hurrell Froude, who was the most fiery and original, but died too soon, or Walter Hook, one of England's greatest parish priests, but he had belonged to the old High Church Party, and was growing old. Or William Palmer, the great authority on liturgies and the offices of the English Church. Or Keble, who at this time enjoyed an immense reputation not only for *The Christian Year* (1827) but for his saintly character and his high churchmanship and his powerful grasp of theological principles, and yet brought some of the poetry of country vicarages into Oxford common rooms which "stank of logic"; or Dr Edward Pusey, fresh from the universities of Germany, the soundest of their theologians and the most learned of their Arabic and Hebrew scholars. Any of these might have been quoted in the 'thirties or 'forties, according to the speaker's own predilections. But for those who study the mind of man through literature, J. H. Newman is, of course, the only satisfying exponent.

If we take Newman as our guide through the mazes of this controversy, it is because his position is unique. He played a double part, in that he received as much as he gave. If he has so unmistakably impressed his personality on the movement, the movement absorbed and remoulded him and not only changed his career but redirected the current of his being. He surrendered to these influences because they seemed to promise him what we are all seeking—the marriage of mind with spirit, of reason with imagination, of scepticism with grace, of modernism with antiquity.

To understand this significance it must be remembered that Newman was endowed with those special qualities which make for freethought. He had an acutely logical mind, a passion for reasoning and thinking clearly, and of reducing emotions to words. So in youth he took a marked interest in science, especially mathematics and chemistry, and all through his life he was on terms of sympathy if not intimacy with the highways and byways of the sceptical mind. As a young man he was almost morbidly shy, and no doubt this sense of inborn diffidence urged him to self-assertion through his intellect. In his own words he wished "to be a firebrand" and "to have a mission". So, whatever his pursuits and persuasions, he was bound to become a controversialist, and in this warfare he did unquestionably develop a genius for exposing the illogicalities and inconsequences of an adversary. Free discussions if not freethought was destined to be the very breath of his thinking life.

So these qualities involved a heavy responsibility in the second decade of the century. Orthodoxy was losing its dignity as well as its persuasiveness, and "infidelity" promised to be more and more attractive because it flattered the pleasures of thinking for oneself. One would have expected Newman to become a rationalist. When he went up to Oxford he devoted his first Long Vacation to studying Locke and Gibbon, and the Law was talked of as his profession. This project was abandoned when they elected him to a fellowship and under that influence he took orders in 1824. But the election brought a change of habits rather than of mind. The common room encouraged criticism; his contemporaries (Copleston, Darwin, Hawkins and Arnold) were *noetics*, that is to say, survivals of the eighteenth century who trusted their piety as far as they trusted their intellects. Newman was not encouraged to do otherwise. He continued to read the books which stimulate and unsettle the mind. In 1825 we find him collaborating with the then Dr Whateley (his future adversary) on his *Elements of Logic* (published four years later), and Blanco White named him his "Oxford Plato".

One imagines that Newman could not for long have persisted in these paths so carefully trimmed by men and paved with probabilities, for there was quite another side to his nature. It has often been noticed that all through life he suffered from a sense of dependency; that he shrank from making decisions on his own initiative, was always quick to see the difficulties in the way of any project; easily resigned himself to inaction, and yearned for the guidance and companionship of a friend. Whether or not the psychoanalysts are right who attribute such dependency to the "filial complex", it is nevertheless true that the human being who yearns for parental guardianship is particularly in need of religion. Such was Newman's case; nor would his religious instinct be easily satisfied. Although his intellect cut like a razor, he was intensely emotional, and his thoughts were not always to be soothed by the violin, which he loved to play. Under the pressure of his feelings his behaviour sometimes became quite unaccountable, and it is surprising to find how often this thorough Englishman sought relief in the un-English outlet of tears. He was not only highly strung, but imaginative. He had a marked poetic talent, though it was never developed. We can see from his verses that he was certainly quick to receive visual and sensuous impressions; and to convert them into ideas. When he visited a strange place, for instance Cambridge or Rome, he at once felt and even visualised what he called the *genius loci*. Even his austere and deeply reasoned prose abounds in figures and symbols. Such a temperament required a faith to match. If his religion was to be large enough for his spirit, it would have to be both scientific and sensuous; it would have to dominate his life purpose and yet leave his intellect free to enjoy its earthly power; it would have to be such as he could preach to his fellow-creatures, for a religion must be shared with others, and Newman in those youthful days was determined to have a mission.

Nor did he come up to Oxford altogether unprepared for his task. His home life had taught him to be content with the Bible and the unimaginative sanctities of Protestant worship, but evangelicalism had been deepened at Dr Nicholas's school at Ealing by the teaching of the Rev. Walter Mayer.[1] This classical master had impressed him at the age of sixteen with the consciousness of God's presence, which one cannot prove but which is as certain as the fact of one's own existence, and had further convinced him that unswerving allegiance to this immanence is the only way to Grace. Thus Newman began his religious life as an enlightened Calvinist; nor did he ever forget the obligation which he owed to the inward silent voice. His problem was to adjust its promptings to the discursive intellectualism of Oxford and to the agnostic intellectualism of the outside world. Obviously, a man so bred and conditioned would not seek the sort of God whom his contemporary Heine preferred and the English Broad Church afterwards cultivated—"ein bescheidener Gott des Volkes, ein Bürger-Gott, un *bon dieu citoyen*".[2]

He would seek a religion which satisfied his privileged position, that is to say, a cult of intellectual and spiritual activity, breathing zeal and sanctity, in which erudition enjoys elbow-room and the heart's desire finds or creates fulfilment in something greater than itself. By 1828 this ideal seemed to be within reach. In that year he was appointed vicar of St Mary's, and began to enjoy sufficient eminence to influence young men. So he gained insight into their difficulties. In those days, as we have seen, the tendency was not so much to question the existence of God, as to question the authority or evidence by which the orthodox professed to

[1] Wilfrid Ward, *The Life of John Henry, Cardinal Newman*, 2 vols, 1912.
[2] *Italien. Die Stadt Lucca*, Kap. VII: "A modest popular God, a citizen God."

know anything about Him. Thoughtful and scholarly undergraduates had learnt from historians, mathematicians and physicists new and searching methods for testing their data. But when
they turned their well-trained minds to religion, they were met
with a conflict, if not confusion, of beliefs and opinions unworthy
of academic standards. As Newman himself had written in 1823:
"Contradiction can be no more true in religion than in astronomy
or chemistry."[1] Those who could not see their God in forms of
worship or the works of nature, would soon become deaf to the
inward intimations of His presence. Newman appreciated this
danger all the more deeply because he had himself not been free
from its menace. Besides, he loved to counsel and guide young
men. In the same year as he was appointed vicar he became
intimate with Hurrell Froude, who introduced him to Keble.
These two friends largely decided the course he was to take. He
learnt from them how to bring the enthusiasms of the romantic
movement into his religious life, and how to look to the Church,
an august and divine structure, for the evidence and intimation of
God's Presence. Thus inspired, he began systematically to study
the Fathers in order to see whether he could learn the true secret
of religious authority from antiquity—from the old theologians
who exercised their intellect without losing sight of their creator.
The result of this concentration was *The Arians of the Fourth Century*
(1833). Following their example, he felt himself henceforth to be
specially appointed to combat all looseness of belief and wilfulness
of thought, all the intellectual and spiritual compromises which
went by the name of liberalism. Henceforth his sermons gained
in depth and power, and he became famous as a preacher. At the
same time he was so conscientious a controversialist that by 1830
he had formed the principle of always copying out the letter which
he was going to answer.[2] Such a man was bound to throw himself
into the movement which was already on foot by the time he had
recovered from his illness in Sicily and had returned home. On
31 August 1833 he writes to J. W. Bowden: "Our objects are 'to
rouse the clergy, to inculcate the Apostolical Succession, and to
defend the Liturgy'. We hope to publish tracts, etc."

[1] *Letter to a Young Man of Sceptical Opinions.* See Anne Mozley, *Letters and
Correspondence of John Henry Newman*, 1891.
[2] To his sister Jemima, Sept. 1830.

CHAPTER V

Newman as tractarian and Protestant reformer—He searches for the truth till his critical acumen and religious imagination find it among the Roman Catholics—So he wins to spiritual peace, but neither Church enables him to reform his fellow creatures.

Renan has compared theology to a Gothic cathedral: "Elle en a la grandeur, les vides immenses et le peu de solidité."[1] Newman might have been dedicated to supply those defects. "We have", he declared, "a vast inheritance, but no inventory of our treasures. All is given us in profusion; it remains for us to catalogue, sort, distribute, select, harmonise and complete."[2] So he made it his task to examine the tangled differences between belief and usage, formularies and revelation, the unwritten no less than the written word. Like the author of *The Analogy*, he based his convictions on the accumulation of probabilities. The initiate would be led on from one likelihood to another, the aggregate of evidence becoming at each step more irresistible. But the final conviction depended on a certain willingness to be convinced; reverence and devotedness springing from a secret and unexplained knowledge that God was in the background, beckoning. "Divine aid alone can carry anyone safely and successfully through an inquiry after religious truth."[3] These researches brought to birth the *Via Media*, that is to say, a religion cleansed of all the "mistiness" and indecision of Puritanism, and on the other hand untainted by what most churchmen would then call the superstitions and idolatries of Rome, for instance, mariolatry and the doctrine of transubstantiation.

So from 1833 onwards Newman gradually became the greatest religious leader of his age, perhaps one of the greatest in our history. He expounded his doctrines in his sermons preached at St Mary's, in the essays which he wrote as editor of *The British Critic*, in the thoughtful and learned volumes which he published from time to time. He surpassed his associates and fellow-workers because of his psychological insight and intimacy with religious experience.

---

[1] *Souvenirs*, chap. v: "It is similar in its grandeur, its immense gaps and its unsubstantiality."

[2] *Lectures on the Prophetical Office* (book form), 1937.

[3] *Private Judgment*, §1, *The British Critic*, July 1841.

Besides, no other teacher had Newman's mysteriously contained personality, his spirituality of manner and bearing, his mastery of incisive and unforgetable phraseology, his genius for puncturing a fallacy, his power of appealing to the deeper sensibilities while conducting an argument with lucidity. You think that you are merely following a concatenation of ideas, and you find yourself admitted to the recesses of his clean passionate sincerity. So he left his mark on all the younger humanists, both those who were destined to resist, and those who were destined to preserve and develop these earlier impressions.

For while his position was supreme and he must have enjoyed the most that a human being can expect from life, intense intellectual activity leading to a vision of what is best on earth and in heaven. He believed that the whole movement was inspired by God. "A flame seems arising in so many places as to show no mortal incendiary is at work", he writes to Froude in July 1835. Trusting in this internal revelation, confident that he can sort out all religious beliefs by the light of the intellect and create a system by the light of conscience, he developed astonishing skill as a controversialist. Sometimes he would tempt his antagonist onward step by step till the unsuspecting theologian found himself confronted by two impossible alternatives, between which he had to choose. At other times, he would turn his opponent's eyes inward into his own heart and lead him to discover for the first time all his opinions accepted and implied—his impulses, intuitions and motives, all that deeper ferment which actuates the reasoning powers and should arise out of contact with God. The height of his triumph was reached in June 1838. In that year sixty thousand tracts were sold, and Newman's latest volume of sermons was sold out in six months. His doctrine of the *Via Media* was elaborated in lectures and published in 1837 as *The Prophetical Office of the Church.* But his greatest victories were won in the pulpit, to which A. P. Stanley, Sir Francis Doyle, Gladstone, Lord Coleridge, Principal Shairp, J. A. Froude, Matthew Arnold, and even Mrs Humphrey Ward, have borne witness. The best were published in 1843 as *Sermons Preached before the University of Oxford* and their author afterwards described them "as a whole, the best things I have written".

A few months later there comes a change. He seems to be realising that he is "finessing too deep" as Hurrell Froude had warned him as early as January 1835. On 21 November 1838 he writes to J. W. Bowden: "I distrust my judgment, and am getting afraid to speak. It is just like walking on treacherous ice." On 5 December 1838 he writes to Keble: "I do not realise things, but am merely drawing out intellectual conclusions." In 1835 he had confidently asserted that we can "embrace, maintain and use general propositions which are greater than our own capacity".[1] In 1840 he writes sadly to Miss H.: "The human mind in its present state is unequal to its own power of apprehension; it embraces more than it can master." On 21 February of the same year he is expecting "a collision with Puritanism which may split the Church" (to J. W. Bowden). On 25 August 1843 he writes to Canon Woodgate: "The fact is, our system is rotten and won't hold together."[2]

We note that this discouragement could not proceed only from overwork, though he used to write so hard that his hand ached, and would sometimes recast chapters "over and over again, besides innumerable corrections and interlinear additions".[3] The character of the tracts had changed. They began tentatively, as quite slim pamphlets, quaintly reminding one of *The Spectator* of Addison, whom Newman so wholeheartedly admired.[4] The import and purport were of course quite different, but the method was similar. The tractarians took one feature after another of contemporary religious life and discussed its significance for the inquiring layman, much as Addison enlightened his fellow-townsmen's curiosity in the society and institutions of their day. Perhaps the best example of this earlier spirit is to be found in No. 8, a mere leaflet on *The Gospel, A Law of Liberty* (the idea derived from Keble), in which God is conceived to be treating us as friends, not servants; trusting to our discretion, telling us "not so much what He would have done in detail, as what are the objects He would have accomplished". This doctrine of reverent and affectionate faith was remembered and celebrated more than thirty years later in *Rugby Chapel* by Matthew Arnold, who nevertheless wrote so much against Newman's position, and it bids fair to be the inspiring principle of a revival in our own day. But the tractarians did not remain contented with such humanistic appeals, for Newman was

[1] Tract 73.

[2] *Times Lit. Suppl.*, "Fresh Light on Newman." 26 Feb. 1935.

[3] To Rev. John Hayes, 13 April 1869. (On the difficulties of composition under which he had laboured all his life.)

[4] J. C. Thirlwall, "Cardinal Newman's Literary Preferences", *M.L.N.* XLVIII, No. 1.

an insatiable controversialist. Within the bare limits of theism, he demanded as much freedom of discussion as did Mill in *On Liberty*. Every authority, ancient or modern, was challenged to produce his credentials. Long ago, on 13 March 1829, he had written to his mother that "the talent of the day is against the Church". He now seemed bent on proving to young Oxford that the intellect could and should be roused to as great efforts within the theological schools as without. Apparently, our spiritual welfare might hang on the interpretation of a single text. So the series of fly-sheets grew into theological treatises, often reaching conclusions far above the heads of the laity. For instance, the ark in which Noah was saved "denotes the Church, upborne by the waters of Baptism, wherein Sin was drowned".[1] This development was particularly noticeable after Pusey joined the movement in 1835. No. 82, his learned tract on Baptism, was admired by Newman till his dying day.[2]

But as the tracts soared in speculation, they sank to a lower plane. They began to arouse the spirit of academic controversy, the Protestant's passion for dispute, the kind of zeal which impelled their grandfathers to accuse Dr Butler of popery because, when Bishop of Bristol, he erected a plain marble crucifix in the chapel of his episcopal house. His influence with the young men was still supreme. On 17 November 1839 he notes with pleasure that there were no less than forty-three communicants at St Mary's. But only the year before, S. Wilberforce noticed that undergraduates were beginning to prefer Cambridge because party division ran so high at Oxford. In fact, religious controversy at Oxford had for some years been accompanied by exhibitions of feeling such as would seem ridiculous, almost humiliating, to the impartial and humanised observer, for instance, to Sydney Smith. There was a rumour that Newman left the Oriel dining hall as soon as he saw Dr Arnold, the leader of the Broad-Church party, enter;[3] another rumour that he wore on his surplice a rich illumined cross;[4] another that he introduced a prayer of his own to the Virgin Mary during service;[5] yet another that the tractarians disliked pews because they wished to shorten and eventually abolish sermons.[6]

[1] Tract 67.
[2] Conversation with his sister in 1876.
[3] R. F. Wilson to Newman, 5 Feb. 1835.
[4] Newman to J. W. Bowden, 6 Oct. 1837.
[5] Newman to Miss Giberne, 4 Nov. 1840.
[6] Mrs J. Mozley to Newman, 20 Feb. 1843.

Dean Close of Cheltenham, while disclaiming personalities, described Newman in 1842 as "a liar and a pickpocket".[1] Dean Goulburn tells us that Golightly one dark night in Oxford was seized with fear that the tractarians were waiting round the street corner to do him grevious bodily harm.[2] When Newman resigned the vicariat of St Mary's and reconstructed and adapted some poor cottages at Littlemore so as to form a suitable residence, where he could escape publicity and find peace in obscure parish work, it was rumoured that the shed built to connect the cottage doors was a cloister, that the small bedrooms were "cells or dormitories". Ecclesiastically minded people journeyed from Oxford to spy on the suspicious place. "Heads of Houses, as mounted patrols, walked their horses round these poor cottages. Doctors of Divinity dived into the hidden recesses of that private tenement uninvited, and drew domestic conclusions from what they saw there."[3] This sectarian and undignified inquisitiveness was not restricted to the man who had unwittingly provoked it. Undergraduates were watched to see what books they read, what houses they frequented, and to what societies they belonged.[4] Far away from these haunts of disingenuousness, in one of the most beautiful districts of rural England, the rector of Lavington and Graffham, the strong Anglo-Catholic, R. Randall, was becoming notorious for his ritualistic squabbles with his curate, the extreme Protestant E. Randall.[5]

Why were educated and pious men thus busied with ignoble suspicions, while a spiritual reformation was at stake? Simply because the ideals of tractarianism were more and more diverted from the broad issues of human development into a narrow and rocky channel which does not concern the historian of literature. As the years advanced the temptations of the *odium theologicum* became more difficult to resist. One of the chief causes is almost too well known to need recording: the Newmanites were tending towards Rome and in 1845 their leader finally took the decisive step which he had been meditating so long. This ardent reformer, labouring to extricate the primitive divine element of the Anglican Church—the *depositum fidei*—from the accretions and suppressions

---

[1] A. Mozley, *Letters of J. H. Newman.* Footnote to letter of 1 Dec. 1842.
[2] In 1842. Recounted in *The Guardian*, 13 Jan. 1886.
[3] *Apologia*, Pt VI, §1.   [4] *Loss and Gain.*
[5] *A Tractarian at Work. A Memoir of Dean Randall.* By J. F. Briscoe and H. F. B. Mackay, 1932.

of Puritanism, had ended by convincing himself that the faith of his university no longer contained what he sought.

The history of his conversion is of great importance to our inquiry for two reasons. It reveals, in the first place, that the religious atmosphere of the nineteenth century was not congenial to the disinterested search for truth. There were too many sentimental associations, vested interests, appeals to self-importance, inherited prejudices, and personal resentments. Religion was so entangled with the claims of home life, citizenship, and academic or class loyalty, that the uncompromising investigators were at a hopeless disadvantage and had to descend to a lower plane. The Church was not sound enough to resist moral contamination. So much of one's best self had to be sacrificed to theological technicalities and controversial bitterness that many humanists, especially among the younger generation, conceived a contempt for the religious temperament, turned their backs on theological research, and sought self-expression elsewhere. But Newman's conversion is even more significant because of the motives which led to his decision.

If we are to believe the letters which he wrote to his family from Italy in 1833, he conceived the strongest distaste for the Eternal City, whose ecclesiasticism was still dominated by the spirit of ancient pagan Rome.[1] Not least amongst his aversions was the sight of priests spitting while engaged in the most sacred part of the services.[2] Even as late as January 1839 he contemplated reprinting extracts of his writings against popery.[3] It need not be added that to sacrifice Protestantism was to sacrifice friends, fame and fortune. But in the summer of 1839, while studying the history of the Monophysites, he noted that they had originated the Puritan dogma that the Saviour did not shed the divine substance and become man, was never actually born of the Virgin Mary, but retained full divinity even after the incarnation. For that reason modern English priests, like the followers of Eutyches in the fifth century, do not mix water with wine at the communion service. But Monophysitism had been disallowed by Pope Leo, the undoubted inheritor of Christ's authority, and if he, or any of his divinely appointed successors, refused to recognise the claims of any religious society, that sect could not belong to the Universal Church. The infallibility of the Church could not be questioned;

[1] To S. Rickards, 14 April 1833.   [2] To his mother, 17 April 1833.
[3] To F. Rogers, 22 Jan. 1839.

its supreme authority was established by "one of the prime oracles of antiquity", St Augustine, who had formally pronounced her judgments to be supreme and incontestable throughout the world.[1] And now it began to dawn upon him that the history of the fourth-century Arians taught the same lesson. Their heresy was being perpetuated by Anglicans, and he reflected bitterly on the subterfuges and reservations, the submissions to earthly governments, by which the modern English Church, like the old Arians, had maintained their schism; and all the time in her "arrogant John Bull way" treated other nations as mere foreigners, not as Christians.[2] Finally, he learnt from St Alfonso Liguori and St Ignatius that no dogmatic symbol, rite or sacrament need obscure the relationship between the soul and its Creator. Man and God was *solus cum solo* in the Roman Catholic Church no less than in the Puritan sects.

Thus, after fifteen or more years of intensive study and dispute,[3] when he looked round on the non-Catholic religions of modern Europe, they all seemed to him to be like upstart and local administrations in a great empire which had broken up, whereas the original and authentic government was that which had always continued united from the first. "The Church only *is* while it is one, for it is individually as *He* who animates and informs it."[4] Only Rome fulfilled these conditions and therefore only Rome was authorised to give access to God.

These ideas were slowly forming in Newman's mind from 1839 to 1845. Many of his friends and enemies foresaw the end after he published Tract 90. Neither the author, nor Keble, expected the pamphlet to create much stir, yet by 6 February, 12,500 copies had been sold and the third edition was in preparation. The Rev. C. P. Golightly bought up copies as fast as the printer could supply them, and sent them to the clergy all over the country. This publication merely contends that the Thirty-Nine Articles do not commit their subscribers to uncompromising estrangement from Rome; they condemn the corruptions but not the doctrines of the Catholic Church; so Tract 90 was bound to rouse the sectarianism of professed and professional Protestants and to enjoy a *succès de scandale*.

---

[1] *Securus judicat orbis terrarum.* Newman had been reminded of this dogma by Wiseman's article on *The Schism of the Donatists* (*Dublin Review*) to which R. Wilberforce drew his attention.

[2] *Private Judgment*, §5, *The British Critic*, July 1841.

[3] He states his position in a letter to Mrs J. Mozley, 24 Nov. 1844. Henceforth his letters to her record his agitations and searchings of heart. Especially that of 15 March 1845. [4] To W. R. Lyall, 16 July 1842.

The true revelation of his mind is to be found in the book which he wrote in retirement after the pamphlet had been condemned, and published in 1845 as *The Development of Christian Doctrine*.

This work is sometimes quoted as being typically modern and progressive because it recognises the principle of growth in theological phenomena.[1] J. Guitton[2] goes much further. He finds in Newman's pages that awareness of time which, he maintains, originated with the eighteenth-century historians, gathered strength from the philosophy of Hegel, was afterwards corroborated by the biological theory of evolution, and found its full expression in the doctrines of Croce and Bergson. Both estimates rather miss the purpose of the essay. It is Newman's first *Apologia*, addressed neither to Kingsley, nor the British public, nor yet to the Roman Curia, but to himself. It is the examination of his own conscience. As such it is an astonishingly determined effort to adapt the Past to the needs of the Present. Here is a man who cannot live without handling and rationalising knowledge, who cannot rationalise knowledge unless it brings the consciousness of contact with a divine power—unless he fuses his erudition with his sense of the sublime and the beneficent. As he had written in 1841: "What wiser and what juster and what more really merciful law than that man shall not be able to receive into his head what he will not receive into his heart also."[3] So he retraces the history of his religion and finds that the authentic word of God has developed in harmony with the development of the mind of man. The Divine Spirit is older than creation yet as young as the nineteenth century. This energising vitality can be found only in the Roman Catholic Church. The book is a model of argumentative power and of chastened intensity of thought, but, as the author admits, the idea is not new.[4]

Newman has sometimes been compared to Renan. It has even been maintained[5] that the one became a Catholic not only in the same year as the other became an agnostic, but for similar reasons. They certainly were alike in one respect: neither desired the change. They went whither the preponderance of demonstration led them. Renan confesses that he let his convictions form themselves, "par une sorte de concrétion impersonnelle, dont on n'est en quelque

[1] E.g. H. Walker, *The Literature of the Victorian Era*, 1913, Pt I, chap. 1.
[2] *Philosophie de Newman*, 1933.   [3] *The British Critic*, Jan. 1841.
[4] Introd. §21.
[5] J. Guitton, *La Philosophie de Newman*, 1933.

sorte que le spectateur".[1] Newman was just as scientifically minded. He followed with equal fidelity "the concatenation of arguments by which the mind ascends from its first to its final religious idea".[2] Yet they arrived at opposite poles because their ideas of a human perfectibility were opposite. Renan applied himself to the German theologians and especially the Christologists, just as Newman applied himself to the early Fathers. Renan began in the Newmanite spirit seeking "la conciliation d'un esprit hautement religieux avec l'esprit critique".[3] But he learnt from these modern investigators and from his own profound knowledge of Scriptural languages and literature, that the Bible, the ultimate authorisation of Christianity, was a collection of very fallible books, riddled with contradictions and falsehoods. That autocratic voice was only a babel of human voices. So Renan's adventurous spirit gave free rein to his intellect. He examined the data as the great churchmen of the seventeenth century had taught him to do, without wishing or fearing any result, and he ended with "la claire vue scientifique d'un univers où n'agit d'une façon appréciable aucune volonté libre supérieure à celle de l'homme".[4] As we shall see later, many were to follow in his footsteps.

Newman was, as we have seen, not content with an intellectual triumph. When we think of some living personality whom we deeply love, we have to admit many considerations besides those sufficient for the appreciation of an inanimate object. So it is with religious truths. We are not only handling facts; we are in contact with essences of more than scientific significance. The keenest research is subject, not indeed to any expressed desire or expectation, but to certain spiritual exigencies which decide their value. Love, reverence, awe, devotion are required, and they must give their sanction to scientific inquiry. The inquirer must approach his subject not only with an unbiased mind, but with a spiritualised mind. We shall examine in subsequent chapters the consequences of the rationalist's attitude, such as Renan exemplifies; but we must first consider the fate of Newman's idealism. Has it justified itself in nineteenth-century life?

There is a temptation to answer "No", because the churchman

---

[1] *Souvenirs d'Enfance et de Jeunesse*, chap. v, §III.

[2] *Apologia*, Pt VI, §II.　　　　　　[3] *Souvenirs, ibid.*

[4] *Ibid*. chap. VI, §II: "The clear-sighted and scientific view of a universe in which, to any appreciable extent, no independent will-power is operative, higher than man's."

who submits to the rule of the Pope surrenders his private right to influence culture. It is forgotten that Newman is chiefly remembered for what he wrote under the shadow of Rome, and that he believed himself to be entering upon a new life. It should always be remembered that he never condoned her corruptions and infidelities; that he never conformed to Catholic authority till he had convinced himself that it was authentic. What he accepted was the Catholic principle rather than its practice. In his Protestant days he had been occupied with the search for the Truth; the Truth had now been found; and had brought him peace and strength. He felt a fullness of satisfaction in its theology, its sacraments and discipline; in its indissoluble unity; in the principle of its indefectibility. "It is the earnest and the beginning of repose in Heaven." Its rites captured his imagination. He has described with fervid eloquence the poetry and symbolism of the Mass,[1] and once declared "that the thought of the Anglican service makes me shiver". With this great power behind him, he felt himself to be called to new efforts. With unusual penetration, he foresaw that rationalism and freethought would continue to increase and could only be met and conquered by equal freedom of thought and exercise of reason.

The first important manifesto was the body of lectures delivered between 1854 and 1858 as rector of the ill-fated Irish University in which he pleaded for unfettered discussion, and unrestricted inquiry, but all deepened and directed by the recognition of religious values. In fact theology—"the science of the One God" —was to be the indispensable subject in a scheme which embraced the empirical sciences. When once students had been imbued with a sense of conscience, duty and the Supreme Intelligence, they could safely be left to verify modern discoveries, and to develop ideas struck out by the collision of mind with mind and knowledge with knowledge. As contributor and editor to the *Rambler* and *Atlantis*, he tried to assure doubters by analysing the relations between faith and reason; admitting that the old principles must be retained, but insisting on new forms of thought and expression adjusted to the new knowledge; still confident that the Catholic mind should be as free as an ancient Greek's, provided that the horror of sin and the reverence for moral law were not obscured. At times he certainly went to extremes to modernise the Church of St Peter. According to Lord (then Sir John) Acton, he appeared

[1] *Loss and Gain*, Pt II, chap. 20.

to think "that it was not so important that people should be brought round to particular opinions, as that they should be taught to think logically".[1]

Yet these and many other efforts produced very little effect, nor was he successful in his various administrative and organising projects, except for the two oratories which he founded. He was too unpopular at Rome. The Catholic world did not want to debate and discuss. They expected their eminent convert to effect spectacular conversions and deliver brilliant lectures, like the course on *The Difficulties of Anglicans* (1850), but not to disturb their beliefs. More than once his published opinions were *delated*. It was becoming more and more obvious that the Catholic, like the Protestant religion, had become too organised and enmeshed to serve as a bridge towards a new world, at any rate on earth. This may be the reason why Newman's later writings, despite their broad-mindedness, are narrow in their appeal.

In one way and another Newman was thwarted for twenty years. He had begun to consider his career to be at an end, and had almost discontinued writing, when Kingsley's attack roused him to reply, and with the tactical skill of a consummate controversialist he saw that the moment had come not only to refute this slur on the Catholic priesthood, but to clear his own character of any imputation, and moreover, to demonstrate how cogent his reasons were for crossing over to Rome.

The *Apologia pro Vita Sua*, on which his fame will rest, is assuredly one of the greatest of the world's "confessions". Yet why does the book command our admiration? Partly because it contains within its two covers an unforgettable impression of that most elusive of all things, the spiritual atmosphere of an age. We know how people thought and felt, we appreciate the tone and tenour of their lives, even though we may have little sympathy with their preoccupations. Partly again because of its style. The author has a genius for lucid exposition. He can straighten and simplify the mazes of theological controversy, and in a phrase, often in a word, can touch the secrets of religious emotionalism. But chiefly beeause this autobiography is a piece of highly artistic portraiture. Newman can put himself into a book. The reader begins with a kind of respectful curiosity in the workings of his mind, and ends with admiration at his single-mindedness, his intellectual self-control and his modesty. But these are not the highest qualities of a book. The *Apologia* does

[1] Sir John Acton to Dr Newman, 8 July 1861.

not reveal the reader to himself. Whenever a writer's mind is expanding to new influences, we can follow him and enjoy the same expansion by proxy, even though we do not agree with his thoughts, nor share the spirit in which he thinks. The student may not be able to pass through the same experiences as did Dante, Thomas à Kempis or Sir Thomas Browne, but he can identify himself with their sense of discovery and conquest. Can he capture that mood while reading the *Apologia*?

The publication of this autobiography revived his fame; his influence, especially in England, was further enhanced by his reply to his old friend Dr E. B. Pusey's *Eirenikon*; Rome fully recognised the value of these services, but neither the Pope nor his advisers felt more inclined to authorise the doctrines of this adventurous thinker, or allow him to influence young Catholics at Oxford as he himself proposed on two occasions. Yet neither success nor failure seemed to blunt his restless, insubordinate mind. He was bent on combating liberalism with its own weapons, and thereby claimed that he was continuing the tradition of the true church. As he wrote to Henry Wilberforce on 21 July 1867: "In all times the debates in the schools have been furious and it is in this way, of the collision of flint and steel, that the light of truth has been struck and elicited." The author of *On Liberty* could have said no more. Take, for instance, his attitude to the question of infallibility. At this time (1867–8) the Papal States were being confiscated, and the faithful, outraged at the spoliation of the Holy See, rallied round the Pope and hotly reaffirmed that he possessed all the authority of St Peter. So Newman at once challenged the interpretation and application of the dogma, and argued that the pious must indeed accept the principle, but that they were always entitled to sift and examine each papal pronouncement and collate it with previous utterances, so as to decide whether the High Pontiff was translating the voice of God, his judgment founded on a definition of faith, or whether he was delivering himself of a mere human opinion which his fellow-mortals had the right, in fact the obligation, to criticise. No wonder the hereditary Catholics resented the reforming zeal of this newcomer; no wonder Newman could complain that "every word I publish will be malevolently scrutinized and every expression which can possibly be perverted sent straight to Rome".[1]

Yet this second period of repression produced not indeed his greatest work, but the one which contains the ruling idea of his

[1] To H. Wilberforce, 12 Aug. 1868.

whole life. For more than twenty years he had been trying to give his doctrine its final and convincing form; he had already made a dozen attempts; and then in 1866, while staying with Ambrose St John at Glion, he hit upon the right avenue of approach and so *The Grammar of Assent* was begun. The purpose of this book is to sanction and sanctify freethought. The genuine student should fearlessly seek the truth, but he will not find it unless he employs all the resources with which we are endowed—especially that process of subconscious reasoning which originates in the sense of awe, love, shame, and the horror of sin. These sentiments are distinct from the reasoning faculties, but ought to assist and complete them. They have a logic of their own, and can penetrate, interpret and even rationalise our moral problems and questions. The modern sceptic is continually wandering in these realms, but guided only by his materialistic intelligence; and his dehumanised powers of scientific observation and deduction are excellently adapted to the study of inanimate objects, but blind to the secrets of the soul. He is not insincere, much less perverse, but only ill-equipped. He lacks the illumination of his own spiritual experiences, the *illative sense* as Newman termed it. This influence, born of our deepest emotions, often contradicts the findings of the materialist and always adjusts his empiricism to its own intuitions. Its enlightenment qualifies knowledge to understand religion and replaces "probability" by "certitude".

This book not only consummates the history of Newman's active life, but marks its close. Though he was destined to live another twenty years and be honoured with a cardinal's hat, he had grown too old to think hard. So it remains to consider the significance of his career. What is the value of his teaching to his contemporaries and to us? Did he really equip the rising generation for the battle of life?

He equipped them, or rather he tried to equip them, for the battle of ideas—"a right moral state of mind germinates or even generates good intellectual principles".[1] It seems at first sight an inspiring idea. The student who exercises his sense of spiritual values, who feels God in his conscience, can be trusted to face historical criticism, science, or anything else. But Newman also possessed an almost uncanny insight into the rationalism which he only half understood. So much so, that one almost suspects him of having never quite effaced in his own mind an unconfessed bias

[1] Newman to Father Coleridge, 5 Feb. 1871.

towards scepticism. Consequently, he had an instinctive fore-boding of the course which freethought would take. He foresaw that it would become increasingly difficult to recognise divinity in nature, society, secular history, industrialism, and the sciences which investigate the human mind. The heart might be full of religion, but this allegiance would not find its justification in culture or in the world of common experience. So, as we have seen, he looked to the authority of the Church for what he could not find elsewhere. Without sacrificing one iota of sincerity or scholarship, he staked his spiritual life on formularies and ritual. Such eccle-siasticism has not proved an equipment for the battle of life.

In the first place, consider the immediate consequences of Newman's conversion. It was followed by many others. Before the end of 1843 Wiseman writes to Philip de Lisle "scarcely a day passes that I do not hear of someone who is on the point or in the thought of joining us and losing often their all". To mention only a few conspicuous names. In 1845 F. Faber confessed in the pulpit that he had been teaching heretical doctrines, flung his surplice on the floor of the church and walked out to join the Catholics. Sir George Bowyer and T. W. Allies crossed over in 1850. After the Judicial Committee of the Privy Council had ruled that G. C. Gorham's Calvinistic views on baptismal regeneration should be no bar to his institution to a benefice, Archdeacon Wilberforce and Manning took the same step in 1851. In 1857 James Marshall, soon after his ordination from Exeter College, sacrificed all emolu-ments and prospects, and brought with him seventeen converts, now reduced to destitution. In 1866 Gerard Manley Hopkins wrote to Newman, who as ever was counselling delay and reflec-tion, and declared that unless he at once became a Catholic, he would have "to live without church or sacraments".[1]

These conversions bear testimony to the prevalence of religious sentiment and also added to its vitality. They roused the Protestant denominations, especially the Broad Church Party and the pro-fessors of muscular Christianity; they may have caused and certainly stimulated the movement towards church-building and restoration. Everyone began to talk and think about religion, but not, unfortunately, as if they were fellow-seekers who agreed to differ. Losses and gains equally exacerbated these learned rivals, provoked them to battles of texts and soon this cultured bigotry degenerated into uncharitableness. Many people at this time held

[1] G. F. Lahey, *Gerard Manley Hopkins*, 1930.

that the Antichrist of *The Revelation*[1] should be interpreted as the Romish Church, and these conversions, explained as the result of Newman's defection, made them fear that the Whore of Babylon, the Scarlet Woman, had crept into their midst. Public feeling first came to a head in 1850 when Wiseman was raised to the Cardinalate, and was appointed Archbishop of Westminster. His Pastoral Letter was read in all the Catholic Churches and that jubilant and indiscreet document gave Protestant sectarianism its opportunity. The Bishop of Durham wrote to the Prime Minister demanding an official protest against this "insolent and insidious" aggression. Lord John Russell's reply and the furious leaders in *The Times* aroused such excitement, that on Guy Fawkes night the Pope or his Cardinal was burnt in effigy over different parts of England, in some places while the band played the doxology.[2] Newman's condemnation in the libel action which Achilli brought is hardly less significant.

Thus the vulgarisation of religious controversy which was noticeable during Newman's Protestant career became more marked after his conversion to Catholicism, and throughout the following decades we shall find an acrimonious preoccupation, whenever the greatest of human issues comes under consideration. Hence Freeman's attacks on Froude's *History*, Carlyle's and Browning's superciliousness towards forms of worship, and Trollope's glimpses of the clerical mind. Even Kingsley's notorious attack on Newman, culminating in *What then does Dr Newman mean?* owes its unscrupulous bitterness not so much to personal motives as to the sense of danger. Or take Newman's overwhelming reply beginning with "Away with you, Mr Kingsley, and fly into space. Your name shall occur again as little as I can help, in the course of these pages", but culminating in the Appendix in "Answer in Detail to Mr Kingsley's Accusations", enumerating the thirty-eight "blots" on his honesty and logic. Surely this saintly and long-suffering man would not have pressed home his intellectual triumph so vengefully if the atmosphere of religious controversy were still such as he had breathed it in the 'thirties. So the waste of energy went on, disguised and accredited as religious zeal.

There was, perhaps, a deeper reason for the failure of the whole movement. Newmanism was based on the older theologians who thought and wrote on the assumption that the Devil was alive;

[1] E.g. *The Protestant Idea of Antichrist*, *The British Critic*, Oct. 1840.
[2] Stephen Gwynn, *Cardinal Wiseman*, chap. x, 1929.

that there was a power for good and a power for evil; both high
above man; and that we are the battle-ground for these two superhuman influences. So it was of vital importance to understand and
cultivate the exact channels through which the good can reach us
and fortify us against the evil. Nor must we ever forget our
liability to sin. But the nineteenth century was beginning to convince itself that the Devil was dead. He died during the romantic
movement, if not before. There was perhaps no such influence as
Evil. There were, of course, evils in plenty, but they were the result
of mistakes; they arose from man's inadvertency and inadapta-
bility. Newman's generation was faced with the problems of an
overgrown and immature society—the increased population, the
development of commercialism, the extremes of wealth and poverty,
the rise of democracy confronted by the power of the squirearchy,
the dissemination of revolutionary and rationalistic ideas, the
enormous multiplication of the reading public. The world must
have seemed to be a chaos of newly awakened forces. These maladjustments, excesses and irregularities looked like Evil, but were
due to the impersonal influences of society and economics. Each
ebullition contained the germs of its own remedy, if only human
beings would cultivate the eyes to see. What they needed (it was
felt) was confidence to master the situation. The conviction of
human worthlessness, the belief in Original Sin, even the acquiescence in Providence, might be appropriate as sentiments, but fatal
as a life rule. Then as always, man needed to recognise the absorption of his own egoism in a supernatural system, but that
system must stimulate his self-reliance and constructive energy; he
must conform to the influence in a worldly spirit. Newman and
his school ran counter to this tendency; not so much because they
vilified liberalism, but because they vilified human nature. In his
old age he declared that the large and deep foundation of religion
"is the sense of sin and guilt, and without this sense there is for
man, as he is, no genuine religion".[1] So he allied himself to those
writers who provided for dangers in which the best or most progressive intelligences did not believe. It is just as an army in
contact with the enemy imposes all kinds of orders and regulations,

---

[1] *Grammar of Assent*, chap. x, §1. He did not, of course, assign to Evil a real
and substantive existence as the Manichees had done. He explained it as "a
defect, or a negation—a negation, a privation, an opponent of good". To
Canon H. A. Woodgate, 23 Feb. 1872. See *Times Lit. Suppl.*, 26 Feb.
1935.

which none but the most fractious of martinets would recognise, if they were not on active service and not in imminent danger.

Thus the Oxford Movement, originating in an age of hope and appealing to a nation's sense of religious responsibility, ended in theological technicalities and perplexity of conscience. It helped to disintegrate the Church which it promised to unite. At first sight, it might perhaps seem that Newman was to some degree the father of "modernism", since he examined every dogma on its merits, and made it prove its right to acceptance: and, moreover, encouraged others to test their religion by their heart and conscience. But in reality he judged it by its theological credentials. What the mid-century needed was less a change of heart than a change of ideology. Ecclesiasticism, under this eloquent dialectician, increased the volume of thought, but kept the swollen stream within the old narrow channels. It provoked new controversies, but did not create new contacts. Newman himself believed in his guardian angel and was sure that heresy involved eternal damnation. So Newmanism dwindles away—a last gesture of the Middle Ages before relegation to museums, lecture-rooms, and such books as the reader now holds in his hand.

There is yet another reason why this earnest theologian, who starved his literary genius, should be discussed so fully in an essay devoted to literature. As a certain type of mind he was both extreme and supreme; and the attitude which he represents was just then awaiting its severest trial; and much literature was to arise out of the ordeal. Newman's theology is a wonderful structure, the work of genius, and none the less architecture because its most material element is words. The system could not have held together without profound research and the constant and skilful exercise of deductive logic. Its maintenance exhausts the resources of scholarship. Yet this edifice rests on two assumptions: first, the consciousness of God no less than of one's own existence; secondly, the consciousness that certain dogmas and formularies, expressed through a certain gorgeous and historic ritual, confirm this inward conviction. The whole dialectical superstructure is founded on the assertions of the spirit. Are such the supreme sanctions? Is reason to be trusted only when it amounts to illumination? Is the soul the dictator and the intellect the master-of-horse? Our inquiry will resolve itself into answering these questions, or in concluding that there is as yet no answer.

CHAPTER VI

Tennyson reforms himself so that he may reform his contemporaries—
Thus enlightened, he looks for the divine influence first in nature and
the world of men and then in the progress of personality after death—
At the height of his fame he loses his influence and with it his vision—
He begins as a prophet and ends as a craftsman.

For the literary student, Newman represents the first effort of
Victorianism to be worthy of the heritage which the romantic
movement had transmitted. He still believed that human beings
were planned to be more than human, and that the only obstacle
to this consummation was their own perversity. So he exercised
all the resources of his intellect to seek out and test the influences
which should raise us above our lot. In the end he found a spiritual
kingdom which commanded the allegiance of his soul, and it was
an idea which appealed to his imagination no less than to his
scholarship. Yet he missed the self-fulfilment which each age offers
to its ablest sons. Was his failure typical?

It may be objected that this was an exceptional case; that others
could and would be more successful; that Newman narrowed his
intellect and his sympathies. To save his soul he sacrificed his
humanism and humanitarianism. Let us then consider the career
of another writer who cherished a no less exalted faith in human
destiny, who schooled his impulses and perceptions with equal
austerity, who was indeed devout but accepted no other creed
than pantheism (which Newman abhorred), and who turned to
the varied activities of this world to prove that God existed and
was beckoning us into His presence.

One might imagine that Tennyson was specially born in 1809
to form these convictions, and persuade England to believe them.
His education encouraged him to observe the tendencies of his age
from a distance and to meditate. As his chief teacher was his
father, and their chief subject the classics, he accustomed himself
to the technique of the best Greek and Roman poets. No English
verse-writer owes more to the daring and laborious felicity of
Sophocles, Virgil and Horace. At the same time, romanticism was
in the air, and he must have learnt from that movement how to
develop his sense of outward things.

But, as we have seen, the romantics were also self-centred; they
believed that the poet must look in his own heart for inspiration;

and Tennyson must also have learnt from their example the duty of studying himself. But as soon as he turned his eyes inward he saw much more than his fair share of failings and misgivings. Our poet had two natures. In some moods he was the aesthete and artist. In others, he was a hypochondriac, in revolt against life, full of spleen, and morbid imagination. There was a devil in his soul, something that he called "a vice of blood", a restless, sullen, fire, smouldering deep down in his consciousness and at times bursting into sinister flame. Some of his poems—for instance *The Kraken, The Vision of Sin, The Dead Prophet,* or *Rizpah*—astonish us by their gloom or wildness. The circumstances of his early career intensified his melancholy. Between 1831 and 1834 he lost his father, his best friend, his money,[1] (and for the next fifteen years) his betrothed. Besides, his third volume of poems, containing some of his freshest and finest work, was as severely criticised, even ridiculed, as the preceding volumes. So we must picture him roaming about the countryside a tall, uncouth figure—"a pirate with a lion's mane"—ruining his health and eyesight by overwork, depressed with the agonies of composition, writhing beneath a sense of frustration and neglect.

These circumstances should be borne in mind in order to understand the tone and drift of Tennyson's earlier work. He was at war with himself, his own private circumstances, and the mammonism of his age, nor did romanticism help him towards self-forgetfulness. But in one respect the poets of the previous generation proved to be his best friends in need. They had shown the world that the impulse to write verses may arise in discontent with oneself. We suffer so much from pity, wounded pride, or an outraged sense of justice, that our minds are apt to become each a separate hell, and we grow sick through hating other people or ourselves. The way to conquer these evil moods is to look outside for an example of the particular happiness that we feel we miss; and that effort of recognition will make it our own. Thus Wordsworth once recognised the purpose of his own life by watching a stream flow to the sea. In fact, all the poets of that generation taught their contemporaries how to externalise the selfhood which they took so seriously. Each doubt, disaffection or disability might become another pair of eyes, wherewith to seek another rectification of oneself. The more a poet lacks, the more he has to look for, and thus motived, he may discover even in ordinary objects and

[1] *Letters to Frederick Tennyson.* Edited by H. J. Schonfield, 1930.

prosaic ideas the healing power which he needs, and which comes as a revelation to his readers. Tennyson followed in the footsteps of these guides, and improved on their range.

Being of a rough and almost violent disposition, somewhat free with his tongue, he schooled himself by celebrating the graces of women (having also learnt much from his mother), especially their delicacy and daintiness. Being at times moody and exclusive he cultivated the companionship of kindred spirits, especially after his residence in Kent rendered London accessible, and through inter-course with, for instance, the Sterling Club, he broadened his mind and humanised his poems. Hence his many conversational pieces, such as *Audley Court*, *Walking to the Mail*, and *Edwin Morris*, in which his own difficulties are discussed under the detached and search-ing light of friendship. Sometimes he recants his evil thoughts by producing a poem in the opposite mood; *Ulysses* is a palinode to *The Lotos-Eaters*, *The Two Voices* to *The Vision of Sin*, *Literary Squabbles* is a self-apology for his gibe about "the padded man" flung at Lytton in answer to *The New Timon*'s "school-miss Alfred". He ransacked the older literatures to learn how other minds had faced his problems. He tested the mentality of such an anchorite as St Simeon, and found him to be full of religious pride. He condemned Goethe for brooding too intently on his own self-culture as if life could be spent in a Palace of Art. Both had missed what he most needed, humility and self-forgetfulness in the love of human nature. He showed in *Dora* how much farmer Allen could make of his narrow life and in *Edward Gray* how little the educated romantic could gain by expecting too much. But the Greek and Latin poets gave him most help, because classical literature is essentially moral. It represents certain types of cha-racter face to face with certain crises and shows how that character acts or how he ought not to act. Hence the series of very remarkable monologues, *Ulysses*, *Oenone*, *The Lotos-Eaters*, *Lucretius*, and later *Tithonus*. In these statuesque figures his mind seemed most suc-cessful in allegorising his own problems, especially the fallacies of Epicurean philosophy which left the moralist and man of action unguarded against treacherous thoughts.

These classical poems are also significant, because none of the characters has an object in life. They are like archers who shoot without a target. Even his Ulysses, at least as much of Homer as of Dante, has only the divine curiosity which possessed Tennyson, without finding the consummation which Tennyson sought. In fact, during this period of maturing manhood, the poet was constantly in quest of something worth living for, and being so often baffled, he was constantly dreaming of suicide. The choice between death and life is argued with extraordinary lucidity and penetration in *The Two Voices*. The poet seems to have realised as clearly as Sir James Jeans, the utter insignificance of man; and to have realised more clearly than Bergson how soon the *élan vital* loses its power. While in this mood he would utterly despair of man, unless he remembered our sense of artistic creativeness and our irrepressible aspiration towards the infinite.

What Tennyson most needed was a religion. His own will was too clamorous to be tamed, too anarchic to be left free, but it could be allied to a higher will. So at other times his poetry became a religious quest. Tractarianism left him untouched; he followed the romantic poets and became a pantheist. Here again he tried to see further than his teachers. The worst of those pantheists was that they were not pantheists. They did not find their Divinity everywhere—not in churches nor among the muddy tracks of modern civilisation. Tennyson carried their researches further. He looked for the God of beauty and nature among all the duties, privations and conflicts of that Victorian world which would else drive him to monomania, as it drove the "tongue-tied poet" in *The Golden Year*.

In this search and during this period (the extreme limits 1830 to 1850) he has been credited with both more and less than he achieved. He certainly found time to read and discuss what other writers were thinking in London. He impressed Carlyle as being full of ideas—"speech and speculation free and plenteous".[1] He even succeeded in bringing something of the new philosophic atmosphere into his verse, hinting, as it were, at their points of view. At times, he caught that touch of naturalism which was to be prevalent in the second half of the century. For instance, he succeeded now and then in escaping from the obsession of physical death, and of the small cold worm which frets the enshrouded corpse, and attained to something like Meredith's kinship with the progress of the seasons—the resignation of a mortal involved in the immortality of nature. One thinks not only of the studied pronouncements of *Tithonus* but of such consolation as

> Then let wise Nature work her will
> And on my grave her darnel grow.[2]

---

[1] *Reminiscences.*   [2] *My life is full of weary days.*

But then comes an answer to that mood, in *On a Mourner*, insisting that nature speaks with a deeper voice, telling of a more mysterious power,

> Till all thy life one way incline
> With one wide will which closes thine.

But he did not at this stage assimilate, much less foresee, the tendency of science. He was in search of a creed that would give him the heart to write expressive and significant poetry. He would not, like Huxley, be eager to accept any hypothesis "which assumed the operation of no causes but such as could be proved to be actually at work". He could never surrender his imagination. On the contrary, he had read Butler's *Analogy* and had convinced himself that the same influences which move so visibly through creation, must also be present in human relationships, though often invisible. Otherwise the modern poet cannot write great poetry. Art in those days must derive its significance and expressiveness from pantheism. If he failed to recognise the hand of God in the works of man it was because his mind was still darkened by self-pity, wilfulness and resentment:

> I am too forlorn,
> Too shaken: my own weakness fools
> My judgment, and my spirit whirls
> Moved from beneath with doubt and fear.[1]

He seems to have "beaten his music out", not in a consistent chronology, but from time to time, according to the promptings of his mood. For instance, in *Love Thou Thy Land*, he can listen to the Spirit of the years, toiling beneath the surface and "yearning to mix itself with Life". In *The Day-Dream* he suggests that the legend of the Sleeping Beauty can be interpreted as an allegory of humanism, after a hundred years, awakening to science—to the secrets of the stars and of the human brain—and he promises himself that the newer knowledge will "bring truth that sways the soul of men". His avowed good-bye to the old angry, thwarted Tennyson is declared in *Locksley Hall*. Its ranting rhetoric has received a full share of censure, but the harangue is nevertheless a fine piece of self-revelation. In a Walter Scott setting the poet gives vent, half satirically, to his romantic grievances and self-compassion, and then devotes his enthusiasm to the wonders of

[1] *Supposed Confessions of a Second-Rate Sensitive Mind.*

progress, leaving the Hall to the gathering thunderstorm which may blast it out of his life, with all its humiliating memories.

Thus the poet had aimed as high as a human being can. He had convinced himself that in order to perfect his art, he must perfect his ways of thinking, and that in order to perfect his ways of thinking, he must prove to himself the presence of a divine influence. Being a man of rare imagination, and very human sensibilities, his religion must be earthly as well as heavenly; something that can be seen without, as well as felt within. He called it, in later years, *The Higher Pantheism*, the clear-sightedness to recognise the influence of God everywhere, both in the wild wastefulness of nature and in the yet wilder contentiousness of modern civilisation. But his purpose had declared itself much earlier, in the poems published in 1842.

These two volumes established his reputation. All readers from that time to the present have respected the conscientiousness of the artist, who could maintain a ten years' silence in order to repolish, recast and almost rewrite—or else suppress—the poems which he loved best and which had been most unsympathetically criticised in 1832. It is forgotten that the corrections were not all made in obedience to Lockhart's scorpion-like censures. Some are due to his newly acquired insight into the secrets of life. Moreover, the new poems in volume II are not only rich in technical effects; they are conceived in an unmistakably philosophic spirit akin to religion. Tennyson is teaching his contemporaries to think classical culture, to think medievalism, to think science—even to think Adam Smith—with an imagination which leads to piety. Knowledge, seen in the crystal of his versification, appeared to become wisdom. Above all, it had become aphoristic wisdom. The poet had completely mastered the art of combining vivid imagery with epigrammatic terseness, so his ideas could be imparted as quotations.

His contemporaries, many of them hovering between the older humanists and the philosophical radicals, welcomed this stimulating and persuasive condensation of thought. It brought order into the chaos of their minds. In too many cases it saved them the trouble of thinking for themselves. But the more penetrating critics, then as now, must have detected that the poet was preaching to himself. His texts and maxims come from the head, not from the heart. One has only to compare Tennyson's monologues and meditative poems with those of the great masters, whose searchings of heart are too deep to be intellectualised. Their thoughts are melted into elemental contact with life. Their voice is the voice of nature. It was from the depth of his being that Hector made up his mind to face the avenging Achilles before the walls of Troy, and that Lucretius convinced himself of the folly of fearing death. In both cases the spirit travels as cleanly and directly as an arrow, because it finds its target in conduct. During the nineteenth century such spontaneity could still be met in real life, as a matter of actual experience, among simple souls who had slipped into their own proper niche in the world's system. But intellectuals were finding it more and more difficult to cultivate the old-time arts of adjustment.

Tennyson *seemed* to show how the miracle could be worked. But whether he speaks in his own person, or through the mouthpiece of legend and history, his pronouncements were unconvincingly epigrammatic; they relied too much on conscious artistry; they were simplified, not simple. They appeal more to one's sense of literature than of truth. By no means "rugged maxims hewn from life". Does he really himself believe that our troublesome, disappointing world is so divinely engineered? Does he find that these ancient heroes and sages can teach us how to make the best use of the nineteenth century? Or are these studied and rather homiletic poems mere enamels and cameos? Does our poet live by the light of his visions? *Does he practise what he preaches?*

The world always asks such questions of its teachers. Some of the greatest—for instance, St Augustine, Sir Thomas Browne, Rousseau, Goethe, Wordsworth, Newman, Mill, Renan—have given a direct answer. They have published confessions, or spiritual biographies, or like Dante and Milton[1] have revealed so much of themselves in their works that we know their lives to have been governed by their principles. Tennyson's position depended on whether he could do the same.

He did. While working on the two volumes of 1842, he was engaged on another set of poems which demonstrate what his philosophy really meant to him. He continued his labours till 1849 and then, after at least seventeen years' work, he published them in 1850 as *In Memoriam*.

This sequence is the poet's history of his soul. Its occasion, of course, was the death of Arthur Henry Hallam in 1833, and the elegies were inscribed in a ledger, wherever a vacant space was

[1] Cf. J. C. Graham, *Autobiography of John Milton*, 1872.

left. But though the composition began in this haphazard fashion —mere swallow-flights of song, at the most blending his sorrow with his subtle sense of atmosphere and his genius for visual effects —the poet gradually became aware of a dominating purpose directing his thoughts. Finally, the poems were grouped and arranged, not chronologically, but so as to give prominence to that idea. The introduction, summing up his idea with such admirable lucidity and condensation, was written last of all.

His inspiration is dominated by the fact that you cannot think of the dead as you think of the living. You must either reconcile yourself to mortality, and let their memory linger in your consciousness as a regret, or else you must face the profoundest mysteries which unsettle a human being's idea of himself. A living friend quickens your sense of life. A dead friend hurries you from the world of physical certainties into the world of metaphysical uncertainties, and keeps you there as long as he keeps your love. So Tennyson could not confine his pen to threnodies and the sorrow "which makes sport to mock itself".

Nevertheless, these elegiac effusions with which the series opens are essential to the progress of the poem. At first his abandonment to grief seems to be unmanly, and one wonders why a poet, who at other times resented the intrusions of the public eye,[1] should be at pains to parade a private and personal grief. But soon it becomes evident that this mourning is the fitting portraiture of the dead man's perfection, and the fitting impulse to celebrate his life after death. "Sorrow makes us wise."

It was also artistically necessary to the spirit of the poem that Hallam should have been perfect. He died suddenly of cerebral haemorrhage at Vienna at the age of twenty-two, before his brilliant promise had reached maturity. Does such unfulfilment typify our destiny? The test was all the more crucial because he seemed to abound in spiritual vitality. His influence on his friends was irresistible. Even now when his body had been laid to rest at Clevedon, Tennyson imagines that he can feel his presence. If such a man as Hallam has ended his career with his life, we must all abandon the hopes and ideals transmitted through the romantic movement.

So bereavement leads on to meditation on the survival of personality and the purpose of creation. In these highly wrought moments the poet becomes aware that when he purges his grief

---

[1] See *To* ——, *on reading a Life and Letters* and *The Dead Prophet*.

of egoism and resentment, and blends it with his poetic sense of beauty, grandeur and righteousness, his mind becomes clearer, and more receptive to spiritual influences. One illumination follows another, till he discovers that if he can keep his thoughts to the high tone enjoyed in Hallam's presence, he can understand that his friend has not died. His disembodied spirit is still alive, continuing its progress towards divine perfection. His friend has been transferred to a kind of "fourth dimension", in which personality persists, released from the restrictions of matter, enlarged and intensified in the widening opportunities of that new environment. At death you do not so much say good-bye to this world (a parting which every man dreads) as good-bye to all that confines your spirit; you are above life yet within it. It was not a severance but a consummation.

Such convictions were not a discovery; they might suggest themselves to any reader of Plato, Virgil, or Dante, not to mention the churchmen of the eighteenth century, or the philosophers of the early nineteenth. Bishop Wilberforce alludes to them, as the commonplaces of consolation, in 1861.[1] Yet Tennyson, without claiming any original or preternatural faculty of insight, felt sure that he could see further into the mystery. He convinced himself that even here, our feet resting on the earth, we can train ourselves to catch some inkling of the next stage in man's progress.

Thus there was more inspiration to be won from Hallam than from Ulysses, Lucretius, or Sir Galahad. When alive, his friend had not only stimulated his intellect and directed his thoughts; he had also intertwined so much of himself with Tennyson's moral qualities, that after his death the poet felt able to follow his spiritual development, to divine his upward course; he could even himself strive towards that post-mortal enlargement, by tact of love and intuition. He now had a target at which to aim. The death of his friend had given him something to live for; in fact the friendship would have lost half its value if it had not been intensified by death. Moreover, he was proving to the world that he was living up to his ideals and had achieved the "faith which comes of self-control".

This demonstration should be of the greatest importance to his age. But before such convictions could be accepted as a rule of conduct, they must be sanctioned by the intellect. Mathematical proof, of course, was neither possible nor requisite, but philo-

[1] *To an anonymous correspondent.* See R. G. Wilberforce. *Life of S. Wilberforce,* vol. II, chap. XIII.

sophical probability was essential. Here again the sincerity and earnestness of the poet are established by his readiness to face the issue. He saw that science was at that time the chief stumbling-block, and some of the most remarkable poems of the series[1] not only restate the arguments against survival after death, but develop them with eloquence and imagination. He dwells particularly on the evidence of biology—the waste of life and lack of purpose in nature—and on the evidence of psychology—the dependence of the mind on the working of the brain—and we know that after death the brain turns to dust. If science is right, we are only magnetic mockeries, cunning casts of clay, fit to be blown about the dust of the desert, or sealed within the hills, and our lives must end with our bodies.

It is generally asserted that Tennyson never even tried to refute this materialism, but only appealed against its verdict. Such an impression is quite natural because he wrote as a poet and not as a controversialist. His rhythms and picturesque flights of sentiment divert attention from a quite solid counter-argument. He claims that science has excluded the most telling evidence, that of our own mental and spiritual experiences. We have the wish to survive; the conviction that we shall survive; the sense of vague contact with the departed, at any rate the consciousness of their presence; in highly wrought moments actual communion with the dead—an absorption of our spirits into their post-mortal enlightenment. When the imagination is calm and fair, the memory like a cloudless day, the conscience like a sea at rest, our spirits can hold intercourse with theirs.[2] Once, and only once, our poet attained to that mystic initiation; it was in the genial warmth of a summer's evening, after re-reading Hallam's letters.[3] Such considerations are quite admissible. If we are to study the human mind we must study all the ways in which it works. These intuitions should carry as much weight as sensuous impressions, for in the end all knowledge about our immaterial selves is subjective. So any Tennysonian who could test and confirm these assertions by his own experiences, was justified in believing that the author of *In Memoriam* had the credentials of a religious teacher. He had humanised immortality by ignoring the supposed relegation to heaven but without sacrificing supernaturalism. The human spirit continued to develop under the conditions misnamed death and

[1] E.g. LIII–LV. [2] XCIII.
[3] XCIV.

we could dimly intuit that development. An admirer might almost claim that the poet had anticipated the doctrine of evolution in the realm of metaphysics.

In Memoriam was published anonymously in 1850, but the authorship was widely recognised and it delighted all classes of readers. Even the scientifically minded were overjoyed to find that the leading poet sympathised with their labours, appeared to understand their subject, and could write as poetically about zoology and biology as about beauty and spiritualism.

So it must have seemed to contemporaries as if the appearance of this volume was the greatest event of the nineteenth century. No one need any longer fear materialism, or despair of human destiny. Nor was his doctrine likely to be superseded. The convictions rested on intimations which do not change with the fashions of culture. A humanist of 1850 might confidently prophesy that we at this present time would still be living by Tennyson's inspiration.

But such is not the case. The influence of *In Memoriam* has steadily declined. By the end of the century it was valued only as a phrase-book, a metrical triumph, a masterpiece of poetic expressiveness, and as such, generally relegated to schools and colleges.

In one sense the poems deserved this fate because their author (through no fault of his own) did not face the spiritual problem of the nineteenth century; he only appeared to do so. The materialism against which he protested was of the eighteenth century. It was Hume, not unaided by Locke and Berkeley, who argued that our minds are a mechanism, that our profoundest thoughts are only the elaborations of nervous activity, that all you find in your head entered through the five senses. It was Joseph Butler who in 1736 wrote: ..."of the numerous seeds of vegetables and bodies of animals, which are adapted and put in the way to improve to such a point or state of natural maturity and perfection, we do not see perhaps that one in a million actually does. For the greatest part of them decay before they are improved to it; and appear to be absolutely destroyed...the *appearance* of such an amazing *waste* in nature with respect to these seeds and bodies by foreign causes, is to us as unaccountable, etc....", and Tennyson may well have had this passage from *The Analogy of Religion* before him when he wrote the famous LIV. Our poet is distinctively modern only when he creates his idea out of *Principles of Geology* (1830–3). The subject was new and captured his imagination, and some of his most felicitous phrases sculpture visions derived from that book. But Sir Charles Lyell was a cautious writer with a wholesome respect for the *odium theologicum*. He had no desire to revolutionise anything but the technicalities of his science. Thus Tennyson has missed the wider inferences which were at that very time being drawn by Darwin and Wallace.[1]

Tennyson did not only confine his strictures to eighteenth-century scepticism, but he protested against it in the eighteenth-century spirit. His insistence that Providence has limited our access to Truth is found in Joachim Böldicker's *Historische Einleitung in die Lehre von der Uebereinstimmung des Glaubens und der Vernunft* (1746). His celebrated LIII ("O yet we trust...") is no advance on Leibnitz's *Théodicée*.[2] His belief in spiritual progress was asserted by Butler: "If the soul be naturally immortal, and this state be a progress towards a future one, as childhood is towards mature age; good men may naturally unite, not only amongst themselves, but also with other orders of virtuous creatures, in that future state."[3] Dante could have taught him that the souls of human beings communicate without words, whether in this world or the next.[4] There is no need to infer that our poet was consciously basing his convictions on these old-world teachers, but he would not have echoed their wisdom unless he felt, as they did, that nothing more was to be revealed; we have explored all the manifestations by which the spirit can recognise itself.

It is no reflection on Tennyson's genius that he ranged himself with the older humanists. The age had not yet produced a more worthy allegiance. One is apt to forget that the ideas which were to revolutionise Victorianism had not yet come to the surface. Darwin was known only to the inner circle of specialists. Huxley, himself unknown, declared as late as 1858 that the only person whose knowledge and capacity compelled respect, and who was, at the same time, a thoroughgoing evolutionist, was Herbert Spencer. Yet in 1850 Spencer had not launched his prospectus of synthetic philosophy, and if known to humanists, it was through his little read *Social Statics* and a few inconclusive essays.[5]

But ten or twenty years later, Darwinism became the burning question, and it was then proved that Tennyson was not one of the

---

[1] *Post*, pp. 213–14; 279–81.   [2] Especially Pt I, §§ 9, 10.
[3] *Analogy*, Pt I, chap. III.
[4] *Purg.* xv, 127: *Parad.* II, 43 and *passim*.
[5] *Post*, pp. 246–50. Also H. V. Routh, *England under Victoria*, § 3, v.

voices which cry "forward". He closed an epoch which began at the Renaissance. After the appearance of *The Origin of Species* (1859), scepticism was no longer a matter of guesswork. It was reaffirmed and established on a system. If not proved up to the hilt, as so many then believed, it could at least be argued with a very high degree of philosophical probability. In any case the hypothesis involved a new and disconcerting idea of man and of his destiny on earth. We, with our ideals, dreams and achievements, might very well be nothing but highly organised animals fighting for our lives against the immutable and unhuman laws of nature. Human destiny was probably in the grip of a mechanism, not of an intelligence. That was the issue which the younger generation had to face, and it demanded a kind of courage alien to the older humanism. Tennyson's convictions were not in themselves invalidated, because (as we have seen) they were sanctioned by internal evidence. Yet his humanism was unequal to the situation. It could not face such a blow to our self-ideals. He had taught the world that the soul was a wanderer, who had gazed on a glorious image of itself in the other-world, who had grown strong in that vision, and would faint and fall if its image could be discerned only among the beasts that perish. For instance, he declares again and again that without the hope of a future life and of reunion with the departed, he would not care to exist, nay more, he would have no motive for self-discipline and self-culture.[1] Compare this self-abandonment of the poet with the fortitude of the mere man of science, a disbeliever in futurity, a believer in man's animalism, who had just lost his son. "What! because I am face to face with an irreparable loss, because I have given back to the source whence it came, the cause of a great happiness, still retaining through all my life the blessings which have sprung and will spring from that cause, I am to renounce my manhood, and howling, grovel in bestiality."[2]

As soon as Tennyson's younger readers awoke to the responsibilities and disillusionments of their age, they were bound to conclude that the author of *In Memoriam* was behind the times. They were taught in school that the Poet Laureate elected in 1850 was the wisest voice in England, and they found that he did not even understand their difficulties. So they began to resent his authority and to discard his teaching. We can, perhaps, trace to

[1] XXXIV, XXXV, LVI, CXIX.
[2] T. Huxley to C. Kingsley, 23 Sep. 1860.

this discordancy the first beginnings of an inclination to divorce literature from the more serious considerations of life. We shall watch the rift widen as the nineteenth century merged into the twentieth. It may have originated in the great poet's inability to think ahead. If so much fine writing fails us, we cannot help feeling that fine writing may take too much upon itself.

In the case of the Poet Laureate, this distrust was not ill-founded. As we follow his career we find him less and less able to justify his convictions. He was now famous, married, and financially assured, yet he can no longer trace the hand of God in the ways of men. His decline was not due to failing powers. He wrote with greater facility and touched on an even wider range of subjects. It was only his idealism which flagged; and with the slackening of his enthusiasm, his mastery of rhythm and metres increased. This artistic pre-eminence, which at first looks like a compensation, weakened his position yet further. It undermined the confidence of his admirers. Their prophet was degenerating into a technician, an experimentalist in words, not in aspirations. For instance, *The Princess* (1847) is a mock-epic in celebration of domestic love, yet the mockery spoils all but the studied workmanship. "A gorgeous piece of writing," notes Carlyle, "but to me new melancholy proof of the futility of what is called 'Art'."[1]

So far the poetry of Tennyson has been considered as if his only preoccupation was religious or at least spiritual, and we have seen that he was overtaken and caught unprepared by the rising tide of modern thought. But we have also seen that in his earlier manhood and up till 1850, he had persuaded himself and others that some more than human influence could be traced in the progress of his country—its politics and commerce. By 1840 these developments were becoming the despair of humanistic and humanitarian Englishmen—Carlyle started the outcry in 1839[2]—and from that time onward novelists and essay-writers kept asking how the industrialisation of our country was to be reconciled to the will or even the existence of God. This wave of indignation and disillusionment need not have caught Tennyson unarmed. *The Wealth of Nations* appeared in 1776, Malthus's *Essay on Population* in 1798, Ricardo's *Principles of Political Economy* in 1817; Mill's *Principles of Political Economy* in 1848. There was no good reason why a poet who used to debate

> On labour and the changing mart
> And all the framework of the land

[1] *Journal,* 9 Feb. 1848.   [2] *Post,* p. 129.

should not have had time to test his belief in divine governance by the economic laws which ruthlessly dominate human society and vitiate peaceful progress with the struggle for life. This issue is faced in *Maud* (1855).

There could be no more convincing proof that Tennyson had lost his hold on modern life. The monodrama is the longest composition in which he speaks in his own person of his own time, and it is the most deficient in moral and intellectual self-possession. He who once celebrated the triumph of peace and progress, now protests against the reign of Mammon more bitterly than Carlyle, Disraeli, Mrs Gaskell, Kingsley, Dickens, or Thackeray, and what he most fears is its influence on himself. The monologist is not so much the poet as what the poet fears that he will become. He revives all his old discontent and misanthropy which he had abjured in *Locksley Hall*; and aims it against the "mud-honey" of modern luxury; he revives all the scepticism out of which he had reasoned himself in *In Memoriam*. But this young man has neither Tennyson's acquired faith in progress nor his determination to cling to supernaturalism. He lapses into apathy; he becomes as self-centred as Werther, the victim of the Everlasting Nay. He has all the weaknesses against which Tennyson fought. Even in his ardent and idyllic passion for Maud, he is still a confirmed egoist. What the poet has added of his own best self is the prosody. The long poem is diversified with an almost endless variety of form and rhythm, and this artistry betrays us into sympathy with the lover, or rather, makes us forget the theme in the lyric sensuousness of the poet. The author now seems more at home with the significance of words than with the significance of science.

Henceforth Tennyson turned his eyes away from the problems of his age, and, like so many of his contemporaries, tried to keep alive his confidence in man by recalling the past. So the final test of his position is *The Idylls of the King*. This cycle of romances represents perhaps the most sustained interest in Tennyson's life. The earliest, *Morte d'Arthur*, was published in 1842, though probably composed early in the 'thirties, long before he had projected the series. *Merlin and Vivien, Geraint and Enid, Guinevere, Lancelot and Elaine* appeared in 1859, four years after *Maud*. He then left the subject and published *Enoch Arden* in 1864. In 1870 he brought out *The Holy Grail, The Coming of Arthur, Pelleas and Ettarre, The Passing of Arthur*; in 1872 *Gareth and Lynette*, and *The Last Tournament*; in 1875 *Balin and Balan*. Thus the *Idylls* follow *In Memoriam* as the third phase in the growth of Tennyson's mind; and, like the earlier poem, the stories originally succeeded one another in a haphazard and rather inconsequential way, according to the mood and inspiration of the poet. At first sight he seems merely to be reviving his older themes in a new form, for instance, his admiration for the grace, gentleness, patience and devotion of women (Enid and Elaine) and their true merit as the inspiration and counterpart to manly virtue; his ideal of manly strength and courtesy; his love of Hallam as the perfect gentleman; his dream of medieval vision and piety; his conviction that all human beings can fulfil their highest destiny only if they live for others and understand them. At times he seems to recall his own youthful enthusiasms, as in the character of Gareth (one of the latest of the idylls) and in the conception of a brotherhood united under God to create a new England. So apart from the influence of Malory, one would have expected no other continuity than that arising from the author's personality and adjustment to life.

But just as, in his period of storm and stress, he discovered a distinct idea running through *In Memoriam*, so it was with these expressions of his period of fame and disillusionment. The stories acquired a more special significance, and so in a final edition he arranged them according to this doctrine and accomplished some skilful fusing and editing to complete the effect.

The issue is almost too well known to need indicating. It is to the effect that society is infinitely sensitive to evil influences; any individual faithlessness, even in the noblest of fraternities, is like the sin of Achan, and slowly demoralises the rest. Nay more, society is as ruthless as nature. It lives on the death of its institutions; the noblest human efforts cannot retain their perfection; they serve their single purpose and, having spent their force in raising mankind, they lose their inspiration, no longer serving the designs of God.

It will at once be recognised that Tennyson had changed. *In Memoriam* rose into an aspiration, *The Idylls* sink into a *moral*, almost a sigh of resignation. Nor are the conclusions new; they were familiar to any reader of Rousseau, Goethe, or Carlyle; they come as a melancholy reminder. Of course the final effect of a poem does not depend entirely—nor even chiefly—upon its argument. It depends upon its atmosphere. It is for this reason that the medieval setting of *The Idylls* is even more significant than the progress of the story. Tennyson had always been fond of medievalism. In that tranquil tinted light he was able to purify his studies in human devotion and mystery, as if on the background of a Gothic window. But since the days of *Sir Galahad* and *The Lady of Shalott*, this cult of romantic feudalism had become less a simplification of life than a refuge from it. The educated classes of the 'fifties and 'sixties enjoyed facilities for reading old books and wandering among old towns. Such experiences became a mark of distinction, and they were valued as a relief from that same commercialism without which they would have had neither the cheap reprints nor the cheap railway tickets. So medievalism became a cult; a compensation for the mechanisation and uniformity of modern life; an outlet for the finer feelings, and more exuberant fancies. The Rossettis were already showing how it might be done. You could even dally with the imagined refinements of war in an age of monotonous peace. It is significant that Tennyson fell under this influence. His hero came to him from the very midnight of the Dark Ages; a chieftain who led the Iberians or Welsh against the Anglo-Saxon invaders. The Table Round was a *comitatus*. Arthur, like any other warrior of the heroic age, gathered adventurers round him, and fed and supported them, while they followed him to battle and died at his side, like Harold's house-carls at Senlac. The theme had proved to be one of the most inspiring of all legends and had been treated again and again in Latin, Italian, French, German and English from Nennius to Spenser. Even Milton contemplated making Arthur the hero of his epic. So there were plenty of schools to follow. But of all the possible atmospheres, Tennyson chose the one most akin to the Pre-Raphaelites and the unrealists. He made of this rude warlike Table Round the study of a small brotherhood united under a godlike leader; he endowed them with the ideals, though not the activities, of the modern Christian gentleman; and he cast over their adventures the glamour of the pseudo-Gothic. The Arthurian wars were fought some time in the fifth or sixth century, after the withdrawal of the Romans, before the Saxons had made good their footing. Yet Tennyson's pages are full of flaunting tournaments, rich carvings, deeply toned organs, vestments stiff with jewels, golden cups and dim rich cities, in which the roofs "tottered towards each other in the sky". Carlyle read it "with profound recognition of the finely elaborated execution, and also of the inward perfection of *vacancy*". Vacant it seemed to be, because contemporary thought was bringing realism to bear on the study of the Middle Ages. In

1856 J. A. Froude began to publish his *History*,[1] in order to reveal the long-standing abuses which the Reformation swept away, and completed the exposure by his studies in fourteenth and fifteenth-century decadence. In 1864 Furnivall founded the Early English Text Society which has contributed so much towards a realistic idea of the Middle Ages. Yet Tennyson is content to follow Malory and the romantic tradition.

And yet the poems have one abiding charm, their background of English scenery. His sense of nature had always been the most brilliant trait in Tennyson's lyrical genius; and no theme could give him a better opportunity, because the story carries him all over the countryside. He is at his best after he settled at Blackdown (1868) and revealed the south country, especially Sussex and Hampshire, as something infinitely strange and reminiscent—curiously sunken, tortuous roads, which once connected long vanished homesteads; clumps of thick jungle; odd and unexpected relics of masonry half-covered with ivy; ancient oaks and yew trees, often found near streamlets which must have wandered through their dells and meadows for thousands of years. Every excursion brings you across something which holds a secret, something suggesting the presence of men and yet something quite untamed and mysterious, because of the little wild creatures, which really do seem to be spirits of the wood and the heath. Such is the soul of south English scenery and such are the experiences which Tennyson recreates. Yet he has lost that deeper insight into the soul of nature—that sense of kinship with the powers of growth and decay—which he had promised to develop in the 'thirties and 'forties. And besides, these beauties may console, even fascinate the reader, but they are holiday pleasures. The problems of nineteenth-century manhood do not find their solution on the road from Haslemere to Midhurst, though Tennyson prized its scenery above any in England.

The other works which accompanied or followed the *Idylls* are even more remote. The dialect poems may seem to be an exception. They certainly are delightful, and so masterly that they helped to establish a new literary sentiment which Barnes, Waugh and Wingate had already attempted and which Kipling was afterwards to consummate. But they are the playthings of culture. In fact this great poet, once the idol of the English-speaking world, the first writer to win a peerage by sheer genius, and almost the last to be buried in Westminster Abbey, was nevertheless, in the

[1] *Post*, chap. x.

highest sense, a failure. He seems himself to have doubted whether
his verses would live, and to have guessed the reason why. In an
early sonnet he begins,

> Mine be the strength of spirit, full and free,
> Like some broad river rushing down alone,
> With selfsame impulse wherewith he was thrown
> From his loud fount upon the echoing lea.

The fount was the philosophy and idealism of the romantic movement, but he could not conserve the power and clearness of the
source, as the stream wound its way among the difficulties of his
age. Late in life he confessed

> I am losing the light of my Youth
> And the Vision that led me of old,
> And I clash with an iron Truth,
> When I make for an Age of gold.[1]

Like Merlin he was always following the gleam. Unfortunately
the mysteries of the other world are revealed only to those who
have mastered this one, to the man who can see the spirit of other
ages in the manners of his own, and Tennyson had lost faith in
progress by the middle of the century. Now and then he caught
glimpses of the new era, as in *Charity, Mechanophilus, Doubt and
Prayer* (which almost reminds the reader of Meredith), *God and the
Universe*; but by then his hand had lost its cunning.

[1] *The Dreamer*: cf. *The Wanderer*.

CHAPTER VII

Robert Browning, the poet of optimism, searches for the will of God in the hearts of men—Even of those who cannot bring it to fruition—Nor can he, unless he looks outside and beyond the experience of his readers—His best poems borrow their effectiveness from the glamour of the storied past—So he, too, in the highest sense, fails.

On looking back over Tennyson's career, one is inclined to say that he missed pre-eminence because he was at heart a pessimist. He kept to the romantic tradition, tried to school himself into optimism, and failed. Browning is a complete contrast. He was born an optimist, and could not have become anything else. For this very different reason we shall find that he also missed pre-eminence. Because he could not help seeing what was good, he did not lead his age, though his resourcefulness was almost inexhaustible.

Unlike Tennyson, he had every reason for optimism. He came of an exuberant, long-lived obstinate stock. His father had set his heart on being an artist, but was compelled to earn his living as a government clerk. Yet he did not altogether miss the culture for which nature had intended him. He found the time to become an omnivorous reader and the cash to collect rare books and prints. Besides, he was one of those men who fulfil themselves by living for other people. So he determined to retrieve his own thwarted career in the life of his son, who was born in 1812.

The younger Robert was lucky in his father. He was no less lucky in his mother—an angel of a woman—from whom he inherited a vigorous constitution and a sunny temperament. He was luckiest of all in the gifts of nature. Besides a genius for humanism, he was endowed with the talents of a designer, a modeller, an actor and a musical composer. When such a son discussed his future with such a father, only one conclusion was possible. They unanimously agreed on the career which would fuse all these activities—the poet's calling. In that choice he was luckiest of all. So Browning, like Wordsworth, went out into the world "a dedicated spirit". His dedication, however, was more professional. On the day that he chose his career he started a systematic study of his language in Johnson's *Dictionary*.

The greatest writers of the nineteenth century seem to have

formed their genius by sublimating some disability such as lesser authors ignore. Browning was also lucky in his faults. He suffered from the inbred scholar's megalomania. He inherited his grand-father's domineering personality and acquisitive powers. These aptitudes had been directed into the world of art and letters, so he ranged through his father's library, not so much as a learner, or an explorer, but as a master among his possessions. He used the heroes and sages of old time as slaves to minister to his ideal of himself. His first temptation was to bend all his authors to his will. It was a blunder, because he did not yet know what to make of life, and they did. He narrowed their wisdom down to his boyish enthusiasms. Yet he was lucky in this megalomania because all humanists worth the name begin by imposing their personality on their books, before it is ripe. The proceeding might be called the first infirmity of noble mind. So, if Browning was to overcome this egocentricity and learn how to learn, he would be fighting every-body else's battle as well as his own. Thus, at the outset of his career he ought to be sure of a following.

He certainly did not shrink from maturing and proving his culture through experience. After commanding the services of the dead he was resolved to share the joys of the living—every one of them, as the day which does not waste a sunbeam. Once again, he was acting for his contemporaries of the 'twenties and 'thirties, as well as for himself. They taught themselves to think in the austere and elevated style of their best library models, and they expected to find some reflection of this grandeur in experience—at any rate a world tinted with romantic philosophy and idealism. Their dis-illusionment was none the less acute because they were not pre-pared for it. Such was especially the plight of Robert Browning, who was overweeningly self-confident and had begun his search for truth in the library of a bibliophile and art collector. He compares his experience to waiting for "a fair girl, that comes a withered hag" or to the glimpse of "strange towers and walled gardens thick with trees", which promise the joys of fairy land, and next day the vision has vanished.

This confession is made in *Pauline* (1833), his first publication, which most Browningites condemn as a piece of romantic senti-mentalism, and do not read. Yet the poem lays a finger on the essential maladjustment of that age—and of ours. It is the com-plaint of a youth who still takes romanticism seriously as the torch of life, and finds that its flame is guttering. He begins with the old romantic remedy, love for a woman. But this Pauline soon becomes elusive and distant, she loses her identity, and fades into a shadowy symbol of poetic idealism. No wonder; the poet cannot reconcile his muse with life. He is not only distressed by its crudity and materialism and the ordinary vices and passions which everybody has to face. He encounters something much more disconcerting: the undiscovered depths of himself. Victorian experience, which he expected to be the complement to culture, was playing on unsuspected impulses and appetencies deeper and more primitive than conscious personality, and some of them very different from what literature had prepared him to expect.

This disquieting self-consciousness was quite out of tune with romantic mysticism. It whispers that we are each a complex of tendencies and urges as elemental and uncontrollable as creation. It points towards the twentieth century and we think of Samuel Butler, Conrad, Virginia Woolf, D. H. Lawrence and Dorothy Richardson. Here, one is tempted to think, was Browning's chance. On the threshold of manhood he had acquired a new insight. Would he press forward with a new recklessness; abandon his preconceptions; explore these human mysteries, objective and subjective; and satisfy his curiosity without fearing the results? That is what modernists profess to do in the experimental mood of the present day. Yet *Pauline* reveals its author hesitating on the brink and then retracing his footsteps till he can find a safer and more frequented track.

To understand his hesitation we must remember that, like Tennyson, he had no inkling of our modernist philosophies; he did not think of the human being as an accidental product of cosmic or natural forces. He had learnt in his father's library to conceive of man as a microcosm, self-contained under the surveillance of God. Within this microcosm there were, of course, many contributory energies (especially the faculties of the brain exercised in penetrating the mysteries of the macrocosm without) but they were all melted into co-operation by the unifying influence of personality. It was this individualised intelligence (compact of will-power, insight and reason) which imposed on the microcosm its distinctively human purposiveness and directed its progress by some higher light. Only thus could we preserve our individuality and ascend towards perfection. Such is the philosophy of Pauline's lover. But what (he seems to ask) if the directing power has lost sight of its own goal of self-fulfilment? The energies under its rule will become as aimless as their master. They will miss their way among the vagaries and deceptions of uncontrolled experience, and end in mockery, cynicism, self-interest or self-worship. So man will lose his own soul. At all costs we must keep alive the consciousness of human dignity and self-direction, and the idea of a destiny which raises us above our mortal selves—some inspiration, congenial both to the intellect and imagination. Otherwise there is too much to lose. One detects, perhaps, a certain timidity in this foresight, but it is the cautiousness of the optimist. The poet is too much in love with life to risk his chances of self-fulfilment. He must hold to a religion, nor was his poetry for that reason to be any the worse.

Such is the upshot of *Pauline*. It missed its public because the reader is led to expect a love poem, and then finds a piece of self-revelation, full of incoherencies, involutions and "intense and morbid self-consciousness". If he had written more clearly and impersonally, the reading public would have recognised that he was also writing about them. As it was, his aunt paid thirty pounds for the production of the edition of which he did not sell a single copy, and Browning gave up his life to the problem which this poem raises but does not solve—how to find a faith, a devotion, in which his spirit could grow to its full stature. Only two years later he propounded in *Paracelsus* (1835) an idea worthy of his quest.

Paracelsus demonstrates how any thoughtful man may fulfil his personality, that is, may catch himself in his highest and most tranquil mood, and stay there. Let any sincere inquirer in his hour of enlightenment look into his heart and ask why he happens, in that clear-sighted moment, to be at peace with himself. It is because he is at peace with everything else. He finds that creation is moving in the same direction as his own spirit, both towards fulfilment. Even the halts, setbacks and disasters are only pauses to gather strength for the next move forward; again, as with himself. In fact the movement pervading the earth and all its inhabitants is the movement within himself. He is at one with creation. He can convince himself that such is the true interpretation—that all science and humanism express his personality—because his spirit is drawn towards this travail and progress. The God within him feels joy and fellowship in the godlike work outside. This affinity is made known to his intelligence as love.

Such is the doctrine of *Paracelsus*. It was not new even in Browning's day. It has been represented as a continuation and application of romantic metaphysics by Sir Henry Jones.[1] But the inspiration may also have come to him from the eighteenth-century optimists—Leibnitz and Christian Wolff—who contended that if critics were dissatisfied with the world-system it was because their view was limited, they could see only half the picture, and needed more insight to understand the design. That insight could also have been learnt from Lucretius.[2] Goethe in *Wilhelm Meister* could have shown him that happiness is willing collaboration with nature and society. The idea was ready for any poet who had the will to take it. Browning's achievement consists in realising that this faith should embrace not only nature but especially mankind; that we attain the serenity of self-fulfilment only if we love all humanity enough to measure our development by theirs. *Pauline* confessed that self-love ended in self-contempt: *Paracelsus* was to demonstrate that self-perfection depended on the perfection of everybody else.

It was difficult to give this idea artistic expression because the real subject of any such poem must be the enlightenment which steals over the reader. The story itself will be only a device to awaken the spirit of discerning love. So the poet was well advised to choose a theme out of the annals of culture, a subject immune to the antagonisms of our daily prosaic life, and steeped in the mellowness of a vanished and imagined age. He was also wise in choosing an imperfect hero, an inexplicable and erratic character, so that his interpretation would force the reader to look deep below the surface, bring to bear all his intelligence and sympathy, and meet the narrator half-way. He was most skilful in that he associated this mysterious and unaccountable personage with three other figures to offset his qualities, and told his story by making them all speak their thoughts. As he said much later, "depend upon it, in a soliloquy a man makes the most of his good intentions and sees great excuses in them".[3]

And what is the issue? They all—Paracelsus, Aprile, Festus and Michal—confess that according to their several endowments and opportunities they have travelled the road which Browning and his contemporaries were tempted to travel. Each has sought self-development and self-expression in a selfish, individualistic spirit. Each fancies that a human being can exercise and improve his own powers as if the rest of the world did not help him, can lead a privileged life, no doubt mixing with other people, but secluded

---

[1] *Browning as a Philosopher and Religious Teacher*, 1891.
[2] *De Rerum Natura*, i, ll. 21–3. [3] To Miss E. Story, 1 Jan. 1870.

from their influence, not sparing them any of his sympathy and interest, not looking among them for reflections of himself, his soul satisfied with the contemplation of his own activities. Even Aprile is confined to his self-enjoyment in what Croce would now call lyrical intuition, but Paracelsus with his Napoleonic intellect is the most egocentric. He seeks to explore and master all Truth, as if it were a treasure hidden within his own spirit. Yet all are failures. Each character is led to discover and confess that this titanism[1] means littleness. It precludes the highest and widest perceptiveness. A human being surpasses his peers only by realising that he is like them, that their halting and many-sided development comes to consciousness in his own head. Without this discovery, the soul is introverted and misses that sense of common love which brings mortals as near as they can get to God.

Human perfection, then, is the emergence of all humanity in oneself; such, concludes Paracelsus, is the only way to become a superman. At this distance we can already divine the emergence of the Browningesque monologue in which both the writer and the reader achieve their own salvation as far as they discover it in some other person. The final speeches in Part V contain some of the best poetry that Browning ever wrote. Yet they did not convince Browning's contemporaries. A small group admired the vision and lyric fervour of the book, but the majority left it alone. Perhaps they were right, for *Paracelsus* promises too much and accomplishes too little. It promises a humanitarian religion by which men ought to live, proclaimed with all the sincerity of a prophet. So one might have expected the rising generation to welcome his doctrine, however erudite and Hegelian. But the man who would convince his contemporaries of something new must appeal to their experience, and Browning does not really demonstrate. He only preaches. His characters reiterate the phases of spiritual failure through which he has passed. But they do not reveal anything about ourselves. They do not make you see in a flash that the truth must be so. Above all, they do not show how the new purposeful and joyous life may be led. In fact Browning has acquired a great style and a great idea, but has still to prove whether or no he is deceiving himself and us. In the meantime he must make an income out of his books.

Macready helped him. In the winter of 1835 he was invited to write a play; in 1837 *Strafford* was produced; and though its success

[1] Goldschmidt, "Der Gedankengehalt von Robert Brownings *Paracelsus*", *Englische Studien*, June 1934.

was small, the poet devoted most of ten years to the theatre. Thus he hoped to gain publicity and a reputation, for in those days the drama was in the tradition of the best literature. Shelley, Byron, Coleridge, Southey and even Keats were arm-chair dramatists. Shakespeare would smile benignly from the distance of two centuries. So the receipts of the ticket office would be sanctioned by the most august authorities. Best of all, play-writing would improve his art. Up to this point, he had propounded ideas, but he had not learned how to make his characters practise what he preached. In an acting drama the personages would have to act, and his method ought to become more objective.

So it became. He acquired the knack of visualising character in relation to conduct. In all his plays you can see that he aims at exemplifying his great doctrine: God's influence on His creations, especially man. And yet these tragedies were a mistake. He had a sense of the drama but not of the stage. He could create a situation yet could not make it theatrical. So in the end Browning returned to the printed page, the only proper medium for his lyric genius. But he learnt from the drama how to make his theories speak for themselves. He was now able to describe a human being's thoughts so that they could be felt and seen.

Yet it took him another ten years or so to find his true vein, if he ever found it, though at first he seems to have achieved effectiveness at one stroke. You open his very next poem, *Pippa Passes* (1841), and you find that there is no preaching. You feel the presence of God through the angelic purity and single-mindedness of the silk-winder, who strays through the picturesque old town and awakens goodness in others by the sweetness of her voice, all unconscious of her influence. The poem is a great artistic achievement, because it seems to be so artless. But if you take *Pippa* as seriously as the author intended, and reflect on your impressions, you find that you have been beguiled. It is felicitous, not convincing. Despite its lyrical touches, dramatic contrasts, and glimpses of passionate, tortuous lives, it is, after all, effective only as an exotic romance. Its episodes do not persuade the reader that "All's right with the world", nor that crooked characters can be straightened by the touch of a fairy's wand—not even in Asolo, Browning's favourite town.

Pippa Passes is another of his dreams which will never come true. So with *Dramatic Lyrics* (1842) and *Dramatic Romances* (1845). They are experiments in expressiveness; mere lyric fancies; or "escapes of my inner power, like the light of a revolving lighthouse leaping out at intervals from a narrow chink".[1] How was this inner power being employed? What was he looking for? Like every other artist, he was still searching within his own circle for the evidence which would justify his philosophy, give shape to his convictions, illustrate his religion. Such are the means by which the spirit comes to life in literature. In this quest he assimilated certain influences, which became the chief materials for his thought (which inspired many of his lightest or happiest pieces from 1842 onwards) and which also decided his future development and his significance for posterity.

In the first place, though he soon outgrew his father's and mother's sectarianism, he learnt from their piety to believe in the personality of Christ. This supreme example of love for its own sake inspired some of his most human poems, especially the best passages in *Christmas Eve and Easter Day* (1850). But it also dominated his intellect. For better or worse, he dismissed Strauss and his fellow christologists, because they divested the man-god of his godlike humanity; and he dismissed Darwin and Huxley because they could not believe in a creative intelligence such as Cleon and even Mr Sludge could grasp. Even in the 'eighties he insisted that *Paracelsus* contained all that was true of evolution.

Browning also learnt from his own experience how to idealise earthly sexual love as the union of two different spirits which complete each other, as in *By the Fireside*. Immediately after the death of his wife he wrote to his sister: "My life is fixed now; I shall live out the remainder in her direct influence, endeavouring to complete mine."[2] This sentiment stimulated his creativeness again and again. For instance, it was the spiritual contact between Caponsacchi and Pompilia which gave him an opening for *The Ring and The Book*. In fact he would often imagine what people had missed because they had missed each other, for instance, *The Statue and the Bust* or *Youth and Art*. Or he would digress into a dirge over a marriage that was no marriage, but the death of two souls, as in the tragic implications of *My Last Duchess*. These studies in frustration served only to demonstrate the prizes we may lose. At the back of his mind there were always the prizes we may gain. The vision of this composite perfection through the marriage of true minds seems to have confirmed his confidence in life; we can follow him as far as he goes; and share his serenity.

[1] To Miss E. B. Barrett, 11 Feb. 1845.
[2] To Sarianna Browning, 30 June 1861.

But much as the reader enjoys these sentiments, he cannot help missing a sense of the irrepressible vitality and resilience of the human spirit, the fascinating wilfulness and inexhaustibility of the impulses which trouble life. Browning's lovers, like so many of his other characters, have been tamed. With the exception of the immortal Caponsacchi they are so true to their soul's mate that they become false to the spirit of adventure. This insistence on domestication excludes many a vista, and, as nineteenth-century civilisation began to weigh heavily on the imagination, it became more and more worth while to realise that the most precious jewels sometimes lurked at the bottom of the most stormy seas.

Browning's poetic sympathies were both widened and narrowed by another condition of his existence. He was born into a cultured circle and he was endowed with an immense capacity for humanistic research. He could accompany the human spirit through all its wanderings over the earth since the dawn of literature. So if actual contact with the nineteenth century failed to reflect his thoughts, he could look for confirmation elsewhere. Thanks to this telepathy, he acquired an unusual insight into the continuity of thought and sentiment. Humanity often presented itself to him as life force, independent of the millions of bodies that it vitalised. It was an aspiration which asserted its energy according to the civilisation of the age; under favourable conditions it attained to its true significance as art, literature and learning. Its expressiveness varied with the aims and opportunities of culture, each virtue enjoying a special faculty at a special time, but the urge was always the same. The student who followed its progress could contemplate every fact of man's genius and end by understanding that endeavour was immortal—a force which pursued God's purposes. This spirit of progress passed from man to man, enlivening his faculties up to extreme old age, till death, in fact beyond death. Having familiarised himself with all that the human race had dreamt and desired, he felt sure, as did Tennyson, that one life was not enough for a man's God-inspired ideal of what he might become. There was too much to learn and to forget. But whereas the author of *In Memoriam* hoped for a disembodied existence in the enlightened and ethereal atmosphere of the after-world, Browning believed in a second chance on earth. "No work begun shall ever pause for death."[1] The spirit which could invigorate old age, could pass into another body and continue its progress towards self-fulfilment.

[1] *The Ring and the Book*, VII, l. 1787.

This faith in earthly immortality has inspired some of his noblest poems, especially because it convinced the poet that a human being need not distrust himself. Man's impulses and ambitions were more than he; his part was to give them their free and natural expression. So comforting an idea was quite congenial to humanists still under the influence of the romantic philosophers. Goethe, who ought to know something about the possibilities of life, had confided to Eckermann[1] that the old age of talented men was a *wiederholte Pubertät*, a revival of youth, and had insisted that each human being had his own capacity for self-fulfilment—his *entelechy*[2]—since nature always accomplishes her ends. Thus Browning was persevering in a well-established tradition. It had recently been reaffirmed by Reveillé Parise, who argued in *La Vieillesse* (1853) that a man did not reach his full development ("toute l'hauteur de ses facultés") till he had lived for seventy years or more. It was to be revived in *Back to Methuselah*. In fact this tradition is always needing renovation, because it is not borne out by experience. Unhappily Browning, in his exuberant confidence, was tempted to write as if wishes were proofs. He was content to encourage a day-dream even if it could no longer be an expectation, nor even a hope. So he dissociated himself from the line of great poets who celebrate the other fortitude of desiring little, and he missed contact with those who were already resolved to conquer disillusionment by conquering illusions. One has only to compare *Rabbi Ben Ezra* (despite its solemn enthusiasm and mastery of rhythm) with Arnold's *Growing Old* (a much slighter performance), to realise which poet is the more prepared to trust to himself. So once more Browning had to pay for his optimism.

Such were the leading ideas which the poet extracted from life. They all provided endless material for his versatile and creative genius, but they all helped to divert his gaze from one half of the world—the aspect which most people have to face. His experiences were congenial to his temperament, for he had "drunk of the cup of life, with the sun shining on it",[3] as his future wife observed. He could not have written otherwise. So for more than half his life he cultivated what is beautiful, noble, heroic and divine, and showed that the grandeur of man is found in his aspiration, perseverance

---

[1] 11 March 1828.

[2] "Ich zweifle nicht an unserer Fortdauer, denn die Natur kann die Entelechie nicht entbehren." 1 Sept. 1829.

[3] E. B. Barrett to R. Browning, 20 March 1845.

and disinterestedness. Some of his speeches, episodes and situations are presented with unforgettable felicity of rhythm and phraseology, and are developed with a virile simplicity of manner which he made peculiarly his own. For many admirers such is the true Browning, and they quote *Saul, The Lost Leader, Abt Vogler, Garden Fancies, Balaustion's Adventure* (in which the inspiration of Euripides is raised to a modern poet's vision), but above all, *Evelyn Hope,* a masterpiece which fuses thought with thoughtfulness and artlessly reveals more of Browning's philosophical religion than you will find in all the tedious and grotesque ruminations of *Christmas Eve and Easter Day.*

But Browning could not always have persisted in this vein. To begin with, the opportunities for discovering human perfection are not inexhaustible. Far from it. Even in the specially preserved gardens of historic culture, we have to look for our flowers among an entanglement of weeds. In the next place, the arts of idealisation have been perfected by too many master hands, and it would become increasingly difficult to escape the comparisons which are odious. Besides, in the search for new beauties there would always be the temptation, sometimes the necessity, to be remote, exotic, hypernatural. It must be confessed that some verses in *Dramatic Lyrics* (1842) and *Dramatic Romances* (1845) have the tastelessness as well as the charm of unreality. For instance, *Waring, The Boy and the Angel, The Flight of the Duchess,* fascinate the imagination, but only if you are in a holiday mood, off-duty, not inclined to reflect whether these personages will cast a ray through the complexities of your own life. They are dramatic in form rather than in spirit.

Such affectations, however poetically legitimate, could not satisfy the younger Victorians determined to enlighten conduct by culture; least of all could they satisfy their author bent on asserting that God was powerful even in the apparent failures. A man of Browning's energy and resolution would not rest till he had found a method adequate to expound his pantheism in all its relations to human beings—at least to his own satisfaction. By the time he published *Men and Women* in 1855, he had learnt how to test his philosophy in the battle of life. With *Dramatis Personae* (1864) his ideas have found the one artistic form which makes them real.

This presentment was, of course, the dramatic monologue. It may be objected that Browning had been practising nothing else since he first put pen to paper, and that in any case this type of poem was familiar to readers of Wordsworth, Byron and Tennyson.

But neither they nor he had realised the possibilities of the *genre*. A drama must represent a conflict; if a monologue, a conflict of thought. Up to the mid-century it had represented a conflict between what the speaker wished and what he knew that others wished; that is to say, between a desire and an external situation; for instance, *Two in a Gondola, The Last Ride Together*. Thus the monologue had to serve as a monodrama. But why should it not represent a conflict of which the speaker was unconscious and about which even the reader would be in two minds—a monologue which made you hesitate between God's view and man's view? Such was the most significant conflict, according to Browning's mature philosophy.

It was in this discovery that the poet realised his peculiar genius and fulfilled the idea projected in *Paracelsus*. He had all along believed that God moved through human beings, vitalising each personality. Filled with this optimism he had studied the mental habits of his fellow-creatures with an almost holy interest, and like all lovers of his kind he loved their idiosyncrasies. But this fascinating investigation by no means revealed an unimpeded stream of divine influence. On the contrary, it looked as if God's presence was strangely at a disadvantage in many people's temperaments and dispositions. Such was the disconcerting evidence, and the character in question seemed quite unconscious of any conflict or two-sidedness. So this human pantheist set himself to examine and explain why and when the divine urge was—not suppressed—but concealed. To elucidate the paradox, he had to dramatise the types of mind which are disingenuous, complex, mixed with base metal.

Such is the unique Browningesque monologue. His first achievements in the new style are *Blougram* and *Cleon* in *Men and Women* (1855). In his earlier efforts his characters are presented either as wholly bad, for instance the speakers in *My Last Duchess*, and *Spanish Cloister*; or men like Paracelsus who slowly and painfully rise to perfection but are always aiming at it; or men who are wholly good even if misunderstood, like Lippi, The Patriot, or David (in *Saul*). But from the mid-century onwards, he begins also to develop an eye for the characters that are both good and bad at the same time; who seem to disappoint the Creator's purpose, to take in hand their own development and quite conscientiously turn it to their own lower purposes. He did not abate one jot of his confidence in the divine omnipresence, but as he was so versed in following that universal influence, he had often traced it to the individual's brain and observed that it sometimes stopped short or lost effectiveness in that temperamental and man-controlled mechanism. But the obstruction was not due to the powers of evil— it was doubtful if there were any such powers—but to a trick of the understanding, a distorted habit of mind, an obliquity which might any day be straightened by some shock or flash of intuition. To demonstrate this conviction, he started afresh to probe men's minds, to follow up their trains of thought, to track their prejudices, inconsequences, and obsessions. Hence his later monologues become not obscure but tortuous and labyrinthine. Occasionally they are difficult because he sometimes found his most promising material among archaic characters, whose thoughts were complicated by a jumble of old notions, quite foreign to the modern mind. For instance, when criticising *Holy Grail and Other Poems* he writes: "I should judge the conflict in the knight's soul the proper subject to describe. Tennyson thinks he should describe the castle and effects of the moon on the towers and anything *but* the soul."[1]

These monologues have great power, because they exact all the reader's talent for intuition and psychological guesswork. Browning is so chary of indoctrination that the inattentive critic is sometimes betrayed into doubting whether the poet had made up his own mind. He had; but he generally left his reader to do the same; he paid him that compliment—gave him the chance of divining his own spiritual problem in the confession or self-defence of an imaginary personage. Some of his best effects are produced by a kind of dramatic irony, by which the speaker reveals himself as infinitely better or (more often) worse than he supposes himself to be. A casual example is *Prince Hohenstiel-Schwangau*, but the supreme achievement is *The Ring and The Book* (1868–9).

When Browning notified his new publisher, Fields, Osgood and Co., that the forthcoming manuscripts contained a mere twenty thousand lines, he added, "it is the shortest poem, for the stuff in it, I ever wrote".[2] It is certainly the most searching and explicit. Part I tells the crude story in its barest outline, and then sketches the interpretation which a poet's insight can extract. The next three Parts show how the unenlightened observer will misread the facts, because his own view is preconceived. And then, since there must be diabolism in such a tragedy, he hunts the evil down to its source in the heart of the arch-villain. There it lies hidden. So

---

[1] To Miss J. Blagden, 19 Jan. 1870.   [2] 19 July 1867.

Guido the murderer is produced and allowed to speak and betray himself, but all unwittingly. He thinks that he is vindicating his motives, and does indeed conceal his wickedness, perhaps from himself, certainly from many others, and would deceive, if it were possible, even the elect. On the other hand, no human encounter can be altogether unblessed. Therefore the poet passes on to Parts VI and VII and reveals the spirit of God springing up in the souls of the other two characters, who at first seem to be no better —Caponsacchi and Pompilia—however much lawyers may confuse the issue. Finally, the old Pope, who had "probed many hearts beginning with his own", probes this mystery also, by his knowledge of good and evil. In one respect the most significant part of the whole poem is to be found in the last forty lines, in which Browning insists that the truth to which he had penetrated could be revealed only by the art of the monologue. It will be noted that *One Half Rome, Other Half Rome*, and *Tertium Quid*, all judge the chain of events without knowing the inner life of the actors. They are viewed from the outside as ready-made types, fixed and set, easily classified; and so Guido judges his enemies. Browning's way is to judge the action by the whole past of the character, scanning every biographical antecedent which survives in the final effect. For him, moral character is movement in time, passed experiences telescoped into present motives. Or, to vary the metaphor, a man's personality is like a slowly constructed mole, his ostensible motives being only the last few inches of masonry, which bring the pier into contact with the obstacle. This insight is an anticipation of Bergson.[1]

His secret was to concentrate his interest on the character's own idea of himself; not God's idea or other people's idea; but his own explanation of his attitude among the circumstances in which he had to live—what Jung would call his *persona*. The artistic problem was to catch the speaker in his truthful moments, in the situations which touch his intimate idiosyncrasies; for instance, Caliban in a thunderstorm, Sludge face to face with exposure, Blougram over his wine, Guido on the eve of his execution. The reader is expected to start with a poet's idea of human values (not the world's idea) and to apply that test to all the speaker's apologies, evasions, and self-assertions. His insight depends on his knowledge of human nature, as well as of God's purposes. Thanks to this realism, Browning's best monologues create an unexpectedly welcome atmo-

[1] *Post*, chap. XXIII.

sphere of worldliness. They appeal to one's ethical sense and also to one's practical experience. The author was so confident in this effect that when a friend at last detected the mystic, he replied in surprise, "Yes, but how did you find it out?"[1]

Browning seems to reconcile The Past with The Present, to blend ancient experiences with modern consciousness. So it is important, in conclusion, to investigate his reputation both with his contemporaries and successors. At first it would seem that he should have exercised a marked influence on the future development of literature. He quickened the imagination of his younger readers by his accessories and backgrounds; he knew how to stage his monologues; he could make a vanished age live through the realistic strangeness of its details, as in *An Epistle*. While Tennyson (especially in touches of *In Memoriam*) was verging towards regionalism, Browning had created *chronicalism*. His success is most conspicuous in such masterpieces as *The Grammarian's Funeral* and in "*Childe Roland to the Dark Tower Came*".

Again, he anticipated realism, since he not only portrayed imperfect characters, but took a profound interest in their imperfections. In his studies of their inner lives, especially their self-deceptions, there was much to prepare the next generation or two for the methods of Meredith, Hardy and Conrad. Even the iconoclasts were likely to be stimulated by his unconventional attitude. He unsettled our way of looking at our literary heritage both in style, for instance, in *Holy Cross Day*, and in sentiment, for instance, in *Lippi*. He unsettled our ideas of duty and self-respect, as in *Fifine*. In fact, it is difficult to read Browning without revising one's values. Even his incorrigible trifling with prosaic details and unpoetic colloquialisms was quite to the taste of the younger generation. Such banalities as Mr Sludge's egg-nogg and cigar, or the ankles of Mr Smith's female model in *Youth and Art*, or Verdi's "Orchestra of salt-box, tongs and bones", or "thingam-bob the new prose poet", were refreshing at a time when the flowers of poetic diction were becoming hot-house plants. One recalls the effectiveness with which A. E. Housman in *A Shropshire Lad* (1895) was afterwards to write of gallows and beer and "chaps"; and Shaw was to introduce on the stage a dentist's chair or a motor-car with a chauffeur busy under the wheels, or Julius Caesar sensitive about being termed an "old gentleman".

[1] W. B. Yeats, *Letters to the New Island.* Edited with Introd. and Notes by H. Reynolds, 1934.

Above all, Browning recognised modern scepticism. He places no reliance on creeds which pass all understanding or faiths founded on the miraculous. He trusts God only as far as his own eyes and intuitions. He was an old man when Renan noticed that such was the tendency of nineteenth-century thought and feared that we should have to return to credulity or lose our ideals. "Je le dis franchement, je ne me figure pas comment on rebâtira, sans les anciens rêves, les assises d'une vie noble et heureuse."[1] The English poet had no such fears. Altogether, one might have expected that Browning would become the hero of the iconoclasts.

At one time, it looked as if he would attain to that "bad eminence". In 1865, even before he had published his "murder poem", he learns from Chapman and Hall that the young men are inquiring for his books, some of which had languished almost unread for a quarter of a century.[2] In 1867 young Oxford proposed him as Matthew Arnold's successor to the professorship of poetry, and in order that he might be qualified, the older men granted him an M.A. by diploma (26 June). In October 1868 Balliol made him an honorary fellow. In 1871 he was offered the Lord Rectorship of Glasgow University. In 1877 *The Inn Album* was translated into German.[3] In June 1879 Cambridge conferred on the poet a D.C.L. In 1881 F. J. Furnivall founded The Browning Society and its publications so far stimulated the book-lovers' interest, that people paid enormous prices for the original volumes which he had printed at private expense and given away.[4] In 1887 W. G. Kingsland published *Robert Browning, Chief Poet of the Age*. So it would seem that at last we have found one of the pioneers of the twentieth century.

Yet such a conclusion is very questionable. It will be noticed that the more adventurous admirers then and now who might have relished his unconventionality and introspection, do not cultivate his optimism nor his learned sympathies. Even *The Ring and the Book* was more discussed than read, and more read than imitated. Besides, there is something unsubstantial about the homage which Browning enjoyed, but by which he was not de-

---

[1] *L'Avenir de la Science*, Préface: "I frankly avow that I cannot imagine how we shall reconstruct the foundations of an honourable and happy life without the former dreams."

[2] To Miss J. Blagden, 19 Aug. 1865.

[3] E. Leo, *Das Fremdenbuch...Aus dem Englischen*.

[4] To W. G. Kingsland, 27 March 1885.

ceived. He seems to have realised that his reputation was founded on what one might call the discipleship of a cult.[1] Outside a small group of kindred spirits, he was a household name only to those who subscribed to the Browning Society, or considered themselves superior to the critical powers of the common herd. He was so sensitive to this estrangement that he refused the most advantageous invitations to publish in magazines; because he would thus obtrude his poems on the adventitious reader. Nor was he deceived by the university honours, which he accepted with reluctance. They were a tardy recognition of his erudition, industry and high moral tone. In fact his life work was more a source of interest than of inspiration.

Why had he lost touch with the deeper, more spiritual influences which shape the thoughts of the future? There are several answers and they will help us to realise the delicacy and elusiveness of literary adjustments. In the first place, as he grew older, his literary indiscretions became more and more unpardonable. In 1845 his intimate friend, Carlyle, had the foresight as well as insight to give "that prodigious advice of his, to write your next work in prose".[2] In later life Browning did sometimes so draft his monologues, but he could not resist turning them into verse, because, even to the end, he was blessed with a genius for flashing out into occasional phrases of sublimely vivid poetry. But, unlike Tennyson, he was not blessed with a talent for self-criticism, and some of his lines are more prosaic than *Paradise Lost* at its pamphleteering worst, and some of his rhymes out-Ingoldsby Ingoldsby. H. H. Hatcher[3] claims that less than one out of every hundred of his 34,746 rhymes is unusual; yet the peccant examples quoted by his apologist are unforgettable. His freakishness lacks a sense of humour, and that defect is always remembered against a writer.

These grotesqueries and eccentricities might have been forgiven if his more thoughtful poems fulfilled one's expectations. But the inveterate optimist has not proved his case—not to the satisfaction of his juniors. The motives with which his characters wrestle are not those of the next two or three generations. The besetting sin of the 'forties and 'fifties was *banausia*. The Brownings knew it well.[4]

---

[1] To T. J. Nettleship, 10 March 1889.
[2] E. B. Barrett to R. Browning, 9 Sept. 1845.
[3] *The Versification of Robert Browning*, 1928, chap. XII.
[4] E. Barrett to R. Browning, 9 Sept. 1845. R. Browning to E. Barrett, 25 Sept. 1845.

Both understood that their contemporaries needed great interests. Yet he did not show them how to live more intensely. He seems so to do, but ends by showing how much more intensely men of former ages had lived. His favourite personages are Athenians, rabbis, early Christians, lovers and artists of the Renaissance, historical warriors and statesmen. Men and women who belong to the storied past, and shame our banality through the mirage of culture. In olden times, we are assured, life was harder and fiercer and therefore the light of heaven streamed into the mind.[1] So if the life of to-day is to satisfy the spirit, it must be through the modern opportunities for rediscovering the world of yesterday. Such was the conviction of the Brownings, as of Tennyson, and (as we shall see) of Carlyle, Froude, Arnold, Fitzgerald, Pater, Symonds. But (as we shall also see) such was not to be the creed of the younger generations. Rightly or wrongly, they were to be conscious of emotions and sentiments which the past could not inspire and were to feel that earlier civilisations had neither their temptations nor opportunities. They wanted to assure themselves that the present was big enough for them, despite its multitudinous littleness. Browning, who at first sight seems so modern, proved to be unable to cultivate modernism on its merits. He was bound by his own humanism and had to rely on its encouragement. He was aware of his own limitations. On 19 August 1865 he wrote to Miss Isabella Blagden: "As I began, so I shall end, taking my own course, pleasing myself or aiming at doing so, and thereby, I hope, pleasing God." As a result, he is more a sign of the times than an influence in their fulfilment.

In one respect his later verse might have started the younger men thinking in new ways. He introduced the ultra-modern spirit of dissection. Each of his monologues is an ethical problem, so the most sceptical investigator can ignore the humanistic associations, and practise his analysis of the moral spectrum. One might quote such introspective experiments as E. L. Masters's *Spoon River Anthology* (1914), T. S. Eliot's *Prufrock and Other Observations* (1917), even the later novels of Virginia Woolf, for instance, *Mrs Dalloway* (1925), *To the Light-House* (1927), *The Waves* (1931), or the unutterable *Ulysses* (1921) of James Joyce, to demonstrate that Browning's example has been followed. These, and other such writers, have buried the dead, and they analyse the living by putting themselves in their place. Yet it is very doubtful whether they learnt even their

[1] E.g. *The Ring and the Book*, x, ll. 1851–65.

method from the Victorian. He rendered the exercise too difficult; he spoilt his manner by his mannerisms. Paul de Reul claims that our poet anticipated some of the twentieth-century innovators in versification, the principle which Cocteau terms *l'esthétique du minimum*.[1] There is the same compression and tendency to speak in riddles. Some of our free verse certainly does rely on the fascination of guesswork, or on nothing else; but such was not Browning's intention. Once when he was going to convince an old friend of his errors, he told his future wife that he would "drive the great wedge through his breast" and deeper still.[2] Such was the treatment to which he subjected his characters. But when he has penetrated to the man's heart, he finds too much in that hidden recess. The examination lets loose more thoughts of his own than he can control. They carry him back swimming to the surface, among the speaker's subterfuges, circumlocutions, parleyings, and self-deceptions. He is so anxious to leave no facet unillumined, that he illumines nothing. His portraits, like Milton's deity, are dark with excessive light. He cultivates *l'esthétique du maximum*. So his readers are apt to become impatient. Alfred Austin described him as "the very incarnation of discordant obscurity",[3] and the poet himself alludes to the "fifty-years'-long charge of unintelligibility against my books".[4] In reality Browning is not obscure, but he certainly is tortuous and prolix. W. B. Yeats was summing up a widespread impression when he concluded: "The world was simply a great boarding-house in which people come and go in a confused kind of way. The clatter and chatter to him was life, was joy itself."[5]

[1] *L'Art et la Pensée de Robert Browning*, 1929, chap. VII, §1.
[2] 1 July 1845.   [3] *The Examiner*, 12 Aug. 1876.
[4] To Edmund Yates, *c.* 1882.
[5] W. B. Yeats, *Letters to the New Island*. Edited with Introd. and Notes by H. Reynolds, 1934.

CHAPTER VIII

Carlyle a pessimist in search of optimism—He cannot find it because he looks for the God of his own soul (and of German poetry) in the social developments of the nineteenth century, or in the historical developments which preceded it.

So Browning was hailed not as one of the latter-day prophets, but rather as the antiquary of the human spirit. Possibly his mind was shaped by the tradition of culture which held sway in his father's household, probably by his marriage with a scholarly poetess, certainly by his fifteen years' residence in Florence. Let us now consider another combined humanist and humorist who entered life with none of these advantages or disadvantages, but was no less determined to learn from culture the way to live, and came even nearer than Browning towards breaking the Victorian tradition.

Carlyle was a transplanted peasant, the son of a master mason who had never received a penny which he had not "picked", as he said, "out of the hard stone". He founded his family on his masonry. So, in the first place, he learnt—none better—that honest work was the one pathway to peace and respectability. He was also a Calvinist, and had enough imagination to fancy himself surrounded by the ominous powers of Eternal Justice "as the unutterable depths of silence, through which flickered a trembling hope". This quivering flame was fed by industry; labour in this life was the one claim to salvation in the next. So with all the force of his commanding personality he impressed on his children the duty not only of working with all their might, as if there was nothing else to do, but of working so that some spiritual enlightenment, some approach to God, should result from every effort.

James Carlyle was as consistent as self-disciplined. Even in his holiday moments of intelligent curiosity he recognised the responsibility of the true labourer. He did not accept the knowledge of other people till he had worked for it himself, nor consent to "putting out the natural eye of his mind to see better with a telescope". The principle also was to influence his son's career.

But however disposed to think for himself, the father had the vision to appreciate a culture beyond his ken. He paid his son's bills at school and college. Thus Thomas started where James left off. "I can see my dear Father's life in some measure as the sunk pillar on which mine was to rise and be built."

It was so; in a moral no less than a practical sense. Our author set out to conquer knowledge in the spirit of the Ecclefechan stone-mason. There were, of course, other ways in which his father influenced him, especially by his gift for picturesque phraseology and mordant witticisms. If the son had been content to imitate his grimly humorous parent in this talent only, he would, with his own genius for vivid and ironical narration, have succeeded much more rapidly. We are apt to forget James's other attribute: "he seldom or never spoke except actually to convey an idea". Nor do we remember that in the mind of this self-educated, self-disciplined Calvinist, an idea was something which concerned man's relation to God. That was Thomas's chief difficulty as an author.

When this raw, earnest boy went up to Edinburgh University in 1809 he was not encouraged to study for the satisfaction of his soul, nor even to believe in God, but in Voltaire, Hume and Gibbon. Such an apprenticeship was an all-too-severe trial for the Ecclefechan spirit. Carlyle's ancestors had been masons or cobblers, and he, their descendant, had entered on manhood with the con-viction that doctrines, sciences, and systems were like the materials out of which you made boots or houses. The craftsman must first test their raw quality; then shape and rework them to minister to other people's comfort and one's own sense of work well done. Such an obligation was easily discharged, if your materials are stone or leather, but not if you are an artisan in knowledge which can often be used to prove that God does not exist. This training unsettled him for the ministry; aroused "grave prohibitive doubts"; but not the confidence of solving them. He tried to become a schoolmaster. He thought of becoming a barrister, but his artisan's conscience revolted against a profession in which your deepest thoughts must be left unsaid and "your intellect, your highest heavenly gift, hung up in the shop-window, like a loaded pistol for sale". Finally, after attempting to take pupils, he drifted towards "the resource of all Adam's posterity, that are otherwise foiled—the Pen".[1]

He made this last venture in what he called a mood of "*desperate*

[1] *Life of Sterling*, Pt II, chap. III.

hope" and he never really succeeded in earning a living as an essayist in humanism. At the end of fifteen or more years of incessant toil, dyspepsia and penury, he was on the point of investing his last few coins in farming implements—though past forty years of age—and emigrating to America. But if the labours and disappointments of this anxious period (from about 1820 to 1837) did not achieve a competence, they forced him to think, explore and experiment, and thus constrained, he found the one thing necessary to his temperament, what he called *acumination*, the concentration on a point, a definite ruling idea on which to work.

As is well known, the enlightenment came to him through German literature, and he approached these studies with a definite question in his mind;[1] and only after he had tried other oracles. His natural taste was for science. At Edinburgh John Leslie's interesting lectures had aroused his enthusiasm for mathematics, and from the age of sixteen to twenty-three, he worshipped geometry. While he was at the University Lagrange's *Mécanique Analytique* and Laplace's *Exposition du Système du Monde* (with its note on the "nebular hypothesis") fell into his hands and captured his imagination. In fact he learnt German in 1819 in order to study Werner's mineralogical doctrines in the original. Sometime in 1820 he drifted into authorship, but even then, he began as a scientific contributor to *The Edinburgh Philosophical Journal*. He next began writing biographies for *The Edinburgh Encyclopaedia*, apparently because he needed money.[2] Thus if his life had been easier he would probably have cultivated science as a second, purified religion. At that period (1820–30), eighteenth-century deism was no longer supreme. The study of natural laws invalidated orthodoxy, but not necessarily the idea of God. The Divine Intelligence could still be recognised in the mechanism of the universe, if one looked with unprejudiced eyes. It was only when Carlyle began as a professional writer to study the ways of modern man, and looked in vain for any scheme such as he could find among the stars or among minerals, that he began to seek guidance from humanists who could think of society in the same religio-scientific spirit as he could think of nature. Madame de Staël's *De L'Allemagne* seemed to show him where to look, and the publishers seemed favourable. Lockwood and De Quincey were already reviewing German books, and *Blackwood's Magazine*, since 1819, had been printing translated

[1] Carlyle to Goethe, 3 Nov. 1829.
[2] See I. W. Dyer, *A Bibliography of T. Carlyle's Writings and Ana*, 1928.

extracts in *Horae Germanicae*.[1] It was Goethe's impression in 1825 that almost every young Englishman of good family had learnt German.[2]

In 1823 he joined the philo-germanists, and during the next nine years he established a restricted but genuine reputation as an authority on the subject. So his early manhood was spent. Goethe in 1827 recognised the spiritual and moral insight of his interpretations.[3] These were services rendered to the culture of his country. But Carlyle would not also have rendered so great and in some respects so questionable a service to himself, except for his peculiar temperament. He made a false start with his *Life of Schiller*, which John Taylor commissioned him to write for *The London Magazine*.[4] Schiller was one of those idealists for whom life has no disillusionments, since he ignored them. Carlyle, on the other hand, had nothing else. He was already infected with a mania for pitying himself and satirising other people. So he had got into the habit of regarding English civilisation as an aggregate of bad workmen; at the same time he brooded over his own difficulties till they seemed to encircle him like the Calvinistic gloom of his father's household without the flickering ray of hope. We are asked to believe in his "fearful wrestlings with the foul and vile and soul-murdering mud-gods of my epoch". Even the higher journalism of his time had spread "into length and breadth, into superficiality and saleability". It was hopeless to look for the depths of the stream beneath the foam.

Carlyle was judging an age of transition much as his artisan ancestors would judge materials which proved to be defective by the established standards. Obviously the influence of Schiller would only intensify his malady. He had to learn that the moralist must work experimentally—should cherish his faith, but be prepared to scrutinise its findings. Such is the only way of discovering whether God can be discerned in the social as well as in the astronomical scheme.

Carlyle achieved this *acumination* through the study of Goethe. He had begun to read *Wilhelm Meister* in 1821 or 1822. After a year's meditation he began to realise its significance for him. On 6 April 1823 he writes to Jane Welsh that its author "does not

---

[1] E. Neff, *Carlyle*, 1932, chap. III, §2.
[2] Eckermann, 10 Jan. 1828.   [3] *Ibid.* 25 July 1827.
[4] Oct. 1923; Jan., July–Sept. 1824. Revised and augmented in book form, *Life of Friedrich Schiller*, 1825.

yield himself to his emotions, but uses them rather as things for his judgment to scrutinise and apply to purpose". A few weeks later, after contributing his first instalment of *Schiller's Life*, he started to translate the novel and worked alternately at the two tasks. When the translation was published in 1824 he sent a copy to the sage of Weimar with a covering letter, and so began the correspondence[1] which lasted till Goethe's death, and reveals so convincingly the Scotman's genius for hero worship.

It took Carlyle another year or two before he learnt to tread in his hero's footsteps. He completed his biography of Schiller in March 1825; then he had the courage to leave London, settle in Hoddam Hill, which his father leased for him, and devote himself to the study of the sage of Weimar. The year which he spent on this little farm, just before his marriage, especially between May 1825 and May 1826, was the turning point in his life. What Carlyle learnt was not so much a new philosophy—Goethe as we have seen[2] disclaimed theories and worked by impressions—as a new religion. The author of *Wilhelm Meister* and of *Faust* belonged to no school. He had severed himself from all illusions, even those of romanticism, and trusted only to his own observation. In this sceptical spirit he studied nature, himself and other people, just as Carlyle was trying to do, and yet never fell a victim to scepticism. On the contrary, being disembarrassed from any prejudice towards either agnosticism or superstition, his mind seemed to work with unrivalled clearness and he was able to distinguish a deeper meaning in phenomena than that which met the eye. He could explain that a supernatural spirit was moving through nature, through himself, but also through other people; yes, and through the whole fabric of society. By the help of philosophy, art and science we could all gain an insight into its range and scope. Over and above human beings, he could discern and understand humanity. Other thinkers had guessed as much, or nearly as much, before. But Goethe had the creative imagination. He did not only speculate, he knew how to describe what he saw in this new significant light, without falsifying the appearance; he enabled others to see the ground plan in its seemingly imperfect realisation. Even error and miscarriage were proofs of cosmic energy. This interpretation of life which Browning was to proclaim so impetuously to deaf ears in *Paracelsus*, is leisurely unrolled in his poems, plays, novels and scientific papers,

[1] *Correspondence between Goethe and Carlyle.* Edited by C. E. Norton. 1887.
[2] *Ante*, chap. III.

and, above all, enforced by his personality. He exemplified what he teaches—not tolerance, but confidence. His insight and genial wisdom made a convert of Carlyle, filled him with the enthusiasm of a religion and gave him something to believe in and to work for. He who lamented the aimlessness of contemporary literature had now something at which to aim. Like his father, he need no longer speak "without conveying an idea".

It is surprising what ideas he found to convey. His first mani-festo was a review of Franz Horn's *Die Poesie und Beredsamkeit*,[1] in which, like Schopenhauer,[2] he argued that art sees deeper into reality than our own experience can, and bodies forth the essence of things under more expressive symbols. In fact it was Carlyle who inaugurated the new function of the critic as the interpreter between the inspired and the uninspired; the physician who opens darkened eyes so that they can see the true import of the poet inside and beyond the mere beauty of his words. It was also Carlyle who began looking into the lives of writers for the credentials of their inspiration, and hinted that the grand style is to be traced to what the grand stylists do or suffer. So Carlyle turned a book-review into a work of genius and devoted the next decade or so to de-veloping and applying the ideas which he sketched in this essay. One might cite the story[3] how Goethe won to spiritual freedom; the attack[4] on the mechanisation of modern life, thus anticipating Arnold's *Culture and Anarchy* (1869), Rathenau's *Zur Kritik der Zeit* (1912), Jasper's *Die geistige Situation der Gegenwart* (1931); how the transcendentalism of Novalis may be used by any plain-thinking man as a guide to life;[5] how Richter's patient heroism may be studied as a demonstration of man's kinship with God.[6] Every-where he seems to be searching and sifting for ideas which will confirm his trust in man's possibilities, efface the "dead Edinburgh Whiggism, scepticism and materialism" of his student days. More important still, he is learning from the romantic writers of the previous generation, how the dreams of yesterday might become the virtues of to-day. On 13 January 1832 he can jot down in his Note-book: "The world grows to me ever more as a magic picture—a true supernatural revelation, infinitely stern,

---

[1] *Edinburgh Review*, No. 92, 1927.

[2] See *Die Welt als Wille und Vorstellung* (The World as Will and Appearance), Bd. III.

[3] *Foreign Review*, No. 3, 1828. [4] *Edinburgh Review*, No. 98, 1829.

[5] *Foreign Review*, No. 7, 1829. [6] *Ibid.* No. 9, 1830.

but also infinitely good; shall I ever succeed in copying a little therefrom?"

In rereading the essays and appreciations of this period which stretches from 1827 to the publication of *The French Revolution* in 1837, one hardly knows whether to admire the width and depth of his allusions or the lucidity and directness with which complex and abstract ideas are summed up in vivid phrases. His occasional writings are mostly free from the pseudo-Tacitean mannerisms and repetitiousness of his historical books and political pamphlets. His style, like his thought, is highly individualised, but not extravagant or eccentric. Yet it will be noticed that this journalism is made up of so many essays in rediscovery. They explore ideals and activities which have already found expression in literature, and what is more, in the literature of a simpler, less scientific age, when towns were smaller, and men had more time and space to study their own minds. It will also be noticed that the sage who initiated Carlyle into the secrets of humanity had never seen London or Paris, had passed the most prolific period of his life in a town of forty-nine thousand inhabitants, the capital of a small German principality. Besides, he was seventy-five years old when the two began to correspond, and was never to see, much less study, the perplexities of the Victorian era. So Carlyle's *Miscellanies* were bound to be retrospective; an assertion that we learn more of man from the past than from the present. According to this picture our worst enemy is "flunkeyism", that is, *thinking in livery*, respecting not the values of things, but their price and importance according to established usage; just as Wilhelm Meister[1] went on the stage because he thought that the most aristocratic and therefore the finest thing in life was to cultivate his individual self. Besides, it must not be forgotten that Carlyle was a critic in search of a religion, and almost necessarily became an inspired phrase-maker. He catches us in our reflective moods and gives us suggestive sentences which we can turn over and over in our minds. Obviously he would be uneasy till he could catch us in our active moods and invent thoughts and phrases which could influence our conduct as well as our meditations. Could the old world at its imagined best teach the new world at its actual worst? He had committed himself to the wisdom of eighteenth-century France and Germany and had now to prove that it held good for nine-teenth-century England.

[1] *Wilhelm Meister*, Buch v, Kap. iii.

So between January and August of 1831, while still at Craigen-puttock, he wrote *Sartor Resartus* to prove that the older philosophers knew what was best for the factory-ridden England which they had never seen. They lived a concentrated introspective life, studying the appetencies and affinities of the human soul. Yet we should be able to discern the essential virtue and wholesomeness of our own chaotic civilisation, if we learnt their secret, and applied it to our own overcrowded and superficial lives. Being so ego-centric, he naturally used his own experiences to explain the needed adjustment. He was well advised, for he was thus speaking as an individual and morality is an individual problem.

Sartor describes first of all the despondency of a man who feels himself to be full of energy, which he must employ; full of intel-lectual aptitudes, so he must employ this energy in thought and research; full of love for humanity so he could satisfy his soul only by serving his fellow-creatures, a faithful craftsman in ideas. But when he goes out into the world to earn his living, he finds nothing worth doing and his fellow-creatures will not pay him for his help because they do not want it. To judge by the selfishness, material-ism, greed and rivalry of his contemporaries, the eighteenth-century rationalists were right: men are highly magnetised machinery; or if they have a soul, it is petrified under modern conditions. We cannot fulfil our best selves under the mammonism of this age. The writer is half convinced; he loses hope; and begins to despair of his age and consequently of himself. He even whispers that revolt is useless, that things cannot be changed. This pessimistic resigna-tion is *The Everlasting No*. So his humanity and religious sense are thwarted, his spirit grows restless and turns inward upon itself; dwells upon its own helplessness, exaggerates its difficulties; shudders at the weight of circumstance.

Suddenly, while nursing these fears, it dawns upon him that he is helping to suppress his own soul, for the spirit lives only in the consciousness of its invincibility. To confess yourself the victim of mortal circumstances, is to deny your immortality; to be afraid of man is to confess that you have no part with God. The individual who sees further and higher than the life around him must be spiritually superior to its influence. He can afford to be indifferent to evil. Such is *The Centre of Indifference*.

But if there are godlike impulses in you, so must there be in other people, for the world is made up of beings like yourself. Consequently, this mammonism, corruption and selfishness are more apparent than real. Perhaps they are only the disabilities of transition, perhaps even the birth-pangs of a newer more perfect order. Byron, a romantic decadent, may have declared the world to be unworthy of his immortal soul, but Goethe had shown that our daily life may give it ample scope. So surely the individual of to-day can find some response to his aspirations, some reflection in experience of the pattern which hangs in his head. Such is *The Everlasting Yea*.

He will find much more. If, like Goethe, he can study the needs of man first as revealed in himself, then as revealed in the contacts of society, he will be able to understand that an immortal spirit— what the German would call a *Daimon*[1]—is still active, bringing our highest qualities into play, unless we are too self-centred to rede the new mystery. Nineteenth-century industrialisation does not really antagonise human beings; it weaves them together and breeds a religion of exalted co-operation, in which we ought to rise above the physiocrats and romantics—"a second all-embracing Life, wherein our first individual Life becomes doubly and trebly alive and whatever of Infinitude was in us bodies itself forth, and becomes visible and active". A grand idea! For this mysticism, certified by the observation of facts, ought to give scope to one's whole nature. Man should now have a target worth shooting at.

The difficulty was to bring this truth home to the imagination. That is why Carlyle, especially in this treatise, avoids the academic note, and does not quote authorities. He was probably thinking of Theresa's pronouncement: "the man, to whom the universe does not reveal directly what relation it has to him; whose heart does not tell him what he owes to himself and others—that man will scarcely learn it out of books; which generally do little more than give our errors names".[2] So the doctrine is embodied in the allegory of *clothes philosophy*. "Whatsoever sensibly exists, whatsoever represents spirit to spirit, is properly Clothing, a suit of Raiment,...the whole External Universe is but clothing."[3] This symbolism was not, of course, an invention of Carlyle's. It is found in *A Tale of a Tub*, in *Faust*,[4] and in Heine's *Reise nach München*.[5] Carlyle may, in the first place, have been inspired by Fichte's assertion "that all things which we see and work with on this earth, especially we

---

[1] See *Dichtung und Wahrheit. Gespräche mit Eckermann. Ante*, p. 37.
[2] *Wilhelm Meister*, Bk vii, chap. vi (Carlyle's translation).
[3] Bk i, chap. ix.   [4] 1er Theil Gothisches Zimmer.
[5] Kap. xxix.

ourselves and all persons, are as a kind of vesture or sensuous appearance". He had probably already played with the idea in the lost *Thoughts on Clothes* refused by *Fraser* in 1830, and he continued to play with it after he had written *Sartor*. In 1848 he projected *Exodus from Houndsditch*,[1] that is from the old clothes of Hebrew Christianity, but abandoned the plan. Even in that later altered mood, he reverenced the wrappings too much to tear them off and leave some souls to perish in spiritual nakedness. In 1831 he was more affirmative. He uses the figure to show that civilisation, with all its failures and crimes, is the vesture by which God humanises society. "Thinking reader, the reason seems to me twofold: first that *Man is a spirit*, and bound by invisible bonds to *All Men*; secondly that *he wears clothes* which are the visible emblem of that fact."

To render his philosophy not only pictorial but picturesque, Carlyle associated this clothes philosophy with a definite personage. In doing so he followed a well-established usage, already practised by F. Schelling, Tieck, Jean Paul, Godwin and Byron, but of course his chief inspiration was Goethe's *Werther* and *Meister*. It is surprising how often the spirit of the latter work breathes through Carlyle's assertions and ejaculations. Under such influences the essay ought to have been quite easy to read, if the author had not insisted on discussing the duties of citizenship in the spirit of a romantic poet. But he did not adhere to their point of view. The romantic philosophers had taught that man has received a designation surpassing his earthly limits and therefore yearns for the infinite, but they insisted that this *Unendlichkeit* is to be cultivated in poetry, art, and the sentiment of love. Carlyle asserted that what he calls our *infinitude* can find full scope only in the nexus of society. For instance, a shoeblack is infinite in soul, but he will become conscious of his infinity not in contemplating Shelley's universe "all vacant azure, hung with a few frosty mournful if beautiful stars",[2] but in blacking shoes. Space and time could and should be transcended amid the commonest and most conventional pursuits of middle-class life. By virtue of his citizenship the average wage-earner should live a transcendental poem. Such an exposition involved many high-flown passages, many paragraphs full of introspection, much apostrophising and ruminating, much

---

[1] J. A. Froude, *Carlyle's Life in London*, chap. xv (1846–7).
[2] The sentence occurs in a letter to Browning, 8 March 1853. Quoted to illustrate the romantic Carlyle's dislike of romantic poetry.

repetition and some confusion. The author himself admits the difficulty. "How to paint to the sensual eye what passes in the Holy-of-Holies of man's soul; in what words, known to these profane times, speak even afar-off the Unspeakable."[1]

The effect of the book is weakened yet further because Carlyle writes only for those who are of his mind. If any reader was predisposed to doubt whether the bigness of modern city-life rendered the citizens big, Carlyle would not convert him. The "Sartor" does not persuade our reason, he exacts our obedience. He is more dogmatic than Newman without the dialectical skill. He convinces only those who have abandoned theism, without abandoning the theistic temperament. He does not, as Spinoza might have taught him, trace back ideas to their original causes, thus explaining and defining them. He exhorts, illustrates and appeals to the reader's self-consciousness for confirmation. Take, for instance, his brilliant definition of society as "the vital articulation of many individuals into a collective individual". Such was to be the conclusion of Herbert Spencer's Synthetic Philosophy, patiently argued through sixteen compact volumes,[2] from the nebular hypothesis to the latest principles of municipal administration. But Carlyle is content to formulate the idea in a few graphic sentences and to exact the reader's consent on pain of having to lose his soul.

Altogether it is not surprising that the author had difficulty in placing this series of essays. He hurried from Craigenputtock to London in the autumn of 1831 to find a publisher. But no printing house, in the depressed state of the market, would take the risk, especially as everyone was talking about the Reform Bill. After two years' delay this inspired and impassioned appeal at last appeared in detached fragments in *Fraser*.[3] It was not till 1836 that James Munroe in Boston published the work in book form with Emerson's preface. It was not till 1838 that Saunders and Otley published the work in London, after the *French Revolution* had made the author famous.

Nevertheless, *Sartor* is immensely significant, because it shows that Carlyle's mind has taken its bent. He seems to realise that modern society will involve the spiritual death of its members unless they realise its meaning. One might almost say that he aims at making democracy safe for the world. But how will he develop his idea? So far he has discussed only the individual's needs, which

---

[1] Bk II, chap. IX.　　　　[2] *Post*, chap. XVI.
[3] Nov., Dec. 1833: Feb.–April, June–Aug. 1834.

are as wide as the universe, if not wider. In Mill's phrase, "his eyes are unsealed",[1] but he has still to discern the channels through which his or his reader's energy should work its way. He counsels hope, not effectiveness. Yet the Carlyles were work-people and believed that human earnestness should be approved by what it produced. Thomas, being a writer, would have to show his fellow-creatures more precisely how to fulfil the scheme of the World-Spirit.

Mill expected him to think out a programme of social reform, or at least propound a reasoned system of practical philosophy on which humanitarians and statesmen could act. But Carlyle always distrusted the modern reliance on calculations and logic-choppings; they savour (so he would say) of earth-bound self-sufficiency; they dabble only in the transitory clothing with which the Time-Spirit enwraps Eternity. The utilitarian could not kindle the spark which reverberates from mind to mind till "it acquires incalculable new light as Thought, incalculable new heat as converted into action". Nor could he find his mission as a churchman; he distrusted established religions because they profess *formulas*, by which he meant ideas which cannot be tested in practice. He respected the physical sciences because facts were sacred; that was why he admired Kepler; but he did not respect the modern conclusions of biologists and zoologists. He refused to believe that the intellect and the moral sense were given to man by a power which had none itself. At the same time he seems to have been deeply impressed with Aurelia's parable that man is like an architect facing a quarry, and that his duty is to "combine with the greatest economy and fitness and durability, some form, the pattern of which originated in his spirit".[2] So he turned to the study of how men had succeeded and could again succeed in shaping life on their inward heaven-sent idea—the study of history.

The possibilities of such an interpretation seem to have grown on him while investigating the spirit, or rather the spiritlessness, of the *ancien régime*. In September 1832 he had begun working on Diderot for an essay which he published in April 1833 in *The Foreign Quarterly Review*, and thus he perceived why man failed to live up to his divine destiny. Diderot had great gifts; yet his genius could only grope within "the thin rind of the conscious". He never found his way to "the deep fathomless domain of the Un-

[1] To Sterling, Oct. 1831.
[2] *Wilhelm Meister*, Bk VI. Confessions of a Fair Saint (Carlyle's translation).

conscious whereon the other rests and has its meaning". What was true of the *encyclopédiste* was true of the age that produced him. Culture was based on logic. According to French thinkers God was an architect who designed a mechanised world and then sat apart and looked at it; not a supernatural vitality permeating all creation and especially human society. This combination of deism and agnosticism blinded that generation to the necessity of keeping pace with the divine progressiveness within "the Sanctuary of Man's Soul". In fact the materialism of eighteenth-century France was very like the materialism of nineteenth-century England, and had collapsed in a conflagration. So it dawned on Carlyle that the French Revolution was not a mere outrage against the wisdom and continuity of the Past, but a reawakening of divine energy, an assertion of the Human Spirit's will to outgrow its clothes, and that it should be the duty and privilege of the historian to examine and reveal this quality. On 1 February 1833 he notes in his Journal how utterly he disagrees with the fashionable school of historians who strive to "sink the Supernatural to the Natural". On 25 March 1834 he records "a thousand voices speak to me from the distance out of the dim depths of the old years. I sit speechless. If I live I shall speak." In September of that year he had indeed begun to speak.

The History of the French Revolution was finally published on 1 June 1837. Despite Mill's early and enthusiastic review in the July number of *The London and Westminster*, the press opinions were at first cautious, even adverse, and this great work might have languished for years, if Carlyle had not prepared the public for its reception. A wide group of educated people had been familiarising themselves with the idiosyncrasies of his genius; but half unconsciously; their appreciation was dissipated and interrupted, like his essays, by the inconsequences of periodical publication. But now these impressions were unified and reaffirmed in the dignity of a three-volume work of which neither the erudition nor the subject could be ignored. So the author returned from a holiday with his family at Scotsbrig to find himself famous.

The French Revolution is the climax of Carlyle's achievement as a genius and a leader of thought. The book is remarkable in the first place because he avoided the modern historian's principle of interpreting events as if they were moves on a chess-board. In his "flaming" pages a whole nation is swept on to its destiny and yet you are conscious of its myriad-headed diversity. Individuality is not lost in crowd psychology, much less in the "tendencies of the age"; you can almost hear the babel of differently pitched voices. Then, of course, there are the epic scenes, and the character-portraits, or, rather, the inspired caricatures, too well-known to need reference. Besides, Carlyle's literary personality was so forceful that he could make his convictions live in every description, and make us believe that the leaders of this terrible upheaval were servants of God. Such dramatisation is generally achieved at the expense of actuality and one would have expected his narrative to be romantic, inaccurate and allusive; a history after the manner of Victor Hugo. Yet Carlyle's authenticity and scholarship have been tested again and again, and though many defects have been found, it has been proved that even his most lurid scenes are based on a careful study of documents—only the study was enlightened by imagination, or as he would correct us, by God-fearing intuition.

These excellences explain the popularity of the book, but also its weakness, and why Carlyle began to lose influence the more he gained in reputation. The history took his generation by surprise; they did not examine its pretensions; and it claimed too much. It does not only demonstrate that accumulated abuses provoke volcanic outbursts, or as Tolstoy would say, that *If you neglect a fire, you don't put it out.* It also in an intensely religious spirit affirms a principle which was then driving thousands to agnosticism: that we can test and confirm our most sacred hopes by the evidence of history. Just at this time Sir Charles Lyell was examining in his *Principles of Geology* the history of the earth's surface, and was proving that nature changes her features slowly and blindly, in obedience to mere physical causes, and apparently quite uninfluenced by any superhuman will or intelligent purpose, such as the Old Testament reveals. Almost in the same year Strauss[1] had applied the historical method to the New Testament narrative, and was persuading thousands of English readers that the life and teaching of Jesus was a national myth, the symbolisation or allegory of a people's hopes and aspirations; a man-made romance. What Christologists and men of science argued out of the Bible, Carlyle argues into the latest European drama, the mere thought of which still made elderly Conservatives shudder. He is not content to demonstrate that the revolution, for all its bloodshed, contained the germs of democratic progress, nor even that Divine Retribution is

[1] See *post*, chap. XVI.

as inevitable as in the days of Jeroboam and of Ahab. He tries to convince us that man has a hidden source of superhuman spirituality on which he can always rely, even in working the guillotine. He is so vehemently eloquent, and his visions were so much of an imaginative adventure for his readers, that they did not stop to consider whether his impassioned phrases were coined only to convince them, or to convince himself also. Might must be right, because might is God's will made active on earth.

This over-emphasis is equally insistent in *Heroes and Hero-Worship*. The book is valuable because his theme gave him the opportunity of explaining why he studied literature and history as if they were Holy Writ. Goethe[1] had remarked: "We do not become free by *refusing* to recognise anything above us, but, on the contrary, by *paying honour* to something which is above us." Carlyle tries to show what it is we should honour. The hero, in the first place, is the man initiated into the eternal realities underlying the world of appearance; that is to say, he thinks and aspires in the spirit of *Sartor Resartus*. In the next place, he is so possessed by this insight that he becomes absolutely sincere and at once effects the cosmic purpose; that is to say, he lives and acts in the spirit of *The French Revolution*. The lecturer illustrates the signs and tokens by which the heroic figure proves his enlightenment and then discusses how we, the common herd, rise to his level, yes, even act in his spirit, as often as we recognise and worship in the hero "a dignity far beyond all others". We reverence him inasmuch as we can see eye to eye with him into the reality of things. The generation familiar with romantic poetry and philosophy, for instance, Fichte's *Ueber das Wesen des Gelehrten*, would find nothing unusually original in the theory, and it could then admire the author's earnestness, eloquence, and erudition as we can still admire them. But the younger, more positivist readers, must have suspected that they were taken off their guard by the literary genius of the lecturer, and were soon to question whether genius burnt with so ethereal a flame, and whether this inexplicable "infinitude" (as he translated the romantic *Unendlichkeit*) was really to be intuited through these figures. Carlyle would not argue with such an objector. He dismissed him as a *dilettante* "who dwells in vague outwardness, fallacy, and trivial hearsay about all objects".[2] So he could lead

---

[1] "Nicht das macht frei, dass wir nichts über uns anerkennen wollen, sondern eben, dass wir etwas verehren das über uns ist." *Gespräche mit Eckermann*, 18 Jan. 1827.   [2] *Hero as Poet*.

only those who, like Nevil Beauchamp,[1] were inclined by temperament to believe in his interpretation of history. Otherwise this course of lectures is chiefly interesting as an appendix to *The French Revolution*.

Thus *Hero-Worship* illustrates the continuity of Carlyle's mind. The same is true of the social pamphlets, which he now began producing. The recent fall of the French dynasty had been described so as to teach amongst other things one of the oldest of Biblical lessons; that accumulated crimes involve their own retribution which we must recognise as divine, however human the agents may be. *The French Revolution* contained an object lesson for the generation which forgot the warnings of the Old Testament. So this modern prophet now proceeded to demonstrate how the lesson applied to England. *Chartism* was published in 1839 with the motto "It never smokes but there is fire".

In this spirit he followed *Chartism* with *Past and Present* (1843), *Latter-Day Pamphlets* (1850), *Life of Sterling* (1850), *The Nigger Question* (1853), *Shooting Niagara: And after* (1867). These essays expose the abuses of his own day, much as the author would have exposed those against which John Knox protested. He had certainly studied his subject at first hand, especially the unequal distribution of money—the physical poverty of the working classes (the creators of wealth), and that other spiritual poverty of the well-to-do who would not use this wealth either for the betterment of themselves or of their fellow-creatures. So England was dying in the midst of plenty. He differs from the other political and social critics in attributing this stagnation not so much to the ineffectiveness of either the Tory or the Whig ministry, as to the irreligion of the educated classes, especially of orthodox divines who could reconcile the teaching of political economy with the teaching of the New Testament.[2] He condemned this "jesuitism" as "pig-philosophy" and at the same time stigmatised the more spiritual revivals of his day as "wretched dead, medieval monkeries and extinct traditions".[3] He even remarked in conversation that Newman had not the intellect of a moderate-sized rabbit.[4] More significant still, he has now lost hope in the average member of

---

[1] Meredith, *Beauchamp's Career*, 1875, chap. I.

[2] *Latter-Day Pamphlets*, No. VII.

[3] *Life of Sterling*, Bk II, chap. IV. For his classic pronouncement on evangelicanism and anglicanism from Coleridge onward, *ibid.* Bk I, chap. VIII.

[4] J. A. Froude, *Carlyle in London*, chap. XXV (1859–62).

society. Ten years after the Reform Bill he has reverted in sympathy to the eighteenth-century ideal of autocratic administration. Like Goethe, he believes in the strong hand. In fact, he seems to have made up his mind that the majority of his contemporaries (including most of his best friends) were poor creatures, almost as limited as the sciences in which they believed, only fit to be dominated, and if necessary enslaved, by the few leaders who from time to time were able to understand the purposes of God. In *The Nigger Question* he maintained that the free labourer exchanged most of his economic value for the freedom to be useless—and to starve.

These denunciations at first impress one as so many proofs of Carlyle's sincerity and practical wisdom, and they certainly speak with surprising force when one remembers the seditious meetings, the public demonstrations, rick-burnings and terrorism of the time, and the European crisis of 1848, with all that it implied. Yet amid all this helplessness he has only one statesmanlike remedy to suggest—a policy of emigration. For the rest he seems to be applying the doctrine of "organic filaments" preached in *Sartor Resartus*; society will be rearticulated when once the tone of its culture has been rehumanised, as in the old days. He asks his own soul how England has lived in the Past in order to show how England should live in the Present. In fact his most effective pronouncement is *Past and Present*, in which he exhorts modern capitalists to revive and practise the responsibilities of the feudal lord of the manor. But the picture of medieval fraternity as seen through the monastery of Bury St Edmunds is all too persuasive with its inimitable touches of historical imagination and literary showmanship. The organic filaments of society did not weave themselves so softly and pervasively in the wild contentious reign of King John.

If there were any doubt that Carlyle had dropped behind the times, it was to be proved by his next important publication. Since 1840 his books had begun to bring him an adequate income, and as he never abandoned the frugality of his peasant ancestors, he could afford to spend time on another three-volume work. So in 1842 he recommenced studying one of his favourite subjects, the history of the Civil War and Protectorate, and in 1845 he published *Oliver Cromwell's Letters and Speeches*. The history of the strong man who rose to the crisis of the sixteen forties had obvious applications to the crisis of the eighteen forties, especially as the Protector made Right to triumph through Might and achieved our freedom by a wise tyranny—according to Carlyle. Thanks to this autocratic position, he was untrammelled, he could take the statesman's long view; "could discern across many consecrated rubrics of the Past, the inarticulate Divineness too of the Present and the Future". Moreover, Cromwell was a standing reproof to the arts and the methods of the modern democratic leader who relied on oratory for power. Carlyle notes in his Journal on 11 November 1869 that according to Aristotle (and the practice of Victorian orators) the first, second and third thing about eloquence was acting—ὑπόκρισις —which may originally have meant *delivery* but often in England justified its derivative—*hypocrisy*. Whereas Cromwell was not a man of words nor even of theories, his letters and speeches strike directly to the fact; the only living ruler at all like him was the Iron Duke. Thus there was ample place for such a book in the thought and culture of the time, especially as its author had a genius for describing battles, plots, death scenes and such episodes as the trial of Hampden. But why write about the Protector as the "armed Soldier, terrible as Death, relentless as Doom; doing God's Judgments on the Enemies of God"? Why describe Puritanism as "the Genius of England soaring sunwards" or even as "the last of all our Heroisms"? and then add that up to the appearance of one's own book, the theme had been "overwhelmed under such an avalanche of Human Stupidity as no Heroism before ever did"? No accurate and disinterested historian could substantiate such pretensions. Once again, it looks as if intuition has been overrated as a guide to Truth, and as if the visionary needs to convince at least himself by his own magniloquence.

In 1853 Carlyle began to write *The History of Friedrich II of Prussia, called Frederick the Great*, "but not in the right tone". After many false starts, volumes I and II were published in 1858, volume III in 1862, volume IV in 1864, volumes V and VI in 1865. There is very little to utter about this "unutterable book". In fact, the longer Carlyle's works become, the less they need discussion. We all admire his vigorous character-portraits and descriptive pieces; his irony, humour and burlesque; the undiminished ability with which he constructs and organises his multitudinous material. Assuredly these well-stored volumes will not easily lose their peculiar place among standard works on the eighteenth century. Nor will anyone dispute that the king of Prussia was so far a "hero" in that he created something which was to continue and endure—the historian lived to see William I and Bismarck committed to their policy of empire-building—and that Frederick was also a "hero" because he undertook what seemed impossible and had the sincerity to persevere to the end. Macaulay would agree. But in other respects this man of action was a double-faced and unscrupulous old scoundrel, filled with inordinate ambition, and Carlyle had to hide half the truth from himself, if not from others. Assuredly one can pay too high a price for clinging to The Everlasting Yea.

CHAPTER IX

When viewed in relation to his greatest contemporaries, Carlyle's significance becomes clear—A rift had spread across European culture—He and they stand on the wrong side.

In the previous chapter we have discussed the teaching of Carlyle on its own merits, and have found more than a suspicion of something insincere in this prophet of sincerity. It remains to inquire what he is worth to the twentieth-century student, all the more as this question cannot be answered without considering him in relation to his greatest contemporaries. His literary position has often been discussed and may be dismissed without further comment. Has he any deeper significance for us to-day?

It will be found that his value is twofold. He helped, in the first place, to bring about a new order, because he unsettled other people's convictions. He questioned anglicanism, evangelicalism, the Oxford Movement, democracy, political economy, metaphysics, Benthamism, biology, zoology, Darwinism. He was really the "spirit that denies", though he would rather have accepted a baronetcy than have confessed to The Everlasting Nay. So he perpetuates the habit of thinking for oneself. He is even more to be valued because this habit did not lead to nihilism. Despite every rebuff, he cannot argue himself out of his trust in supernaturalism. He presented himself to the world as a God-fearing man in search of God. Not finding what he sought elsewhere, he learnt from German literature to look for it in his own heart. There he discovered influences and aspirations which seemed to be other than himself, though known to him through his intellect. These satisfied his sense of mysticism. Late in life he declared: "It is in the soul of man, when reverence, love, intelligence, magnanimity have been developed there, that the *Highest* can disclose itself face to face in sun-splendour."[1] Such illumination, vitally necessary to himself, was equally necessary to his contemporaries, so Carlyle concluded that it was the author's duty to substantiate this inward vision—to look outwards on the works and ways of other men; in the phrase of the pantheist Hegel to look for the divinity which sleeps in stone, dreams in animals, and is awake in man.

[1] Journal, 13 Nov. 1869.

Thus Carlyle had no new gospel to proclaim when he taught that men could and should be demigods. It was a literary tradition, a religious creed becoming more and more secularised in the mouth of each succeeding preacher. As we have seen, the idea began with the romantic philosophers; they merely speculate and affirm. It continues in the romantic poets; they recognise the truths in their hearts, then prove them through their imagination; their lyricism brings joy, and is not expected to convince. Then came the Oxford Movement, and Newman, like the philosophers and poets, directs our eyes into our consciences, where God is first to be found and, for proof, refers us to Scripture, theology and Church history. There, by the light of your conscience, and the keen but reverent employment of your intellect, you will find the same true God as you found in your hearts. You will find that what we call the Church is the embodiment of Christ. But as the prototype was one, so must his substantiation be. Therefore our destiny is to find the one pure indivisible Church and cling to it. Thus mysticism becomes a motive for conduct, and in this practical application it does not suit the age. Tennyson, for instance, will have none of it, but he also has learnt to feel the need of God in his heart. So he looks for confirmation in his poetic experiences, embracing the whole culture of his age. Yet it is only in friendship that he finds the promise of immortality and of spiritual progress; not a certainty, but a hope; and he gives up the rest of the world in despair. But Tennyson, it may be urged, was moody and passionate. Then let us take Browning, an optimist and a man of action. He is temperamentally inclined to believe that the world is worthy of our best aspirations. Being a sociable humanist, he is sure that he will demonstrate the presence of God by studying the minds of his fellow-creatures. His researches are fascinating but inconclusive, for he can confirm his ideals only by embodying them in figures resuscitated from some vanished age. His portraits are the products of the historical imagination, not of experience.

So it appears that the leaders of Victorian culture were still living on the inspiration of the romantic movement, but each applied it to his own world in his own way. They looked within themselves for a divine pattern on which to model their thoughts; they looked on conduct for a reflection of that pattern, describing what they saw so as to make it fit in with their ideal. They tried to adjust ethics to metaphysics. There is a rather ignoble temptation to belittle the achievement of these geniuses whom we can no longer imitate. They were great as artists and yet greater as a moral force. Whoever is scholar enough to yield to their magic, must also yield to their high sense of duty. Yet their influence will not stay with the admirer because these moralists protest too much. None wholly convinced themselves, nor their contemporaries, much less us. They express a tension, a yearning, not a realisation. They show us how they think we ought to live, not how we can live.

Carlyle is conspicuous amongst these figures because he is the most aggressively practical of them all. He insists as vigorously as any on the evidence of his own conscience, but much more vigorously on the evidence of his eyes, that is to say, on conduct as observed in past and present events. He asserted the superiority of the "poorest historical fact" over fiction, even over imaginative poetry.[1] He was so intolerant of "windy sentiments" that he would not tolerate any theories at all. As such he exercised an enormous influence in the 'forties and 'fifties. He got as close as he could to life without renouncing his visions. He was a realist in ideals. But he is much more significant for us as a realist who could not substantiate his ideals. Thanks to his pragmatism he ended by finding himself in a false position. In fact, towards the end of his life he seemed to fear that he would become as he described his contemporaries, "destitute of faith and terrified at scepticism". For instance, earnest and adventurous thinkers in the 'fifties and 'sixties were trying to explain the mysteries and anomalies of human nature by tracing its origin. Carlyle did not examine or even consider their hypothesis, though crowded with facts. He merely betrayed the animosity inspired by fear, caricaturing their conclusions as "man made chemically out of *Urschleim* or a certain blubber called protoplasm". On another occasion, near the end of his life, when Froude remarked that one could believe only in a God who did something "with a cry of pain which I shall never forget, he said, 'he does nothing'".[2]

So Carlyle joins the other great Victorians of the earlier period who lost heart or effectiveness because they clung to their inward convictions. His failure completes the impression that there was something specially uncongenial and disconcerting in that epoch, from which we perhaps are still suffering. Mystics of the previous ages seemed quite convinced of the truth of their intuition and seemed able to convince others. It is only in the nineteenth century

[1] *Past and Present* (1842), chap. i.
[2] J. A. Froude, *Carlyle's Life in London*, chap. xxix (1866).

that really great men seem compelled to be at odds with themselves, and unable to reconcile insight with experience. This two-sidedness is all the more worth considering because it is not peculiar to the reign of Victoria or even to the civilisation of England. The plight of modern poetry was first noticed in the 'twenties of last century by Heine, who explained that a rift had spread across the culture of all Europe and is felt most deeply in the heart of the poet because he is the centre of the world. "Once", continues Heine, "the world was whole, in antiquity and the Middle Ages; despite external conflicts, there was an all-embracing unity, and the poets also were whole. We are ready to honour these poets and to take delight in them; but all imitation of their wholeness is a lie, which the healthy eye detects and which cannot then escape derision."[1] Such was Heine's impression; he does not analyse the dichotomy. He merely draws attention to the divided aims as the vice of the age. Poets are no longer absorbed by a single faith or enthusiasm which sustains their inspiration. He feels this distractedness (*Zerrissenheit*) in his own spirit, but his chief example is Byron.

Is not such the disability under which the next generation of authors laboured? They certainly abjured Byronism, and tried to recover wholeness of spirit. Nay more, they loudly profess their faith, but they gradually relapse into Byronic effusiveness and irresolution. So it seems as if there really was a rift in nineteenth-century culture and that it was widening.

We have already seen that it was bound to widen. The great mid-Victorians took as their centre of unity the idea of God; the name of the Deity recurs in their pages with almost tiresome frequency; they claim that the divine influence is manifested in their conscience and consciousness. Yet they do not attach any definite meaning to the word. If you asked Dante, Spinoza, Milton or Dr Johnson what he meant by God, his answer would have been clear, almost precise. Ask any of the authors whom we have discussed and you will recognise their religious instinct only in a wish, a cry of the heart, a maladjustment to worldly things. One might almost say that they know God only by knowing what is not to be found in civilisation or even culture. This divine discontent would not in itself produce a rift; on the contrary it might have produced great lyric poetry if only the poets had kept their aspirations for

[1] *Italien*, 1828–9. *Die Bäder von Lucca*, Kap. IV. The idea is developed by M. Arnold (*post*, chaps. XII and XIII) and by many others since, notably by J. Benda, *La Trahison des Clercs*, 1927. *Discours à la Nation Européenne*, 1933.

their moments of self-communion and other-worldliness. But the rift sprang and widened as soon as they insisted on judging the world in this exalted and unsympathetic mood. For instance, Carlyle writes in his Journal on 9 February 1848: "Life consists, as it were, in the sifting of huge rubbish mounds and the choosing from them ever with more or less error, what is golden or vital to us." But by what signs and tokens does he distinguish the gold from the rubbish? What is his criterion? It is as well that he admitted the possibility of error, since we find that he judges England as if he were the old Biblical deity. He expects from earth the sentiments which his forefathers associated with heaven. The humanists of Carlyle's generation wanted to find in secular life the kind of inspiration which was once found in sacred literature. So they missed what inspiration really could be found. They were like men who start to explore a new country with an old map. Maps must be used; the Past had taught that lesson; but not the same kind of map. It would no longer serve. So they underwent the disappointment of finding that their charts were useless and they missed the experience and encouragement of feeling their way and gradually constructing a new map which explained the district. What the nineteenth century needed, and we still need, is the spirit to create new values.

We shall see later what these new values might be. By way of anticipation one might hint that the virtue of modernity consists in prizing the act of conquest above its results; self-analysis above self-perfection, since the two attitudes seem antagonistic. For instance, in 1842 Tennyson quite innocently declared that the highest task of man was

> To follow knowledge like a sinking star,
> Beyond the utmost bound of human thought,

and then had not the heart to follow it himself. If he had done so he would have achieved a new self-reliance: the conviction that humanity is strong enough for any verdict. Like Carlyle he needed the freedom to worship something higher than himself. Did he miss the freedom to need nothing higher than himself to worship?

So the problem of the nineteenth century is resolving itself into the question: Can we develop the imagination within the limits of earthly experience? Can we believe in ourselves without believing in a Divine Power? Or will it be found that the individual's most intimate and integral possession is a certain spiritual content, which he will sacrifice if he search for realism—that he will lose his best self in order to know his worst? The experiment was to be inaugurated in the last few decades and still continues, and we shall see that much was to be risked. The issue depends on whether the experiences of the new world (however perplexing) will produce an alertness and openmindedness which begin as materialism but may lead to another kind of spirituality.

CHAPTER X

Froude, like Carlyle, despairs of ritual, dogmas, and formularies, and turns to history to learn morality—Yet he is more than a second Carlyle without the genius—He has fewer illusions; more insight into upper-class culture and he understands that circumstances make or break the spirit.

What one most misses in Carlyle is the cult of the microcosm. He is so possessed by macrocosmic ideas that he had no genius left for making the best of his personal self. He does not seem to have caught sight of Thomas Carlyle as a self-controlled and self-adjusted unit; he could not taste and enjoy his private dignity as a human being who knows his place on earth; he had not found the right model for his own behaviour. To that extent, he misunderstood his age. The educated classes, with whom he mixed and for whom he wrote, insisted on feeling that they played their full part, free from reproach. It was at that time the Englishman's personal ideal and it was realised by the way the upper middle class cultivated gentility and especially religion. Carlyle did not understand either cult.

In early manhood he acquired some inkling of one of the two secrets. In February 1929 he wrote in his Diary at Craigenputtock: "He who would understand England must understand her Church—for that is half of the whole matter. Am I not conscious of a prejudice on that side? Does not the very sight of a shovel hat in some degree indispose me to the wearer thereof? Shut up my heart against him? This must be looked into." But it never was looked into, any more than he learnt to distinguish gentility from dilettantism. For both those reasons amongst others he lost influence over his contemporaries and posterity. But his place was taken by his friend James Anthony Froude, who lacked his genius, but had travelled step by step over that particular tract which Carlyle had only skirted, especially the gentlemen with shovel hats, and therefore knew much better how to direct the footsteps of other people.

Fate seems to have appointed Froude specially to supplement Carlyle and to attune his ideas for the younger generation. To begin with, he was born twenty-three years later, in 1818, and began to enter upon the moral responsibilities of life just when the ferment of ideas became acute. In the next place, his preparation for that ordeal was as many-sided as it could be. His father, the accomplished horse-master and Tory-gentleman-parson of the old school, had an excellent library and all his sons were encouraged to read and to think. Young Anthony was withdrawn from Westminster in disgrace at the age of fifteen, and during the most formative years of his adolescence he was left to educate and amuse himself at home. We know nothing definite about this period, but it must have involved some wonderful experiences, for Froude did not only acquire the imaginative way of thinking about books, but an astonishingly generous way of thinking about his family. He never disowned the traditions of his caste. He retained a sincere admiration for his father, who first neglected and then disowned him; a profound hero-worship for Hurrell, the gifted and pious brother who shamelessly bullied him; and to the last he valued as a national heirloom the exacting standards which the English gentry of his youth imposed on themselves and theirs. That is to say, he learnt somehow in boyhood to understand that the gentleman's point of view had a wisdom of its own. In all his subsequent acts of iconoclasm and apostasy, this habit of mind was to broaden and humanise his thought, and enabled him to disseminate liberalism in a tone and manner which half persuaded conservatives.

His religious experiences were even more important. He went up to Oxford in 1836, when the "Counter-Reformation", as he afterwards called it, was at its height. As befitted Hurrell Froude's brother, he threw himself with ardour into the movement, and it was under the great tractarian's guidance that he first learnt to examine and test religion as a spiritual power. Controversy was indeed the very air which intellectual undergraduates breathed; but Froude soon developed the scholarly aptitudes which enable a student to keep such questions within the province of the intellect, especially as he had an ample allowance, and did not forget to enjoy spending it. In 1842 he was elected to a Devonshire fellowship at Exeter College. In 1845, as was customary with resident fellows, and appropriate for the member of an old clerical family, he was ordained a deacon. Thus his early manhood appeared to be passed as a leisurely and congenial initiation into the fraternity of cultured theologians, and he might be expected to settle down to the life of a scholar qualified to instruct youth and to hold the balance between the views of Pusey, Bishop Wilberforce, Gorham and F. D. Maurice. Yet in 1848 he had discovered that he could not conscientiously teach the doctrines of his Church, and by 1849 his *The Nemesis of Faith* was publicly burnt in the lecture-room—an idiotic proceeding!—and he at once resigned his fellowship. His father now stopped his allowance, and so this promising scholar, still a deacon without the credentials of orthodoxy, went out into the world to support himself and a newly wedded wife by higher journalism.

Froude was determined to start life over again because he had grown suspicious of culture. The young men of his time were bred to live in two worlds. One was the world of actual outward conduct, in which their training was confined to the cult of good manners—the gentleman's world as it ought not to be. The other was an inward world of theories, sentiments, and historical facts— the so-called liberal education. Froude complains that these two worlds have now lost contact, and that consequently the realm of thought is no better than a dream: "a great game played out by book actors; we do not think, we only think we think". That is to say, we study the characters, creeds and conflicts of the past without inquiring whether they help us to make the most of the present —to understand human nature; to distinguish truth from error; to establish the best standard for judging conduct.

This attack on the gentleman's education is delivered in *The Nemesis of Faith* which purports to be a series of confidential letters (apparently modelled on *Die Leiden des Jungen Werthers*). A youth enters the Church (as did most young men of Froude's position) and then finds that ordination has not prepared him for the doubts and difficulties which present themselves. So he reviews all that he has learnt, retraces his steps and asks help of literary history, and finds that he is appealing for guidance to a system of academic ghosts and sentiments, which have no value for his own moral and spiritual responsibilities. Unable to solve his difficulties, he takes refuge in the Roman Catholic Church only to find a worse disillusionment, which ends in suicide. The book has since been forgotten because it is loosely and rhetorically written and much of the same ground was travelled thirty-two years later in the series of trenchant papers published in *Good Words* as *The Oxford Counter Reformation* (1881). Nevertheless, *Nemesis* is significant because it contains some penetrating glimpses of clerical life, which anticipate Trollope, and much more because it struck at the very core of Newmanism. It implies that the most sacred truths have no other test or sanction than their effect on the conduct of individuals, both past and present. The authority of God depends not on the arguments of apologists—for instance, Newman's *Development of Christian Doctrine*, or Archdeacon Robert Wilberforce's *Doctrine of the Incarnation*—not even on the intimation of one's own conscience, but on the evidence of civilisation and the light of one's own experience. As Froude said in the preface of his second edition (1849): "The one great Bible which cannot lie is the history of the human race."

Such was the disconcerting result when a young man of the 'forties began to test the old-fashioned methods of culture. He ended by testing religion and finding the same vice. James Anthony Froude has never explained why the men of his generation had acquired new spiritual wants which could not be satisfied by the faith which was popularly supposed to have served men for over a thousand years. He merely insists again and again on the breaking up of beliefs and traditions. But another humanist,[1] who best understood the spirit of Europe, has indicated in his own whimsical manner what progress meant in those days. "The old fairy-story of the three (*sic*) brothers is coming true. The one runs one hundred miles in an hour or two; the other sees things a hundred miles distant, the third shoots as far, the fourth blows armies away— railway, telescope, cannons, powder or press." Thus the ever-advancing knowledge of physics was creating a modernised fairy-land and putting man in possession. Under its influence, as Emerson[2] also saw, the forces of nature were being reproduced and combined to serve human purposes. One might almost say that physical science had a consistent volition of its own. These inferences were all the more perplexing because in other fields of research, for instance in geology and biology, science seemed to disprove theoretically the existence of the old god, whom its inventions were supplanting. And, as if to clinch these conclusions, the labours of two generations of German christologists came to a head in Strauss's *Leben Jesu* (1835), which argued that the Jesus Christ of the Gospels was a man-made myth. It looked as if human beings, not singly and individually, but by infinitely complex systems of co-operation, were becoming the composite God of this world— as if the Biblical deity were abandoning his prerogatives—as if we petty men must in future pin our allegiance to some grand abstrac-

[1] H. Heine, *Gedanken und Einfälle*. IV. *Staat und Gesellschaft*.
[2] *Nature*, chap. II.

tion called Man. Whatever the issue, the old forms and formularies could never more be sufficient. On the contrary, it might be enough, as Mill and Comte thought, for men to worship Man; no other worship need be considered.

On the other hand, young men of Froude's stamp, especially Oxonians, had to make quite sure that an earthbound religion was enough for human nature. They had to ask of the world's literature and philosophy whether there were not something at the heart of man deeper than science and higher than his idea of himself; some inward sense of the supernatural or at least of the superhuman, in itself evidence that man is not the only spiritual power in the universe. If such be the truth, the scholar's task is to learn from humanism how these wants can be supplied, and Froude's writings almost inevitably shaped themselves into an answer to the question. He began life in an age of revivals, or so it seemed, in both literature and religion. He set himself to inquire whether the rediscovered ideals held good for the modern consciousness. He was trying, by the light of his own and his ancestors' experience, to distinguish between the false and the true continuity.

As a young man he acknowledged Tennyson and especially Carlyle as his sources of inspiration, because both traced a certain superhuman influence outside the consecrated paths, active here and there, among the efforts and aspirations of unsanctified humanity, from the earliest times to the present day—witness Tennyson's *Morte d'Arthur* as well as Carlyle's *Revolution*. What most impressed Froude were the opportunities they created of finding one's own religion for oneself, and in this pursuit he was content to be their disciple. Yet he developed an originality of his own, because he had more insight into the mentality of the rising generation. He had trod the path which they would have to tread; and he knew how to touch the springs of fancy and sentiment which release the intellect of young men. Besides, he did not aim so high as Tennyson and Carlyle. He was more conciliatory, content to appeal to the intelligence, and succeeded in conveying nearly as much as his masters, though without their mysticism and exaltation. Consequently, he was still read as an influence when Carlyle was already cultivated as a myth.

The best of Froude's mind can be traced back to one of his earliest efforts, *The Cat's Pilgrimage*, composed in 1850, while he discharged a tutorship at Manchester, and studied free trade and the theory of private enterprise. In this little fable the unexpectedly Shavian touches of common sense and commonplace rather blind us to its serious meaning. It is the result of his investigations and illustrates what is wrong with Victorian culture. We might call it Froude's Everlasting Nay, his Mephistophelian fling. The ox, the bee, and the fox represent the spirit of "enlightened self-interest"; the business of existence absorbs their thoughts; in this best of all possible worlds, they do not even have to search for their special place in life. But if commercialism condemns some classes to take interest only in themselves, it enables others to take interest in nothing at all. These fortunate unfortunates are typified by the owl and the dog. The owl is privileged with the responsibilities of an intellect. But just because life is so comfortable, this speciously omniscient bird allows the meanness of his nature to predominate, and he becomes a metaphysician. That is to say that he preens himself on posing questions which he cannot and does not want to answer. The dog also has fallen a victim to self-indulgence and complacency. One can only conclude that not having the talent to think, he has one faculty less to waste.

The cat is the only type who offers us any hope. Though a member of the comfortable classes, she feels something within her which refuses to be satisfied by the constitution of society. Moreover, she has the faculty of thinking for herself. Like Carlyle, Froude and some others of that generation, she starts on her pilgrimage with an open mind. But hers is also a vacant mind. If she is free from shibboleths and prejudices, she is devoid of culture, and does not know where to look for it. As she restricts her inquiries to sociology, economics, utilitarianism and metaphysics, she learns nothing about herself and returns more resigned, but no more instructed. For the rest of his life, Froude was to continue her researches for her, and to reveal what she might have found.

The cat ought to have noticed that this predatory and above all spiritless way of life is not untouched by religion. On the contrary it is accompanied, almost sanctioned, by a cult of sects and observances which imply much interest in the forms of worship. Then she should have referred to the immense erudition which a modern university renders so accessible, to find out whether there is generally a connection between the demoralisation of society and its preoccupation with doctrines and dogmas. Such is partly the object of Froude's first series of essays, produced in the 'fifties.

Our author lets his mind rove through the history of culture to certify the conditions under which religions have ennobled human beings, and he finds that worship renders the worshippers great only so long as it instils the horror of being little. For instance, the old Achaean gods of Olympus,[1] inspired the Homeric heroes; the childish fairy-stories of the hagiographers,[2] and the scholastic system of philosophy[3] which established the doctrine of Original Sin, must once have been true, because they encourage what is true to the best in man—the fear of not becoming better. Why, on the other hand, does *The Book of Job*[4] fascinate the modern mind? Because it can still rouse the modern spirit. The drama represents the struggle between the established belief (so familiar to orthodox Victorians) that all misfortune is a judgment on sin, and the discovery (just dawning on humanists like Carlyle and Ruskin) that fortune and misfortune have nothing to do with blessedness; that we must apply a much more exacting standard: the test whether we can rise above our material selves in "a steady love of God and a steady scorn of evil". This rule will always keep the votary struggling and is therefore a true religion. Much more true than the doctrine of Spinoza,[5] who taught that all actions and experiences are attributes of God; that we ought always everywhere to recognise the divine spirit, even in our own instincts and desires; that consequently there is no such thing as evil—no hell, devil or positive and active agency at enmity with God. Froude condemns this pantheism as treacherously reassuring; it relieves us of responsibility; even if we can act as we choose, it is doubtful whether we really have free choice. Such is the upshot of metaphysical thought. But the student who ignores these insoluble speculations and searches knowledge, particularly history, with his own moral experiences for comment, will soon convince himself that whether we can choose or not, we feel that we ought to; nay more, we feel more strongly than any fatalism the obligation to act in certain ways, regardless of consequences. This conscience is also ingrained, and if we are to believe the record of humanity it is our chief inspiration in the ascent of man.

In these essays the influence of Carlyle is too obvious to need emphasising. But their significance will not be appreciated unless

[1] *Homer, Fraser's Magazine*, 1851.
[2] *The Lives of the Saints*, 1850.
[3] *The Philosophy of Catholicism, The Leader*, 1851.
[4] *The Book of Job, Westminster Review*, 1853.
[5] Review of Boehme's edition of *Tractatus de Deo et Homine*, 1854.

the reader remembers that the earnest dominating figure of Newman is hovering in the background. Any sincere Churchman of that period, but especially the great tractarian, was almost bound to insist that God is a mystery only to be approached by the paths of initiation. Froude implies that such is the explanation of England's decadence. She has religiosity but no religion. Ceremonies and creeds have power only when they instigate a moral crisis; when they are new and symbolise a conscious effort towards resisting some specific evil and achieving some specific good. For religion is an undecided battle. As soon as the victory is won, worship becomes an institution, a habit of mind.

All through his life, Froude continued to be interested in the conflict between religious sentiment and religious conduct. Quite late in his career,[1] perhaps under the influence of Renan's *Origines du christianisme*, he investigated aspects of the ancient world which favoured the rise of Christianity; how Euripides dramatised the demoralising power of dogma;[2] how Lucian[3] demonstrates that beliefs, which were once symbols of piety, may become superstitions, worthy only of ridicule; how Cicero in the *De Natura Deorum* discusses man's immemorial scepticism about a just providence;[4] how the Romans really came to believe that their emperors died as men to live as gods.[5] So his researches proceeded. He was not in the least a materialist, nor even an anti-religionist; if pressed for a definition of himself, he would probably have replied that he was a religious pragmatist. Such was his idea of higher journalism. Yet after the publication of *Spinoza* he ceases to search so widely and indiscriminately. For the next ten or fifteen years he rarely voyages into ancient or medieval civilisation. The reason is that he had found what he wanted in the history of the English Renaissance and Reformation.

The first sign of this concentration was the famous *England's Forgotten Worthies*.[6] One of the narratives is supposed to have suggested to Tennyson[7] the idea for *The Revenge*; but it more concerns us to note that the series convinced Froude of the truth which he was seeking, because the facts confirmed his own ex-

---

[1] *Sea Studies. Fraser*, May 1875.   [2] *Ibid.*
[3] *Lucian.* (The dialogues which Froude translates might have been written by Hardy.)   [4] *Divus Caesar.*
[5] *Ibid.*   [6] *Westminster Review*, 1853.
[7] For discussion of Tennyson's indebtedness see *Times Lit. Suppl.* 15 and 22 Oct. 1931 ff.

perience. These Elizabethan buccaneers dared and died at a time when England was breaking through the crust of a system which had been frozen on to her spirit. That is just what Froude had done and what he rightly foresaw that many other men, younger than himself, would soon be doing. So he gave them the chance of perceiving how life moved in those great days. Above all, he could point to Protestantism (now, to his mind, a petrifaction) as it ought to be. He could show that it once took possession of men and made them heroes, because it was then new; it had just been created out of the destruction of older formulas.

If our historian had lived in our own day, he would probably have confined his energies to essay-writing. But it was inevitable that this dispossessed fellow of Exeter, now a mere Grub Street author, should wish to write a big book. Such an effort was expected of a literary man, and he would be able to show that he had not resigned the scholarship of Oxford as well as its beliefs and benefices. Besides, histories were in fashion. Voltaire, Montesquieu and Turgot had first taught humanists to study a nation's destiny through its manners, morals and movements. Gray, Walpole, Mrs Radcliffe, Lewis, Scott, Landor, Lytton, Tennyson, Browning —not to mention Schiller, Goethe and the German romanticists— had accustomed their readers to think of the past as of the present. The rapid reconstruction of society since the Reform Bill of 1832 was warning the serious-minded to follow Burke's example, and to refer to the experience of previous generations, not only for guidance in the study of cause and effect, but in order to learn how far the nineteenth century was after all fulfilling the tendencies inaugurated in the seventeenth and eighteenth. Besides, the development of post-Napoleonic Europe had created a new idea of nationality. So there were many reasons for joining Hallam, Grote, Thomas Arnold, Milman, Macaulay, Carlyle, Freeman and Stubbs. It was beginning to be surmised in the mid-nineteenth century that history held the secret of man's destiny and duty. By a lucky chance no member of this unfraternal fraternity had attempted the one great human crisis which seemed to contain the most inspiring secret of all.

. Now every secret has to be guessed. In history, as in other investigations, there is some neglected or apparently negligible clue which the inquirer must appreciate if he is to understand what really happened, and every newcomer is bound to feel that his predecessors have not quite found the line which threads the labyrinth. Froude was well versed in the methods of his contemporaries, he understood that for the most part they put faith in mass movements which could be systematised—what one might call the impersonalities of history. It was not merely in the spirit of reaction that he avoided these scholarly considerations. He was intent on penetrating to the moral and spiritual issues involved in the reshaping of events. So far he was Carlyle's disciple. But he did not look for the same kind of evidence as did his master. He directed his research towards statutes with their preambles, the correspondence between statesmen and their ministers, the speeches, private comments, and minor decisions which generally pass unnoticed in campaigns and council chambers. He turned to such data because they revealed not only the temporary expedients and adjustments, but also the fundamental duality of human nature— fortitude and cowardice, self-devotion and meanness, perseverance or vacillation, all the conflict between good and bad, often in the breast of the same man. Viewed in this light the manœuvres of a statesman make clear the deep spiritual tendencies which he tries, unwittingly, to guide or misguide, to use or abuse. Often the same administrator by his hesitation or duplicity represents both sides of the conflict; often by his single-purposed persistence in what was wrong, he brings out into relief what was right.

At the beginning of his history he describes in glowing phrases the change which was then coming over the world and in which he and his contemporaries were still participating: the new prospects which were opened to thought, the new principles which were to govern morality, social responsibility and legislation. But he does not adhere exclusively to this orientation. His narrative sub-divides into ramifications, into the gropings of individuals along these new paths, not only the designs of the rulers but also the actions, impulses and self-assertions of the common folk, even their mode of life. As is well known, his industry was enormous. He searched the Cecil papers at Hatfield and even travelled to Simancas in order to study the dispatches sent from the Spanish ambassador in London. But the chief value of this documentation arises from his genius for illuminating character. Amongst other touches of independent thought, he surprised his readers by his admiration for Henry VIII, his indifference to Elizabeth, and his picture of Philip organising the invasion of England with the zeal and faith of a crusader. Besides his imaginative insight into the thoughts of men, he handled his plethora of details so as to render the action unforgettably vivid. His descriptions of battles and expeditions, though far less rhetorical than Macaulay's or Carlyle's, are far more realistic. No historian since Thucydides (unless it were the chronicler Froissart) has succeeded so well in reconstructing an epoch-making event from the ordinary participator's point of view. The general effect is humanitarian and humanistic. This voluminous history, despite its elaborate research, despite the "rooms piled to the window sill with bundles of dust-covered dispatches", which he was the first historian to read, and despite the transcripts which he bequeathed to the British Museum, belongs more to the world of literature than to the world of historical scholarship, because the whole study culminates in an issue of equal importance to all educated people of his own day. "My object, as I defined it at the outset, was to describe the transition from the Catholic England with which the century opened, the England of a dominant Church and monasteries and pilgrimages, into the England of progressive intelligence."[1] But at every turn the reader is reminded of the nineteenth-century conflicts between High Church and Low Church, Romanism and Anglicanism, Christianity and science, sentiment and intellect, love of heaven and love of truth, conscience and consciousness—"those trying periods of human history, when devotion and intelligence appear to be opposed, and the metal of which men and nations are composed is submitted to a crucial test".[2] The antitheses have not lost their interest for our day.

Since 1850 Froude had been living with his wife at Plas Gwynant in North Wales. As often as he visited London, he saw a good deal of Carlyle, who revised his proof sheets. *The Reign of Henry VIII* (2 vols.) appeared in 1856; *Edward VI and Mary* (2 vols.) in 1860, *Elizabeth* (5 vols.) in 1870. In 1860 his wife died and he settled in London. In the late winter of that year Carlyle called on him and suggested that they should be "companions", and for the next twenty years the two men met several times every week, either for walks, riding, or indoor conversation.[3] In 1861 he was appointed editor of *Fraser's Magazine* and held the post for thirteen years. Both circumstances are important. His new position was not only an inducement but an obligation to resume the essay-writing—The *Short Studies on Great Subjects* at which he excelled—

---

[1] *Reign of Elizabeth*, chap. xxxvii.
[2] *Ibid.*
[3] J. A. Froude, *Thomas Carlyle. A History of his Life in London*, chap. xxvi.

and besides the surplusage of his historical researches, he now had the ferment of Carlyle's mind on which to draw.

Under these auspices, Froude entered upon the third phase of his career. At first sight one is tempted to underestimate the new series of essays which he now began publishing, because they seem to be mainly echoes of Carlyle's social and moral pamphlets. Yet on a second reading it will be found that the resemblance is superficial. Unlike his master, the disciple was entering upon a second youth and was reflecting the new spirit of the 'fifties and 'sixties.

This younger generation was destined to travel one of the most critical periods in the history of European culture; and its influence on posterity will be discussed in a later chapter in the proper connection. For the moment it is enough to record that Froude was one of the few seniors qualified to understand their situation, and to explain it to them. His younger readers had been brought up in an atmosphere of collective self-congratulation—surely no epoch had ever been so consistently praised to its face, at least by Macaulay, H. T. Buckle and the newspapers—and now to their astonishment and dismay they found themselves entering upon a very old world which betrayed beneath its surface of material progress all the symptoms of decrepitude and obsolescence. Froude had devoted so much energy to the study of younger and more vigorous ages that he could still criticise his own times from the standpoint of youth. So we shall find that our ageing historian rearranges and reasserts his old ideas to suit their point of view. He shares their distrust in enthusiasms, their disinclination to believe in the intimations of the spirit, in a word, their indifference to the pneumatology of the romantic movement. Like them, he prefers to examine and discuss, and does not lose his faith.

England's senile decay was to be proved by the routine of her intellectual and spiritual life. Take first of all her way of worship. As a student of history he is convinced of natural and moral law. Religion is, or ought to be, the light by which we first perceive and then pursue these ordinances. But after a generation we become so accustomed to the illumination that we forget its moral purpose.[1] Instead of looking at the path, they look only at the lantern which ought to light it, and our dimmed eyes are dazzled. It is so much easier to make a habit of ritual than of right conduct. So religion becomes "a hard nutshell round a shrivelled kernel". The Roman Catholic Church had been the first to petrify; the Reformed

[1] *Calvinism: An Address to the Students of St Andrews*, 17 March 1871.

Church was created as a protestation, but Protestants were now too old to remember the defective morality against which it began by protesting and English churchmen busied themselves (only too zealously) about the verbal correctness, not the spirit, of the Bible, or the authority of bishops.[1] Thus both the great Churches of Christendom were dead because they lived only as a theme for theological speculation. And now, in Froude's own day, there had arisen "a knot of Oxford students", who believed that the strength of the Church rested on the priesthood and the sacraments and its weakness arose from their neglect.[2] So the Oxford Movement also failed to rejuvenate our reverence for the laws of moral obligation. Nor did it help to revive our nationhood. It neither conquered Rome; nor resisted atheism; it merely annihilated the Evangelical Party and disseminated the priggism "that dissent is vulgar, and that to be an Anglican, if not a Papist, is essential to being a gentleman".[3]

In thus diagnosing the disease, or rather the degeneracy of his country, Froude is much more progressive and adaptable than Carlyle. For instance, although he disliked the tone of Mill's *On Liberty*, he did not inveigh against the essay as did his master; he claimed the right to apply its principle to the discussion of religious problems.[4] More broadminded still, he paid a tribute to "the now notorious work of M. Renan, which is shooting through Europe with a rapidity which recalls the era of Luther"; and he wonders whether the sources of Christianity, as of all other living things, are buried in mystery, or can be explained by the methods of *Vie de Jésus*.[5] He is free from the bitter sectarianism so rife among the older men of his age. In fact the pages in which he describes Newman's powers and personality are as good as his best. More notable still is his freedom from any touch of mysticism. Unlike Carlyle he does not even appeal to man's own consciousness of the God within him. But he believes in the moral law which (as Sophocles averred) was born in heaven and holds its sway as powerfully now as of old.[6] He cared little for Darwin who "is looking gravely to the courtship of moths and butterflies to solve

---

[1] *Conditions and Prospects of Protestantism.*
[2] *The Oxford Counter-Reformation.*
[3] *Revival of Romanism.*
[4] *A Plea for the Free Discussion of Theological Difficulties.*
[5] *Criticism and the Gospel History.*
[6] *The Science of History,* and *On Progress.*

the problem of the origin of man and prove his descent from an African baboon". He held fast to the superterrestrialism of personality. "The νοῦς, the intellectual spirit, being an οὐσία—an essence—we believe to be an incorruptible something which has been engendered in us from another source." Yet he admits that science is undermining our faith in immortality as was probably the case in ancient Egypt, that the doctrine "may have generated once more a practical infidelity"; and that "our Father in Heaven may have ordered the belief in a life beyond the grave to be withdrawn".[1]

Thus Froude seems to hover between two attitudes. Compared with Victorian orthodoxy, his attitude is pagan, compared with the neo-pagans of the nineteenth century, his attitude is that of a humanist all-but orthodox for lack of scientific certainties. He seems to have felt that true wisdom is to be found in compromise. If our intellect relies on the new world our spirit relies on the old. This two-sidedness is significant because it proceeds from a man of action, or at least from a man who thinks and writes about actions. His dominating interest is conduct in the past and present, and as a result he abjures not only the theories of library students but also their definiteness and (it must be added) their consistency. So his mind seems at first to be indistinct, and this indistinctness, as we shall see later, was to a certain degree an anticipation of our own age, an age of action. Froude was beginning to see things as we do because he wrote history with imagination but (unlike Carlyle) without preconceptions. As a result he was always best able to think and express his thoughts within the limits of portraiture and narrative. Just as the early *Cat's Pilgrimage* is his best pronouncement on what Spencer would call "social statics", so *The Siding in a Railway Station* is his most comprehensive inquiry into "the whole duty of man". And now in the last stage of his career, while Carlyle was inclined to ask whether the nineteenth century was about to shoot Niagara, his friend answered by parading Past and Present in two parallel processions.

The Past is recalled to life in his essays[2] on medieval and early sixteenth-century history. It was as if he wanted to corroborate and amplify the lessons of his *History of England*. Of all these

---

[1] *On Progress. Fraser*, Dec. 1872.

[2] *The Dissolution of the Monasteries* (1857), *A Bishop of the Twelfth Century* (1870), *Annals of an English Abbey* (1872), *Times of Luther and Erasmus* (1867), *Life and Times of Thomas Becket* (1877).

themes it might be observed, as he said of the will of Henry VIII, that they are worth studying "as shedding some light upon a disposition which an altered age will never fully comprehend, but which is pregnant with indirect suggestions".[1] They are indeed like flashes of lightning in a dark night; human nature in its grandeur or perversity suddenly stands out revealed in the perennial outlines but amid almost inconceivable surroundings. The essays certainly warn us how inevitably custom and negligence lead us into the most unexpected predicaments and while revealing the medieval abuses which led to the Reformation, he reminds the reader to draw an inference as regards modern abuses which are leading to anarchy. What most impresses the literary student is the author's zealous renunciation of medievalism. In Froude's early manhood the two mysterious strangers among the ruins at Marney Abbey had praised the humanitarian and social disinterestedness of monastic institutions.[2] In his mature manhood, Ruskin and Morris had celebrated the domestic and civic faithfulness of that vanished civilisation, and its artistic piety. Froude abstains from either cult. He belongs to the movement which aimed at understanding the things which other people used to enjoy; he devoted himself to his theme in the disillusioned and exigent mood of the modern realist. He did not go unrewarded. His studies have a vividness and an intensity which were achieved by few writers of historical novels, certainly not by George Eliot, perhaps only by the author of *The Cloister and the Hearth.* Yet they are founded on painstaking research and keep (at any rate as far as intentions go) to bare facts. Is it too much to infer that these brilliant papers opened our fathers' eyes to a new function of culture and prepared the way for the Early English Text Society?

The historical essays prove that though Froude took an almost passionate interest in the Past, he harboured no illusions. He appreciated grandeur of character, whether in a twelfth-century bishop or in Luther, because such heroism was a protest against decadence and depravity. The Middle Age produced good men because it was bad. This phenomenon opened his eyes to the true state of Modern England. Froude is progressive because he distrusts our progress. He parades the Present,[3] and is able to see as

---

[1] *Reign of Henry VIII*, chap. XXIII.   [2] *Sybil*, Bk II, chaps. IV, V.

[3] *England and her Colonies* (*Fraser*, Jan. 1870), *Reciprocal Duties of State and Subject* (*ibid.* March 1870), *The Colonies Once More* (*ibid.* Sept. 1870), *Progress* (*ibid.* Dec. 1870), *England's War* (*ibid.* Feb. 1871), *Party Politics* (*ibid.* July 1874).

many decayed institutions as in the sixteenth century; not so depraved as the effete monasteries and the church system which some sectarians still admired, but just as soulless. But modern institutions did not produce great men, not even in protest, and the social and political essays are valuable as far as he explains the causes of this modern littleness.[1]

There is a special significance in these parallelisms. Unlike Carlyle, Froude insists on the decadence of both eras; he implies, again unlike Carlyle, that the centre of moral gravity has shifted. He does not want to revive the good old days; their problem is not ours. In the pre-Renaissance world, monasticism decayed because the spirit could find free vent elsewhere. In the modern world politico-industrialism is decaying because the spirit *cannot* find free vent elsewhere. It must permeate our material civilisation or expire. If we are ever again to become as great as the Puritans of Henry VIII or Elizabeth, we must not revive their habits, but spiritualise our own. We must live the modern commercial and democratic life so as to create a purpose different from, but worthy of, the sixteenth-century Protestants. Froude, now a veteran, writing under the pressure of journalism, did not develop these implications. He hardly seems conscious of them. Yet such are the conclusions corroborated by his train of thought. We must better our souls by making the best of this world. Quite late in life he revived Carlyle's idea of emigration,[2] this time under government encouragement, but not as a mere escape from the overcrowded labour market. He wakes to a vision of men who could employ all our appliances and inventions, and enjoy our ever-rising standard of living, so as to become more self-reliant, truthful, and generous —bound to the earth because they see hopes of changing it into heaven.

[1] For an appreciation of their content, see H. V. Routh, *Money, Manners and Morals as revealed in Modern Literature*, 1935, chap. III.
[2] *Oceana*, 1888.

CHAPTER XI

Culture is disconcerted by civilisation—Ruskin tries to reunite and solemnise both, first through art and then through social and economic reform—He fails.

So far we have discussed the authors reputed to be the greatest in this period, yet we leave them with the feeling that they might have been greater. None seems to have done full justice to the genius within him. Each labours under a secret sense of weakness. The defect is obviously not due to lack of industry, nor to any technical difficulties with style or subject, such as beset lesser writers. These giants of productivity were masters of their material. But they all have something on their minds, as if discontented with what they have achieved or could achieve. A little further study will reveal the cause of their self-distrust. Not one of them has wholly succeeded in reconciling culture to civilisation.

This reconciliation was one of the most critical problems of the later nineteenth century, and we must understand its significance if we are to understand the developments which have led to our own era. Civilisation tends to unite the community in the bonds of mutual dependence and therefore involves one serious disadvantage. It threatens to render an individual less and less master of himself. He does not only divide and distribute his actions among all the claims of social service, but he dissipates and diminishes his consciousness of his indivisible self. He has too many parts to play. He sometimes loses sight of his identity among failures, humiliations, mutual comparisons and acts of self-abnegation. Fortunately, civilisation also brings, at most epochs, an influence which counteracts this disintegration—some interest, art, allegiance or exaltation which restores a man to the consciousness of his intimate self. Such is culture. If civilisation unravels our personality into a hundred threads, culture reweaves them into a new and fairer design. Failing this synthesis, culture becomes cultureless.

The history of literature illustrates this formative power a thousand times. In every country and epoch we find men of genius bearing witness to our ideal of spiritual self-possession in some imaginative cult or system which atones for the follies, passions, failures, misfortunes, self-effacements betrayed in their letters, journals, autobiographical confidences and even in the asides of their formal works. Conspicuous examples are Cicero, Dante, Milton and Goethe. One of the earliest recorded cases is Achilles, always thwarted, humiliated or bereaved in his short mortal life, yet rising to his full stature as often as he thinks of the immortality of fame. One of the latest is Condorcet, an outcast from society, not master of enough food to nourish his body already forfeited to the guillotine, yet master of a dream of human fraternity in which his own existence is gloriously fulfilled.

A hundred other similar examples might be quoted and in every case another quality will be noticed. The culture which restores and fortifies a personality may be the corrective of civilisation, but is not its antagonist. The two influences, though so different, seem to serve each other. The true man of culture seems endowed with a zest for the distractions of civilisation; he possesses himself without sacrificing the world's multiplicity. Culture does not disqualify him for the many-sided battle of life, with its divided aims, but entrusts him with a pocket-mirror in which from time to time he can contemplate his scattered self as it should be—unified in a picture of something else.

The nineteenth century seems to have failed in this compensation. The men who lent themselves to its varied activities, who distributed their emotions and intellects among its perplexingly rapid and ramified developments, found an increasing difficulty in rallying their true selves. They searched, apparently in vain, for some leading idea through whose tone and tint their sporadic experiences would become part of their own essential indivisibility. Newman, Tennyson, Browning, Carlyle or Froude did not confess to this disability in so many words. But their plight can easily be understood after we have studied three other authors who inherited their difficulties, Ruskin, Clough and Matthew Arnold.

Ruskin is not otherwise an important figure in this inquiry. His achievements as a stylist and a critic of capitalism hardly claim our attention. But his career is also interesting because it was a struggle for culture; a struggle, moreover, which exemplifies, almost epitomises, the humanistic problem of his age. By birth and position he laboured under every disadvantage typical of the Victorian era. He was born in 1819 and so he began to grow up just as the Reform Bill of 1832 introduced mediocrity into the national character. He belonged to the triumphant middle class

which had most to gain by this introduction. His father had
acquired considerable wealth by close attention to business. That
is to say, the inmates of the Ruskins' house in Brunswick Square
were expected to take life seriously as a task in which worldly
success was the proof of merit. As if to exclude any other possibility,
both parents (like so many of the successful commercial class) were
rigid Calvinists, and had the strength of mind to impress their
convictions on their receptive son. In such a household at such an
epoch it would seem that culture, in the true humanistic sense,
was utterly excluded. Of course there was no objection to the boy
dabbling in the arts, since he would one day inherit a position of
considerable wealth and importance. In fact his parents willingly
sent him to Oxford, and began to take him abroad as early as
1833. They were, indeed, conspicuous among their class, because
they made a practice of visiting the continent, enjoying museums
and mountain scenery. Besides travel was good for the boy's
health and it gave him the air of being as well educated as a
nobleman's son. But there was nothing in the traditions of his
home or his class to reveal a deeper value in the art of the continent
or the humanities of Oxford. Life at its best meant the management of money and the study of the Bible.

Under these conditions it would seem that John Ruskin had no
choice between breaking utterly with this civilisation, like Browning's hero, Waring, or resigning himself for ever to the character
of a *dilettante* such as Carlyle abhorred. He did neither. He
stayed in his Victorian middle-class world, he continued to cultivate the Bible with its revelation of an all-powerful Creator and
Ruler whom we cannot worship unless we understand, he continued to meditate on the pictures and scenery of the continent
and on the English and foreign classics which he studied at Oxford.
He continued to spend his father's money. But he managed to
follow these middle-class pursuits in such a way that his imaginative instincts found a liberal outlet, forced their way into the upper
air and assumed a form such as the brain could grasp for itself and
communicate to others.

The difficulty was to bring all these varieties of experience under
a single idea. Ruskin succeeded, or thought that he succeeded,
when he analysed the technique of Joseph Turner. So he started
to expound the "infinitude" of the human soul by apologising for
the methods of an unpopular artist.

Joseph Turner was the son of a London barber, born near

Covent Garden in 1775. He had the good fortune to merit the patronage and protection of the great Sir Joshua Reynolds. He made a reputation as a more or less academic though self-opinionated landscape painter of the eighteenth-century school. But after two visits to the continent (1800 and 1820) he abandoned his conscientiously acquired classicism and he indulged his passion for far-flung colour schemes and huge cloudy symbols—all the majesty and mystery of the elements. These savage effects were created by a technique no less savage. He hardly tries to design or delineate; he seems to dash his brightest colours on the canvas anyhow. Instead of outlines you get daubs seen through a haze. An admirer of Balzac might have been reminded of *Le Chef d'Œuvre Inconnu*. Yet Ruskin convinced himself that this romantic splasher of colours had brought the human spirit into contact with God.

What most impressed him was the activity of his own spirit when he studied anything created, or rather suggested, by this artist. Turner's technique was a puzzle, in which the solution depended on one's knowledge of oneself. Ruskin found that all his own scattered memories of nature's elusive and mysterious charm —such indescribable and inimitable effects as evening twilight, the sunrise between banks of clouds threatening storm, the sea roused to its own disorderly yet rhythmic activity by the wind, some wild landscape lashed by rain—all came to life again, evoked by Turner's art. In understanding the artist's purpose, his own far-fetched experiences became an intellectual possession. He realised much more. In Ruskin's circle, the beauties of creation were not so much ignored as referred to the glory of the Creator and it was agreed that one object of man's existence was to understand the Will and Wisdom of God within the limits of human attainment. But this awe-inspiring power was not made known through scenery. On the contrary (according to John Ruskin's elders) Godhead and Grandeur were to be divined and worshipped in the Bible. Ruskin knew that intricate and many-sided book—a whole literature and national history between two covers—from childhood; and some of his profoundest emotions and aspirations were obscurely associated with its strange texts and stories. A hundred impressions gathered from records of a thousand years culminated in the vague consciousness of a divine Presence, somewhere at the heart of life, imposing unity of design, completeness, infinity, and repose. Such a conception must have remained indistinct if it had to be traced through the rambling and often contradictory labyrinth of Scriptures. But all these intimations came back to mind with all their religious awe and exaltation as soon as he learnt to analyse and explain to himself the artistry of the great and misunderstood painter. In his best work you could find the grandeur, beauty, tranquillity and power which you felt to be implicit in Scripture. A single masterpiece by Turner expressed to the eye, as a mere matter of sense, all that the Bible suggested through religious meditation—an insight into the plan of creation—to that extent into the will and wisdom of God.

Accordingly, Ruskin's defence and explanation of Turner was much more than an excursus into art-criticism. The great painter of storms and sunsets is prized as the symbol or exposition of what culture ought to be—the knowledge of one's whole varied self through one's most active and concentrated faculty. Ruskin had an acute appreciation of that discipline, as his mind was otherwise abnormally uncontrolled and his temperament unbalanced. Application to art was his chief hope of steadying his wits. But he also valued Turner because he found his secret to be that of the established and recognised masters. They also called on their admirers to relive their happiest moments in order to appreciate art. Even literature, which the average *dilettante* still enjoyed in the eighteenth-century manner, as a source of apposite quotations and graceful or pointed epigrams, was now found to partake of the significance and suggestiveness of pictorial art. Just as great pictures often produced their effect by *composition* ("help of everything in the picture by everything else"), so quite ordinary phrases, in view of the situation and character of the speaker, might have for the alert reader "an awful undercurrent of meaning". Ruskin was particularly fond of the "He has no children" of Macduff and the "quel giorno più non vi legemmo avanti" of Paolo. Turner, then, was not an innovator but the artist who revived a great tradition. He was the latest of the prophets and one of the most effective in that his technique exacted the liveliest collaboration from the onlooker.

Turner's greatness could not be fully demonstrated without reference to the past. But the nineteenth-century landscape painter was great enough to fill a book by himself. Ruskin proposed to call his volume *Turner and the Ancients*, but changed the title to *Modern Painters* and added a few notes on other contemporaries only because his friends assured him that the essay was more likely to be bought and read. He ought to have called it "Modern Culture" or "Modern Religion", for obviously he could not have confined himself to one art, much less to one school. There was too much at stake. When Turner had shown you how to study atmospheric and topographical effects—a sunset, a stormy sea, a mountain pass, the evening star—he had taught you how to possess yourself of their glory, grandeur, blessedness and calm. So *Modern Painters* of 1843 was followed by a second volume in 1846, by two more volumes in 1856 and by a fifth in 1860. His essay grew into an expert and learned treatise on aesthetics, carefully based on psychology—one of his first precautions was to study Locke's *Essay concerning Human Understanding*—and seeking its data anywhere among the highways and byways of humanism. One feature of his long inquiry is the analytical acuteness with which the technique of painting is examined: the craftsman's secrets of this mystery. Another feature is the interest in the metaphysics of art. Ruskin has to some extent anticipated Croce in that he recognises art to be aesthetic concentration of mind. The value of the artist is in his aim—in his desire, not to deceive the eye, but to suggest on canvas the love or wonder or happiness that he feels in understanding the external world. As is well known, the upshot for the specialist is his contention that art is expression not imitation (an abuse which had crept in towards the decline of the Renaissance), and that Turner was, as we should now say, the first of the impressionists. But for the humanist the upshot rises much higher, for Ruskin described art as "a passionate and whole-hearted endeavour to fathom the mysteries of the deeper things of life; not only of beauty, but also of truth and goodness". He begins by discussing the effects of colour, perspective, distance, composition, tone, and atmosphere. He ends by proving that these are only suggestive of the spiritual world, though essential to its realisation—the devices by which we rise out of our petty distracted selves, into an understanding of the Divine Intelligence.

Modern Painters, despite its digressions, apostrophes, and pretensions, is a great work for another reason; it corrected or rather counterbalanced the narrowing tendency of mid-Victorian rationalism. Ruskin was resisting, perhaps unconsciously, the limitations of systematised and logical thought. He was no enemy of science for its own sake; on the contrary, he was a painstaking student of crystallography and botany; but he must have realised that physicists, mathematicians and, of course, economic and social thinkers, were imposing mental habits, methods of reasoning and stereo-typed phraseologies which were very convenient for the conveyance of their theories, but were otherwise inadequate to satisfy the whole man. They preferred the formula to the image. Reality might be infinitely complex and elusive, but they tried to catch it in artificially simplified concepts and laws. In opposition to these influences, Ruskin, though himself a careful and consequential thinker, had nevertheless trained his spontaneous consciousness and thereby had discovered that he became more fully and realistically himself. He achieved this realisation by keeping all that he had ever learnt within reach of his sensations; all his emotional and intellectual experiences accompanied his appreciation of the passing moment; his whole mental past crowded into the present.

In this concentration he was, in some sort, a fellow-worker with Robert Browning,[1] and, like the poet, he was also working for the future. He was vaguely anticipating the inductions of Bergson,[2] which were in so many ways to influence the twentieth century, for instance, D. H. Lawrence, Virginia Woolf and E. M. Forster, but especially Marcel Proust,[3] who went in search of lost time, collecting the impressions and experiences which had accumulated and combined since early childhood, each new thought coalescing with the ever increasing background to sustain his identity. In fact Proust himself has confessed that Ruskin taught him the secret of life "que la bonheur véritable consiste à tout sacrifier à la dé-couverte, à l'expression des réalités éternelles qui se couchent sous les apparences".[4]

To this extent *Modern Painters* is a valuable contribution to culture. It steadies and concentrates our selfhoods; it exacts the kind of effort by which someone else's wisdom becomes our own; it gives ample scope to the imagination. Yet the book did not go far enough. It guided the reader through only half of his journey, for it savoured of solitary masterpieces achieved without apparent effort. Solipsism could not be enough. Even Bergson had admitted in *Matière et Mémoire* that all mentality is good only for action—not solely muscular exertion—but for interest in the pursuits and

[1] *Ante*, p. 108.

[2] For explanation and discussion see *post*, chap. XXIII.

[3] General title for his twelve volumes of introspection, i.e. novels, *À la Recherche du temps perdu*, 1913–25 (volumes after 1922 posthumous).

[4] *Pastiches et Mélanges*, 1919: "That true happiness consists in sacrificing everything to the discovery and expression of the eternal realities which underlie appearances."

avocations of men; the artistic expression of energy, creativeness adjusted to conduct. Ruskin, with his strong social and moral sense, seems to have realised this defect and to have felt, instinctively, that *Modern Painters* for most Ruskinians would never be more than an exercise in aesthetics.

But it is one of the virtues of art-criticism that each study leads on to another; so Ruskin's eyes were soon wandering from pictures to the buildings which originally contained them, and so on through all the various features of an art-city; its town-hall, its streets, its citizens' houses and especially its churches, chapels and convents. All these, like pictures, spoke of piety or great-heartedness. They were not only constructed to suggest the assembling and sheltering of human beings, but to suggest in the noblest way all the emotions and aspirations with which they should be entered. That is to say, an edifice is so disposed and adorned that it expresses the same kind of sentiments and enthusiasms as are expressed by a picture. But there is one great difference. A painting is the work of one artist and each onlooker enjoys it by himself according to his aesthetic experiences. A building is the work of many artists, often, as in the case of some cathedrals, continued from generation to generation. So it represents a national, not merely an individual experience, and belongs to the community. Thus architecture expresses something more than pictures can; it expresses the common difficulties and responsibilities of life, the growth of national faith and domestic virtue, the collective piety and perseverance of many people who have attained to their highest, working together and helping each other through many centuries—the social and racial energies which are (according to Ruskin) the crown of human nature. Full of this idea he produced *The Seven Lamps of Architecture* in 1849, *Lectures on Architecture and Painting* in 1853, the two volumes of *The Stones of Venice* in 1851 and 1853.

These essays expand and supplement *Modern Painters*. They are written with the same power of analysis, the same eye for details (for instance, tracery and sculpture), and for technical considerations (for instance, the laws of construction and the uses which artist-architects can make of light and shadows). As in *Modern Painters*, the critic devotes his expertness to emphasise the moral significance and he comes to a similar conclusion, that Gothic, in its widest sense, is the supreme architecture, because in the Middle Ages architects were still content to symbolise their tragedies, hopes and sufferings. It was during and after the Renaissance that edifices began to flaunt the pride and vanity of the age. Ruskin takes Venetian architecture as the supreme Gothic, because it expresses most unmistakably the lessons of national virtue.

If this series of treatises, first on the arts of painting and then of architecture, had fulfilled the purpose of their author, they would have ranked amongst the greatest works of the nineteenth century, for they would have concentrated in one focus the essential virtues of the ascent of man. We should have been able, through the eyes of the art-critic, to identify ourselves with God's purposes. The aim of culture would have been achieved, and the nineteenth century could then have turned to its problems with a vision cleared, simplified and redirected. Such was Ruskin's life-work. It is useless to pretend that he succeeded.

The least unsuccessful effort is *Modern Painters*. In these five volumes the author discovers something about reality through self-consciousness. Yet one cannot help wondering whether pictures can any longer keep ahead of thought; whether the accumulated experience of civilisation has not created expectations and urges which no visual figure, however pregnant and suggestive, can satisfy; whether it is possible for the strongest artistic personality to impress its sovereignty on the labyrinth of modern humanity. Goethe apparently thought so,[1] but Goethe did not visualise the thousand conflicting forms under which nineteenth-century life was to assail us. Ruskin claimed to think so. Great personalities, he argued, had done so in the past and might do so in the future. But it is to be noted that he did not easily persuade others, nor himself. His aestheticism did not fully stand the test of association with human activities. While he was protesting, consciously and unconsciously, against the utilitarianism and economic preoccupation of the times, his younger contemporaries were developing an even more adventurous restlessness. Under the influence of modern literature, the mind was becoming too agile, experimental and self-resourceful to seek a sense of reality through the outward forms of art. The demand was for an art of life, only to be discussed and projected in the printed page.

Ruskin's inadequacy becomes unmistakable as soon as he turns from painting to the arts of building and decoration. He is just as expert and enthusiastic but he ceases to convince. He is fanciful and humoursome; while more is asserted, less is proved. The facts are not so well established. We know much about the lives and

[1] *Ante*, p. 33.

labours of painters, but little about the growth and completion of medieval buildings. It is not always so certain that they arose, as it were, out of the heart of the community. *The Seven Lamps* and *Stones of Venice* are another case of the modern highly sensitive intellect trying to read into wood and stone the significance which can be created only by winged words. In fact one feels more and more that our author only pretends to discuss what was and is. He is really describing what should be. The conclusion is at least forced upon us that these studies in art and especially in architecture belong not to history or aesthetics but to the literature of utopias.

There is always a double weakness in an utopian. He does not have to prove the practicability of his schemes; he is morally obliged to assume that they could be imposed on the conditions under which his contemporaries live. Ruskin gave the death-blow to his influence by yielding to both of these temptations. He not only assumed that medieval architecture was the fruit of man's noblest and most moral effort, but exhorted us to repeat that effort by reviving the ancient spirit. At first sight, the prospect did not seem to be unreasonable. The old spirit of the painters had been revived by Turner, and (as Ruskin thought in 1851) by the Pre-raphaelites. So with the medieval workmen who created gothic architecture—why should not their spirit be revived in our factory-ridden and steam-driven age? Ruskin insisted that it could, and should, and would, if certain impediments were removed. Modern commercialism could be converted into medieval expressiveness. So he wrote *The Political Economy of Art* (1857),[1] *Unto this Last* (1862), *Essays on Political Economy* (1863), *The Crown of Wild Olive* (1866), *Time and Tide* (1868).[2]

This was the next and most disastrous stage in Ruskin's career. He assumed that his utopia could be established on earth and therefore set himself to analyse the causes which prevented its establishment. Up to a certain point he was still true to himself and to the tendencies of culture. For instance, he was keeping to his dominant idea of art as self-realisation; he was trying to make its wisdom an influence in the lives which his contemporaries had to live, especially the millions of wage-earners who seemed to be furthest removed from such a possibility; he was also true to the

[1] Third and later editions entitled *A Joy for Ever*.
[2] For discussion of Ruskin's economic and social influence, see H. V. Routh, *Money, Morals and Manners*, 1935, chap. v.

more recent and less recognised aspirations of his generation. Moreover, his arraignment of English decadence exposed certain abuses, and so hastened their reform. His devotion to the cause of socialism has, since then, awakened some spark of heroism in many a disciple. But he insisted on trying to rehandle civilisation to suit his own plan, and thus sacrificed culture to utopianism. If the nineteenth century abandoned its industrial system the workman of that period would not express his soul in his work, he and we would starve for lack of the comforts and conveniences of modern life. Mass production was necessary for mass population. But in any case, it is not the duty of the humanist to devise ways and means. His task is to find creative ideas which give his own soul freedom and on which others can act. He creates the public will or at least unifies and points it. The people then devise the means. The thinker who mistakes administration for morality only increases disunion.

In one respect Ruskin's transition from art-critic to socialist is very significant. It indicates a stage at which culture could no longer be a personal private matter. Those who must do justice to themselves must do justice to their fellow-creatures—social and educational inequalities had become too glaring. We can also recognise the stage in which thinking human beings began to look again to the state to consummate their self-culture. Ruskin, like Carlyle and (as we shall see) like Arnold, Mill and Spencer, feels that his philanthropic enthusiasms must radiate through the organic filaments of society. Unhappily this radiation only created friction.

In another less speculative aspect, Ruskin's career illustrates the difficulty of his age. The true army of progress—those knights of the Holy Ghost celebrated by Heine—was no longer a small straggling band; on the contrary it was being crowded with camp followers who pretended to serve the cause but served only their own vanity. Ruskin's art-criticism was fatally accommodating to these pseudo-intellectuals. He insists on making up your mind for you. He arouses your spirit, melts it into the fluid enthusiasm of his own heat, and then pours it into his own moulds. You must feel the divinity within you meeting the divinity without. This attitude was old-fashioned; it belonged (as we have seen) to the romantic tradition. The new spirit (as we shall see) cherished no such illusions. Science and sociology were already convincing us that we are quite different from what we thought we were—the product of obscure social and biological causes. The mystery of human nature arises out of our distant and labyrinthine origins. So we have to face the wonders of life without preconceptions or ready-made standards; we have to watch our reactions, prepared for anything.

Many shrank from such a view, and again, Ruskin's influence was bad. When one flees to a great writer for protection, one has to obey his orders, and so it is difficult to think for oneself. The followers of Ruskin found themselves in the Alps, or in front of a Tintoretto, and instead of forming their own judgments they searched their memory for the master's impressions. So they fell into that habit of docility and repetition which became the vice of drawing-room culture. The intellectual insincerity was but the counterpart to a kindred vice in the teacher. The great humanist who indoctrinated his admirers ended by indoctrinating himself. He was dominated by the majesty of his own message and per-suaded that there was more in his revelations than he himself could find. So in old age his ornate and imaginative prose won him a vast reputation just at the time when his humanity and humani-tarianism were arousing his bitterest enemies. He was most admired by superficial readers who cared nothing for his deepest aims and sensibilities. In fact he is unintentionally responsible in no small degree for the sentimental poses and affectations of late-Victorianism. Meanwhile, the new generation was becoming particularly sensitive to pretentiousness and biassed in favour of intellectual caution. So Ruskin's enthusiasms did not deceive them even if they deceived Ruskin, and before his death he was dismissed as a coiner of phrases.

CHAPTER XII

Clough and Arnold both begin life as academic poets—Both try to live with the sincerity and intellectual freedom of the great masters, so as to write after their manner—Both fail; Clough almost at once, Arnold after some magnificent attempts aided by Goethe and de Senancour—H. T. Buckle illustrates his difficulties.

We saw in the last chapter that Ruskin, like the other great writers of his time, failed to lead his generation, much less the generation which was taking its place. Some, as we shall see later, were to follow the rationalists and inductive reasoners who trusted nothing beyond the reach of logic or observation. But there were still many others who clung to the old culture without sacrificing the new sense of truth. Where were these younger people to look for their leaders and we to look for their spokesmen? Not among the writings of William Morris, Ruskin's fellow-socialist, interested in man only as a splendid creature who would always find an outlet for his best self, if only his ideas were few and his civilisation simplified by brotherly love. The way of spiritual culture is not quite so simple. Nor yet among the aesthetes and aestheticians—Pater, Symonds and Wilde—who may in the first place have been inspired by Ruskin, and to the end talked much about the soul and spirit, but borrowed the courage of their attitude from the Darwinism which they affected to despise. We must first consider how far it was still possible to reconcile mystery to experience, to cherish sacred enthusiasms among critical habits of mind, and, thus exalted and focussed, to exercise authority over the spirits of others. We shall find what we want in the failure of Clough and the success of Matthew Arnold.

Clough is of importance because of the peculiarly intimate and unobtrusive difficulties of his career. He was gifted with an enthusiastic and exuberant temperament, the love of exercise in the open air, and an unmistakable talent for verse-writing. What a lot he could have made of his life, if he had been a contemporary of Davies and Rupert Brooke! But he was born in 1819 and entered Rugby in 1829. Here he learnt the new intelligent way of interpreting the classics: how to assimilate their simplicity and grandeur of style, so as to become oneself a great writer; how to cultivate their clear-headedness, fortitude, self-reliance and disinterested discur-

siveness, so as to become a great man. From Dr Arnold's religious
teaching he learnt how to combine these classical virtues with the
love as well as the worship of Jesus. From the public school system
he learnt the meaning of morality; it was the conscientious devotion of all one's powers to the furtherance of the public good. What
better equipment for the battle of life? Indeed, life need not be a
battle but a clearly marked pathway, smooth if steep. Both his
mind and spirit would find their fullest scope in pursuing the same
idea; and the English university system would provide the opportunity. So congenial was this equipment to the boy's nature that
he won every possible prize at Rugby and went up to Oxford in
1837 with his Balliol scholarship and the formidable reputation of
being Dr Arnold's favourite pupil.

He lived at Oxford for the next eleven years. His academic
career did not quite fulfil the promise of his school-days, but in
1842 he was elected a Fellow of Oriel and there seemed no reason
to the less progressive of his well-wishers why he should not have
pursued a distinguished and useful career, maturing his own
powers as a scholar, poet and priest, and handing on his culture to
the rising generation. Yet he was granted none of these felicities.

It should first be noted that he produced only one poem worth
considering, *The Bothie of Tober-na-Vuolich*. This original and spirited
composition is most significant, partly because it is full of promise,
and partly because that promise was not fulfilled. Perhaps no
work has celebrated more felicitously the true spirit of academic
youth. Clough, like nearly all Arnold's favourable pupils, has
been accused of being a prig. *The Bothie* is redolent of College
culture, yet it is absolutely free from priggishness. Even the adaptation of the hexameter is so natural and lighthearted that it
hardly seems to be the achievement of an Homeric scholar, who
could interpret the prosody of the *Iliad* and the *Odyssey*. And
again, though *The Bothie* is the work of a studious poet, and celebrates a studious fraternity, yet no other English poem gives a
better sense of the open air, and the joys of health and strength
among streams and mountains. Nor is it easy to find another
scholarly composition, in which the humour is so unsophisticated.
Above all, the poem culminates in action. It tells how an Oxford
scholar discovered that the end of culture is to be natural and
started on his manhood in that spirit. Thus the poem has a value
which transcends literary criticism. It turns the reader towards
this most intimate and pressing problem, the conduct of his own

life, and plays upon his own motives and aims with the clear and inspiriting light of art.

Why did Clough never surpass this achievement; nor even repeat it? His university career sapped his inspiration, and in tracing this decline, we see how impossible it is for any man to play his proper part in the material world unless he understands his place in the spiritual world, and can clearly see where his soul owes its allegiance. When he went up to Oxford he was amply armed against Newmanism by Dr Arnold. But, like all the gifted and imaginative Oxonians of this generation, he was soon converted to the great tractarian's earnestness, to his dream of a devout and God-fearing England, strong in the universality and divine authority of the unsectarian pre-Lutheran Church, glorious in its sumptuous symbolism, its mystic communion and human fellowship, its historicity, its humanism, and its duty of self-examination—all so attractive to a schoolboy who kept a diary. No young man of Clough's temperament could be true to himself without hovering between this appeal to his idealism and the rather austere Calvinism and religious isolation which he had previously been taught to prize as the earthly crown of the Christian gentleman.

So Clough's thoughts were unsettled, his buoyancy and creativeness oppressed, his academic studies distracted. Then came the inevitable reaction. He found himself unmistakably searching here and there for definite proofs, for authorisation which will stand the test of logic, and modern experience, and so discovering the joy of exercising his brain in the disposal of his life. In order to make a free choice in his religion he fell under the tyranny of his intellect—the alternative was to fall under the tyranny of Rome. As was usual in the England of those days this new spirit came to a head in conflict with an old institution, the subscription to the Thirty-nine Articles. "It is not so much from any definite objection to this or that point, as a general dislike to subscription, and a strong feeling of its being a bondage and a very heavy one and one that may cramp and cripple one for life."[1]

Those words are significant. Clough is the first case we have met of a genuinely religious temperament in search of a religion, trying to create a religion out of suspended judgment. Unlike the freethinkers whom we have discussed, his mind was too free. He

[1] *Prose Remains*, quoted by H. F. Lowry in *The Letters of Matthew Arnold to Arthur Hugh Clough*, 1932, to whom I am indebted in making this character sketch.

could not find an allegiance to take the place of the Thirty-nine Articles. Having resigned Oxford he resigned himself. He wasted his life seeking a livelihood and, what for our purpose is most significant, he did not succeed in giving to his new state of mind the clear outline of poetic expression. His remaining poems have excellent ideas, for instance, *The Music of the World and of the Soul, The Questioning Spirit, Dipsychus*. Some have excellent passages, for instance, in *Amours de Voyage*. But one feels that none of them really expresses what the poet was feeling. One can only divine his greatness in his unfulfilment. Amid all his intellectual disappointments, financial worries, the humiliations of job-seeking and death from consumption in the prime of manhood, he persistently searched for some definite idea or cause in which his whole being could find its scope, but without success. He sacrificed his literary career to this concentrated lack of concentration. That is why "*Say not the struggle nought availeth*" is not only the most popular but the most perfect of his short poems. That is why he was the favourite correspondent and perhaps most valued friend of Matthew Arnold, who was himself treading the same path.

Matthew was born at Laleham in 1822. Like Froude and Clough he was a public schoolboy, being educated at Rugby and Harrow, and followed his friend to Oxford. There, despite his father's teaching, he fell under the influence of Newman; so much so that in his old age he ranked the apostle of tractarianism with Goethe, Wordsworth and Sainte-Beuve, as one of the four people from whom he had "learnt habits, methods, ruling ideas which are constantly with me".[1] Like Clough he discussed, ruminated and read so widely that he missed his first class in the Schools of 1844; again like his friend, he won his fellowship at Oriel, and before his academic career was ended, he again resembled Clough by doubting the Thirty-nine Articles. But he differs from his friend and from other writers whom we have discussed in a certain rather disconcerting two-sidedness. In manner he was self-contained and aloof, and consequently inconsiderate and as quizzical as a dandy. Yet few writers have cultivated a more graceful vein of intimacy, nor shown themselves more ready to confide in their readers. During his early manhood he wrote verse, much of which laments that his age was overwhelmed with new theories; during his

[1] To J. H. Newman, 28 May 1872. (First published in *Times Lit. Suppl.*, March 1921: reprinted A. Whitridge, *Unpublished Letters of Matthew Arnold*, 1923.)

mature manhood he wrote prose, complaining that his age was inaccessible to ideas. Sometimes one hardly knows whether to take him as a man of profound impulse, who disguised his yearnings beneath an urbane and chastened style, or as an extremely skilful craftsman who husbanded a thin vein of inspiration, and suggested more than he had to say. His individuality seems to be at one and the same time suppressed and expressed. We shall probably get nearest the truth if we picture him as the most impressionable and responsive mind of this age, and for that reason the most important and difficult author to study. He tried to preserve and assert his own identity by reflecting his environment, and there were too many things to reflect.

His contemporaries might have been pardoned for not understanding him. He was endowed with a profoundly religious instinct which had come under the most enlightened theological influences of his youth and early manhood. He was gifted with an extraordinary power of assimilating other men's wisdom, and these talents had been admirably trained in the old-fashioned humanism of his day. He really knew and understood the greatest Greek and Roman classics, and these councillors had filled him with confidence in their clearheadedness and flexibility of mind. So Arnold acquired the arts of percipience, that is to say, the skill to assimilate other people's ideas, then pull them to pieces and make them his own. But he had also learnt under Dr Arnold to study history in a practical spirit and to study modern languages, which direct our attention to the age in which we happen to be living. So when he set himself to acquire the knowledge of his own time in the combined spirit of ancient Greece and modern France, he soon realised that there was in culture as much to resign as to acquire. Neither Dr Arnold's nor Newman's teaching could survive investigation applied with the penetration and humanism of pagan and rationalist thinkers. Nor would it seem to an admirer of ancient civilisations that Victorian England was any the better for her modernised creeds and faiths. Thus some great thinkers who had stood firm in their faith did much to unsettle the convictions of their disciple. In 1849 we find him studying Aristotle's character of the φρόνιμος (the man of judgment),[1] and in 1850 he is reading Locke, since reason was the only "rock of refuge to this poor, exaggerated surrexcited humanity".

Like Clough, he succeeded in authorising himself not to deny

[1] To Clough 23 Sept. 1849 and 23 Oct. 1850.

God, but to seek Him by the light of human learning and intellect, and was less unsuccessful in the search. He began by seeking the master impulse which so many great poets and humanists had celebrated and which he now in his turn received from them—the urge to be better than the world around you, to cultivate the will to perfection. At the same time he realised acutely that this universal spirit of self-direction must become intimately his own, an acquisition adopted to his particular individuality, before he could join in the great tradition. On 23 September 1849 he writes to Clough that he is seeking interests and themes which give "a distinct seeing of my way as far as my own nature is concerned"; in 1852 he enters in his Note-book a quotation from Gonville on the duty and profit of understanding and applying one's own special qualities.

This self-study and self-discrimination became the dominant quest of his mature life. Our nobler impulses whencesoever derived must become consciously our own, before they can be cultivated—to the exclusion of all that is base or selfish in our animal natures. So only could God be found on earth, and the proof of our reunion is release from self-conflict, the sense of perfect adjustment, the calm of the spirit which has conquered the recalcitrant instincts and is at peace with itself. No doubt Arnold was helped by his own susceptibilities as a nature-poet; in fact all through life he longed for that rest from friction and wasted effort, that tranquillity which sometimes seemed to him to be the very expression of nature. Hence his love for rivers, dew, the stillness of twilight. Hence also his almost unique sense for mountains, not only "the cheerful silence of the fells", nor the far-flung purity of glaciers, but even the winds and storms whose energy was simple and always young. Yet one also realises that he was not at heart a true poet of nature. She is only cultivated as a symbol or imaginative expression of something higher, of what in man can be described as "strife divine".[1]

So here we meet the first of those unsatisfied longings which are both the glory and the blight of Arnold's verse. He can learn from nature an ideal of serenity which is granted to man only after the most painful self-examination and self-adjustment. Such reconstruction of one's life involves the mental habits of an eremite, an isolation in which the poet is thrown on his own resources and on the resources of all the great writers who have faced his

[1] Cf. *Self-Dependence, Morality, Harmony with Nature, The Youth of Nature.*

difficulty—Arnold, like Shelley, often laments the essential loneliness of every human being—and then, in the end, he finds that
to be his best self he must be in touch with his fellow-men. Some
of man's finest faculties are social or at least only blossom and
flower among human sympathies.

That is why Wordsworth exercised so great an influence in the
forming of his mind. The Lake-poet had lived through the passions
and misdirections and follies of youth, and the disappointments
and narrowing influences of manhood, and had learnt how to
ennoble and simplify all this human pettiness and folly by breathing
into it the grandeur and significance of nature. So he had achieved
classical serenity in a modern setting, medieval self-dedication
purged of medieval emotionalism, spiritual fixity won from a
piteously secluded and prosaic existence. More noteworthy still,
he could share his affections with the humblest human beings.

Arnold, therefore, was always a Wordsworthian, but it was
necessary that he should try to be a great deal more. Though the
Lake-poet never lost the human touch, yet his range was too
restricted. He seemed unable to think great thoughts except
among little people in a little world. Arnold, a lesser poet, needed
a bigger sphere. To begin with, the mid-nineteenth century with
its enormously increased opportunities, its industrial inventions,
social aspirations, economic developments and intellectual possibilities, was sounding a trumpet-call to action. One could not for
long continue "along the cool sequestered vale of life" without
sacrificing half one's manhood. Self-fulfilment was too inextricably
intertwined with the activities which civilisation imposed. In the
next place, Arnold was by temperament a man of action. He was
by common consent the most worldly member of his family. All
through his life he took a lively interest in politics and gave up half
his life to the public service of his country. His mind seems to have
been divided between two desires, the scholar's natural longing for
leisured seclusion, and, since solitude left half his energies unsatisfied, the active man's instinct for managing other people. This
dualism introduces an unusual note into much of his poetry,
especially during his later phase; but for us it is most important to
notice that he aimed at overcoming his regrets (occasionally,
perhaps, a trifle disingenuously) and at making his mark as a poet
of action.

This is the second stage of his development, and if one author
more than another influenced his course, it was Goethe. The

German poet had himself described this two-sidedness in *Faust*,[1] and Arnold was certainly indebted to him for the spirit which conquers retirement into self. Goethe, as we have seen, despised the rumination, introspection and melancholy of the German romantic movement. He believed that life was action, the assertion of personality over nature, or circumstances, by conduct, by what Spencer called "acts adjusted to ends",—*Im Anfang war die That*.[2] Art, especially literature, should express, interpret and encourage this urge; it should recreate and purify the thoughts and emotions which lead to action. It should tell stories and propound situations in such a way that human beings became conscious of the impulse to impose themselves on life and fashion its conditions according to their inborn and preconceived ideal. Arnold followed this lead. He is generally described as a lyric or elegiac poet, yet it is surprising how many of his best pieces celebrate, if not action, the desire for action, an endeavour, the study of self-devotion, the exercise of the will. One thinks not only of *Sohrab and Rustum, Tristram and Iseult, Saint Brandan, The Neckan, Balder Dead*, but of *East London, Immortality, Morality, Switzerland*, even *The Strayed Reveller*. It is significant that *Rugby Chapel*, provoked by an unfavourable review of *Tom Brown's School Days*,[3] is really an ode to a man of action. Even if he had not thought deeply he had read widely; his choice of subject is often surprisingly recondite; yet he always seems to be searching for some character suggestive of a clear purpose and a well-directed life.

A poet who thus sought to wake within us the fundamental springs of action and self-expression would need to exercise the utmost insight and tact in selecting both his theme and its poetic form. We have already, in the case of Ruskin, discussed the difficulty which a modern writer experiences in finding the focus which will unite all his contributory ideas and enthusiasms into one allegiance such as the mind can visualise. In this delicate task Arnold again followed Goethe. Even in the comparative retirement and provinciality of Weimar, the author of *Faust*, had recognised the difficulty of disentangling one's own petty egoisms and preferences so as to extricate the universal motives and clear-cut human ideals which unite men with the purposes of God. The Greeks had shown Goethe how it could be done. On 11 April

[1] 1er Theil, ll. 1110–23, *Vor dem Thor*.
[2] "In the beginning was the deed."
[3] H. F. Lowry, *The Letters of Matthew Arnold to Arthur Hugh Clough*. Appendix I.

1827 he had explained to Eckermann where the modern world should draw its inspiration. On 3 May 1827 he had shown why. It was because of the character which pervades Greek literature and art. "Dies ist der Charakter des Grossartigen, des Tüchtigen, des Gesunden, des Menschlich-Vollendeten, der hohen Lebensweisheit, der erhabenen Denkungsweise, der rein-kräftigen Anschauung."[1] Arnold must have had this passage in mind when he wrote to Clough: "A thousand things make one compose or not compose: composition seems to keep alive in me a cheerfulness— a sort of Tüchtigkeit, or natural soundness and valiancy which I think the present age is fast losing—this is why I like it."[2] The problem was to cultivate the mood in which to write poetry is to dream of action. Goethe[3] had said "study Molière, study Shakespeare, but above all the ancient Greeks, and always the Greeks". Arnold as a young man believed that he could do the same. He chose as his models Homer, Dante and Milton, and by the beginning of 1849 he had developed his theory of "the grand moral effect of *style*. For style is the expression of the nobility of the poet's character."[4]

So the first thing to notice about Arnold is that he definitely aimed at recapturing in concrete form the atmosphere of an earlier, simpler and more heroic age. He tried to adapt and subdue to his modern purposes the spirit of Greek epic and drama. The next thing to notice is that he did not wholly succeed—not even in finding what was best in himself. Take his most studied and sustained epic, *Sohrab and Rustum*. Opinions will always differ about the merits of this remarkable effort, which he took such pleasure in composing and thought the best thing which he had so far done.[5] Yet surely the only part which is purely of the poet is the epilogue with the vision of the river. The rest is a supreme literary effort, a skilful and conscientious harmonisation of a romantic theme with the techniques and sometimes the phraseologies of Homer and Virgil. He certainly has succeeded in portraying two statuesque figures intent upon a quest, exotic and romantic, no doubt, but ennobled by their single-heartedness. But are they not too statu-

---

[1] "This is the stamp of the grand, the valiant, the healthy, the humanly-perfect, the high worldly wisdom, the lofty habit of thought, the clean vigour of contemplation."

[2] H. F. Lowry, *op. cit.* No. 51. 30 Nov. 1853.   [3] 11 April 1827.

[4] To Clough, 1 March 1849. From H. F. Lowry, *op. cit.*

[5] To his mother, Monday (May 1853).

esque and single-hearted? He certainly delights the stylist, but has he, as he hoped, told a great story in such a way as to help people to live through mid-nineteenth century life more courageously and intelligently? Take *Merope*, produced as late as 1858, his last sustained effort at poetry. By that time Arnold was a recognised literary figure, the drama sold well and attracted much attention. Some reviewers accused him of insulting the sacredness of the romantic tradition and of presuming to impose classicism on his age. That was precisely what he wanted to do. He wrote to Miss Arnold on 3 February 1858: "What I meant them to see in it was a specimen of the world created by the Greek imagination." That is to say, a drama in which the conflicts and discords of the plot do not arise of themselves, but are manifestations of universal law; the work of Fate and the Olympic gods, as interpreted by the Chorus. Yet no one can imagine that the poet produced the effect which he intended. This antique story of Theban dynastic intrigue does not inspire and encourage the modern reader; the author has not the gift of dramatic narrative. We can only enjoy the scholarly imitation of classical form. Yet hardly that. *Merope* is too conscientious a reproduction of Greek mannerisms to give a true impression of the Greek manner in English; it lacks lyricism and intensity.

Since the publication of Arnold's letters to Clough, it is clear why the poet missed his mark. Between 1848 and 1849 he had asserted that poets "must begin with an Idea of the world in order not to be prevailed over by the world's *Multitudinousness*".[1] In the same letter he had described Browning as "a man with a moderate gift passionately desiring movement and fulness and obtaining but a confused multitudinousness". It was the poet's function to dominate these many-sided experiences and to impress them with his artistic personality, and for that reason Arnold had been at such pains to cultivate his own individual bent of mind and to express it with Greek simplicity and directness. Despite this self-discipline, he was failing as we have seen that his great predecessors failed. They, however, had continued on their way, though with a somewhat halting gait, and had held their own. Arnold was still a young man when he began to confess that his muse was deserting him, and all through his poetic career he laments the storm and stress of modern civilisation, which sweeps over us like the waves of a heavy sea. At other times he talks of the "sick hurry" of his

[1] H. F. Lowry, *op. cit.* No. 24.

times or its "hopeless tangle" or of "the petty dust" which each day brings to choke our souls. Gradually he discovers that the simplified world of high endeavour as cultivated by Greeks and Grecians was not sufficiently pregnant to symbolise or suggest modernism. Assuredly he was being mastered by life.

At first his plight seems already to savour of the twentieth century, for such is the burden of our own time. Life is a task-master which disposes of our thoughts as well as of our actions. Arnold must certainly have had sympathy with such a feeling, for he also was a slave to mechanisation, and from 1851 a bread-winner in a not very congenial profession. So his inspiration must often have flagged from moral and mental exhaustion; and he must sometimes have feared that he would lose his self-hood to become a function. Yet such is not the usual tenor of his revolt. As a poet he does not so much protest against the dullness of his age (that complaint was to come later) as against its over-active distracted-ness. It could not have been otherwise. As we have seen, Arnold had acquired remarkable powers of adaptability and assimilation. But so had hundreds of other thinkers, and many of them were quite as capable as Arnold of choosing and experimenting for them-selves. Beneath the grimy, clanging pall of industrialism, many minds were busy forming new ideas, and even more pens were busy disseminating them among the ever-growing army of book readers. So in any case a scholar who took an interest in modern thought would find himself faced by a conflict of opinions and theories.

It was this many-headed hurry and irresponsibility of thought which disheartened the poet, and his perplexity is one of the most important facts in our inquiry. It comes as a surprise; there ought to be something bracing in a plethora of controversies; we should have expected a man of Arnold's calibre to be more than equal to the test. One is almost tempted to conclude that his surrender was due to material preoccupations and moral exhaustion—merely personal causes. Yet others, with less excuse than Arnold, were just as conscious of the same disability. Take for instance H. T. Buckle, a man with a very different temperament, but born only a few months earlier than Arnold, who settled in London in 1842 to study the cross-currents of the modern intellect, and by 1853 had fused all the varied tendencies of culture into the plan of his *History of Civilisation*.[1] This monument of learning is nowadays

[1] 1st instalment 1857, 2nd instalment 1861. Buckle died before the work was finished exclaiming, "My book! my book!"

neglected, no doubt rightly so, since it is a fragment and bound to be misleading. Yet no other Englishman of this period has made so consistent and comprehensive an effort to systematise and even unify the thousand paths by which Europe has found her erratic way down to the nineteenth century. He is not at a loss for the one effective element which has dominated this progress: it is the human capacity for intellectual legislation, for classifying and interpreting facts till we become their master. So his book is an enthusiastic but none the less reasoned tribute to the sufficiency of logic and observation. In this spirit our forbears have gradually eliminated superstition and created ideals which are humanitarian.

When such widespread and profound erudition leads to such cheering conclusions, the author is not likely to fall a victim to disillusionment. Yet it is most significant that Buckle at the height of his triumphant record has to admit the same defects and blemishes as troubled our poet. The historian confesses that "the complications of modern society, and the immense variety of interests into which it is divided, have done much to distract the intellect, and to prevent it from dwelling upon subjects which a less occupied people would deem of paramount importance".[1] He, too, complains of English materialism. "Our facts have outstripped our knowledge and are now encumbering its march....We hear constantly of what nature is doing, but we rarely hear of what man is thinking."[2] And, lastly, Buckle observes that there is among scientific inquirers an avowed intention to separate philosophy from poetry which is a part of philosophy simply because the emotions are a part of the mind. In one of the most striking passages of his book he asserts that the huge treasuries of learning stored up during the last two centuries will be useless until connected by some presiding idea, and that "the most effective way of turning them to account would be to give more scope to the imagination, and incorporate the spirit of poetry with the spirit of science".[3]

In a certain sense Arnold was treading the same path as was Buckle. When looking back on his poetical career, he once wrote: "It might fairly be urged that I have less poetical sentiment than Tennyson, and less intellectual vigour and abundance than Browning; yet, because I have perhaps more of a fusion of the two than either of them, and have more regularly applied that fusion to the main line of modern development, I am likely enough to

[1] Vol. I, chap. VII.   [2] Vol. III, chap. v.   [3] *Ibid.*

have my turn as they had theirs."[1] That is to say, Arnold recognised his calling as a poet of modern intellectualism. He had to think nineteenth-century thoughts, and breathe contemporary enthusiasms, whatever the form or subject of his verse. So he was more or less conversant with the material which Buckle was handling with such laboured skill; and was just the man to fulfil the historian's wish—to inform and enlighten philosophy with the poet's vision. Yet he tries and confesses that he has failed.

Are we then to conclude that there is in each individual something which cannot be adapted to corporate movements or material experiences—some spiritual egocentricity which only thrives on what it can imagine? Does rationalism by creating self-reliance destroy that other confidence in a superhuman allegiance? Was the substance of nineteenth-century thought too stubborn for idealists? These questions have obtruded themselves into the study of each great Victorian figure; they are essential to our inquiry, and must be discussed for their own sake. But as Arnold is the last of the old guard, we must observe his reactions before considering (in the next chapter) the influences against which they all reacted. He is our immediate difficulty.

In the narrower, more personal sense we may say that he was perplexed, because experience disproved his religious trust in a miraculous and superhuman system, such as the Oxford Movement championed; and because the philosophic or scientific alternatives came so quickly that he had no time to co-ordinate and spiritualise their findings, so that he could recover his own sense of personal unity. In trying to grasp ideas he nearly lost hold of himself. It was impossible to envisage all these contributory streams and dig for them a single channel, such as the great poets of a simpler age had done.

In February 1849[2] he begged Clough to reflect "how deeply unpoetical the age and all one's surroundings are", and two years later he gave unmistakable proof that he had failed to adjust the spirit of poetry to his age. In 1852 he published his second volume, *Empedocles on Etna and other Poems by A.*, and when in 1853 he republished much of his earlier work with many important additions as *Poems by Matthew Arnold*, *Empedocles* was omitted. In the remarkable preface to this edition—his first public effort at criticism, which ranks among his most suggestive pronouncements and finds a place in every collection of his prose passages—he justifies this omission because the subject, though Greek, contains no action,

---

[1] To his mother, 5 June 1869.   [2] H. F. Lowry, *op. cit.* No. 25.

and consequently is not in the tradition of great poetry. His dissatisfaction with this dramatic poem implies an interesting revelation, not only of Arnold's character, but of the influences which controlled his development.

Empedocles is one of Arnold's most sustained and individual pieces, with many felicities of phrasing and some unforgettable passages. He seldom wrote with more eloquence and insight. It was praised by *The Times*, it was even sold on the railway bookstall at Derby; Browning insisted that it should be republished in the *New Poems* of 1866. Yet the author wished it to be forgotten, and not without reason, because it records a defeat. He was probably attracted to the philosopher of Acragas because he saw in G. H. Lewes's *Biographical History of Philosophy* (1845–6) a verse translation of some hexameters on the vanity and instability of human knowledge and because this passage (which Arnold imitates) supplied a more convincing explanation for the Greek's suicide. At any rate Arnold recreates Empedocles as the crystal figure through which to allegorise the modern poet trying to impose his personality on experience; and all unwittingly he finds himself describing with the eloquence of sincerity how the modern poet sinks beneath the influences which he should master, if he is to remain a poet. It is most impressive, the feeling with which Arnold describes the modern sensitised consciousness, fixed on the conquest of spiritual happiness and penetrating into the tendencies of his age, only to find proofs of his limitations. How are we to look for the inner purpose and plan of life when "the wind-borne mirroring soul" is spinning among new doctrines, winning a thousand glimpses and never striking to the core? So we are robbed of our quest of inward righteousness and find no response from without to what we yearn for within—only the perception of an inhuman nature and at most of a finite god, "the o'erlabour'd Power".

So (according to Arnold) we lose sight of what is true and permanent in the human soul, and spend our emotion railing at Fate and God, or reverse the scheme we ourselves have spun. Rationalism may be a stimulant to the mind, it may be more—a duty, since every good man must seek the truth. But can he thus find the truth about himself?

> To see if we will poise our life at last,
> To see if we will now at last be true
> To our own only true, deep-buried selves,
> Being one with which, we are one with the whole world.

This quest of spiritual self-possession amid the welter of intellectual distractions, thus proclaimed by Arnold, has continued to be one of the problems of culture up to the present time. Among the last to echo Arnold's sentiment are E. M. Forster and D. H. Lawrence.

One is reminded of Nietzsche's insistence on the need for creativeness[1]—that human beings must invest all they learn and do with their own ideals sprung from their own hearts. Culture still purified and intensified those ideals but civilisation ceased to give them scope. No borrowed inspiration could compensate for this lack of purpose, not even the genius of the grand style. You cannot live for long on the spirit of Homer, Sophocles, Shakespeare or Goethe, unless that spirit is felt to be still alive. So our poet was left with the impulse to create but not the power, the longing for spiritual fulfilment, but no vision. While casting about for help he found another kindred spirit who had suffered as much or more than he, and had, moreover, given literary effect to his moral ineffectiveness. So Arnold came under the influence of *Obermann*.

The author, E. P. de Senancour, was and is very little read. Lanson does not mention him in his *Histoire de la Littérature Française* in 1894; Lanson's successor, D. Mornet, in his *Histoire de la Littérature et de la Pensée Françaises* in 1924 dismisses him in an undiscerning phrase. In 1862 M. E. Grant-Duff could find a copy of his works nowhere procurable except from a circulating library at Geneva.[2] Arnold may first have heard of this obscure writer in 1846, when he visited George Sand at Nohant,[3] or he may have read Sainte-Beuve's two essays in *Portraits Contemporains*.[4] But whatever the source of his knowledge he always spoke of de Senancour with the profoundest admiration and gratitude, and sometimes echoes his figures and phrases as well as his sentiments.

The reader of our own day who seeks out this philosophical sentimentalist will probably be disappointed. Yet for our inquiry the author of *Obermann* is important. Even his life is noteworthy. As a boy he was trained for the priesthood. At nineteen years of age he revolted, quarrelled with his father and fled to Switzerland. He wrote *Obermann*, his second book, between 1801 and 1803, in a mood of complete agnosticism and discontent with the spirit and prospects of civilisation. In middle age he returned to Paris and,

---

[1] *Der Wille zur Macht.*
[2] Arnold to his mother, 28 June 1862.
[3] J. E. Sells, *Matthew Arnold and France*, 1935.
[4] Vol. 1, 1832; 1833. Also cf. *post*, pp. 191–3.

as in the case of Arnold, reverted to a liberal Christianity, which he tried to inculcate on his contemporaries but with even less success than his English admirer was to achieve.

De Senancour had broken away from orthodoxy for the same reason as Arnold had done: he wanted to live creatively. He cherished an ardent longing towards happiness, righteousness and tranquillity and he tried to read and interpret the world in accordance with these desires. He needed an intellect which would convince his spirit of the divinity underlying the human scheme. Did he find anywhere this moral and intellectual fulfilment? Not among men, only now and then among the tranquil grandeurs of nature, especially the awful magnificence of Alpine scenery.

Thus Arnold found his own moods re-echoed, multiplied and illustrated in a hundred turns of French phraseology. For years he remained under the spell; possibly there is a certain disingenuousness and affectation in his discipleship. Anyhow, the obscure author, of whom he had apparently read only one or two books, exercised nearly as much influence on our poet as did the Olympian and voluminous Goethe. In fact Arnold impresses one in this next phase as a man

> Whose insight never has borne fruit in deeds,[1]

who is always seeking for a motive within himself.[2] He does not completely find what he seeks, but every now and then the spirit of the man springs to light in response to some impression, and flashes of insight and sympathy gladden our eyes, as if by the way. But he is perhaps at his best when he evokes the intimacy and homeliness of a familiar landscape—what we now call regionalism; and what he described as "the peculiar sentiment of this country and neighbourhood".[3] The two classic examples of this quality are *The Scholar-Gipsy* and *Thyrsis*, in which the manner is faintly inspired by Theocritus, but the scenery is so felicitously created out of memory and loving observation that for once we elude the melancholy of the theme, and the poet himself seems to forget it.

But the more he writes, the more clearly he perceives that he cannot spiritualise the thoughts which the world puts into his head. So he explains in poetry, why poetry has left English culture. The effect is well illustrated by his literary or purely didactic poems. While searching nature, history, biography and common experi-

[1] *The Scholar-Gipsy.*   [2] E.g. *Dover Beach.*
[3] To his wife, Sunday, Oct. 1854.

ence for the encouragement he rarely found, he did not overlook
the great writers of the previous generation who were now beginning to attract attention. He approaches them more as a poet than
as a critic, since he asks them for a satisfying sense of reality,
tinged with emotion, and finds the same kind of sentiment as he
derives, for instance, from Dover beach. His impressions are based
on careful reading and hard thinking and some of his estimates are
as searching as can be found; for instance, his pronouncements on
Goethe, Byron and Wordsworth. These excursions into critical
lyricism[1] are generally overlooked in eulogies and anthologies, yet
they exercised no small influence on the rising generation, both in
unsettling old-fashioned convictions, and in raising the study of
literature to the dignity of a religion. *Obermann Once More* is
particularly noteworthy.

These didactic verses belong more or less to the last phase of
Arnold's poetic creativeness. It should be noticed that, like his
earlier work, they are also remarkable for their technique. Our
poet is an original as well as a painstaking and fastidious craftsman.
Of course he has perpetrated a few horribly prosaic lines, and he
abuses the exclamatory "Ah!" as often in verse as Zola does in
prose; and besides he is not always conspicuously successful when
he employs the older and simpler metres. But he has shown unmistakable independence in some of his experiments. He has
produced some haunting and impressive rhythmic effects, and,
following Heine's lead in *Nordsee*, he has at any rate ventured on
free verse.

Thus in every sense Arnold is a memorable figure in the history
of English poetry, and is particularly significant, as far as the
present inquiry is concerned, because he describes with eloquence
and insight the difficulty of adjusting the ideals of culture to the
march of progress. Compared with Clough, his achievement is
undeniable. Yet he had hardly reached the prime of manhood
when his inspiration began to flag. His most active period was
between 1845 and 1853. By that time he had produced three
volumes containing much of his best work. He published another
volume in 1855 containing *Balder Dead* and *Resignation*; *Merope* in
1858, and one more volume in 1867. From that time onwards he
produced a few compositions in periodicals; for instance *Thyrsis*
was published by *Macmillan* in April 1866, after more than two

---

[1] *Heine's Grave, Stanzas from the Grande Chartreuse, Memorial Verses, Obermann,
Obermann Once More.*

years' meditation;[1] but as a poet he had almost ceased to write. The explanation is that in the latter phases of his poetic career his inspiration was derived from the frustrated longing for action and the sense of isolation; and Arnold was (even in imagination) no longer inactive or isolated. His spirit had found scope among the works of his fellow-creatures and his intellect had found expression in prose.

He began to start life afresh, and this redirection brings into relief one change which among many others was stealing over English culture. His contemporaries were, for the most part, unaware of its trend; we at this distance can perceive its inception, since we are still living in the consequences. This tendency did not aim at arguing the spirit out of existence but at arguing its energy into a new sphere of action. The human being must realise his intellectual and imaginative self not only by studying men but by participating in their ordinary activities—their pleasures and pursuits. While declaring that his age was unpoetical, he must have felt that the defect lay with those who looked for poetry in the wrong place: in an old-world atmosphere existing only in books. The soul must look for its mirrored reflection in contemporary civilisation however materialised. The series of poems entitled *Switzerland* bear testimony to this two-sidedness.

Arnold, despite his fellowship, left Oxford sometime in 1846. During the next four years he paid frequent visits to France and Switzerland, in fact he seems to have indulged himself in an extended, if intermittent, *Wanderjahr*. Much of his best poetry was composed during this period, perhaps under the influence of foreign travel, and it has been suggested that of all his work the poems on Margaret, so full of spiritual and emotional experience, are the most significant. They are certainly the most enigmatical. It seems[2] that he really did meet and perhaps fall in love with some such person probably between 1846 and 1847, though whether a waitress, café-singer, schoolmistress, lady-companion or simply a French woman without any more intriguing attribute, remains a secret. What really matters, of course, is not the authenticity of the episode, but the quality of its poetry, and Arnold has invented or applied the episode to define the rival claims which distracted his

[1] To his mother, 7 April 1866.
[2] See H. Kingsmill, *Matthew Arnold*, 1928; L. Binnerot, "La Jeunesse de Matthew Arnold", *Revue Anglo-Américaine*, août 1930; J. E. Sells, *Matthew Arnold and France*, 1935.

life. Margaret may or may not stand for some real enchantress, but she does stand for the Circe of modern culture—intellectual self-indulgence, the sensuousness of romance and sentiment. The poet is constrained to leave these attractions, he is constrained to leave the world haunted by Obermann. He obeys the call of duty, and possibly to some extent the pressure of circumstance, but more than all the urgency within him to mix in a more strenuous and competitive world which will employ all his faculties and engage all his interests. These confessions of a divided spirit have been much admired; H. W. Garrod[1] thinks that they mark the beginning of Arnold's best work. They are certainly conspicuous among his verse for flashes of imagination and felicities of rhythm, but one cannot help noticing that they are in places almost absurdly self-centred. The poet exhausts the resources of the eloquence of self-importance. At one time he compares himself with Patroclus thrust down from the wall of Troy by Apollo. He appeals again and again to the glaciers and whirlwinds of Europe's mightiest mountain chain as if they were monitory voices, were not inadequate symbols of the destiny immanent in his nature. Arnold had much too much common sense and good taste to be satisfied for long with these Wertherisms. The mature Goethe, whom he cultivated, would not have approved. After all, when stripped of its rhetoric, the crisis is not unlike the situation which Maggie Tulliver had to face or even Tony Buddenbrook.[2] It is at least likely that the poet was to find it more and more impossible, in nineteenth-century life, to concentrate and develop his spiritual personality through the study of himself.

His academic training might still retain its hold; he might continue to regret the past and indulge from time to time in melancholy contemplation. But even the Greek classics, Dante, Milton and Goethe, though themselves old, had helped to persuade him to look for something new. They had moved with their times: he must move with his. We shall find another influence, where it was least to be expected. In 1851, in order to marry, he accepted an inspectorship of schools.

[1] *The Poetry of Matthew Arnold I.* In *Poetry and the Criticism of Life*, 1931.
[2] Thomas Mann, *Buddenbrooks*, Dritter Theil, 13er Kap.

CHAPTER XIII

Arnold, who began his career as an artist-poet, ends as a popular moralist—He invokes the wisdom, intelligence and imagination of the Past in adjustment to the intellectual and religious environment of the Present, thus preserving the continuity of culture—Sainte-Beuve points the way and Macaulay obstructs it—If Arnold had been less conscientiously intent on seeing the Present he would have foreseen more of the Future.

We saw in the last chapter that Arnold could not develop his best self in a library, however scholarly the choice of books. Even one's own Platonic archetypes are not to be cultivated by renouncing the world. The great "masters of the mind" had moved with their times: Arnold must move with his. Modern civilisation, for all its philistinism, had secretly suggested certain desires—the consciousness of certain aptitudes—which craved satisfaction elsewhere than in academic bowers. He had not really changed; in fact (as we shall see) he retained to the last his classic idealism; but his idea of the world's opportunities had changed. The old allegiances claimed only half himself, since the stream of rationalism had redirected his thoughts. They were also being redirected by the duties of his inspectorship.

So he settled down to the new projects of organising elementary education. It might be an obscure and laborious career but it was certainly varied. He had to travel all over England. Several times he was sent abroad. He met Quakers, Methodists, Wesleyans, shopkeepers, members of Parliament, lawyers and judges. He came to understand, as few men of culture then could, the prejudices and aspirations of the middle class. His headquarters were in London, but his temporary abode was anywhere, and he might be meeting any type of humanity, from girl pupil-teachers to Cousin and Sainte-Beuve. On one Sunday, having lunched with Lady de Rothschild, he dined with Monckton Milnes and met "all the advanced liberals in religion and politics", including Lewes and Spencer, besides Froude, Browning and Ruskin, "and a Cingalese in full costume".[1] These distractions and avocations, by no means lessened by the hurry of catching trains and dressing for

[1] To his mother, 16 June 1863.

dinner invitations, were intensified by the routine of school inspection in dissenting schools, the drudgery of elementary examination papers, and the pedestrianism of writing reports. Yet the
life suited him. In its earlier phases he complains both in his letters
and his poetry of the pettiness and provinciality of his pursuits.
Yet under their influence he found his place in the scheme of
things, and thereby learnt how to employ that master-impulse
towards self-perfection which he believed every human being to
possess.

To begin with, the exigencies of his career compelled him to
resist distraction, to create the will-power to keep his inward self
alive; "to make habitual war on depression and low spirits, which
in one's early youth one is apt to indulge and be somewhat interested in".[1] In the next place, this profession taught him one of
the secrets of this latter modern world—how to adjust the needs
of the spirit to the concrete realities of a mechanised existence;
how to keep the balance between what Von Robert Musil, in his
very modern *Der Mann ohne Eigenschaften*, calls *Möglichkeitssinn* and
Wirklichkeitssinn. The more he learnt this lesson, the less he seemed
inclined to write poetry about himself and the aridity of his age.
He tells Mrs Forster:[2] "It is only in the best poetical epochs (such
as the Elizabethans) that you can descend into yourself and
produce the best of your thought and feeling naturally, and without an overwhelming and in some degree morbid effort." The late
'fifties was the period during which he gradually wearied of his
own pessimism, and gradually acquired the will and skill to make
what was bad better. At the same time his Note-books begin to
record entries suggesting that he must begin all over again to
adapt himself to the claims of his life. Again and again, all through
his later career, he keeps repeating the words of Thomas à Kempis:
"semper aliquid certi proponendum est".[3] In 1858 he records:
"The three things that improve genius: proper exertion, frequent
exertion, and successful exertion."

It must have been while in contact with the world that he made
his first step towards mastering the "multitudinousness" of life, by
analysing the influences of contemporary civilisation. If Oxford
had taught him that men of learning were divorced from the
Present, London was teaching him that men of the world are
divorced from the Past, not from its routine but from its convic-

---

[1] To Mrs Forster, April 1856.   [2] 6 Aug. 1858.
[3] "Let there be some clear purpose ever before thee."

tions and experiences. What afflicted this age was not so much the multitude of ideas, as their suddenness and discontinuity. There is a significant passage in *Empedocles* in which the philosopher recalls the genealogy of the human mind—the racial, social and family influences which prepare the individual for the adventure of life. "So each new man strikes root into a far fore-time." These roots were, of course, biological and national; but not all of them; the most vital sprang from an intimate and spiritual source—the sense of purpose and continuity which culture had grafted onto the hereditary system. Every man interprets and assimilates his experiences according to the habit of mind which has been fostered in him. Arnold himself had been trained to develop this subtler, more imaginative self-consciousness among the formularies of Protestantism, the moral tone of Homer, Sophocles, and (in early manhood) Epictetus; among the sanctities of home life, the obligations of gentlemanly conduct, the companionship of local surroundings which are the silent and sympathetic witnesses of one's development. Such was the older European culture, founded on observations and ideas which did not imprison the mind, but kept it open and adaptable to the finer influences and presences in nature and society. This background was too good to be sacrificed, for it kept the soul alive. As Arnold quoted from Guérin, "vivre c'est penser avec de l'âme".[1]

Having partially recovered from his poetic despondency, he could face the malady of his age more judicially and could perceive that the ideology of the nineteenth century was threatening this hereditary inwardness which is (according to him) the finer breath of culture. Civilisation was becoming cosmopolitan, co-operative, and mechanical. In order to think like Hume, Helvetius, Malthus, Ricardo, Bentham, Mill, Spencer, Cobden, Strauss and Lyell, one had to accept premises, propositions, and syllogisms as if they were appliances manufactured ready for use, utterly disconnected with the thinker's past associations, and of equal value to everybody. Their triumphs had been celebrated by Buckle, and by W. E. H. Lecky, whose *History of the Rise and Influence of Rationalism* (1865) is in some sort a sequel to the *History of Civilisation.* But Arnold seems to have realised that a man cannot safely adopt new ideas unless he holds himself spiritually responsible for their truth and applications. As Maurice Barrès was afterwards to explain: "the same formula varies according to the places and

---

[1] "To live is to think with the spirit."

circumstances in which it falls. A principle produces different fruits according to the minds which receive it."[1] So in this age it was more than ever necessary to recover the old-fashioned steadiness and clear-sighted vision, before a nineteenth-century citizen could trust himself to live by nineteenth-century standards. If he could not adjust the new phrases to the old aptitudes, his intelligence lost its flexibility, penetration and broad-mindedness. It was not a question of conservatism, of clinging to old beliefs and customs, but of clinging to the efficiency, insight, sympathy and individual responsibility engendered by those customs and beliefs, of preserving one's cultured personality.

Arnold addressed himself to readers capable of this effort. He was often to write as if he were preaching to tradesmen, stock-brokers, dissenters and to any others too absorbed in their own pursuits to care for the things of the spirit; content with tradition because it was too much trouble to live according to reason. But it was not Arnold's habit to write for people who had probably never heard his name, and would certainly never read his magazine articles nor books. In 1858 he enters in his Note-book: "The 3 things that support genius: prosperity, social acquaintance, and applause", and assuredly he intended to win those who could appreciate him. He had to teach others at the same time as himself, how to face the present with the steady penetrative eyes of the past. If he were to find his own way he needed companions who might become admirers. So he wrote for those who could join him in cultivating calmness of judgment and vigour of intellect.

Nor must one suppose that Arnold, or any other humanistic reformer, was a voice crying in the wilderness. His main difficulty was not the apathy of the reading public but its divided attention. These middle and upper classes had rival gods to worship; they were now sufficiently well instructed to enjoy the older writers for more superficial reasons—for their style and historical significance; they preferred education to culture. This counter-tendency has so much to do with Arnold's career, and with those who carried his ideals into the twentieth century, that it must be clearly understood. Its representative and exponent is Macaulay (1800–59).

Macaulay was brought up in a comfortable and affluent home, the centre of domestic affection. With such a father as Zachary and such an environment as the Clapham Set, he would naturally be trained to take a certain form of unorthodox orthodoxy for

---

[1] *Les Déracinés*, 1897, chap. VII.

granted, to give his best self to social service and humanitarianism, and the business of making England the leading champion of Christendom. To that extent he would not be prepared for the inner meaning of art and the undertones of poetry. Yet, on the other hand, never was there a man of business and affairs, a public character, more devoted to humanism for its own sake. Even on his voyage out to India he read or re-read Richardson, Voltaire, Gibbon, Homer, Horace and *Don Quixote* (in Spanish), and he devoted the home journey to mastering German (Schiller and Goethe as well as Niebuhr). During those four busy years as Commissioner of the Board of Control, President of the Committee of Public Instruction, and President of Law Commissions, he reserved his early mornings for study of the Greek and Latin classics, and late in life, when writing his history at highest pressure, he spent half his day in re-reading his favourites, especially Greek. During the last twenty-five years of his career there was hardly a public honour to which he, so self-assertive by nature, might not have aspired, yet now that the family fortunes were restored, he deliberately chose the scholar's secluded and leisured existence. All through his career, in all his trials and troubles, as in his triumphs, his greatest joy or consolation was "to converse with the dead".

By such converse he brought the dead to life and treated them just as we treat our contemporaries, creating an intense interest in their personal affairs, their manners, prejudices, accomplishments, successes and failures. He took some of them to his heart because of their sterling virtues, and others because their intellects stimulated his; especially because he liked to play the part of a prosecuting or defending counsel. As a young man he had been called to the Bar, and its methods seem to have become a part of his mind, though he earned only one guinea in the profession. Being a vivid, as well as a thoroughly sincere writer, he taught his generation how to enjoy the same mental exercise in the same books. So his *Essays* have encouraged hundreds of thousands to read history and literature.

It was unquestionably a great achievement, and in the so-called philistinism of the nineteenth century he reaped his reward. One hundred and forty thousand copies of his history were sold within one generation; he made a fortune as well as a reputation; and, notwithstanding, he pursued culture as whole-heartedly as did Cicero or Sir Philip Sydney.

But not with the same result. He was really retrogressive. He studied literature as it was studied in the eighteenth century, as an exercise in taste, not for the thought, but for the performance. He liked to judge authors who do not persuade you to judge yourself. All he read made him more confident in his own success and in the success of his country. Otherwise books meant nothing to him. For instance, he admired Plato solely for his rhetoric, descriptive power, humour and excellent Greek.[1] He could find nothing worth reading in *The Prelude*—"the old flimsy philosophy about the effect of scenery on the mind; the old crazy, mystical metaphysics".[2] Newman was to him merely a divine who edited *Lives of the Saints*, and afterwards became a Roman Catholic.[3] It is not on record that he ever made an important allusion to Carlyle, Froude, or Ruskin. On 11 February 1854 Mill had already noted in his Diary the fear that "the present age will be known and estimated by posterity as the age which thought Macaulay a great writer", and yet four years earlier Carlyle observed on 24 July 1840 that Macaulay had no vision, and looked on life with spectacles instead of eyes.[4]

Such was the real philistinism which Arnold and his fellow-workers had to face. He admitted as much when he described this prominent essayist and historian as the apostle to the philistines. To mitigate his influence it was requisite to confront the false gods with the true; so this poet, now himself turned essayist, began to discuss the authors who cause searchings of heart and to write about them in such a way that the reader has to revise his values. With this aim, Arnold called to life generally his own favourites, but always those most likely to enlighten or steady his contemporaries, often revealing an unexpectedness, even capriciousness of choice. Just as Wordsworth, Goethe and de Senancour influenced his poetic creativeness, so through his second phase as an essayist he followed Sainte-Beuve.

Sainte-Beuve was born eighteen years earlier than Arnold, in 1804, and began life by studying medicine, and just like Arnold, he first tried to make his mark as a poet. He too passed through his religious crisis and was thereby inspired to write a novel, like Froude. During this early period his work was self-centred, composed in the spirit of romanticism, and it failed. The author had not succeeded in self-expression through self-study and he realised

[1] Diary, July 1853.　　　　　[2] *Ibid.* July 1850.
[3] Trevelyan, *Life and Letters of Macaulay*, chap. xiv.
[4] J. A. Froude, *Carlyle's Life in London*.

his failure too well to repeat the effort. At this juncture private circumstances, mixed with politics, made it necessary for him to earn his living, so he lectured at Lausanne in 1837 and Liège in 1838, and thereby discovered that he had a genius for literary criticism. Apparently he had changed the whole current of his intellectual life. In 1850 he started for the *Constitutionnel* his famous *Causeries du Lundi*, passing on to the columns of the *Moniteur* and *Le Temps*. Owing to his often-quoted confession: "Je n'ai plus qu'un plaisir, j'analyse, j'herborise; je suis un naturaliste des esprits",[1] he is generally taken at his word and described as the man who made literary criticism a science.

Such is not the case. Sainte-Beuve remained an artist. He still searched experience for the ideas which could be reduced to the most suggestive form, but he changed his method and material. He became a realist. Instead of studying the world through his own dreams, he examined it through the reactions of other people, and what is more, of those people who had already proved themselves to be the most sensitive connoisseurs of life, and had left their impressions in a form which was already art.

Thus, for Sainte-Beuve, the study of literature meant the study of interpretative personalities. He concerns himself with individuals, more than with schools, movements or epochs, and at first it seems as if his aim is merely to establish the truth about this or that author's life or the value of his works. So far he was only keeping pace with Carlyle. In fact he sometimes grew weary of jumping from one subject and century to another; like a horse continually jerked from left to right.[2] It is only when the essays have been carefully read and compared that a single composite individuality seems to form itself beneath this multitudinous succession of individual portraits—the spirit which lives on its brain-power. Sainte-Beuve, like any other realist, is concerned with human idiosyncracies, but they are those of the intellect—of that quality which becomes peculiar in each individual, yet moves through all cultured men; which is broken into thousands of flashes as it passes from generation to generation, yet retaining its continuity; culture's common hold on humanity. We know our best selves in so far as we enter into the spirit of Molière, Madame de Staël, Sieyès, Ronsard, Racine. This line of study has proved to be

[1] "My only pleasure is to analyse and botanise; I am a naturalist of the human mind."

[2] *Journal des Goncourt*, 18 Oct. 1861.

of immense importance. As we have seen, the mechanisation of life and apparent lowering of individual initiative was being accompanied by an ever-multiplying body of knowledge and opinion. If the educated classes could not act so freely or so nobly as in former ages, their brains were as busy as ever. Cerebration was the note of the age. Obviously, the old epic and dramatic enthusiasms were difficult to adjust to the new mood (as Arnold himself had found). But here was another unexpected kind of inspiration—the history of innumerable minds which remained centred in intellectual matters, yet exercised their powers with the uttermost effect and achieved the highest perfection of which the cerebrated character is capable. Literary criticism restored our sense of permanence and reality by revealing the energies of the spirit directed into the noblest as well as the most enduring channels.

Arnold had probably been conversant with Sainte-Beuve's writings for years. He possessed and annotated the 1847 edition of *Portraits Contemporains*,[1] and he now undertook with his help to bridge the gulf between the Present and the Past. At the back of his mind there was a well-digested system of philosophy not untouched by mysticism. Like all the great intellects which we have so far discussed he was a confirmed dualist. He believed that we have certain capacities for good and for evil. He also believed that a supernatural urge, coming we know not whence, "permeates this twi-nature"; concentrates and redirects all our faculties according to its divine impulse, harmonises our whole being—soul, spirit and intellect—according to its idea; raises us above our ordinary selves. This influence which enters each one of us and is known only as so many individualised manifestations of human worth is eternal and universal. It might be described as human perfectibility amounting to superhumanity.

The conviction is not uncongenial to Plato, Spinoza or the romantic philosophers. In 1858, when fairly launched on this fresh voyage, he makes several entries in his Note-book from Kant, and on the constructiveness of the human mind. But it is hopeless to attach so eclectic a writer to any school of thought. That is because our author never expounded his intuitions as a system. He never advanced any argument at all. He is so simple, and direct, so anxious to leave us to discover our own souls, that the reader does not always realise what he is expected to discover. He thinks that

[1] H. F. Lowry. *The Letters of Matthew Arnold* 1932. *Introductory II.*

he is being academically exercised in ethics or criticism, when he is invited to remodel his own life. Arnold wrote as a moralist but did not escape being taken for a critic.

His first attempt as a latter-day prophet is a striking example. He was elected Professor of Poetry 1857–67. At first his new duties rather worried him, and complaints were made that he did not lecture enough. But by 1859, under the pressure of this obligation, he had found, or thought that he had found, a way to catch the conscience of his contemporaries; and this avenue was nothing more promising than a course of lectures *On Translating Homer*.

His discourses interested his audience, especially the more youthful part, by his disrespect for authority, his witty and quite ruthless criticisms, the combination of a rather affected manner with an unaffected and colloquial style of address, and his air of starting the whole inquiry afresh. They have interested posterity because they are his first and most emphatic manifesto of "the grand style". This idea was derived possibly from Longinus, more probably from Goethe,[1] and Arnold had been familiar with it for years. He had aimed at cultivating it in his own verse—perfect plainness of speech allied to perfect nobility of thought—and since the age no longer gave the impulse towards preserving or recreating the tradition, he was now showing where it could be found. There is in Homer a spiritual dignity, an aspiration of soul, which makes itself felt across and above the superficialities of the narrative. Style is more than man, it is spirit. To help his audience yet further he gives some admirable illustrations chosen from Sophocles, Dante and Milton, as well as from Homer, and some even more admirable comparisons with those who miss the manner, such as Tennyson, Scott, Macaulay and the old balladists. There the lecturer leaves his audience, present and future. They are invited to cultivate the grand style in order to cultivate a nobleness of spirit. It is now known that the poets of the *Iliad* really were of the same race as the men they describe, perhaps a royal caste. It is remarkable that at a time when most students imagined Homer to be a noble barbarian with "the lively eye", or without any eyes, or a wandering minstrel of the Iron Age retelling the legends of the Age of Bronze, Arnold, by sheer literary tact, should have appreciated his nobility and high culture, so many years before Chadwick's *Heroic Age*.

So it is hardly too much to say that these lectures, by their wit and insistence, were intended to inaugurate a new phase of

[1] Eckermann, 3 May 1827. See *ante*, pp.174–5.

humanism: the recovery of spiritual qualities through literature. If there was one virtue more than another which according to Carlyle, Froude, Mill, Thackeray, Trollope and Meredith the Victorian lacked, it was the grand style in thought and conduct. Arnold, who began by talking about the technique of the translator, ends by showing his contemporaries where they can save their souls. As he wrote to Mrs Forster on 21 June 1865: "A nation is really civilised by acquiring the qualities it by nature is wanting in." It was a magnificent, if presumptuous gesture, and no one who goes to Homer with this expectation will be disappointed. Yet *On Translating Homer* has probably never exercised the influence which its author intended. The book attracted much attention and no little criticism, but as Arnold himself protested in his penetrating but not too tactful *Last Words*, criticism that was sectarian, pedantic, or personal. The volume has of course survived this buzz and babblement, in fact it has been eagerly studied ever since its publication, but too much as a manifesto of the author's critical position; as a means of classifying and labelling him in the academic portrait gallery. People appreciate that "the greatness of a poet lies in his powerful and beautiful application of ideas to life"; but they do not go to Homer to learn "how to live". The reason is partly that since Arnold's day a new and absorbing interest has arisen round these poems, with a romance and mystery of its own. Since Dr Schliemann began excavating the Acropolis of Mycenae in 1876 we have gradually become conscious of the vanished world of rising and falling dynasties, ancient races blending or extinguishing each other; strange legends and beliefs, cunning artists in gold and bronze as well as in poetry, long lost trade routes, and savage quarrels; a whole chapter of human history and evolution is being slowly and laboriously unrolled. So the students of archaeology rifle Homer for glimpses of these vanished ages; like a man searching his memory for hints of a forgotten dream. By now we can almost be sure that Agamemnon really besieged Troy in revenge for the rape of Helen, we can actually see the wall from which Apollo thrust Patroclus, and we can even guess at what spot Odysseus landed in Ithaca or Corfu. We no longer ask Homer for a commentary on our life, because he can tell us so much about his own. So the interpretation of Homer has passed from Arnold to Professor Bérard and Sir Arthur Evans.

Even those who care nothing for archaeology and folk-lore will find it difficult to bring the Homeric spirit into their conduct. He is so much a poet's poet. For that very reason he did not serve the purpose at which Arnold was beginning to aim. Our poet wanted to teach others his own practical philosophy by the means he was teaching himself. He was bent on inculcating intelligence more than exaltation, so he would be bound to search for authors who would help to solve Victorian problems. By 1863 he had made unmistakable progress. In that year he writes to his mother about "saying imperturbably what one thinks and making a good many people uncomfortable" (19 May). He reflects that "it is very animating to think that one at last has a chance of getting at the English public" (29 October). More significant still, he feels "an inward spring which seems more and more to gain strength, and to promise to resist outward shocks" (24 December). For all this time, since the publication of *On Translating Homer*, he was producing in various periodicals the essays which appeared in 1865 as *Essays in Criticism*.

Thoroughly to understand this volume, it must be remembered that it is published as the Englishman's guide out of his present difficulties. Yet although salvation is to come from literature, no essay is written directly on an English author, and though English prose and poetry are occasionally alluded to, quoted and even discussed in parenthesis, it is not the English literature of the nineteenth century. In fact Arnold, though so wide-awake, and so thoroughly in sympathy with the modern spirit, had always been rather distrustful of his elder contemporaries and immediate predecessors. By 1849 he described Carlyle to Clough as a "moral desperado". By 1852 his mind seems to be made up. Modern English poetry is weak because it imitates the Elizabethans; produces "exquisite bits and images...whereas modern poetry can only subsist by its *contents*: by becoming a complete *magister vitae* as the poetry of the ancients did".[1] On the other hand, our author is not looking for manuals of instruction on how to live; each man must make these out of his own head, following the tendency of his own nature. What he wants to instil is a point of view and method of thought—"sensitiveness of intellectual conscience, respect for right reasons, broad-mindedness of judgment, unfettered thinking". Wherever the reader can appreciate these qualities, however expressed and exemplified, in the subject-matter of his book, he is in contact with ideas in the Platonic sense; his own

[1] H. F. Lowry, *The Letters of Matthew Arnold to Arthur Hugh Clough*, No. 40.

mind moves freely; his own judgments are solid and secure. He can solve his social and moral problems.

So according to Arnold the most needful thing for modern Englishmen was to be neither modern nor English in their reading but, as he afterwards quoted from Georges Sand, "to be in sympathy, across time and space, with a multitude of honest wills which interrogate their own conscience and try to put themselves in accord with it".[1] It was best to consult continental writers, who had developed flexibility of intellect, and the insight of human sympathy. For instance, Maurice and Eugénie de Guérin reveal an intimate and confident insight into Nature, which no rationalism can destroy; and illustrate the possible grandeur of Catholicism, freed from the possible narrowness of the Protestant. Marcus Aurelius reveals the tranquillity which the most preoccupied business-man may enjoy if he copies the Roman emperor's example, and retires into his own soul. To appreciate the essay on Spinoza, it must be remembered that the consternation over Colenso and *Essays and Reviews*[2] was at its height and Arnold explains the doctrines of the great Dutch heretic to prove that a thinker can propound a system utterly untenable to the broadest intelligences of the present day, and yet retain the piety and earnestness which alone justify the treatment of such subjects. The most memorable is the essay on Heine. Arnold had first become acquainted with *Reisebilder*[3] in 1848 and had been disgusted with their blend of Byronism, mockery and gloom. Since then he realised that the German Jewish poet had the disinterestedness and human insight to understand why we persist in a system of institutions and dogmas, a legacy of the past, which by no means corresponds with the wants of our actual life, and for the modern world is "customary, not rational", and why so many people have allowed themselves to be one-sided, clinging exclusively to the Hellenic spirit of beauty or the Hebrew spirit of sublimity. He developed his idea in the lecture which he delivered at Oxford in February or March of 1864 and published next month in *The Cornhill* as *Pagan and Medieval Religious Sentiment*, contrasting the spiritual emotion of the hymns of St Francis with the idyll of Theocritus which describes a religious festival, yet expresses only the joy of life. His brilliant translation almost makes us forget his broad-minded tribute to the culture and universality of the Catholic Church, as

[1] *Mixed Essays.* [2] *Post*, pp. 218 ff.
[3] To his mother, 7 May.

also his glimpse of the age of Pericles when for once morality and intellect were harmonised into a strain of "imaginative reason", by which the modern world must live.

How was the world to be won to this way of thinking? That duty was explained in the last of this brilliant series: *The Function of Criticism at the Present Time*. Arnold insists that the critic is himself an artist and that his material happens to be that aspect of the spirit which is perceived through the medium of books.

All unconsciously Arnold was devoting his wit and learning to an effort in what his contemporary Herbert Spencer had recently termed *adaptation to environment*. The mid-Victorians (as everybody knows) had been born into a social and industrial order for which they were unprepared, and they seemed to have lost the power of adjustment which each generation hands on to the next, if the race is to survive—in this era a flexibility of mind rather than of body. Culture meant the survival of the intellectually fittest. Arnold was endeavouring to revive the disused qualities so that his generation could meet the exigencies which conditioned its existence. These diarists, saints, philosophers and poets must be read because they represent the stream of human thought flowing at its purest and clearest along the channels which lead to perfection.

But, of course, examples were not enough. This lucidity of spirit must also be the fruit of high motives and a firm purpose, and as the years advanced Arnold seems to have been more and more impressed with the importance of mental discipline. By the time we reach the year 1868, there are an especially large number of entries in his Note-book bearing on the duty of self-direction. One of the most memorable is "He that will not obey the laws of God must obey his own passions, which are the worst tyrants; he must obey the world, and the humours of others." More remarkable still are his quotations from medieval ascetics, for instance, "Quanto quisque plus sibi moritur, tanto magis Deo vivere incipit",[1] which he writes down twice. Obviously, he is not thinking of self-mortification, but of self-concentration in a higher will; of eliminating personal preferences (as Newman had taught), of acquiring that "power of self-management" which, as he told Miss Arnold in a letter dated 9 October 1870, was the hardest power in the world to acquire; "half the wasted lives one sees are due to the want of it". This consummation, as his poetry implies, can rarely be achieved by solitary self-study. It was society which had nearly always

[1] "The more each one dies to himself the more he begins to live to God."

imposed the most salutary restraints on the individual's personal bias. As he notes again in 1868: "L'œuvre de notre perfectionnement est une œuvre collective et éternelle", and "Les Grâces étaient chez les Grecs le symbole de cette harmonie sociale qu'établissent la bienveillance et la mutuelle sympathie."[1] Man becomes nearest to God through contact with his fellow-creatures.

All these entries made at this point of time are significant, because from the beginning of 1866 to the end of 1870 Arnold had been engaged on the two series of essays which appeared in book form as *Culture and Anarchy* in 1869 and *Friendship's Garland* in 1871. With his usual eye for conduct he had perceived that since the modern community necessarily controlled our thoughts and actions, it must also become the rallying point for the highest intelligence and worthiest instinct of the individual.

It is true that other influences helped to shape his mind. He had been sent abroad to report on continental popular education in 1859 for the Newcastle Committee and in 1865 for the Taunton Committee, and he had come back impressed not only with the need of secondary education, but with the need of raising the dull level of British society. He even feared that England might decline into a secondary power like Holland "for want of perceiving how the world is going and must go, and preparing herself accordingly".[2] These criticisms and forebodings colour *Friendship's Garland* with his inimitable cartoons and caricatures of British domestic administration and foreign policy (especially the Black Sea question) and colour *Culture and Anarchy* with delicious satires on middle-class self-importance and individualism, the disturbing insight into lower-class turbulence and the unforgettable classification of British society into barbarians, philistines and populace. But both these volumes and the *Mixed Essays* penetrate much more deeply into nineteenth-century culture.

His fundamental proposition is that culture can become perfect only in the perfect state. The individual must complete himself by helping others to be complete. This consummation was to be reached by the cult of charity, suppressing the lower instinct for competition, but much more by the practice of social, almost socialistic virtues, which refine our subtlest sensibilities and per-

---

[1] "The effort towards human perfection is collective and eternal—The Graces were to the Greeks the symbol of social harmony, founded on goodwill and mutual sympathy."

[2] To his mother from Zürich, 24 Oct. 1865. To Miss Arnold, Nov. 1865.

ceptions. In that sense the State became "the only appointed frame and prepared vessel for our best self".[1]

Thus Arnold had brought himself to believe (as Plato, Aristotle and Cicero taught) that the individual cannot attain to a complete selfhood, unless he has also attained to a complete nationhood. This conviction was another advance in his work of adaptation. Socialism was already in the air, partly thanks to the example set by Engels, Marx and Ruskin.[2] As early as 1853 Frederic Harrison, an ardent student of the classics and of history, just after taking his degree, notes in his Diary that the really honourable contest of numbers against property is just beginning and that the true appeal to the individual's responsibility is coming to light. In 1861 he notes that the literary classes are so enslaved by pedantry that the reformer must rely on work-people.[3] In 1867 he blames the author of *Essays in Criticism* for his academic aloofness.[4] Arnold must have felt the justice of that reproach. As early as 1852 he had confessed to Clough that the educated class did not deserve to be comfortable, since they did not try to reform the world but only to please it.[5] As late as 1868 he was making in his Note-book several entries from Bunsen on the duty and failure of scholars to devote their learning to the service of the masses. These circumstances must be borne in mind in order to understand Arnold's new position. *Culture and Anarchy* is his first direct contribution to social service, all the more noteworthy because it is not socialistic. Our author does not appeal (as other moralists were doing) to the Great Unwashed; he appeals to their unrepentant employers. Nor does he try to prove that the monied classes are mismanaging their business or their government, but that they have completely missed the classical idea of the perfect republic. He was trying to apply the hereditary spirit of man to the most despiritualised of modern problems.

His theories would probably have exercised more influence on his contemporaries and on subsequent generations if he had been content to argue more practically or more theoretically. He had come to value ideas only so far as they could be applied to life. But on the one hand he would no longer leave the applications to

---

[1] *Culture and Anarchy*, Conclusion.

[2] H. V. Routh, *Money, Manners and Morals*, 1935, chap. VII.

[3] *Autobiographical Memoirs*, vol. I, pp. 165, 248.

[4] *Culture; a Dialogue, Fortnightly*, Nov. 1867. Reprinted *The Choice of Books*, 1891.   [5] H. F. Lowry, *op. cit.* No. 39.

his readers. He directed their attention to the most conspicuous political disorders and religious quarrels including Edmond Beales's breaches of law and order and Murphy's anti-romanism, and he held the upper classes to be ultimately responsible for these pernicious vagaries. At the same time, he has no other more direct and active remedy to prescribe than a heightened interest in culture. One might almost accuse him of believing that the railings of Hyde Park will be safe as soon as we have all read Bishop Wilson. Besides, in order to reason his countrymen—however sweetly—out of their habits, he had to bring these errors home to their consciences, and so ended by involving himself in the necessity for establishing his general accusations. He became a prosecutor. Not content to remind his readers that the State had missed its function—no sensible man would disagree—he had to prove why that was so; why everybody was doing just what he liked instead of what was best for his fellow-citizens and consequently for himself. So he came to the conclusion that the source of England's anarchy and demoralisation is to be found in the way she worships God. The series of essays which begins as a treatise on the uses of government ends as an exposure of the abuses of religion.

One cannot help feeling that Arnold's motives were in some degree personal. When his *New Poems* appeared in 1866, Swinburne welcomed them in his usual enthusiastic way; that was enough; the guardians of orthodoxy, already suspicious of Arnold's liberalism, concluded that a publication enjoyed by a professed atheist must be an attack on religion, and issued their warnings. *The Contemporary Review* and *The Christian World* even accused him of disowning Christianity and propagating pantheism, and based their accusation on *Empedocles* and *Obermann Once More*. When such prejudices have been obtruded on an author's susceptibilities, he develops a keen eye for their influence elsewhere. So Arnold was not slow to discover that there was something in Puritanism uncongenial to expansiveness, progress and the free play of the best impulses and aspirations. He would find many sympathisers. One has only to read Mrs Oliphant's *Chronicles of Carlingford* or W. H. White's *Autobiography of Mark Rutherford* and *The Revolution in Tanner's Lane*. In *Culture and Anarchy* he does not make it his business to penetrate to the roots of the evil. He is more inclined to insist that the State should broaden and liberalise the Puritans by multiplying and sharing out the spiritual blessings of life, especially the perception of beauty hidden behind our daily experiences, and the confidence in man's innate power to rise above his animal self. So there arose his celebrated chapter IV on Hebraism and Hellenism, of which Heine had already suggested the idea.[1] The British religionist was unable to blend these two compensating streams of culture. He was not sufficiently humanised to pursue his own doctrine of spiritual perfection; he was not educated up to his own ideal. So Englishmen took refuge behind their dogmas and commandments (as Froude had already proclaimed),[2] refused the help of beauty, charm and kindliness and lapsed into spiritual defeatists. Having once believed themselves to be sinful, they really became so, as far as envy and uncharitableness are sins. Many entries in his Note-books bear witness to these impressions, especially "L'Absorption hiératique ou marchande amoindrit le rayonnement d'un peuple",[3] extracted from *Les Misérables* in 1863.

Arnold prided himself on his urbane persuasiveness, so it is rather amusing to watch him gently but firmly rasp the nation's religious susceptibilities, at a time when churchmen were still nervous about the aftermath of the Oxford Movement and the premonitions of *Essays and Reviews*. He had now gone too far to hang back. To pass strictures without substantiating them was to embroil the fray. If Arnold was to raise and spiritualise Puritanism he must convince Puritans of all that they missed. He must show them what their religion ought to be. So he was led quite logically, almost inevitably, to the next phase of his career.

It seemed to him to be quite the natural thing to do; he was but following in his father's footsteps. Dr Arnold had taught the older generation that the Bible contained all we need for our religion; his son was to teach their successors that it also contained the wisdom and aspiration which we expect from the greatest literature. Moreover, this seemed the moment to make the attempt. *Culture and Anarchy* had not only prepared his arguments but had prepared a public to receive them. On 5 December 1869 he tells his mother: "I think nearly all the new periodicals have something or other about me, which shows how much more what I write is coming into vogue." In 1870 the author was granted a D.C.L. In the same year, on the strength of his reputation, the Inland Revenue rated his book profits at £1000 a year.

[1] *Ante*, p. 197. [2] *Ante*, pp. 145–6; 150–1.
[3] "A nation absorbed in business or ecclesiasticism ceases to live by the light."

Thus, though already forty-eight years of age, there seemed to be many attractive reasons for devoting his later manhood to this new task of reforming the Reformation. But the most attractive reason was this: the task was not new. It was the consummation of his philosophy. Even as a young man he had displayed impatience with the traditions of the romantic movement, especially with its monistic doctrine that God, man and nature were all the same force; all different aspects of the one universal reality. As has been said, he was a dualist. Like Sophocles, he believed in "laws which in the highest empyrean had their birth, of which Heaven is the father alone".[1] Like Goethe, he believed in the "daemonic element which underlies and encompasses our life", though we can continually penetrate its encirclement and push our outposts into the darkness beyond.[2] In the next place, man himself was a dualism in that he had a higher controlling nature ("our best self") and a lower nature which must be controlled, and it was only by an effort of will and intelligence that he could achieve this merging of the human in the divine. So man must first find God and then school himself. Such a double task could be discharged only with the uttermost disinterestedness, perseverance, imagination and literary insight, and it was in the exercise of these qualities that culture was so indispensable. Both impulses came within the reach of our comprehension as the thirst for righteousness. The Bible pointed the way.

So Arnold achieved his sense of reality, of what Babbitt afterwards called "an ultimate datum of consciousness". He understood the meaning of life by recognising that, if left to ourselves, we are highly organised animals, but in contact with God (known to us as righteousness) our spiritual destiny is consummated. This philosophy would seem to be particularly helpful at that time. It saved the believer from the subjectivism of Kant, leading to unfaith; from pragmatism, which finds truth only in particular experiences; from positivism which denies the reality of truth altogether. These same ideas are now being canvassed in a philosophic spirit as part of the humanistic revival of the twentieth century. Arnold made them known without academic terms; he brought them within the comprehension of the ordinary reader, whose interests were Biblical, ritualistic, and to our mind hopelessly old-fashioned.

[1] *Oedipus Tyrannus*, ll. 863–71. See *Pagan and Medieval Religious Sentiment*.
[2] Letter, 3 March 1863.

But why go to so difficult a book, the cause or occasion of so many wars and schisms, when humanity can learn all it needs of the spirit from profane literature; from Sophocles as well as from Isaiah? Because the Bible had long ago forestalled the great pagans in the heart of the nation. For over two centuries it had been associated with the average Englishman's most serious thoughts and most earnest endeavours. Besides, the Bible and the Church were so intimate a part of British culture that they did not only influence the nation's piety but suffered from its perversions and perversities. They had become so much a part of the people's thoughts, that they served as pretext and justification for their animosity, baseness, and philistinism. The Englishman was generally faithful to his Bible, even in his faithlessness. Whoever wanted to reform the spirit of the age—so it seemed to Arnold— must approach the Englishman through this Book.

The prospect was not unpromising for the way had been to some extent prepared by *The Rise and Influence of Rationalism* (1865). In this history Lecky has asserted that "each dogma is the embodiment and inadequate expression of a moral truth, and is worthless except as it is vivified by that truth",[1] and had prophesied that the age would soon witness three transformations. The first is the gradual evanescence of doctrines which clash with our moral sense. The second is the decline of the influence of those ceremonies or purely speculative doctrines, which without being opposed to conscience are at least wholly above its sphere. The third is the substitution of the sense of right for the fear of punishment.[2] Arnold hoped to endow this practical wisdom with the aspiration and self-sacrifice of religion.

His thesis was quite simple. The religious sentiment springs from the inexhaustible resources of the human spirit, which the Infinite Being is always rousing and raising towards Itself. So our destiny on earth is to bind our fleshly impulses and egoistic wills to a Higher Will. So far he was only in accord with teachers as different as Coleridge and Newman. When he comes to tell his countrymen all that can be known about this Higher Will, he refers to its most inspired and humanistic·exponent. In the case of the English Church the profoundest light was also the established source and authority: St Paul and the Gospels. This interpretation was published in *The Cornhill Magazine*[3] and reprinted in book form as *Saint Paul and Protestantism* (1870).

[1] Chap. II.   [2] Chap. III.   [3] Oct., Nov. 1869; Feb. 1870.

His book is certainly an advance on the essays in which Carlyle and Froude were so vehemently protesting against the petrification of anglicanism, without showing how life can be restored to the dead formulae. But Arnold could not be at his best on such a theme, unless he were writing for those inclined to believe him. He could reason, exhort, and ridicule with delicious irony, but was not skilled at adducing proof, or at undermining the logic of his opponent; and this time he knew that he was not addressing an indulgent audience. The middle-class of the 'seventies did not like their morals to be discussed with the same freedom as their literary taste. So Arnold writes with less grace and unction. Thus, this fourth phase of his career has generally been regarded as a mistake. He seems, like many another, to have resigned art for propaganda. But such a misapplication—if so it be—should not blind us to the lucidity with which he exposes the claims of the spirit, nor to the precision and penetration of his definition of, for instance, God as "the stream of tendency by which all things seek to fulfil the law of their being", or of faith as "a power of holding fast to an unseen power of goodness" or of heretics as "separatists for the sake of opinions".

This freedom of discussion on the part of a clergyman's son and a public servant surely marks the consummation which Mill so devoutly wished, when writing *On Liberty*, and it brought with it the advantage which Mill foresaw. The more Arnold argued and refuted, the clearer his own ideas became, and the firmer his hold on what he considered to be the truth. He spent the next two or three years in reading reviews and refutations and in developing his own theory, and then in 1873 produced the most complete and on the whole convincing of his exhortations as *Literature and Dogma*. This book is the most satisfying of his treatises because it lives up to its title; it really does demonstrate the power of literature over dogma: how literature leads the humanist, without controversy or conflict of soul, to exercise his judgment on dogma, to strip off the luxuriances of rhetoric, or fairy-tales of sentiment, and to grasp the moral significance often hidden beneath archaisms and historical allusions. So the leading idea stands out clearly and we thereby discover that contrary to all appearance religion (as Sophocles has taught us) aims at conduct and *conduct is three-fourths of life*; that prayer (as Rousseau might have taught him) is an energy of aspiration towards the divine *Not Ourselves*, and of co-operation with it; and that the *secret* of Jesus, was that of Socrates in *The Phaedo*; self-examination, leading first to repentance and then to self-betterment. He admitted that the *Zeitgeist* (that convenient word which Carlyle used but Arnold made current) would for some time yet encourage agnosticism or conversion to Rome, but that the next age of enlightenment would recognise that the truth of the Bible is the truth of experience.

God and the Bible appeared in 1875[1] to develop and defend the position which he had taken up, and to insist that the truth of Christianity lay in its power of engaging "for the government of man's conduct, the mighty forces of love, reverence, gratitude, hope, pity and awe". He continued his advocacy in *Last Essays on Church and Religion* (1877) and in *Mixed Essays* (1879). Among these latter productions the most lucid and comprehensive is "Bishop Butler and the *Zeitgeist*". So we are again assured that the wisdom and piety of the ancient world will save modern Europe. Arnold is still persuading his contemporaries to use their reason, yet the result is not what he expected. One forgets his theories in his attacks. One feels especially that Tractarianism is in the background as one of the influences to be opposed. Yet Newman, as we have seen, was named with Wordsworth, Goethe and Sainte-Beuve as one of the four writers who had contributed to shape his mind, and assuredly Newman's spirit presides over this fourth phase of his career. Arnold has learnt from the great Churchman and apostate how to refute his teaching.

He resembles Newman in his recognition of the Church as a living, progressive organisation which should keep fast hold of the essential and elemental truth, and should yet move with the times and adapt itself to the advancing culture and intelligence of Christendom. He resembled Newman in that he abhorred the coldness and melancholy of Puritanism and admired and envied the universality of the Roman Catholic Church, its internal peace and union, the consequent freedom of its members to develop the joyousness of worship, or as he would put it, "its charm for the imagination—its poetry". He agreed with Newman that godliness was a supernatural force, borne in upon our souls by the intimations of our consciences. And finally, he agreed with Newman that religious insight was acquired only by those who read the Scriptures with sympathetic intelligence and imaginative thoughtfulness— with the quality which both agreed to call φρόνησις.

[1] Previously published as *Review of Objections to "Literature and Dogma"*, Oct., Nov. 1874; Jan., March, May, July, Sept. 1875.

But in Arnold's mind it was φρόνησις as exercised by Plato and Aristotle; that is, wisdom arising out of intelligence and disinterested curiosity; a habit of mind which recognises the truth only through consciousness that one's thought is accurate and impartial. Such a man has to reason with his own preconceptions and fallacies, but not with the authority of other saints and doctors; in fact, he recognises no other authority than his own powers of intuition and judgment.

Guided by this light, Arnold had produced a thinly veiled paganism which satisfied no one. Not the ritualists, because, like his father, he was ready to accept anybody's ritual, provided that the formula excluded sectarianism; not the practical moralists, because he talked much about righteousness, and defined it as "morality touched with emotion", but gave no inspiring idea of its quality, nor satisfied any open-minded reader that St Paul was the supreme type and practitioner of its virtues; still less did he satisfy the most modern freethinkers. They had indeed argued themselves out of anglicanism, but they had replaced its tenets by the doctrines of science and social philosophy, whereas Arnold clung to the older humanists. Though in touch with continental writers, he found the surest confirmation of his modernism in the classics and took his direction from them. Aristotle had taught that nature (φύσις) is matter struggling and growing into form. Each species partakes of the species beneath, but tends towards the species above; thus the vegetable soul rises out of the clod, the animal soul out of the vegetable, the human soul out of the animal, and God, or pure reason, out of the human soul. Plato had taught that we and our world seem to be imperfect because we are only imperfect copies of perfect patterns, schemes, and types—the divine projections of what experience ought to be—which exist in that other metaphysical world called ultimate reality, the dwelling-place of God. Plato termed these entities ideas and discussed how the human intelligence could encompass them. Arnold, either by an unmistakable stroke of originality, or by a very skilful adaptation of *Longinus on the Sublime*, perceived that we do encompass them, since we apply them to experience—in poetry. Poetic creativeness is the rereading and rearranging of experience by the light of the divine scheme, the imaginative fulfilment of God's will and of our salvation upon earth. The recognition of this significance involved the awakening of our best selves. Thus religion was poetry brought into conduct. When he at last took leave of religious controversy, he announced that he would devote the remainder of his life to literary criticism, "to a field where work of the most important kind has now to be done, though indirectly, for religion".[1]

So we come to his last phase about which there is little to be said, though some of the essays written during this period are those most often read and quoted. Perhaps the most remarkable is *The Study of Poetry*, published in 1880 as introduction to Ward's *The English Poets*, in which he returns to Goethe's suggestion of test passages.[2] Arnold had employed this method with effect in *On Translating Homer* to illustrate the grand style; he now employs it to show how the Platonic *idea* transforms the poet's impressions and ennobles the spirit in which he reproduces them; how his style introduces you into a perfect world, using the familiar, imperfect materials. His specimens have often been discussed as whetstones of taste and it is doubtful whether they serve any higher purpose. On the contrary they started a controversy on the range and function of poetry in which Swinburne, Alfred Austin, E. Gurney, Courthope and J. R. Lowell took part. All plead for the mystery and magic of poetry as against its moral significance, and deny the legitimacy of classifying poems. Arnold's own intention can, perhaps, be deduced from his advice to William Steward, the working man of Bedford, to whom he wrote on 8 May 1872: "And as to useful knowledge, a single line of poetry, working in the mind, may produce more thoughts and lead to more light, which is what man wants, than the fullest acquaintance (to take your own instance) with the processes of digestion."

So here we leave Matthew Arnold as we approached him, in a mood of uncertainty. He remains an enigmatical character. His career as a religious reformer is particularly unsatisfactory. He had certainly grasped a great idea of no small importance to the nineteenth century, if we may believe Heine. That physician of cultural maladies wrote in the winter of 1853–4[3] one of his finest prose passages, prophesying that a widespread knowledge of the Bible will destroy sectarianism and found the great spiritual kingdom of religious feeling, brotherly love, purity and true morality which can only be learnt by means of portraiture and illustration such as are found in Holy Writ. Arnold may well have read that passage and certainly gave effect to its spirit, and it looks as if his self-devotion has borne fruit since his death in 1882. The kingdom

[1] *Last Essays on Church and Religion*, Preface.
[2] Eckermann, *Goethes Gespräche*, 26 Feb. 1824.   [3] *Geständnisse*.

has to a certain degree been established. Among the faithful, dogmas and doctrines have lost their vital importance and piety generally means possession of "the mind of Christ". Among the unfaithful, respect for orthodoxy has certainly spread and for the morality of the New Testament. Among all classes there is less intolerance, and, as some think, an even excessive indulgence for human nature. However much nations may hate each other, individuals are more conscious of an international membership. Yet it is doubtful whether this revival of the human fraternity (according to some the true Kingdom of God on earth) is directly due to the older forces of culture. Nowadays even classical quotations are not understood; the greatest English literature seems to be read only for examinations; the Bible is certainly an unfamiliar book to the majority of educated Europeans. The change is probably due to science which induces even literary folk to start revaluing the prospects of life in a spirit of racial and cosmopolitan humility. But Arnold had no sympathy with the culture which will have to be elaborated from science. He professed a friendliness to this new comprehension and interpretation of the world. He even admitted that the study of literature embraced "the grand conclusions and main principles of science".[1] But, despite his assertions, he was thinking of science as understood by Goethe, not as understood by Darwin, Huxley, Haeckel or even Butler.

These reflections bring us back to the convictions which dominated his literary career, and which it has been the object of this chapter to estimate. What he really valued in culture was the opportunity to study his impressions till he knew himself. Only great literature seemed to give him this power, so he endowed it with all the virtues of all the studies. If his insistence now seems to be extravagant and eccentric, it is because he felt that he would otherwise lose his best self, overwhelmed by a world in which industrialism mechanised our actions, science our thoughts and sectarianism our spirits. Of these influences he confronted only sectarianism, which was, in any case, fighting a losing battle. He glanced sideways at science and industrialism. So it must be our next task to inquire why nineteenth-century civilisation created so unfriendly an atmosphere for nineteenth-century culture, thereby perhaps preparing the way for a twentieth-century philosophy and literature.[2]

[1] *Literature and Science* in *Discourses in America*.
[2] See also H. V. Routh, *Money, Manners and Morals*, 1935, chaps. XI–XIV.

CHAPTER XIV

How rationalism impinged on reason before Darwin had made his influence felt—The conflict and chaos of thought—Geology, biology, the christologists, *Essays and Reviews*, Colenso—The godlessness of society and the finite god—Spinoza *redivivus*, and Schopenhauer—The cult of the Classics and of Shakespeare.

We have discussed Newman, Tennyson, Browning, Carlyle, Froude, Ruskin and Matthew Arnold, seven of the most representative and influential writers of the nineteenth century, and we have found that they differed from the moralists of previous ages, in that they had no definite quarrel with human nature and destiny. On the contrary, they all started to write more or less under the inspiration of romantic philosophy and they all more or less added to this theoretical optimism a practical faith in our future possibilities, if only we could make the best use of nineteenth-century civilisation. Yet whether or not these seven authors retained their faith in *man*, each seems to have ended by despairing of *men*. Dickens, Thackeray, or Trollope would have given a similar impression. The early and mid-Victorian novelists have not been brought into the discussion because they offered no special guidance on the arts and duties of life. They wrote to please. But it is to be noticed that as often as they gave pleasure by depicting the good side of human nature, they kept very far from dwelling on features peculiar to the nineteenth century. All the great contemporaries of Queen Victoria seem to have quarrelled with the country which they claimed to love so well. Nor did they confine their criticisms to those who fell short of the modern standards; they all criticised the standards themselves; not only the actions of their contemporaries but their hearts and their heads.

They were the most candid of friends. In fact they were too candid; they were prejudiced against their own age. We are now at last sufficiently distant from the reign of Victoria to bring some kind of perspective into our view, and we can see that while the nineteenth century created many evils, as we know to our cost, it prevented as many other evils; achieved no mean victories over death, disease, pain, injustice, insecurity, and civic incompetence; it sustained a long and resourceful struggle against the consequences of over-population; it widened culture; it rendered our intellectual life a hundred times more varied and adventurous; it bequeathed powers which have enabled us to enlarge the conquest over space and time. All this has been achieved by the intellectual energy of the nineteenth century. Yet the most eloquent and humanised writers of that epoch speak of modern England about as bitterly as Juvenal and Tacitus speak of ancient Rome.

What was it that these humanists sought and could not find? An inward and unconquerable conviction, not only that the world was wrong, but that they had the wisdom and that therefore their followers would have the power to set it right. This is no question of literary self-confidence and aggressiveness, though both those qualities were needed and generally displayed in the nineteenth century. It is rather that the writer must have something within him which may have germinated as a thought but has expanded into an idea, an enthusiasm and a vision absorbing his whole personality—a pattern of reality which he holds within his head and re-shapes every day because it belongs to his imagination. This idea must give the individual a sense of permanence and continuity: it must be of such a kind that he can see the sources of his own intellectual and moral strength active in the great spirits which have preceded him, and can count on the continuance of that strength among those who come after. Otherwise he will not be convinced of its authority, nor feel himself authorised to give it effect.

It must be such that he cannot hold and appreciate its significance without distinguishing in himself as in everything else a lower and a higher, a retrograde and a progressive, and this higher and more progressive must not only be the offspring of an argument; otherwise the humanist will not serve it with his imagination and self-devotion as well as with his common sense. The writer must feel that his themes, that is to say, his allegiances, the convictions that he champions, his devotions, loves and idealisms, make him a better man. Not, of course, better in the narrow trivial sense of better-conducted, but brought nearer, more intimately assimilated, to some spirit of perfection, which somehow permeates one's best impulses and which one tries to bring within the comprehension of the intellect, whenever writing.

Thus, a great writer is much more than a man or woman with a talent for literary expressiveness, more even than the gifted interpreter of an artistic school. Such accomplishments were of course indispensable in order to command the attention and respect of the reading public, and, indeed, to give adequate expression to his thoughts. But the essence of his genius depended on his belief in himself, not as an infallible authority, but as an adventurer on the threshold of a more spiritually perfect existence, which could be shared by others. His mind was not only inspired by its own sense of power and freedom; it thrived on the vision of activities beyond its reach. Without this double sense of remoteness and reality no man can give his whole self to the quest, nor write with such confidence and common sympathy that his readers will spiritualise their own experiences with his dreams. The Victorians lacked this magic because they lacked confidence in their dream world.

For the purposes of this inquiry we need not stop to ask whether this inspiration is really an influence from God or only a kind of physical vitality, so immaterialised that it finds its proper scope in the superphysical, energising the intellect. But whatever the origin of literary genius, its possessor was then almost bound to believe it to be nourished on something greater and purer than his ordinary self. Therefore, in the past, great writers have generally associated their inspirations with the religious sentiment. The idea of God presented a kind of standardisation by which their ideals could be at once communicated and shared, a power so sublime and remote that it sanctioned an ambitious belief in one's own soul. Nor did that Godhead always remain hidden even from the most resigned deist. The Ruler of Creation had made His will and purpose known, at least to Englishmen, through the Bible, which could always be interpreted to illustrate what was most generous and disinterested in the man's or the nation's moral sense and religious instinct.

Thus the intellect was used to interpret spiritual experience and thereby to preserve the soul's heritage. Such had always been its way. Yet this pious office was now proving to be the death of true religion; without any violent reversal, simply by the law of cause and effect. Victorians used to talk airily about the ages of faith. There never were such ages, if faith implies the submission of the intellect. From the days of the Christian Fathers onward, every word of doctrine has always been subjected to a rigorous examination. In the later Middle Ages the divinity schools were debating societies. For at least a thousand years churchmen had tested their beliefs by the best knowledge and argumentative skill of their age, till this sacred duty had become a habit. But their conclusions had depended on the range of their learning and intellectual experience. For centuries these interests had extended no further than the transmission of authority and its interpretation. Such were the materials on which the reason could exercise itself. Gradually the materials became unmanageable. Newer and newer knowledge continued to fill the human mind, and, as before, the reason continued to draw on these acquisitions to illuminate faith. This stronger intenser light revealed crevices and flaws which no one would have guessed. Serious-minded men did not therefore abandon their spiritual ambitions, but abandoned confidence in the means of fulfilling them. So we have watched the great Victorians gradually loosen their hold on these treasures and on the genius which sprang from them.

The course of rationalism, materialism and even atheism has often been traced and there is no need to discuss their origin or advocacy in the eighteenth century. It is enough to remember that agnosticism and heterodoxy seem to address themselves to the reasoning faculty but do not usually prevail to any great extent unless they also capture the imagination and court the sentiments. For instance, Locke, Berkeley, Hume, d'Holbach and Helvetius asked their readers to suspend the awe and wonder which constitute half the nature of man. What was the result? They might attract specialists like themselves, but offered to the ordinary humanist nothing in exchange for his sacrifices but arguments much too difficult to be followed unwillingly. Fielding could go so far as to suggest that if a "philosopher" could find no divinity in the world, he must have looked for it in "the nastiest of all places, *a bad mind*".[1]

It was geology which turned the scale because this science satisfied the intellect without sacrificing the claims of the imagination. The study of the earth's surface was broached in the eighteenth century by Generelli (1749) and Nicolas Desmarest (1777), and especially James Hutton, whose *Theory of the Earth* (1785) called up a picture of the surface of the globe without beginning and without end, slowly changing from form to form till it had reached its present shape, only to change again. Yet this theory of natural and continuous transition, so prophetic of evolution but then called Uniformitarianism, only aroused the opposition of the experts and left the humanists cold. None of these pioneers could write so as to kindle the imagination and enlist the sympathies. So with G. P.

[1] *Tom Jones*, Bk VI, chap. I.

Scrope and von Hoff. On the other hand Cuvier far surpassed his contemporaries in influence and popularity. Like them, he was a "catastrophist" and a "neptunist" and argued that man was a recent creation, not more than five thousand or six thousand years old. But he also opened an endless world of imagination. Balzac styled him the greatest *romancier*[1] of the century.

So we come to Sir Charles Lyell. He studied the ways the sea altered the English coastline and the ways plant life with infinite slowness was depositing limestone identical to some of the earliest rocks. He demonstrated that the most ancient causes which shaped the globe were the same kind of causes which are active now. So he appealed to the imagination as well as to the instinct for logical induction. Besides, he was most anxious to avoid a direct attack on Mosaic geology; he sapped it by deductions and inferences. His *Principles of Geology* (1831–3) established the "metamorphic theory", that is to say, he taught that the whole surface of the earth was and always has been in a state of slow modification. Darwin declared that the book "altered the whole tone of one's mind".[2] Yet Lyell laid so little emphasis on his conclusions that the most rigid fundamentalist might read his pages without noticing any break in the continuity of culture.

Any humanist has the right to apply such a test. The mind is so constituted that it must engage all its resources before it can decide between right and wrong. We have in the last criterion only the sense that the proposition suits or does not suit the requirements of our mental being. It must suit our emotions and aspirations no less than our deductive and inductive faculties, for the spirit is known to us only as thought. So geology at this stage was not suffered to lead on to materialism, even though it led on to ideas on organic evolution.

In fact organic no less than inorganic evolution was already in the air. Buffon, Kant, Goethe, Lamarck and Linnaeus had already guessed that species are not immutable, that new forms of life are derived from those already existing. The idea so far fascinated Robert Chambers that in 1844 he published anonymously the celebrated *Vestiges*, which began with the nebular hypothesis of Kant and Laplace and then passed on to the origins of life and suggested that the whole living creation had begun in the simplest types and had gradually multiplied and diversified so as to

---

[1] *Peau de Chagrin*, 1831, chap. I.
[2] *More Letters of Charles Darwin*, vol. II, p. 117.

continue and prolong existence amid the changing environment. Again, it is most significant that while the experts condemned the book the general public, who ought to have been outraged, nevertheless read it as they read Lyell, for its vision.

Such were the scientific data which came within the range of the humanist before 1859. As far as we have gone, there was nothing to shake the Victorian faith in eternal verities. Geology and zoology were so many new horizons over which the mental vision might wander. Most of the scholars, humanists and leaders of thought knew of these hypotheses and conclusions only at second-hand. Nor need they do more. The discoveries of science partook of the fallibility of all human experiments. It did not shake one's innermost reliance on what was eternal and omnipotent. As Carlyle could say: "All that is good, generous, wise, right—whatever I deliberately and for-ever love in others and myself, who or what could by any possibility have given it to me but One who had it to give? This is not logic; this is axiom." Biology, zoology and especially geology, if known only by hearsay, ought to have widened the powers of imagination and thought; if studied at all closely they ought at this stage to entrust their adherents with a vast intellectual responsibility—the duty of eliminating from their thoughts all that was unworthy of their religion, because untrue.

But this severe application of the intellect, this disinterested investigation of the truth also played on the most interested of all propensities, the self-satisfaction of exercising one's reason. Nothing gives the complete man a more sustaining sense of his completeness. He was bound to avail himself of the facts and methods of this new learning, to make sure that the older more divine allegiances merited the high aspirations with which he bowed to them. This self-assertion would inevitably lead him to re-examine certain credentials of the Old and New Testaments. If they were worth believing they were worth examining with one's best intelligence. Nor would his loss be great; there was much folk-lore and mythology which might be sacrificed without sacrificing any beliefs essential to the old world superconsciousness.

But the situation became much more difficult when scientific habits and self-reliance induced earnest and inquiring minds to reconsider the New Testament. Disquieting rumours for the last two generations had been reaching them from Germany. Reimarus had interpreted the whole Bible narrative from Abraham to St Paul as so many examples of human depravity, error and disingenuousness. His assertions were far too strong to produce much effect. It was another matter when Schleiermacher explained Jesus to be only so far superhuman as representing the better side of human nature in its fullest perfection, and threw doubt on the authenticity of the first three Gospels because they lacked the inwardness and spiritual significance of St John's portrait. Schleiermacher, once the most confirmed of Platonists, marks the first stage. Henceforward Christians, who could not resist exercising their critical powers, were to be invited by a succession of German christologists to test the strength of their faith by examining the authority and authenticity of its founder. First of all the rationalists endeavoured to satisfy modern judiciality by explaining away the miraculous. For instance, that the Tree of Knowledge was forbidden because its fruit was really a poison; that Christ was believed to have risen from the dead because He had never really died, but was only unconscious when entombed. Then the historical critics began to question the records, which needed such far-fetched interpretations. It was contended that the Gospels were composed centuries after Christ's death, and reflected the atmosphere of a different age and culture, perhaps the conflict between Jewish and Pauline Christianity. The Fourth Gospel might have been written to prove that the *Logos* of Alexandrine theological philosophy had become flesh in Jesus. The so-called Synoptic Gospels (where if anywhere we must look for a reliable biography of Our Lord) were full of discrepancies, inaccuracies, and actual misstatements, often actual contradictions. In fact the New Testament narrative was invalidated by that most human of all failings, a bias for the controversies and prejudices of the time.

All this scepticism in 1835 came to a head in David Friedrich Strauss's *Das Leben Jesu*. Its author is one of the great figures of the nineteenth century. As a young man he entered the ministry; as soon as his intellect matured he became an apostate, and throughout his career was sufficiently in earnest to taste something of modern martyrdom. Strauss did not deny the existence of Jesus. There was such a prophet—not a doubt of it—and He gave His life for His ministry. But the record of His life and teaching apparently died with Him. What we have received through the New Testament is the Jewish dream of a national hero, the allegories of a man-god fulfilling the Law and the Prophets, a theological romance, which satisfied the persecuted nation's yearning for continuity; a beautiful story no doubt, and full of moral edification but not the authentic word of God. Its message was only the aspiration of an antiquated and despised race. The book seems to have aroused great interest in England, even before it was translated. A Unitarian minister summarised the arguments in a course of lectures which completely convinced A. R. Wallace before he was twenty-one years old.[1] When rendered into English by George Eliot in 1841, the *Life* became a best seller and continued to be read and discussed during the 'forties.

Having thus robbed the Bible of its glamour and authority, and having persuaded his contemporaries to choose their own morality, Strauss returned in later life to teach the younger generation what to choose in *Der alte und der neue Glaube* (1872). He was then under the influence of Darwin and insisted more than ever on the essential monism of human nature, and explained that consciousness of self at its best is consciousness of God,[2] that religion was true for mankind only so long as culture subsisted on the imagination and not on the reason.[3] In the meantime Ludwig Feuerbach, who sacrificed the world in order not to follow Christ, had eventually the good luck to marry a rich wife, retired into the country and taught by the light of science that religion was a day-dream, a poem of what human nature desired. So his contemporaries learnt one more lesson in intellectual self-reliance, and lost one more escape into ideals which might become real.[4]

Renan was perhaps the last who contributed directly or indirectly to create a new mood in English culture. S. Laing in his once widely read *Modern Science and Modern Thought* (1885) ranks the author of *Vie de Jésus* with George Eliot and Carlyle as one of the three best examples of modern liberalism. The turning point[5] in Renan's career was the conviction formed in 1846 that there exists in the universe no intelligent will-power higher than man's, and the rest of his long life was largely devoted to consolidating that position. With this object he subjected Christianity to the sovereign judgment of human reason, beginning with the career of its founder. His *Vie de Jésus* was received with grave displeasure

---

[1] A. R. Wallace, *My Life. A Record of Events and Opinions*, 1905, chap. xv.

[2] *Das höhere Selbstbewusstsein ist das Gottesbewusstsein*, § 17.

[3] *Der alte und der neue Glaube*, § 43.

[4] *Das Wesen der Religion*, 1845. *Gottheit, Freiheit und Unsterblichkeit vom Standpunkte der Anthropologie*, 1866.

[5] *Souvenirs d'Enfance et de Jeunesse*, chap. VI, § II. See ante, pp. 66–7.

by the experts. A. Schweitzer[1] condemned it as an "erotic romance" because, Frenchman-like, he dwelt on the sentiments which some women may have brought into the life of the Messiah. Nevertheless, his book inaugurated or illustrated a redirection of rationalism. He did not explain Jesus away. On the contrary he maintained that whoever could saturate himself with the atmosphere and environment of New Testament history, could familiarise himself with the cults, customs and creeds of the people, could keep before his eyes the landscapes of Palestine and feel the warmth of its sun, such a realist would master his subject and be able to see that mysterious figure as he really was; his genius, his personal magnetism, his immense self-sacrifice and his fallible humanity. He would be able to appreciate everything, even the agony in the garden, and he would come to the conclusion that as Jesus was a man, the charm and heroism of His career can be equalled if not surpassed by other men.

The teaching of the christologists might have become a genuine inspiration in the modernising world. The humanisation of Christ gave ample scope to the most exacting intellect and, when once the myths and miracles had been eliminated, the imagination was left free to appreciate the moral tone in all its vivid lights. Even Renan speaks of his *goût vif pour l'idéal évangélique*.[2] The idea easily survived Darwinism and has persisted to the present day as a resource for moralists who have a sense for history and a talent for characterisation. Interpretative and untheological lives of Jesus have become almost a literary type. As we shall see later, George Moore's *Brook Kerith* was a conspicuous example. So England has learned much from christology and yet has contributed little towards its advance. This is partly because the holy vessels were too sacred to be touched, and partly because they were not worth touching. In this country the gulf between theological and secular thought was becoming too wide to be bridged.

To understand this tone and temper we must consider two other publications which created no small stir by the way. In the early 'sixties everybody was talking about *Essays and Reviews* and *The Pentateuch and Book of Joshua critically examined by the Right Rev. J. W. Colenso*. The excitement was intense because even if religious thinkers were averse to Christology, they were taking German theology seriously, as we see from the translations published in *Clark's Theological Library*. Even the more daring and unrecon-

[1] *Von Reimarus zu Wrede*, 1906.   [2] *Souvenirs*, chap. v, § v.

cilable, for instance, De Wette and Ewald, were being read and discussed. Thanks to their influence a group of scholars, including Jowett, Temple and Mark Pattison, published in 1860 *Essays and Reviews* which discussed problems of doctrine and of hagiography in a reverent but acutely critical spirit. Even philology and palaeography were enlisted to complete the triumph of scholarship over tradition. *The Quarterly* went so far as to declare that "the whole apparatus is drawn bodily from the German Rationalists".

The Pentateuch critically examined is in a sense much more interesting. It was partly inspired by *Essays and Reviews*, and the author was versed in German scholarship and had carefully compared his conclusions with Bleck and Kuenen. But the book does not only represent the difficulties of trained reasoners. It represents the difficulties of half-civilised heathens who approached the Old Testament with no other prepossessions than a natural sense of justice and fitness and a willingness to be converted to Christianity. Colenso was a missionary bishop to the newly settled colony of Natal and the first critics to shake his faith in the infallibility of the Bible were the intelligent Zulus who asked searching questions about the improbabilities of Genesis and the inhumanities of Deuteronomy. The scientific theologians confirmed these doubts. So the bishop set himself in five volumes, issued serially from 1862 to 1879, to expose the inconsistencies, anachronisms, errors, in fact the very human failings of the first six books of Holy Writ. "I cannot, as a true man, consent any longer to shut my eyes to the absolute, palpable, self-contradictions of the narrative."

Both publications appeared subsequent to *The Origin of Species* (1859), but though Baden Powell in *On the Study and Evidences of Christianity* alludes to Darwin, while refuting miracles, both works are pre-Darwinian in the sense that they would have been just the same if Darwin had died of the fever which nearly prevented him from embarking on the *Beagle*.

The reception accorded to these works reveals the transition through which England was passing. For instance, Dr Moberly in *Some Remarks on Essays and Reviews* admitted that "those who have the means of knowing, must not be content with a religion on sufferance". In *Aids to Faith*, a collaboration issued in answer to *Essays*, Professor Mansel declared that the controversialists must be prepared, if necessary, "to sacrifice our most valued convictions at the demand of Truth". Others, amongst them the Rev. Prebendary Cook and Dr Davidson, were prepared in a reverent but uncompromising spirit to face the consequences of research. In fact after reading their utterances one can see no reason why earnest men should not "try the spirits, whether they are of God" and "prove all things, and hold fast that which is good". Here were two works quite in sympathy with the spirit of the Christologists; surely they would not only reconcile religion to reason, but also make it part of our intellectual and moral habits.

Despite this free atmosphere *Essays* and *The Pentateuch* aroused the bitterest opposition. Baden Powell died soon after the publication of the former, but the editor (H. B. Wilson) and R. Williams were condemned for heresy in 1862 by the Court of Arches. It was proposed at Oxford to deprive Jowett of his fellowship and Dr Temple of his headmastership. Arnold himself admitted that "certainly the wine of the Essays is rather new and fermenting for the old bottles of anglicanism". Still, these contributors were too highly placed to be easily overthrown; it was otherwise with Colenso, a mere colonial bishop, before the days of fashionable imperialism. He was condemned by the Synod of South Africa, excommunicated by Bishop Gray of Cape Town, and when he appealed to the English Church, he was cited before the Ecclesiastical Court for heresy. Are we to believe that such animosity arose solely from men who always had to be professionally in the right, and who, in any case, could hardly renounce doctrines from which, since early manhood, they had derived an income and a sense of importance? Much of the controversy was due to the fear that holiness could not survive secularisation. The Rev. H. J. Rose has perhaps supplied the best explanation. "We must never forget the difference between the German and the English mind. The paradise of the German appears to consist in unlimited license of speculation, while the practical element is the prevailing characteristic of the English. And thus it often happens that a German will not cast off a certain phase of faith, when he has demolished every ground, which an Englishman would deem a rational and logical foundation for holding it."[1] Many of Colenso's contemporaries (as he himself declares) held to their extravagant creed, because this ancient literature, which they could not interpret and dare not rationalise, for that reason supplied the mystic intimation by which they could feel that they were something more than mortals bound to earth. So to some believers the sacred vessels were too sacredly fragile to be touched.

[1] *Replies to Essays and Reviews*, p. 65.

For some others, the vessels were too sacredly remote and exotic to be of moral significance. Since if God was misrepresented by fallible hagiographers, it soon appeared that He was utterly obliterated by the civilisation of the nineteenth century. Renan might claim that he had always found "une bonté extrême dans la nature et dans la société" and might trust in "l'effort inconscient vers le bon et le vrai", but then Renan also confessed that he was a recluse who lived to think, and in quitting the Séminaire of St Sulpice had only exchanged the spiritual for the ideal. Colenso himself might assert: "Our belief in the Living God remains as sure as ever, though not the Pentateuch only, but the whole Bible were removed. It is written on our hearts by God's own Finger, as surely as by the Apostle in the Bible that 'GOD IS, and is a rewarder of them that diligently seek Him'." But Colenso had once been a poor Cornish boy who spent his early manhood at Cambridge and a country vicarage, absorbed in theology and mathematics, till he devoted his life to missionising South Africa. The majority of thoughtful Englishmen were, as the Rev. H. J. Rose had explained, more practical. They had long ago sloughed any touch of German *Schwärmerei*, which had clung to their more romantic fathers and they turned to experience to test and confirm the aspirations and convictions which were believed to raise man to be "a little lower than the angels".

The verdict of experience was not reassuring. As we have seen, the findings of biology and zoology contributed to their disillusionment and political economists had already made it plain that the Deity was not to be found in the tendencies of society. The classic period of this science begins with Adam Smith's *Wealth of Nations* in 1776 and ends with J. S. Mill's *Principles of Political Economy* (1848), or with J. E. Cairnes's *The Character and Logical Method of Political Economy* (1857), and it is most instructive to watch the faith in a beneficent Providence gradually fade away till even the belief in a directing Intelligence disappears. In fact it is discovered that individuals are no longer free to choose the way which they feel to be right. For instance, according to Malthus the poor will always continue to multiply and compete against each other for employment, thus reducing wages to the starvation limit, and according to Smith, the rich will always continue selfishly to seek their own advantage, for by denying themselves they can do no good to their fellow-creatures. "Enlightened self-interest" was the one secret of progress. Society, sinewed by industrial wealth, had acquired an impersonal will of its own, neither human nor divine, but metallic; as unspiritual as the new machinery which was actuating its progress. Carlyle, Froude, and Ruskin might protest, but the mathematically minded philosophers were not easily refuted. In fact Harriet Martineau and Henry Atkinson were emboldened to publish *Letters on the Laws of Man's Social Nature and Development* (1851), which reduced man's self-determination to the control of his body and God's influence to nothing at all.

While some confessed that the Will of God was not to be traced among the ways of man, others hoped that it need not always be so. The rationalisation of the New Testament might have dimmed the old ideologies, but it had thereby shown what could be achieved by earthly means. If the world was bad Jesus knew how to make it better. If His nature was human, His insight was divine. Historians like Seeley had explained the project as it might fit modern European conditions and even in this eleventh hour, practical idealists, of the school of Charles Kingsley and F. D. Maurice, might learn from the Master and from His interpreter how to create something like the Kingdom of God upon earth. If so, Miss Martineau and H. Atkinson were assuredly wrong: we could each within our own small circle, adjust our conduct to the Will of Jesus. At first sight there would appear much to encourage this aspiration. The Age of Victoria was an age of hopeful reform. An outwardly religious and inwardly humanitarian middle-class was successfully challenging the power of the nobles and of the squirearchy, and this pre-eminence had accrued to them (as they thought) by a divine right, more blessed than that once granted to kings. They had only to point to all that democracy had achieved and that the oligarchies had mismanaged, and it was not without good reason that Victorian thinkers placed so much importance on legislation and the extension of the franchise.

But those whose insight was sharpened by the wisdom and morality of the New Testament found little cause for self-congratulation. Democratic progress was vitiated by a taint which precluded any future realisation of Christ's ideals. The triumphs of the middle-class were not due to disinterested humanitarianism, nor to the statesmanship of this or that political leader, nor even to the skilful tactics of this or that election, but to certain social and economic forces (quite unchristian) which had been applied to self-aggrandisement. It was the will of the people which (despite appearances) was bad. The power of the new governing class was founded on its ability to invest capital, and this money had arisen out of the economic necessity of the millions beneath them. The commercial and professional classes had won freedom by enslaving the masses and, in effecting this mastery, they had unavoidably made over their power to their slaves. A civilisation founded on factories and warehouses is in the hands of those who work them. Thus any business man with humanitarian instincts could not help confessing that the welfare of his own class—at that time most would add of England—depended on the degradation of the majority; any humanitarian with business instincts could not help confessing that only ignorance prevented the majority from realising how much it had lost and might so easily regain.

All these considerations did not lead men to despair of themselves; the test of self-reliance was to come later when they had digested Darwinism; but in the 'fifties and 'sixties they were learning to despair of God. The divine influence might rule their hearts, but could not rule the world outside. Man could see further than God could effect. So the nineteenth century which was witnessing the revival of so many other creeds, revived also the idea of the Finite God. To give only three instances, Ruskin, writing in 1860,[1] represents the creed of the average Englishman to be: "There *is* a Supreme Ruler, no question of it, only He cannot rule. His orders won't work. He will be quite satisfied with euphonious and respectful repetition of them." In 1864, Newman confessed: "I can only answer that either there is no Creator, or this living society of men is in a true sense discarded from His presence...*if* there be a God, *since* there is a God, the human race is implicated in some terrible aboriginal calamity. It is out of joint with the purposes of its Creator."[2] About the same time Mill was working intermittently at his *Theism* and came to the conclusion that if there was an author of the Cosmos he "worked under limitations; that he was obliged to adapt himself to conditions independent of his will, and to attain his ends by such arrangements as those conditions admitted of".[3]

It is worth remembering that the idea of the Finite God was no creation of the nineteenth century. In the ages of polytheism such appears to have been the most natural way of facing life. Monotheism, of course, opened men's minds to a much nobler and more

[1] *Modern Painters*, vol. v, Pt IX, chap. XII, paras. 5–9.
[2] *Apologia*, chap. v.
[3] Pt II, "Attributes", 1873 (posthumous).

transcendental conception, and at the dawn of the nineteenth century one would have expected the battle to be won. As we have seen,[1] German philosophers taught us to recognise God in our hearts by a kind of inspired sympathy, almost an identification, which transformed experience or transcended it. George Eliot in 1843 "considered herself a revelation of the mind of the Deity".[2] These speculations were too romantic for many thinkers and quite incomprehensible to the unthinking, and besides the horrors of the Napoleonic wars followed by the other horrors of expanding industrialism reawoke or encouraged the old lingering doubts, especially among the victims. A. R. Wallace, then a youth struggling to make his way in this competitive civilisation, recounts how he and his young friends at the "Hall of Science" in Tottenham Court Road, used to discuss not only the plans of Robert Owen but such dilemmas as "Is God able to prevent evil, but not willing? Then He is not benevolent. Is He willing but not able? Then He is not omnipotent. Is He both able and willing? Whence then is evil?" After reading R. D. Owen's tract on consistency, they came to the conclusion "that the orthodox religion of the day was degrading and hideous".[3] These were poor folk who read such books as Paine's *Rights of Man* and *Age of Reason*. What they and their more fortunate brethren alike needed was a religion sufficiently congenial to the imagination and to the reason to reawaken the will to believe. That religion was offered in endless variety during the first half of the nineteenth century. There was something for everyone's temperament and intelligence from Newman's catholicism to Browning's humanism. Yet the idea of the Finite God persisted and spread. Tennyson could not altogether escape its influence, and, before Tennyson was dead, Thomas Hardy was writing or meditating such poems as *God's Funeral* and *God-Forgotten*.

We have seen what reasons a doubter had to confirm his doubts, but we have yet to see why he was inclined to accept them and why future generations will probably think as he did. The mid-Victorian could have found just as many arguments for the opposite conclusion, except that his generation had acquired a new habit of mind. They believed that God had failed them because they felt as if they themselves were gods. We have already noticed this

[1] *Ante*, chap. II.
[2] John Cash, *Reminiscences*. See J. W. Cross, *G. Eliot's Life and Letters*, vol. I, Appendix.
[3] A. R. Wallace, *My Life*, 1905, chap. VI.

spirit of self-reliance and self-wonder which sprang up in Froude's youth and complicated his own attitude to life,[1] and it might be added that in 1853 Goncourt recorded: "Gavarni me dit aujourd'-hui 'chaque jour la science mange du Dieu...n'a-t-on déjà pas mis la foudre du vieux Jupiter en bouteille de Leyde?'"[2] Such notes of wonder and pride refer only to unspiritual achievements, but they also mean that the more man doubted of God's miracles, the more he believed in his own.

He believed in his own miracles, because they enlarged his vision of what he might and must go on to achieve. The wonders of the nineteenth century, for instance the steam-engine, steam-boat, telegraph, gas, photography, chloroform, are the kind of inventions which do not let the mind rest. The knowledge which had made them possible had also demonstrated that they were only the beginning of progress, for science cannot satisfy one old wish without creating ten new ones. Even before Butler wrote *Darwin among the Machines* (1863), it was realised that machinery has a life and growth of its own. For instance, Tennyson had hardly accustomed himself to railway trains before he began to think of flying.[3] This knowledge was entirely man-made. Bishop Colenso of all people might plead that "God had given us the light of modern science",[4] but it had not been given through the sacred books, and was often condemned by the god-fearing; not without some show of reason, since every triumph over space and time could be represented as a triumph over the heavenly dispensation. Sturmius affirmed that no man after studying the human eye could persist in atheism, and Paley agreed.[5] Yet Helmholtz a century later declared that the human eye was an instrument such as any scientific optician would be ashamed to make.[6] Divine discontent was leading to discontent with what was divine.

But it is the verdict of literature that men do not often succeed in worshipping man. It is so difficult to unify one's impressions of oneself unless they are reflected in some grand and mysterious idea, high above our fallible nature, worthy of our reverence and

[1] *Ante*, pp. 142–3.
[2] *Journal*, 1ère série, 1er vol. ["Every day science takes a bite out of God... has not the lightning of old Jupiter been put into a Leyden jar?"]
[3] *Locksley Hall*.
[4] *Pentateuch and Book of Joshua*, Pt II, Preface.
[5] *Natural Theology*, chap. III.
[6] *Popular Lectures*, 1893, vol. I (see J. Ward, *Naturalism and Agnosticism*, 1899, Introduction).

allegiance. Even if the inquirer pictures himself, in Emerson's phrase, as "a faggot of thunderbolts", he will need a Jupiter to show him how to use them. It is quite possible to glory in the collective achievements of man, and yet despair of one's spiritual integrity amongst these conflicting pursuits. Kant and Goethe had offered a solution. Each in his own way had insisted that man imposes his personality on experience—describes, interprets, adapts his circumstances according to his inner light and formative power.[1] But how was their advice to be followed without reliance on something more comprehensive and enlightening than one's own distrusted self? You had only to look on mid-century life to feel that your fellow-creatures, like yourself, had lost spiritual self-control and self-determination amid this babblement of doctrines and plethora of material powers.

As the philosophy of the romantic movement was proving inadequate, thoughtful observers, dissatisfied with deism and theism, were beginning to revive the teaching of Spinoza, who died in 1677. Several translations of his works had been produced before the end of the seventeenth century, and he had been studied and quoted by Goethe and Coleridge. On the other hand, he had been disparaged by Voltaire and Bayle, and effaced by Kant; nor was his pantheism congenial to the religious revival of the early Victorian era. So, by the law of reaction, an inquisitive and disquisitive age was ripe for his influence. Not without good reason, for Spinoza promised to reconcile the new to the old. He lived for the freedom of thought; he underwent excommunication rather than consent to what the reason denied. He discarded the inconsistencies and improbabilities of the Bible as effectively as did Colenso; he insisted that without understanding our place in the scheme of the universe, without exercising to the full our capacity for analysis and inquiry, we could not live rightly, could not be ethical. Yet he did not lead one to think of a world without hope, without God, but of a world, if anything, too full of God.

In a pious frame of mind he set himself to think out phenomena, to estimate the moral value of experience. He found that we explain an object by explaining its causes; that is to say, we understand a thing as much as we understand how it originated from something else. So he worked backwards, till he found an essence or energy which was self-sufficient, which could not have been created out of pre-existing material. This was God; the something

---

[1] *Ante*, chap. II.

out of which everything else proceeds. God is everywhere, the permeating energy of all substance and thought, and therefore all we think, see, feel or hear is really in its essence a part of God; phenomena are neither past, present or future but an illustration of the eternal mind and therefore to be contemplated *sub aliqua specie aeternitatis*. So we should view all life, including ourselves. We are all offshoots of the creative energy called God; God is *natura naturans*, nature understood as a creative force; we are *natura naturata*, a part of nature, as far as it has realised the plan.

Once this relationship with creation (or nature) is realised, we understand how to live in the purpose of God. It is by being ourselves, by freely developing the divine impulse. We fulfil the nature of God in fulfilling ourselves. Peter must always be Peter, he cannot become Paul. Then there is neither Evil nor Good, but only self-fulfilment? Yes, there is evil, or at least decline and degradation, for life ought to be a spiritual effort towards accomplishing this Divine Tendency. Every failure is a relapse into incompleteness. We feel joy when we achieve divinity on a higher plane, sorrow when our achievement falls to a lower plane.[1]

There is much of nineteenth-century thought in these doctrines. One recalls Carlyle, Tennyson, and especially Browning. One even catches glimpses of evolution viewed as ethics, and it must be viewed as such in the end. This idea of human life as a *conatus*, as an effort towards self-fulfilment, was vital to the age. There is in it something of Goethe's and Arnold's guesses at "the Spirit of the World" which realises some purpose of its own in each one of us. There is much of Arnold's prose and something of all great poetry in this doctrine of ideas, of seeing everything as outlined in the Divine Mind, *sub specie aeternitatis*, and of thus being raised to the vision of reality and to the joy of realising the vision. At the same time Spinoza had an almost nineteenth-century distrust in the reliability of our perceptions. He had reduced our sensuous consciousness of reality to our consciousness of matter. His epistemology suited the suspicions of modern science. Haeckel, the monist and materialist, could accept the doctrine and reconcile it to his theory of hyloism.[2] Yet Spinoza insisted on the omnipresence of God. His watchword *Deus sive Natura* admitted of natural

---

[1] "Ipsa hominis essentia est conatus quo unusquisque suum esse conservare conatur.... Felicitas in eo consistit quod homo suum esse conservare potest.... Tristitia est hominis transitio ad minorem perfectionem."

[2] *Lebenswunder*, Kaps. IV, XIX. See *post*, chap. XVIII.

philosophy yet proclaimed a pantheism in some respects congenial to nineteenth-century hopes and ideals. George Eliot read him eagerly and declared that he reminded her of a recluse "who says from his own soul what all the world is saying by rote".[1]

Yet George Eliot was mistaken. Spinoza was worth discussing in these pages because certain elements in his thought supplied a modern need, but he is more worth while because in other respects he left the age unsatisfied. All the world was not repeating his theories by rote. Froude complained (as would Carlyle) that his teaching savoured of the metaphysicians, "a class of thinkers, happily, which is rapidly diminishing".[2] Matthew Arnold disapproved for the same reason: Spinoza's philosophy was monistic. Both these humanists, like so many other Victorians, wanted to retain the inwardness and vision of older times and yet cultivate a religion which preferred conduct to contemplation.

Those who discarded Spinoza together with Anglicanism, Romanism, dissent, the comtists and the utilitarians, had no alternative but the pessimism of the spiritually unsatisfied. This attitude must have been prophetic of the future, for we have been fighting against it ever since. Once again we shall find the commentary in a philosophical system[3] which was attracting much attention, for the problem had been faced by Schopenhauer.

Schopenhauer (1788–1860) was the disciple, and, as he thought, the corrector of Kant. He realised as well as any eighteenth-century philosopher that experience is only appearance; that we cannot rely on the evidence of our senses. On the other hand he understood that the mind is not merely a mirror which reflects the outside world according to its many-sided facets. The mind is a creative force which shapes all objects, in fact, almost models them according to its own capacities and capabilities. For that very reason the mind can never find the truth about objective things; the mind makes them all subjective; turns them into expressions of itself. Thus, the only reality within the range of human thought was subjectivity. The mind could acquire some inkling of its own processes, of the formative influence which refashions all external things according to its own light. What do we find when we seek by devious ways to be conscious of our own creative impulses? We feel a straining towards a result. In other words, the fundamental

[1] To C. Bray, 4 Dec. 1849. [2] *Spinoza, Westminster Review*, 1854.
[3] *Die Welt als Wille und Vorstellung* (1819) (The World as Will and Appearance).

reality of which we can become conscious is will. Each thing, living or dead, has a tendency towards realising its quality. Such is the only objective reality of which we can become conscious, since it also partakes of our subjectivity. So we can be sure of this much: that we go through life struggling to fulfil ourselves, to realise our essential qualities. Art supplies the only satisfying insight into this reality, especially music.[1]

Thus Schopenhauer, no less than Spinoza, illustrates the difficulties of the time. The Dutch Jew taught that man should live for his own spiritual betterment, and that this end was achieved by a pious lucidity of thought—the subordination of one's whole distracted passion-ridden self to clear-headed collaboration with God's purposes, the redirection and concentration of one's whole life on an intellectual plane. It would seem to be the one cure for us moderns. But Schopenhauer shows that some such ideal could not fulfil itself under our conditions. He is not attacking Spinoza, he is not even thinking of him. He is looking for a similar solution with a nineteenth-century habit of mind and he finds, indeed, the influence of a plan, a will, an urge, but it is not of God; we are each one of us minute atoms flowing in a vast stream; but it is not a stream-like God. We are each our own will, fulfilling our own purposes, because we cannot help doing so, thereby creating endless friction, antagonism and mutual destruction. Every effort of volition is provoked by opposition, so the essence of life is conflict. Our only escape from this destiny is either the disinterestedness of pure contemplation, or the renunciation which the medieval Saint practised. Such (some might comment) are the consequences of verifying ancient, especially Oriental, culture by modern thought.

At first one is surprised that Schopenhauer was ever known in our practical progressive country, or indeed was ever recognised in his own. Nor was he in the prime of his manhood, when *Wille und Vorstellung* was published in 1819. Hegel's influence was still supreme. It was only after 1851, when *Parerga und Paralipomena* was interesting the younger generation, that Germans began to find something sympathetic in his pessimism. So much so, that F. Paulsen in 1900 could group the philosopher with Hamlet and Mephistopheles as one of three figureheads in the natural history of pessimism. England followed Germany as soon as she had caught the mood. In 1875 Miss H. Zimmern published *Arthur Schopenhauer his Life and his Philosophy*, and in January 1876 the

[1] *Op. cit.* Bd. III.

Westminster Review examined the philosophy of his disciple K. R. E. von Hartmann. Then in 1877 J. Sully produced *Pessimism: a History and a Criticism*, arguing that Schopenhauer's theory was no logical development of European thought, but satisfied an emotional want. But R. B. Haldane and J. Kemp produced their translation *The World as Will and Idea* in 1883; all through the 'eighties T. B. Saunders translated excerpts and selections from *Parerga*; by 1903 G. B. Shaw in *Man and Superman* speaks of the philosopher as a cult. The Schopenhauer spirit was, indeed, abroad from the 'seventies onward. In fact the German becomes not so much an influence as a figurehead and epitome of what the *fin de siècle* was experiencing. Some who had never read him were in sympathy with his tenets. It is surprising how many aesthetes and decadents were losing faith in the future and caring only for the pleasures of the present and the art of the past. Others, unable to find the world without losing themselves, sought refuge in the accumulation and refinement of knowledge (fortunately for them an inexhaustible pursuit) or in the study of personalities which history and literature revealed in preternatural simplicity.

To prove that this resignation did not merely evaporate in "decadence" one has only to consider how many less conspicuous writers and readers returned with a new zest to the study of the classics and of Shakespeare. As has been shown,[1] the cult of Latin and especially of Greek was favoured by the romantic movement, but we should have expected these interests to lose force among the developments of the nineteenth century. Science, political economy and the literatures of contemporary Europe ought (one would think) to have taken their place. Even Dr Arnold introduced modern languages into his school curriculum. And yet we find that Homer, Sophocles, Thucydides, Plato, Virgil, Horace, Catullus and Cicero were honoured as one of the best preparations for modern life, and were studied with increasing appreciation, sympathy and even discipleship.

It was felt in the first place that the mastery of two such difficult and intricate languages, with their fine distinctions, pregnant phrases and lucid reasoning, would subtilise and quicken the intellect better than any other study could. In Greek and Latin we learnt how to handle thoughts and interpret ideas by passing them through the genius of these two clear-speaking nations, which had mastered the elusiveness of the perfect expression. So it came about in this age of scientific progress and religious controversy that the

[1] *Ante*, pp. 24–6.

best years of one's life were sometimes consecrated to practising prose and verse in languages no longer spoken by laymen.

There was another reason. The Greeks were a group of states which had risen with unexampled rapidity from primitive conditions; in fact, their civilisation was an effort to intellectualise the ways of prehistoric man. They had inherited the savage's fearful consciousness of evil or at least of treacherous powers around him, and they all believed that man has to play his part within the rigid limits of destiny, encompassed by ghostly influences which helped or harmed his progress along the narrow tortuous way. But one race, apparently sprung from the original Ionians of Attica, and not from the Northern invaders whether Achaean or Doric, succeeded (for various reasons) in transforming without destroying this uncultured civilisation. The range of their literary experiences and achievements had been rediscovered and appreciated in the seventeenth century; their artistic vision and sense of sculptured form had been eagerly studied, almost worshipped, in the eighteenth century. What fascinated the nineteenth century was the directness and penetration of their thought, at any rate as revealed through their great masters. Despite their short-lived commercial empire, their world was the single city-state, and its simple framework, exempt from the complicated problems of over-population, had left their bright intelligences free to put faith in reason. They brought all the phenomena of life (for us so overwhelmingly multitudinous) with the range of ὁ λόγος. Philosophy for them meant the unity of learning; unimpeded thought was indicated by σχολή which ordinarily meant leisure. So far from anticipating the modern man's arrogant self-sufficiency, they still recognised that man's besetting sin was ὕβρις, a vice of the mind, not merely the inclination to crime or sin, but self-willed recklessness, due to over-confidence, forgetfulness of the supernatural powers—once thought of as spirits of the corn, the stream and the tree, then as "auxiliar gods" in battle—but now understood to be eternal sphere-born laws of justice and righteousness. This view of life dawned with such divine simplicity because it was apparently achieved in two or three generations. Traces of the old religion of terror are still to be marked in Aeschylus (*c.* 525–456). In Sophocles (*c.* 497–405) the Athenian of the age of Pericles stands out in all his simple grandeur and sweet reasonableness; in Plato (*c.* 428–347) they have learnt through the art of dialectic how self-discipline and disinterested thought may lead to contact with ultimate reality. Distracted moderns had plenty to learn from Hellenic wisdom and inspiration, but more from their moral attitude or their *ethos* or what Keyserling called their *tenue*[1]—their self-respect and insight, the harmonious adjustment of soul and intellect to a world which gave ample scope to both. These virtues had been acquired by the Romans and transmitted, more or less at second-hand, under the name of *constantia*. Newman, for instance, specially admired Cicero and Horace, whereas Browning preferred Euripides, and Arnold Sophocles. But whatever their varying preferences, it was agreed by all moderns that this pristine perfection could not be regained. Nevertheless, its effect on the human spirit could be cultivated. We could not be Greeks, but we might become Grecians.

So it was with the study of Shakespeare. The genius of England's greatest dramatist had been amply recognised and established, from the age of Dryden to the age of Coleridge. Consequently one might have looked for the inevitable reaction, which always seems to overtake any author, if adequately appreciated. The reading of Shakespeare should therefore have lost the charm of discovery. Yet his influence continued to grow all through the nineteenth century; often it amounted to idolatry.

This intense interest and enthusiasm was partly due to the intellectual problems which the poet raised—the looseness of the plays; the obscurities of the text; the many locked doors for which scholars, in Schücking's phrase, had to find the key; the curious disinterestedness of the characters, who (as Hardy observed) discuss their own intense egoisms as if solely of interest to the spectators; the glimpses of sublime other-worldliness in a world made up of dramatic properties. But there was another reason. Shakespeare spoke through a medium which had not become academicised; he suffered from no literary inhibitions; his choice of words was not limited by their associations. Best of all, he was not burdened with erudition. For all these reasons his imagination expressed itself with a wider freedom and a more native impulsiveness than has ever before or since been granted to a human being. This spontaneity is contagious and the most culture-ridden expert can at times slip his chain and enjoy by proxy his half-submerged self.

So much for those who faced experience by the well-tried lights of the older humanism. The prospect was, indeed, distracting and chaotic. Let us now see how the rationalists were faring before Darwinism was supreme, especially Mill, Spencer and George Eliot.

[1] See *The Recovery of Truth*, Pt II, *The Ethical Problem*, 1929. (Translation with author's co-operation of *Wiedergeburt*.)

CHAPTER XV

John Stuart Mill, the man who believed that society could be so well administered and intellectualised that the best in man would find scope within its limits.

When John Stuart Mill died in 1873 a grateful nation was at first eager to erect some public monument to his memory. But when the elder and more influential authorities began to examine his claims, headed by Gladstone, they found that Mill's critics and opponents, for instance Carlyle, Ruskin, and Arnold, were right. The logician and social reformer did not deserve any national expression of gratitude; he was a second-rate thinker, who used other men's arguments to disparage our great heritage; he was almost a traitor within the ranks.

Such a change of opinion is natural, for Mill's position is an enigma, all the more perplexing because he took great pains to be explicit. He writes as if he had tidings of great joy to bring, almost a new religion such as one associates with the Victorian exponents of art and literature. No poet or humanist could labour more zealously to reform and enlighten our conduct. Educated opinion was ready to acclaim such idealism, so people respected his aims and his admirably lucid style. But when they began to ask whither his arguments led them, the majority found only the negation of what they most valued. His promised land was to be reached by destroying the time-honoured and reliable approaches in which their fathers had learnt to trust. He claimed the high office of a moralist and proved to be a philosophical radical.

Mill was, and is, often misunderstood because he refused to be abashed by the overwhelming responsibilities of nineteenth-century civilisation. He knew enough and more than enough to be appalled, as were Tennyson and Ruskin, at the vulgarity, mammonism, maladministration and overgrowth of his own age. But he also understood that the modern thinker's duty was not so much to expose these abuses as to rectify them; and he further recognised that modern civilisation had brought with its abuses a whole new armoury of doctrines and expedients wherewith to fight its vices and replace its losses. So he wasted no time in protesting against what was bad. He wielded, or tried to wield, the recently forged weapons with the skill and penetration of the bygone humanists.

He approached political economy, or social reform, or religious controversy, as if he were a disciple of Plato. So he joins in the nineteenth-century effort at uniting the Present with the Past in order to face the Future. Such is his significance for us.

He would have been less significant if he had been left to himself. But in reality Mill did not originate his career, but continued it. The track which most reformers have to engineer after many false starts had been blazed for him by his father. James Mill seems to have been a genius in everything but in his own writings. After resigning in Edinburgh his chances of a career in the Church, he finally settled in London in 1802 to make a living by journalism. He succeeded in supporting a large family and in starting theories in government, finance and education which played their part in the development of Victorianism. But the greatest and most permanent of his works was his eldest son.

John Stuart was born in 1806, at a time when philosophical radicals still believed in the unlimited perfectibility of human nature, and the father educated his son accordingly. His aim was partly preventive. He had himself learnt how difficult it was to overcome other people's preconceptions, and how much more difficult to overcome one's own. So he started his son where he left off. He taught him to trust nothing which he had not made his own by a creative effort; to distrust, for instance, those intuitions and intimations authorised by the romantic movement, which flatter the soul with a sense of spiritual security. For this reason John Mill received no religious instruction whatever. The Thirty-nine Articles meant no more to him than did the *Bona Dea*.

But in a wider, more metaphysical sense, no thinking man or woman can escape formulating a system which, for want of a more distinctive word, we must call a religion. He must satisfy what Haeckel was afterwards to call "the intellect's need to know the causes of things".[1] To supply that want the father's system of education must be constructive, and James Mill's first step was thoroughly to ground his son in the ancient classics as early as was humanly possible. His aim was to familiarise his pupil with their independence of thought, their lucidity of exposition, and their trust in the powers of the intellect; so much so, that John Stuart always felt a Platonist to be more rightly one who practised Plato's method of investigation than one who accepted his conclusions,[2]

---

[1] *Kausalitätsbedürfniss der Vernunft. Weltätsel*, Kap. XVI. *Lebenswunder*, Kap. III.
[2] *Autobiography*, chap. I.

and that conception was afterwards to inspire *On Liberty*. As soon as the boy had learnt the habit of questioning dogmas, testing generalisations, and defining his own terms (some when between the age of fifteen and of eighteen), his attention was directed towards the real problems of life. He was taught to reason out the principles of colonial administration, political economy, the philosophy of the mind, and especially Benthamism. It will be noticed at once that these are subjects in which dogma and tradition cannot play a large part, that the thinker is necessarily thrown upon his own resources and must out of himself create his own assurance and sense of power.

That was as far as the teacher could go. In the opinion of some contemporary educationalists he had gone too far. Such would certainly be the case at the present time when the battle in which the Mills fought has been won. But a hundred years ago imagination and sentiment were more dangerous than they are now. James Mill had aimed at rendering his son independent of illusions so that his mind would be free to work for the good of humanity. With this end in view John Stuart had learnt to consider his own ideas and ideals as subjective, existing only within his own head. Honour, truth, justice, humanity, love, destiny, all that mystics call the soul, and theists call God, he believed to be concepts of his own brain, originating in his own sense perceptions and powers of association. Thus among all the greatest issues of life and death which have filled some of the strongest spirits with holy dread, this thoughtful and introspective young man had been taught to stand alone and self-reliant. Such was his religion, founded on the search for causes. It was certainly an ambitious gesture; and it involved a tremendous responsibility to oneself. So inevitably John was trained to use his intellect as if it were a knife. But the moral side of his nature was not starved. The motives on which he was bred to rely were the noblest and the highest that an agnostic could conceive; such as a man could not obey unless he were a great deal more than what Carlyle termed a logic-chopping machine. James Mill was an austere and rather unsympathetic father, but he gave his son a mission in life, and equipped him to fulfil it.

Yet there was something which the teacher could not bestow upon his pupil, and so John Stuart found that this preparation for life was insufficient. On the verge of manhood, particularly in the winter of 1826-7, though still possessed of the moral grandeur of his mission, he lost all zest in its accomplishment. In fact his religion had now become "morality *untouched* by emotion". He could not visualise his own aims in such a light as to kindle his enthusiasm. Having exposed so many of other people's illusions he was too much afraid of his own. Like his father, he even doubted whether life were worth while.

This crisis is of more than biographical interest. It raises the question whether disinterested speculation for the future welfare of mankind can or cannot prove to be enough for the individual's happiness; whether such self-devotion fails to confer the sense of personal fulfilment, even though all the powers of the intellect are called into play. Mill, with his specialised training, is a test case. If he was so busy devising happiness for others and missed it himself, there must always be some deeper, more fundamental *psyche*, even in those who are taught to disbelieve in its presence. Each human nature seems to have a content and significance, a purposiveness within itself, an aim involving more individual and intimate activities than those shared between all educated intellects.[1] John Mill had apparently neglected this inner identity.

Without knowing it, Mill stood at the crossways in the progress of nineteenth-century culture. He was facing a crisis which is alarming humanists at the present time. We do not know much about the working of the human mind, but it is at last being realised that the intelligence operates by two antithetical processes which compensate each other, and that a thinker who seeks truth solely through logic is as likely to be deceived as one who trusts solely to his imagination. It is one of the distinctions of mid-Victorian thought, that it managed to get the best out of both faculties, and this harmonisation, which Mill accomplished for himself, was his first service to his fellow-creatures.

He recounts[2] with a certain restrained emotion how he effected this completion of himself; it was by the study of the great master of contemplative poetry, of Wordsworth. He chose well, for the lake-poet had travelled the same road some twenty or thirty years earlier. Like Mill he had once hoped to look through the "frailties" of the world and guide an independent intellect by the light of circumstances;[3] and far more than Mill he was disillusioned and lost "all feeling of conviction".[4] What interested Mill was the way Wordsworth recovered from this despondency, not by relinquishing

[1] *Ante*, chap. xiv.
[2] *Autobiography*, chap. v.
[3] *Prelude*, xi, ll. 223-58.
[4] *Ibid.* ll. 303-5.

his philosophy, but by blending it with his imagination and human sympathies. He looked for and found the divine Presence in nature and the divine Spirit in humble folk, thus also finding his own essential self. Nor was there any inconsistency or falseness in his train of thought. Whimsical as the expression may sound, Wordsworth was a pragmatist. His poetic convictions were founded on inductions since they were derived from personal experiences, dating from earliest childhood. Mill's education was completed by following the workings of this mind. In fact he retained a lifelong interest in creative literature, and was one of the first to appreciate Tennyson. But it is more important for us to note that he brought something of Wordsworth's humanity into his own work. He kept, of course, to his proper subjects, the problems of clear thinking and just government, and was thus always dealing with generalisations, if not with abstractions. Yet he imitated Wordsworth in that he learnt to put the whole of himself into his speculations, especially a certain imaginative sympathy. He acquired the faculty of visualising his conclusions in the lives of people around him. Poetry to him meant the associating and linking of ideas by emotion,[1] and he learnt to satisfy his emotions by blending them with his intellect. This harmonisation is not generally recognised, because Mill did not write as one expects from a man thus inspired. He continued to cultivate an austere and impersonal style. It could not have been otherwise. Mill had to exercise his insight into the errors, delusions, prejudices and miscalculations of the human mind; the misjudgment of facts, the misinterpretation of motives, the wrong estimate of results. These consequences seem to arise principally from man's projection of his own egoism into some creed or institution which acts differently from what his heart leads him to expect. It is the function of reason to dissect these impressions, to strip them of their figures of speech, to dissolve their emotional effluence. Neither the destructive nor the constructive reason can apply this discipline to others without practising it himself.

Within this circumscribed field, Mill worked wonders. His first great work was nothing more inspiring in title than *A System of Logic*. Yet Mill spent twelve of the best years of his life on its composition (1830–42). At that time he was much under the influence of A. Comte, and believed that the human race had passed through the theological and metaphysical phases of culture

[1] *Thoughts on Poetry and its Varieties, Monthly Repository,* Jan., Oct. 1833.

and had now reached the "positive" stage. Positive Philosophy holds that we know nothing about noumena; we know only phenomena. But we do not and cannot know all about phenomena. We know neither their essence nor their mode of production. All we can know about phenomena is whether or not they resemble each other and whether or not they are antecedent and consequent to each other, that is to say, constitute cause and effect. All the rest is inscrutable. Yet this insistence on our limitations really brought about a great expansion of intellectual activity. It opened a new direction for thought. Instead of trying to understand facts, it was now proved to be more desirable to study their effects; to observe, classify and differentiate them according to their similitude and succession. So he had recourse to the time-honoured science of Logic, which had long fallen into disrepute, till Dr Whewell had somewhat revived its credit. Mill used this ancient instrument to review the possibilities of human power, to demonstrate how a rigorous and unimaginative process is to lead to the betterment of the human race; how an imperfect knowledge of facts, but perfect handling of their relationships, will enable us to think out the best way to govern, to distribute wealth, to lead moral lives, and to cultivate self-assurance. For those who can familiarise themselves with the technicalities and formalities of these thousand or so pages, the book stands forth like a statement of the world which this adventurer hopes to conquer. It demonstrated that his thoughts were tending towards the analysis of nineteenth-century civilisation, and that in such a task hard-headed reason would be the motive-power. Yet within these limits, imagination accompanies his inductions and enables him to allow for the human factor, to detect the misfits, inadequacies, and privations of the systems which society was elaborating. Already his voice was being raised against the institutionalising of man.

Similarly, the *Principles of Political Economy* (1848) was not a book merely of abstract science, but also of application. It calculated the influence of social arrangements, institutions and individualities. The subject must especially have appealed to Mill because it took human nature with all its defects (as W. E. H. Lecky[1] pointed out) and adjusted its passions, jealousies, enmities and even vices to the progress of civilisation. He uses it to discuss the far-reaching effects of commercial civilisation and at least hinted at some of the problems so prominently discussed in Shaw's plays and Galsworthy's

[1] *History of the Rise and Influence of the Spirit of Rationalism*, chap. VI.

novels. However, it is not till the publication of *On Liberty* in 1859 that Mill's significance as a humanist becomes evident.

The historical significance of this essay, his best and most thorough attempt to get to the essential human nature, has already been indicated,[1] but it remains to consider its value as the expression of an individual's soul. The inspiration comes from Plato, not only because the Platonic method aimed at the truth through free discussion, but because Plato in all his speculations visualised the idea of the perfect man behind the imperfect copy. Mill's aim is hardly less ambitious. At the back of his mind is the ideal citizen for the nineteenth-century state. He had studied his own shortcomings with enough insight to realise that his chief disability was a certain artificial direction of thought, and therefore suppression, due to his father's influence and his own inbred self-discipline. So must it be with other people. They were not free, not fully developed, nor true to type, because they were mentally inhibited. Being a social reformer, he dwelt mostly on the practical causes and consequences of this stagnation. It was an almost inevitable consequence of industrial evolution, which implies that happiness is not a condition of the mind but is due to the combined action of society and that therefore the individuals should be as like each other as possible and subordinated to the composite functioning of the State. As Mill admitted, "the greatness of England is now all collective; individually small, we only appear capable of anything great by our habit of combining".[2] When happiness, or rather the appearance of happiness, can be centred in the enjoyment of this world's goods, the spirit is not tempted to roam beyond. Nor does society encourage such independence. An instinct of self-preservation (no doubt mistaken) prompts the collective will to impose uniformity of thought as well as of conduct.

This instinct was misdirected because each human nature is not the millionth part of a unified machine. The individual can function only if he has thought out and justified his own reasons for conformity; has examined error in order to know the truth. Even within the practical province of economics and administration, every possible outlet should be left open for individual initiative and spontaneity. But the insistence on self-reliance and personal responsibility becomes far more significant when we consider the problems of that second life which every human being has to live face to face with his own spirit. Each individual has an obscure

---

[1] *Ante*, chap. I.   [2] *On Liberty*, chap. III.

fund of volition, a subterranean ramification of appetencies and impulses, a tendency towards eccentric expansion. He cannot enjoy the necessary consciousness of power and dignity, the satisfying sense of reality, unless these urges (as far as they are not antisocial) find expression in thoughts and actions, in the assertion of the right to be himself. His highest, perhaps his only real happiness consists in developing and gratifying these instincts. Such seem to be for us the important aspects of *Liberty*. The author himself is inclined to emphasise the good that would thereby accrue to society—the chances of evolving a more energetic and progressive generation of citizens. As reconstruction and consolidation were the chief problems of his age, such a bias was inevitable. But Mill had not forgotten that mastery of speculation is mastery of life; and that thereby, moreover, mankind might perhaps find nobler ideals for which to strive.

It was agreed, then, that human beings never make more than casual and intermittent steps in progress, unless they know their own minds, unless their changes of opinion arise from a change of spirit, unless they are born again. And so, while Mill and his wife were revising and reconsidering this same essay on liberty, the author began to put his own principles into practice. He set to work to show men how they should constitute their minds with regard to that most fundamental and august of conventionalities, the orthodox religion of the age. The discussion was rendered difficult by the emotional atmosphere which (as we have seen) had gathered round the subject and also because the controversial data were changing every year. So Mill hesitated to proclaim his views, and had not published any of his three essays when he died in 1873. This reluctance seems to us rather meticulous, for Mill approaches his subject with the only query which makes the subject worth while. He does not so much question whether religion keeps people good, as whether it keeps them from becoming better. Having established the intellectual responsibility of man, it became of immense importance that he should help us to analyse and interpret those more vague and imaginative motives, often implanted by training or hereditary, which possess the soul like waking dreams, colouring all our mental life, and often escape our introspection. We will then find that we have imprisoned some of our noblest impulses and finest feelings in forms and beliefs which will not let our nature grow to its full height. Nay more, we have to restrain what is best in ourselves because those articles of faith involve compromise, and will not allow us to look forward as far as our unfettered reason would carry us. Thus man temporises with some of his greatest problems instead of facing them.

Of such is the cult of nature. The idea had been associated with the belief in Providence or at least with man's yearning for self-fulfilment in righteousness. So it had become a moral obligation to live according to nature. And why not? What matter if the conviction be illogical, provided that the dream savours of godliness? Because, thereby, man is not only blinded to the true significance of natural phenomena, but also to the part which he should play towards them. Nature, on examination, will be found to be in her general scheme no boon goddess but a wasteful and ruthless criminal; not a model for us to imitate, but a design lamentably imperfect which we ought to amend. In fact, progress consists in conquering or reforming nature. By a train of pure reasoning, and without any other data than can be gathered from unprejudiced observation, Mill thus corroborated the attitude of Huxley, annihilated at a blow what vitality still lingered in the pantheism proclaimed by the romantic poets, and cleared the way for the new cult of nature which was to arise during the last thirty years of the century.

But his inductions and deductions led him much further. Nature is believed to be the handiwork of God; so perhaps the same grounds which lead us to investigate the imperfections of creation should lead us still further to examine our idea of the creator. So Mill started to inquire whether the theism of his day was indeed the highest wisdom to which man could attain, or only another of these dreams which prevent man from awaking to the business of life. This inquiry comes to the conclusion that there are evidences of design in the universe and that on the whole the design aims towards perfection, but that it is fatal to persuade oneself that the purpose has been perfectly carried out. To compliment the Good Principle with the possession of infinite power is hopelessly to limit our own energies and resolution to better human existence. There may well be a God, but one who needs our co-operation, and he calls in as evidence the inspiration which many derive not from the divine God of Nature but from the almost human figure of Christ, and argues that the personal originality and profound insight of that historical figure may well serve as the ideal for all human endeavour. By such contentions he is in sympathy with our twentieth-century interest in the life of Jesus, and with "that

real though purely human religion which sometimes calls itself the
Religion of Humanity and sometimes that of Duty". These *Three
Essays on Religion*,[1] now superseded, are of importance in the history
of thought. They mark that epoch when human beings could once
more consider the worship of God, solely with regard to their own
moral, spiritual and even social advancement. Perhaps the treatise
which is most culturally significant is *The Utility of Religion*. In this
essay Mill questions whether respect for supernatural authority
does not involve "torpidity if not a positive twist of the intellectual
faculties". If so, the cause of humanity would gain more by a
human creed such as "the sense of unity with mankind and a deep
feeling for the general good", perhaps even the conviction that we
do not end with our own Death (in itself not an Evil) but continue
as it were in the lives of those who follow us. Here again it is easy
to recognise an ideal which was to inspire Meredith, Samuel
Butler and Trench.

Mill's purely social and political controversies hardly concern
us, and much of his time in later years was given up to interpreting
theories of other thinkers. But it might be remembered that in *An
Examination of Sir W. Hamilton's Philosophy* (1865) he argued against
the intuitionists that a man's conduct, feeling and even impulses,
are often less a part of his elemental nature than the product of
circumstances and association, leaving it to the next generation of
novelists and playwrights to infer that many an eccentric or even
criminal so acts because he is in a position in which neither he nor
anyone else could act otherwise. In *Auguste Comte and Positivism*
(1865) he emphasises the resources which the mind has at its
disposal for investigating and thus controlling our destiny on earth,
thus hinting at an idea which Bergson was to develop in *Matière et
Mémoire* (1896),[2] and he writes some really eloquent pages[3] on the
Frenchman's religion of the *Grand Être*, "ghastliest of Algebraical
Spectralities" according to Carlyle,[4] according to Mill a vision "of
the vast unrolling web of human life", of the intimacy between the
dead, the living and the not yet born, with all its call to duty and
appeal to the imagination. In fact this religion of humanity was
perhaps the ruling idea of Mill's life. He had already dwelt on it
two years earlier in *Utilitarianism* (1863) and had explained that by

---

[1] J. S. Mill, *Nature, The Utility of Religion and Theism*, 1873.
[2] See *post*, chap. XXIII.
[3] Pt II, *The Later Speculations of M. Comte*.
[4] Journal, 8 June 1868.

the usefulness of an action he meant its value to mankind. Moreover, when the instinct toward right-doing fails, it can best be
revived or substituted by the thought of social service, by habitually
calculating the effect of our conduct and testing its *altruism* (to use
the word which Comte coined).

This hurried and incomplete review should be enough to prove
that John Mill was not, in the ordinary sense, a materialist. He
was an idealist and Utopian who distrusted the things of the spirit,
a self-styled Platonist out of sympathy with Plato. He broke the
first rule of dreamland, in that he believed that his dreams could
come true. He and his father were convinced that the age of
emotion and of heroism had ended with the French Revolution
and the rise of democracy, and that henceforth Europe, or at any
rate England, had entered upon a new epoch in which development would take the place of adventure. Civilisation would consist in an ever-increasing complex of mutual advantages, leading
not to apathy, much less to self-indulgence, but to an expansion
and intensification of thoughtful enjoyment. Our interests and
opportunities would multiply with the multiplication of inter-
course. Mill was not devoid of poetry, but he assumed that in such
a world poetry would be lived not written; intellectual responsibility would be the prime virtue. If this network of contrivances
and adjustments was really to satisfy the best in man, it must be
investigated and administered with the uttermost care and delibera-
tion. Then it would absorb our spirit and imagination in a religion
of mutual service and progress. The artificialities of life would
render us human and natural. Mill did not work out these possibilities. He was engaged in the intermediate task of persuading
others that they were possible. Most of his contemporaries followed
him up to a point and then dropped behind. Hence the decline of
his reputation, though not of his influence, after his death.

CHAPTER XVI

Herbert Spencer possessed a constructive imagination which found its scope in the unification of knowledge—So he tried to repeat the achievement of St Thomas Aquinas, in which Hunter and Montesquieu had failed—However, he gave a new meaning to the ethics or rather the religion of human perfectibility—Yet he fails, through attempting too much without the aid of art and literature.

Mill had tried to spiritualise his thought. Truth, to him, meant a train of reasoning which should enable himself and others to act with greater effectiveness and realise themselves more fully He must have perceived that he had not altogether succeeded. Meanwhile, a contemporary had created a system of philosophy which seemed to be founded on common sense yet conferred an imaginative lordship over creation and enabled the thinker to play with facts as French children play with *châteaux en Espagne*. It is as such that the author of *Social Statics, Education, Man versus The State*, and the *Synthetic Philosophy* now claims our attention.

Herbert was born on 27 April 1820. His father, William George, was a schoolmaster, a man of great physical and moral energy, with a marked gift for synthesis as is proved by his *Inventional Geometry*, and an even greater talent for aggressiveness. He bequeathed these characteristics to his son, and Herbert, to his dying day, was self-assertive, tactless, anti-governmental and so censorious that he criticised everything from inkstands, arm-chairs and medicine bottles, to public-school education, British foreign policy and evangelicalism.

What is yet more to the purpose, the father imposed no special education on his son.[1] He merely encouraged him to read widely and rather indiscriminately for himself. There was only one thing on which he insisted. As he never accepted on faith the current explanation of a phenomenon, but always investigated the cause for himself, he expected Herbert to exercise a like independence. From time to time he also impressed on his son the duty of becoming "a useful member of society".[2]

Such were the ideals which the father must have hoped rather

---

[1] H. Spencer, *Autobiography*, Pt III, chap. XI.
[2] *Ibid*. Pt II, chap. V; Pt IX, chap. XLIII.

than expected to see realised. For Herbert showed a talent for mathematics and for drawing, and a marked interest in mechanical contrivances; otherwise he was indolent, self-willed and unfilial. But, luckily, he had the talent, even as a boy, of attracting attention and inspiring confidence, and in November 1837 his uncle William procured him a post under Charles Fox, who was then permanent resident engineer of the London division of railways.

So Spencer came into touch with the great world as an engineer on the latest extension of the London and Birmingham Railway, where trains had already reached the speed of thirty miles an hour, and at once he developed surprising energy and resourcefulness. But the most remarkable feature of this period is that as soon as he plunged into the world of action and conflict his smattering of science began unmistakably to develop into a philosophy. Almost at once he discarded his belief in God because the quaint anthropomorphism of the Old Testament could never be an adequate explanation of phenomena as revealed by Laplace, Lyell, Lamarck and Adam Smith.[1]

Many Victorians were coming to the same conclusion at about the same time and then made no further progress till about the 'sixties, and one would have expected Spencer to do the same. Why should he trouble his head to create a religion out of science, especially as his time was fully employed in a practical profession, and he already knew enough physics and geology to feel assured of his place on this globe? Because, unlike most freethinkers, he had a profoundly active imagination. As a child he was often so absorbed in his "castle-building, that he talked aloud to himself, forgot the errands on which he was sent, and looked forward to bedtime because his fancy would then be free".[2] By the time he reached manhood, he had begun to be practical and to give his full attention to the claims of his waking life; but he did not therefore unlearn to see visions and cease to dream dreams. On the contrary, the faculty remained with him till his death. But it did not develop in the usual way through poetry and fiction. Instead of constructing castles, he constructed theories, and his materials were the laws of causation. He was not content to collect and classify facts, as A. R. Wallace at one period of his life was content to do, "bitten by the passion for species and their description, and amassing the record of 8540 different species".[3] Spencer is signi-

[1] *Autobiography*, Pt III, chap. x.   [2] *Ibid.* Pt II, chap. v.
[3] *My Life*, chap. XXII.

ficant because his first and last interest was that of a humanist—
the nature of human beings, their conflicting ideals, their varying
standards of righteousness. He brought all his imagination and
creative talent into play and blended this self-expression with
scientific methods, reduced humanism to sociology, studied individualities, redirected and transformed under the influence of
their corporate existence and their chances of progress. The more
he studied this complicated and imperfectly adjusted organisation,
the more he visualised its fundamental regularity of structure, and
in order to convince himself and others, he enlisted all the science
at his command.

It was a wonderful conception, this imaginative reconstruction
of life on its essential outlines. As early as 1842 he had got so far
towards explaining modern society, as to establish an analogy
between the corporate life of human beings and the lower forms of
nature, and to argue that as all phenomena developed according
to one universal law, none could be reconstructed or adapted at
the arbitrary will of man,—political institutions, no more than
geological phenomena. These ideas, first published as letters to
The Nonconformist and reissued next year (1843) in volume form at
the author's expense as *The Proper Sphere of Government*, attracted
no attention at the time; but five years later the work prompted
James Wilson to offer Spencer the sub-editorship of *The Economist*.
As the railway boom had collapsed like a bubble in 1847 and
Spencer at the age of twenty-nine was left without a profession,
and even thought of emigrating, it did not take him long to close
with the offer. Thus, after ten years devoted to the enterprises,
expedients, negotiations and conflicts of railway building, he settled
down in London to a literary career. And now the really fruitful
and formative period of his life began.

His first step was to improve on *The Proper Sphere of Government* by
explaining the true nature of society. It was a difficult subject
because a community seems to be made up of individuals and yet
develops a character of its own which impinges on those of its
component parts. In fact, society grew as fast as the individual,
and the problem of every citizen was to maintain an harmonious
relationship: to see that man served the institution and that the
institution did not restrict the development of its members. An
equilibrium must be preserved. This explanation was published in
1850 as *Social Statics. The Conditions essential to human Happiness specified,
and the First of them developed.* One can at once see that as regards

psychological insight and social sense, this treatise was not un-congenial to the ideas of the nineteenth century, yet *Social Statics*, like *The Proper Sphere*, passed almost unnoticed. This neglect was partly due to Spencer's originality of presentation. Many people were ready to recognise society as a contract and some few as the gift of heaven. Spencer argues that this vast and complex pheno-menon is in its origin neither human nor superhuman, but organic. He even employed the expression "social organism" and went so far as to establish an analogy between the physiology of the in-dividual, and the constitution of the body politic, comparing the members of a community to the cells of a living body. This idea is still so unfamiliar that even in the twentieth century, men of science have thought it worth while to call attention to Morley Roberts's two books[1] in which he throws new light on cancer by comparing the organisation of the body to the government of a state. So it is not surprising that the mid-nineteenth century was unprepared for the analogy, and did not understand that the social system might be a matter of health or sickness, and like our bodily condition must be treated professionally, thus realising that one more mystery was coming within the range of our comprehension.

All depended on whether one could understand phenomena sufficiently well, that is to say, could in each case discover and appreciate the antecedent phenomena which were the cause. Apparently, at this period, Spencer had no more definite plans of study. His researches or rather his deductions seem to be conducted almost at hazard. Yet, as if of their own accord, they all tend towards the same result: they explain some human interest by some biological or physical fact, apparently outside the immediate range of human influence, and therefore the subject of disinterested examination. Gradually, it dawned upon him that all things con-tain within themselves the laws of their own development, pro-gressing "from homogeneity to heterogeneity", thus moving along lines which we can foresee if we cannot control. This theory was first expounded in 1852 in *The Leader* as *The Development Hypothesis*. But he had still to find the cause of this tendency. Almost at once he thought of the pressure of population which, as Malthus had shown, and as he himself had noted in *Social Statics*, starves some people, but stimulates others to develop and survive. The same might well be true of the lower orders of life and "a

---

[1] *Warfare in the Human Body* (1920), *Malignancy and Evolution* (1926). Cf. *The Times*, 21 Nov. 1934, letter on "Malignancy of Cancer".

universally operative factor in the development of species" might be found. Thus Spencer was treading on the path which seven years later led Darwin to immortality. But, like Mill, he was less interested in biology than in its applications to the nature of man. He contented himself in 1852 with publishing the idea as *A Theory of Population deduced from the General Law of Animal Fertility*, his first contribution to *The Westminster Review*. So for once in his life, on the very brink of a great discovery, he missed following up an idea of his own and turned to the discussion of Victorian politics. In 1856 he published, also in *The Westminster, Progress: its Law and Cause*, reaffirming with ample illustrations Von Baer's theory that all progress is a transition from the simple to the complex. The idea was not unfamiliar to other thinkers. Carlyle notes in his Journal on 3 October 1841: "What is life, except the knitting up of incoherences into coherence?" and often illustrated this assertion in his pictures drawn from history. Spencer's peculiarity was his passion for constructing frameworks for his visions. Next year his idea becomes yet more definite. *The Ultimate Laws of Physiology*[1] introduced the term *evolution* so much more picturesquely appropriate than the word *progress* and showed why the transition was bound to come. The simpler the organism, the greater its adaptability. The primary cause was "the instability of the homogeneous".

Meanwhile, he was making a more important advance in his system of beliefs. He connected the history of bodily organisations with the history of the mind. Having established that all life is adaptation (or, to use his favourite definition, "a continuous adjustment of inner relations to outer relations"), he argued that the adjustment finally becomes more than mechanical and material; it becomes spiritual and immaterial. In prehuman organisations environment stimulates the nerves, and the nerves generate action; in the latest stages of development this stimulation produces a consequent and more complex nervous state; hence joy, sorrow, instinct, memory, belief. Finally, the organism, now definitely human, becomes aware of an order of things different from its own. Hence self-consciousness, thought, reason, the emotions, the will. Yet again it must be noted that there was nothing fundamentally original in this empiricism. It was the case of a man of imagination pulling the human mind to pieces according to eighteenth-century methods of analysis and putting it together again, according to

[1] *The National Review*, Oct. 1857.

nineteenth-century methods of synthesis. His work is most remarkable because it struck a blow at Kant's doctrine of *a priori* ideas, arguing that all mentality was, *a posteriori*, the aftergrowth of experiences handed on from generation to generation and gradually evolved into thought. Spencer did not dissipate the mystery of spirit, but he shifted its incidence. Mind (he would say) is inexplicable but the miracle can be traced to the process of adaptation. We cannot explain this process, but we can reduce it to system and calculation. We can ascertain its effects and to that extent be masters of ourselves. These deductions and inductions were finally offered to the public in 1855 in a compact volume entitled *The Principles of Psychology*. Spencer could never have given the time to its composition, nor have guaranteed his publisher against financial loss, except for a legacy from his uncle Thomas. As belief in a special creation was still almost universal, the book met with a cold reception. At the end of nine months only 200 copies out of 750 had been sold.[1]

By 1857 Spencer had also produced a sufficient number of detached essays to be worth reprinting in book form. His ideas had been put forward one by one as they occurred to him, more or less independently, but he now had a chance of contemplating their continuity, and his constructive imagination had been so developed during these years of scientific guesswork that each theory seemed to fall into its proper place as parts of a common scheme. Then he was confronted by a new problem: what is the explanation—that is to say, the cause—of this scheme? Up to this point it had been enough to speak of "The inheritance of functionally produced modifications" as the moving power. But now he began to realise that these causes must be the product of something more universal. Almost at once he found his answer. Helmholtz had just read his paper on *The Conservation of Energy*; Sir William Grove had just published *The Correlation of Physical Forces*, and the whole scientific world was talking about this mysterious something which produces motion, which cannot be increased or decreased but only transformed and which cannot be defined except through its results. So it dawned on Spencer that "the instability of the homogeneous" and "the multiplication of effects" are only derivative laws. The first cause, and therefore the final explanation of all phenomena is Force.

One would expect him to write another of his vigorous and lucid

[1] *Autobiography*, Pt VII, chap. XXXII.

essays in order to popularise this doctrine. It would have made an excellent sequel to his article *Progress: its Laws and Cause*. But the chance of another and infinitely greater imaginative effort was not to be missed. So he devoted the rest of 1857 and most of 1858 to constructing the skeleton outline of a complete system of philosophy in view of his latest deductions. His aim was social and moral. Neither he nor his contemporaries would see their way to their true happiness and advancement till they understood the influences which had slowly created their own natures and the world in which they had to think and act; that is to say, the laws of evolution. Thus inspired,[1] he set himself to redevelop and readjust his former ideas and arranged them in their ordered sequence, beginning with the forces which shaped the solar system; he then tracked their manifestations through the earliest forms of vegetable and animal life to the more highly developed vertebrates and so on to the gradual evolution of the human mind; his climax was to be the complex organisation of society, with all its administrative activities and moral obligations. Thus, while apparently founding a system on the common-sense study of scientific facts, he was able to rehandle and rearrange his speculations and hypotheses as so much material wherewith to build a new edifice of the world within his own mind. He styled this ambitious design *synthetic philosophy*, because he hoped to combine all the elements of scientific learning into a demonstration of the laws of conduct. Philosophy was for him "the unification of knowledge".

But how were these doctrines to reach the general public? Hitherto Spencer's books had not even paid for themselves. His financial resources were of the slenderest. He was now proposing to devote the rest of his life to a monumental work for which he could hardly expect to provide the expenses of publication, much less find the means of decent existence while the books were being written. In this difficulty he actually applied for a stamp-distributorship at Derby, as the duties, in those pre-Gladstonian days, "could be to a considerable extent performed by a subordinate".[2] Finally, in 1859, he decided to bring out the work by subscription in periodical parts. His name enjoyed a consideration

---

[1] For a statement of Spencer's position, see letter addressed in 1862 to J. S. Mill who in *Utilitarianism* had classed him with the anti-utilitarians. Essential parts of letter quoted in Bain's *Mental and Moral Science*, and Spencer's *Autobiography*.

[2] *Autobiography*, chap. xxxv.

denied to his books, since all the great scientists subscribed to his series of worst-sellers, and many notable humanists and men of letters, including George Eliot, Monckton Milnes, Goldwin Smith, Kingsley, Buckle, Lewes, Masson and Froude.

So then this unconventional and controversial agnostic, who ten years earlier had drifted into higher journalism, had now undertaken to expound a system of philosophy for which Darwin's newly published *Origin of Species* was, in his opinion, merely a corroboration. At this stage he was thirty-nine years of age, already so far a valetudinarian that any mental strain brought on a serious nervous crisis, and he could compose only by dictating to an amanuensis for a few hours every day. What on earth induced him to attempt this task, which in the end was to prove an impossibility?

The question has already been partly answered. It was because Spencer had a constructive imagination; he had the architect's instinct. He has explained[1] that he did not sit down to a problem and puzzle over it, but let his ideas slowly take shape of their own accord. As the thoughts were already elaborated and systematised it was very little trouble to dictate them, almost as fast as his amanuensis could write. It was indeed a great joy to feel that the edifice was slowly rising, each set of facts fitting into its place, each argument working out in congruity with the rest, till the structure seemed to be complete. Such are the enthusiasms of the artist. His thoughts united themselves on this foundation; his life became possessed by a single purpose; health, wealth and domestic happiness became of no importance, compared with the urge towards philosophic self-expression.

So this interpretation of Force inspired his intellect because it satisfied his soul and gave him the key to a religion which to Spencer meant knowledge of the truth necessary for moral and spiritual development. To understand the significance of this aspiration, it must be remembered that the last man to achieve the feat was Thomas Aquinas. About the middle of the thirteenth century the *Doctor Anglicus* had gathered up, as it were in the palm of his hand, the physics of Aristotle, the metaphysics of the neo-platonists, and the logical subtleties of his own age—all the sound learning available through the prism of medieval culture—and had proved the universe to be an hierarchy. He completed this synthesis in order to establish the eternity, unity, ubiquity, and omnipotence of God. St Thomas believed that the more human

[1] *Autobiography*, Pt VI, chap. XXVII.

beings gave themselves up to the contemplation of so much grandeur, truth and goodness, the more their intellects would expand and their souls be inspired to save and complete themselves.

The *Summa Theologica* was a triumph partly because its doctrine was based on all the known facts of the world, safely stored between the covers and clasps of manuscript folios, their validity not to be questioned; partly because the logic based on these data was a masterpiece of sheer intellect; partly because the system transcended anthropomorphism. Nevertheless, its spirit died with the death of scholasticism Later ages had not been able to synthetise knowledge either to the glory of God or to the satisfaction of man's soul. The more knowledge multiplied, the more uncertain and defective the data became. Two notable attempts were made in the eighteenth century. John Hunter tried to complete his study of the human frame from the knowledge he had amassed of lower animals and tried to explain these lower animals from his knowledge of inorganic matter. Thus he hoped to unify all the physical sciences, beginning with the simplest (the morphology of crystals) and ending with the most complex (human pathology); thereby demonstrating that all supposed abnormalities can be reduced to law. "Centuries may elapse", remarks Buckle in 1857,[1] "before that conception will be consummated." At about the same time Montesquieu was trying to combine all we know about nature with all we know about man. His initial purpose was to investigate the relations between the jurisprudence of a country and its social conditions. But in order to show that people frame their laws according to the influences of climate, soil and food, not to speak of their national characteristics, he had to invoke all the sciences to elucidate the history of society. Yet he, too, failed, partly because meteorology, chemistry, and physiology were still too defective for his purpose, and partly because political economy, and the science of statistics were not yet invented. So he achieved no more than *De l'esprit des Lois*. Hegel and Comte had also perhaps dreamt of bringing all knowledge beneath their rule. They both got as far as to frame laws, but they did not attempt to conquer the subjects who should bow to their legislation.

Time and human labour were filling in many gaps in the world's heritage since these ambitious attempts were made. But only the most self-confident representative of a self-confident age

[1] *History of Civilisation in England*, vol. III, chap. v.

could imagine that the time had come to repeat the achievement of Thomas Aquinas. Yet such was the dream of Herbert Spencer's constructive imagination. The discoveries of his brother scientists had been confined to the world of facts; whereas Victorians (he was convinced) ought to discover something in the intellectual conquests and acquisitions of their age, which carried their imagination beyond the limits of facts, something which lent vision and spirituality to their busy complex world, without sacrificing scientific truth. Spencer believed that his philosophy supplied the touch of sublimation which others lacked. In reality his hypothesis was not altogether uncongenial to the orthodoxy of the thirteenth century, however opposed to that of the nineteenth. The God of St Thomas was an essence, not a person, the *primum mobile* which out of itself created motion. But there was this difference. Whereas the medieval scholastic put over man an Intelligence which dwarfed him into insignificance, Spencer recognised an universal and eternal mystery—The Unknowable—which need never overshadow the human spirit, since we are the highest manifestation of its power. In fact the more we grow wise in contemplating this profound enigma, the more we are discovering ourselves. Whatever may be thought of *Synthetic Philosophy*, it was true to a certain attitude of mind, which was to become more and more prevalent as the century advanced. No wonder G. H. Lewes[1] found Spencer to be an inspiring companion.

So Spencer's writings, even more than J. S. Mill's, mark the advent of what we may call the nineteenth-century superman. It now remains to notice the immediate fortunes of his venture, for a glimpse at their reception will illustrate another aspect of the age. The prospectus was finally issued in 1860, and Spencer, having received rather unexpectedly a substantial legacy by the death of his other uncle William, was able to work uninterruptedly at *First Principles*, which appeared in 1862 (revised edition, 1867). The volume was intended to make clear the general lines on which phenomena evolve;[2] but in order to show that their origin could only be indicated and not explained and that he felt as deeply as any theologian the existence of a mystery behind creation, he commenced the book with a short dissertation on Force, which he characterised as *The Unknowable*. That heading had just the touch of singularity which attracts unwelcome attention. The moralists

[1] W. L. Cross, *George Eliot's Life*, chap. VIII.
[2] *Autobiography*, Pt IX, chap. XXXVII.

scented agnosticism (though the word was not yet coined) and the wits smiled at the author who began a series of ten large octavo volumes with an explanation of what he did not know. The real import of the book passed unnoticed. In 1864 he published volume 1 of the *Principles of Biology* after getting Huxley to check his zoology and Hooker his botany. He substituted the neat phrase "survival of the fittest" for Darwin's "natural selection", and showed how the "origin of species" was but another manifestation of evolution, of "the redistribution of matter and motion everywhere and always going on". The book was so inadequately reviewed that henceforth for several years he discontinued sending copies to journals. The second volume of the *Biology* gave him more pleasure than any other of his labours, because he was able to break new ground in the subjects of morphological and physiological development. But by the time the book was finally passed through the press in 1866, the author at last realised that he would soon be faced with ruin. He had sunk £1100, most of his small fortune, in his enterprise, and so far from recovering any of his outlay, let alone an adequate return for his capital, the number of subscribers (originally 430) was steadily decreasing. So he issued notices that the termination of the *Biology* would be the termination of the whole series. Just at this juncture the death of his father in 1866 and of his mother in 1867 relieved him of certain responsibilities and a number of American admirers invested seven thousand dollars in securities in his name (1866). Once more he was in a position to resume his unremunerative work, but towards the end of 1867, owing to a slight effort of over-concentration, he had a nervous breakdown which incapacitated him for a year, so he went abroad.

By the end of 1868 the tide had definitely turned. His publications were now earning an income which steadily increased and translations of four of his books were in commission. In 1869 *First Principles* and *The Principles of Biology* were prescribed at Oxford as text-books, and questions were set out of them for examinations. In 1871 he was nominated for the rectorship of St Andrews, and the senate contemplated conferring an LL.D. In 1873 Arnold could write of the philosophical liberals "who believe neither in angel nor spirit but in Mr Herbert Spencer".[1] In *The Dancing Girl* (1891) Sybil Craig compares Spencer to Dante, and the author, H. A. Jones, used to say constantly "any

[1] *Literature and Dogma*, chap. XII, § 2.

clear thinking I've done, I owe to Herbert Spencer".[1] Besides, his labours in due course had reached subjects on which he could write (or rather dictate) with more authority. By the end of 1870 he had completely revised and republished his *Principles of Psychology*. In 1873 he brought out *The Study of Sociology*, perhaps the most characteristic and at the same time most readable of all his books, and one which proved to be a good seller. Though dogmatic and prejudiced, it is valuable as an introduction to a then unfamiliar subject, and because it champions with much humour and insight the rationalist's attitude to humanism. If he is far from just to literary and theological habits of thought, he demonstrates that logic and science will sometimes lead to a fuller and more intelligent mode of life.

He was now (1874) well embarked on the vast and complicated labour of directing *Descriptive Sociology* and compiling his own *Principles of Sociology*, of which the first instalment appeared in 1876 and the last in 1896. These volumes were intended to be the modern democrat's guide to social and political reform and the author's own demonstration of how to study history. The need of them was not far to seek. Both the people who went to hear sermons and those who went to hear political speeches were in danger of thinking that nineteenth-century England was an aggregate of accidents and could be reconstructed according to desire. The impulse might come from literature, history or religion, and in that case the reformer was sure to be misguided, because the wisdom derived from these sources was wise only for some earlier stage of development, not for society as it is now. Or again, the desire might come from trust in Acts of Parliament, from confidence in short cuts, which by one movement could bring about a redistribution of property or a transference of political power. Such a persuasion was equally delusive, because, as Spencer had already explained in his essays, society is a growth, no less so than natural phenomena, moving along its own lines of development, taking its own time. As was argued in *Political Institutions* (1882), it must not be hurried or diverted. What then is the Spencerian to do who feels the will to control his destiny? He must acquire the knowledge which ensures the control of his social life. Amongst other things, he must learn that each stage in the forward movement is characterised by its own special features. For instance, as shown in *Descriptive Sociology*, despotism is accompanied by elaborate

[1] D. A. Jones, *The Life and Letters of Henry Arthur Jones*, 1930, chap. VII.

ceremonial in social intercourse, military activity by the degradation of women, commercial activity by the "relaxation of coercive
institutions". By these and such like tests the sociologist will be
able to discern whether any tendency is retrograde or progressive.
To put this insight within the reach of public opinion, Spencer
compiled these immense volumes. Incidentally, the book discovered the romance of folk-lore, with its picturesque superstitions,
its glimpses of nature poetry, its flights into the mysteries of
archaeology and its wholesome reminders that human misery is
generally self-inflicted.

Meanwhile, the philosopher had begun to realise that he would
never live to consummate his project by the production of *The
Principles of Ethics*. So in 1878 he started dictating memoranda for
the most essential part of that work, *The Data of Ethics*. In this
essay he postulates "that Ethics has for its subject-matter the most
highly evolved conduct as displayed by the most highly evolved
being", and he tests this social evolution by the individual's ability
to get the best out of life. If this condition is to be fulfilled, society
must apply all the wisdom of all the sciences. From biology we
learn that no act should be committed or thought entertained
which weakens the body, for thereby the human being is rendered
unfit for the duties of life. Illness and unhappiness are crimes
against society, whatever their motive.[1] Psychology teaches what
these motives too often are and what they should be.[2] Sociology
teaches us how to trace these effects and how to develop "faculties
which by their exercise bring positive benefit to others and satisfaction to self".[3] Above all, he clears away the old Victorian ideas
that certain lines of conduct are wholly good or bad in themselves;
since in our present stage we cannot wholly condemn egoism or
commend altruism. Hence a compromise is the only possibility.[4]
And this compromise must be effected by forgetting the Bible and
the theologians, and studying ourselves by the laws of evolution,
as we should study every inferior creature. In a future state these
social and biological needs will have become identical. So this
middle-aged valetudinarian ended his career with a book from
which Butler, Shaw and Wells might have drawn ideas.

And now, in conclusion, what are the lessons to be drawn from
this sketch of an heroic life? In the first place, we learn something

---

[1] Chap. vi, § 37. Cf. S. Butler in *Erewhon*.
[2] Chap. vii, §§ 45, 46.   [3] Chap. viii.
[4] Chap. xiii, § 82.

about the reception of scientific theories in the age of Victoria. It will be noticed that Spencer employed the word *evolution* and championed the doctrine some years before Darwin and Huxley were occupying everyone's attention; but his books did not sell nor his reputation spread till late in the 'sixties. And yet, as we have seen, and as he himself points out in his *Autobiography*, there was much in his comprehensive and philosophic treatment which ought to have appealed to his contemporaries. For instance, Haeckel declared as early as 1866 that "alle wahre Naturwissenschaft ist Philosophie und alle wahre Philosophie ist Naturwissenschaft",[1] and all through his life, especially in the immensely popular *Welträtsel* and *Lebenswunder*, insisted that ethics is the lens which concentrates all the sciences onto one focus. Even before Haeckel, such books as Alexander von Humboldt's *Kosmos*, which appeared in 1844 and was translated in 1849, had familiarised the world with scientific surveys. So Spencer's age must have been ready for his message, but would not take it from him.

He made his own reception difficult because, in the first place, he had too much to offer. Though not himself a specialist, he required his readers to specialise, for the nonce, in half a dozen sciences. However, his polygraphic inclinations might have been forgiven except that the age of comprehensive thinkers had not returned; the age of intellectual and imaginative curiosity had taken its place. People were on the look out for picturesque and provocative assertions. There were still a few polymaths, and quite a large class of thinkers—at any rate among the younger genera-tion—but these, the majority, wanted to visualise their ideas in a paradox or anomaly, in some pregnant epigram or proposition which raised an issue and inspired discussion. We have watched this disposition develop from Goethe to Arnold and Mill and we shall next consider how the most revolutionary of all became very influential because his name was associated with apes for ancestors and the earthworm as man's best friend. Spencer did not exercise these arts. He was too desperately intent on what he called "scientific definiteness" and he was too much in earnest to preserve a sense of humour. So, instead of a war-cry, he offered his disciples a definition of evolution which can more easily be parodied than understood.

These considerations bring us to another inference; the philo-

---

[1] "All true science is philosophy, and all true philosophy is science." *Gene-relle Morphologie*, chap. IV. For Haeckel, see *post*, pp. 288–92.

sopher of the future must not alienate the humanists and men of
letters. The new gospel might be based on logic and science, but
it will need art to win its way "to men's bosoms". Spencer ought
to have accomplished this feat. He had his full share of what
De Quincey called "superstition in the sense of sympathy with the
invisible".[1] Up to his death he repudiated the imputation of
materialism nor would he allow that he was merely an utilitarian.
Besides, as we have seen, his gospel was worthy of the arts of
humanism. He perceived that his fellow-creatures were beginning
to live for themselves and not for the ideal of a combatant. Instead
of a life disciplined to face enemies both within and without, in this
world and the next, they were now learning to give themselves to
their own pursuits, to indulge their temperaments, to exchange
and mutually to enjoy the good things of this world and to serve
the commonweal in order to fulfil the law of their being. Industrialism, as he saw, should not be the goal of modern progress.
In its turn, it imposed almost as many limitations as it removed,
especially the strain of over-cerebration. It was only a necessary
phase through which civilisation must pass. The future had in store
an ideal of more natural and harmonious development, in obedience
to the law of evolution. What he wanted to create was a new idea
of one's self and of one's fellow-creatures, a new dream of this
world's possibilities. Such enlightenment needs spiritual contact
with poets, novelists and picture-painters. Yet Spencer regarded
humanists and humourists as his enemies. He hated those arts
which had adorned the old regime and were still supposed to
cherish the old warlike sentiments and he believed that they would
always be an obstacle to progress. He could not see that literature
might also follow the laws of evolution and become the most
powerful influence in the transition which he was preparing. Other
ontologists were of his opinion. "They have never", declared
Leslie Stephen in *An Agnostic's Apology*, "made or suggested the
barest possibility of making a bridge from the world of pure reason
to the contingent world in which we live."

Yet once, just by chance, he caught the gregarious general
reader. In 1860 he had the happy thought of reissuing in volume
form four essays on education which he had contributed to
periodicals. In these articles he argued that the training of the
young should follow and subserve their line of growth and not
control it, and that the best guide to the pupil's real need was the

[1] *Modern Superstition, Blackwood's Magazine*, April 1840.

pupil's own preferences. Children should be nourished, exercised and taught in the ways they liked best. The tone of the book is quite anti-puritanical, in fact almost epicurean and hedonistic. Yet all the wisdom and learning of *A System of Synthetic Philosophy* is behind these lucid, colloquial pages. The explanation is that Spencer, like many bachelors, was a lover of children's society (or, as he would say, his propensity for philoprogenitiveness was highly developed) and so he wrote with that touch of humanity, that freedom from formulas and that insistence on significant details which are the very soul of literature. As a result, the brochure has been translated into thirteen languages, and still deserves to be in the hands of every father and mother. Perhaps it was too much to expect that the human nature which enlivened his love of billiards and of children should also adorn his scientific deductions and inductions.

Herbert Spencer pleaded for happiness and Oliver Elton remarks in his *Survey of English Literature* that he himself had all too little. Yet fortune was his firm friend. At every financial crisis some deceased relative or some friend or group of friends brought him money, and thanks to these ever-recurring windfalls, he achieved the only happiness vouchsafed to mortals—self-fulfilment. This invalid, "his brain crippled at thirty-five", and almost without private means, lived to compose half a library and to lay down the law on God, man and the universe.

CHAPTER XVII

Marian Evans acquires what wisdom and self-reliance the new rationalism can inspire—She tests and deepens her theories in conflict with family sentiment and love for her fellow-creatures—She intellectualises her imagination and develops her genius for literary expressiveness—So she becomes George Eliot, and preaches a morality worth practising but not worth living for—A glance at De Quincey will show why.

When George Eliot died suddenly in December 1880, several obituary notices mentioned the current opinion that Spencer had influenced her education. The philosopher wrote at once to the papers to remove this impression, and pointed out that their friendship did not begin till 1851, "when she was already distinguished by that breadth of culture and universality of power which have since made her known to all the world". But he admitted in a subsequent letter to an American friend that *Principles of Psychology* may have helped her in the analysis of character and that she actually did read and reread *The Data of Ethics* and *Study of Sociology*. Spencer had indeed been one of her earliest friends in London. He used to take her to concerts and sing duets with her, and had introduced her to G. H. Lewes. Were they in intellectual sympathy? Did she belong to the same movement as these positivists, utilitarians and social philosophers? Was she giving imaginative expression to the new outlook on life?

The answer is not far to seek; it can be gathered even from her first tentative effort, which she was urged to undertake at the instance of Lewes and, in some measure, of no other than Spencer himself.[1] Let us consider why *Scenes from Clerical Life* (1858) was so immediately successful. In the first place, because the stories appealed to the kind of sentiment which Dickens had made popular. Again, because there was something of Thackeray in the tendency to moralise, and in the mock-heroic circumlocutions and the witty allusiveness of the style. Possibly, too, the admirers of Trollope were gratified to find here and there an insinuation of motive, a little exposure of human vanity or meanness, the dissection of some pose or hypocrisy. In all these respects, as in a certain epigrammatic incisiveness, *Scenes* is in the best Victorian

[1] *Autobiography*, chap. LIX.

tradition, and for that reason was bound to meet with applause. And yet there was something unmistakably new in the manipulation of these familiar effects. To begin with, the scenes are placed in the immediate past, one, two, or three generations backward. This revival may seem merely a device to lend picturesque charm, to cast an aroma of other-worldliness on the narrative. But in reality nothing keeps the reader more conscious of change and progress; nothing reminds him more insistently of what he has gained or lost on his parents and grandparents, as Galsworthy was afterwards to discover. And in the next place, the stories themselves convey the moral that whoever trusts tradition ought to distrust himself. George Eliot described her purpose to be "the presentation of mixed human beings in such a way as to call forth tolerant judgment, pity and sympathy",[1] and she produced this effect by shedding on them the best and clearest light of modern rationalism. It must be noticed that her characters "had that salt of goodness which keeps the world together, in greater abundance than was visible on the surface".[2] The authoress shows how this surface had been encrusted and frozen by the conventionalities of civilisation, so the feelings could not find their proper channels. Thus the characters had fallen into the habit of confining their better selves to certain isolated and selected sentiments, for instance, love of their children, regard for their special friends, and had taken their other relationships at a face value. Whenever they come to a situation requiring praise or blame they refer to a mental pigeon-hole, in which habit or tradition had deposited a certain memorandum. Their association of ideas was defective or rigid. These are the kind of vices against which Mill was already arguing in his yet unpublished *On Liberty* (1859) and which Spencer was to expose sixteen years later in *The Study of Sociology* (1873). But theorists can only protest and generalise. The story-teller can exemplify and George Eliot anticipates both these and other moralists by revealing the maladjustments which they only expose. She creates a number of individuals whose social aptitudes are frozen by routine; then leads them up to a crisis and suddenly deprives them of something precious which had always been taken for granted; for instance, the Rev. Amos Barton finds himself standing by his wife's grave, Janet realises that she has no longer a home. So the reader perceives in a flash how few of us really fill our role in the tragedy or comedy of life. Such a method gives full

[1] To J. Blackwood, 18 Feb. 1857.   [2] *Janet's Repentance*, chap. II.

scope to the author's emotion and the reader's imagination and many must have felt that so vivid a demonstration carried a deeper and wider conviction than a reasoned treatise could.

In fact George Eliot inaugurated a kind of fiction which has since become conspicuous in twentieth-century literature. She makes characters interesting because of what they think, not because of what they do. The climax is no change of fate but a change of soul; a rapid transition from the unconsciousness of routine to the consciousness of spiritual needs; the significance of each story arises out of this effort at readjustment. So the novel of insight began to be written and our authoress would not have been followed by so many practitioners, mostly without conscious imitation, unless such were the tendency of culture.

There is another important feature of her work, which is peculiarly illustrative of her age. In all her novels, the spiritual awakening culminates in human sympathy; in the comprehension which forgives; and it will be remembered that the majority of men who undergo this change are clergymen. *Scenes from Clerical Life* might almost have been entitled "The Rebaptism of the Anglican Soul", and throughout her later work she continued to be profoundly interested in the mentality of the priesthood. There is nothing bitter or controversial in her portraiture, but it is significant that she singles out this class of men (with a few exceptions) as particularly weak in the virtues which rationalism values. Trollope depicted many priests who loved the pleasures and prizes of this world too well, who were, in fact, too human. George Eliot portrays many who were not human enough. Those ordained to the ministry of God seemed to be particularly in need of the religion of humanity.

Here we meet another signpost on the broad highway of nineteenth-century culture. The most irresponsible and the least disquisitive of all forms of literature[1] has at last confronted the established religion. After criticising slums, lawyers, snobs, politicians, financiers, domestic tyrants and highwaymen, it is now criticising orthodoxy. Such an attitude was natural in the case of Bain, Paine, Comte, Carlyle, Froude, Mill and Spencer for, as *Alcidamas* reminds us, philosophy is a stronghold thrust into the territory of law and order.[2] But the tension between rationalism

---

[1] *Post*, chap. XIX, pp. 295–6.

[2] ἐπιτείχισμα. *See* Aristotle: *Rhetoric*, III, 3–4. Heine notes the appropriateness of the figure in *Deutschland*.

and reason must have entered on a new phase, when the imaginative and emotional temperaments join forces with the invader, especially such a personality as George Eliot. So we must glance at the early life of this woman least of all destined to further the cause of non-conformity unless the spirit of the age had compelled her.

Marian Evans was born in 1819 in the house of a farmer, land-agent and carpenter, well-educated for his class, who still belonged to the eighteenth century and, like Uncle Pullet, never dreamt "that the British constitution in Church and State had a traceable origin any more than the solar system and the fixed stars".[1] His daughter was sent to a good school where she astonished her teachers by her readiness to learn, though she was quite ready to devote herself to the management of her father's household. In fact, she displayed a genius for home life. But in 1841, when farmer Evans moved to Coventry, and Marian at last met culti-vated and progressive people with whom she could exchange and develop ideas, she began to lose faith in evangelicalism, and to question the divine authority of the Bible. She even refused to accompany her father to church, in those circumstances a gesture worthy of Lucifer. The actual moment of her apostasy is marked by her letter to Miss Lewis, her friend and school-teacher, 13 November 1841.

What had happened to this ardent, affectionate girl, for if there ever was a human being possessing the genuine religious instinct, it was the future George Eliot? She loved animals, and natural scenery; she had a confidence in human goodness as profound as Browning's; she displayed in her youthful letters that kind of reasoned austerity and idealism which can only proceed from temperament; to her dying day she studied the Bible, believing it to be, in J. W. Cross's phrase, "a very precious and sacred book".[2] Then why did she turn agnostic?

Miss Evans renounced her faith for the same reason as Herbert Spencer did, whom some people afterwards expected her to marry. The old orthodox religion was imposed on her in its most restric-tive and depressing form; the new religion of reason and social service was offered in so novel and stimulating a guise that it

---

[1] *The Mill on the Floss*, chap. VII.

[2] *Life and Letters of George Eliot*, chap. XIX. For evidence of her youthful affinities, *ibid.* to Miss Lewis, 18 Aug. 1838; to Mrs S. Evans (the supposed original of Dinah Morris), 5 March 1839; to Miss Lewis, 17 July 1839 and 17 Sept. 1840.

promised more than (to judge from the evidence of literature) it was able to fulfil. It offered new worlds to conquer. Its discoveries brought that sense of expansion and of growth which Goethe valued. So she passed from a devout evangelicalism to an equally devout agnosticism.

The book which occasioned the first crisis was Charles Hennell's *An Inquiry Concerning the Origin of Christianity* (1838), which once enjoyed sufficient importance to be translated as *Untersuchungen über der Ursprung des Christenthums*, with a preface by Strauss. But there can be no doubt that the seed fell on ground only too well prepared by the diversity of her reading. She had read the English classics widely, but had also studied entomology, chemistry and metaphysics. At the same time she followed the theological controversies of the 'thirties and 'forties, and then turned to early Church history to follow up the problems which they raised. As one would expect, such conflicting and divergent pursuits reduced her growing mind to chaos.[1] She had embarked upon these varied inquiries because she had talents which could not otherwise be used. She had to be erudite if she was to feel her own identity to the full. In such cases one is generally helped by the esteem of other people, and for that reason one does not need to press one's studies beyond the point of winning applause. Marian had her full share of this weakness; in a letter written to Mrs Samuel Evans on 5 March 1839 she styles it her "besetting sin". As she had little chance of impressing any but her very narrow circle of friends, all her intelligence seems to have gone towards achieving her own self-consideration unaided. That could be done only by welding this chaos of theories into a whole and stamping it with the impress of her personality and moral will. Hence her perplexity. Like Matthew Arnold,[2] this country girl was being overwhelmed by the multitudinousness of life.

It was indeed life, not learning, which troubled her most, for this farmer's daughter insisted on bringing her principles and theories to the test of daily conduct, and all unwittingly anticipates or concurs in the conclusions of the most advanced thinkers. At thirteen years of age she reads about "a very amiable atheist" depicted in Bulwer's *Devereux* and, like the neo-pagans, she decides "that religion was not a requisite to moral excellence".[3] On the

---

[1] Letters to Miss Lewis, 20 May 1839, 4 Sept. 1839, 5 Dec. 1840, 3 Sept. 1841. See J. W. Cross, *op. cit.*

[2] *Ante*, chap. XII, pp. 176-9.　　　　[3] To Miss Lewis, 21 May 1840.

other hand, like J. S. Mill, she was equally impressed with the
laxity and meanness of some devotionalists who made such strict
professions of faith. Who can forget the case of the woman who
when convicted of lying replied "I do not feel that I have grieved
the Spirit much"?[1] Nineteenth-century morality recognised that
parents owed a very definite duty to their children for having
brought them into the world. This was a claim which Herbert
Spencer urged and on which Samuel Butler was afterwards to
harp insistently, and which was even then being urged as the plea
for instituting schools. George Eliot was one of the first to see that
if we interpret the Bible in the old-fashioned way, a similar
responsibility must rest on our heavenly Father and that many of
the acts of divine retribution can only be condemned as negligence
and injustice. "But we have no claim upon God", objected
Mr Sibree. "No claim upon God!" she reiterated indignantly,
"we have the strongest possible claim upon Him."[2]

These examples are enough to show that Marian Evans (despite
her secluded life in an old-fashioned household) had learnt too
much from nineteenth-century culture to be reconciled to nineteenth-century orthodoxy. Her powers of reasoning were dangerously alert, and were sure to be directed towards the fundamental
problems of Christianity, all the more because they meant so much
to her. And now rationalism was offering what home-bred piety
had failed to bestow: the triumphant mastery of her thoughts, but
only on condition that she sacrificed her dearest associations. No
wonder that she was ready for Hennell's *Inquiry* and that she spent
the rest of her life seeking and imagining the sanctities of home life
which she had lost in early womanhood.

So ended her first phase. Meanwhile her friends at Coventry
introduced her to literary circles and to the sphere of higher
journalism. She began to write for magazines and periodicals.
Near the beginning of 1844 she went to stay with Dr Brabant at
Devizes and it was proposed that she should undertake the translation of D. F. Strauss's *Das Leben Jesu*.[3] The work was completed
by July 1845 and published on a subscription of three hundred
pounds. This translation marks the second phase of Miss Evans's
advance, because Strauss taught her how to associate the austere
and inspiring figure of Christ with her science, philosophy and

[1] J. W. Cross, *op. cit.* Appendix containing the recollections of Mrs John Cash.
[2] *Ibid.* (Mr Sibree, a Nonconformist minister, was her father.)
[3] *Ante*, chap. xiv.

historical knowledge, as formerly with her bedside prayers and nursery theology. In July 1848 she wrote to Miss S. Hennell, "the Galilean is nothing less than the genius of the future". Strauss's influence was to some degree completed by her translation of Feuerbach's[1] *Wesen des Christenthums*, which appeared in July 1854 in Chapman's *Quarterly Series*.

Next year, in 1849, her father died; she spent some months at Geneva, where she formed some valuable friendships; finally, in September 1851, she settled in London, as assistant editor of *The Westminster Review*. Her life now became intensely active and laborious, but she found time to meet interesting people such as Spencer, Huxley, Miss Martineau and especially G. H. Lewes. Most remarkable is the conquest which she achieved over herself. All her life had been a series of revolts. Up till 1840 she had struggled against the illiteracy of her home; from 1841 to 1846 she had resisted its religious atmosphere; from 1847 to 1849 she had sacrificed her best energies to nursing the father who stood between her and her self-realisation. Yet she survived this ordeal without retaining the least taint of bitterness, or, on the other hand, the least trace of world-renunciation. Many years later, on 8 May 1869, she wrote to Mrs H. B. Stowe: "For years of my youth I dwelt in dreams of a pantheistic sort, falsely supposing that I was enlarging my sympathy. I have travelled far away from that time." How far she had travelled by 1851 can be judged from her review of Mackay's *Progress of the Intellect*, published in the January number of *The Westminster*. She complains of the old world bondage to terms and conceptions which have lost their vitality and are mere *idola theatri* but yet obstruct the truth, because they are associated with our better sentiments, and at the same time allied to the vested interests of the dominant classes.

Miss Evans was developing into an humanitarian humanist. This achievement was due in the first place to her nature, which found expression in her delightfully informal and expansive letters to her friends; in the next place to the study of Spinoza whom she read, discussed or translated between 1849 and 1855. But the turning point in her life was, of course, her union with G. H. Lewes, whom she could not marry, as his wife still lived. That story has been told hundreds of times. As A. Paterson[2] points out, the alliance completed her nature as a woman full of love. She

---

[1] *Ante*, pp. 215–18.
[2] *George Eliot's Family Life and Letters*, 1928.

now had a home, four foster-children to care for, and a companion whose temperament just suited hers. Even this happiness was won by a revolt against the social law. Yet, unlike Maggie Tulliver, she could write to Miss S. Hennell on 8 June 1857, "the positive result of my existence on the side of truth and goodness will outweigh the small negative good that would have consisted in my not doing anything to shock others".

It would seem, then, that Miss Evans had been specially prepared and endowed by destiny to associate the cause of rationalism with the deepest and tenderest experiences of her fellow-creatures. How far would the novel serve this purpose? *Clerical Life* was, of course, immature. What would she produce in the plenitude of power and public applause? We turn to *Adam Bede* (1859).

This great novel is created more out of the self-discipline and self-education of her life than out of her experiences.[1] George Eliot (as she was now known) is drawing on her *nostalgia*, on the peasant life in Warwickshire as it survived in her day-dreams. But there is another reason for the pervasive actuality of these domestic and rural interests. She has realised that her readers are also town-dwellers and she has learnt to write from their clever, sophisticated point of view. She does not trust them to fill in for themselves the details, at her suggestion. That is to say, she has become an artist, skilled to create not only the pictures but the feelings they ought to inspire. Hayslope was an imaginative experience. In fact, George Eliot may claim to have struck an unfamiliar note in the culture of her age, what we might perhaps call neo-pastoralism.

While the transplanted country-woman was describing the simple life to complex readers, she also discovered that rural scenes and characters can carry the weight of modern thought. Without losing their pastoralism they can suggest the culture of the city. It is noticeable that we are spared the abominations of country life which Kingsley depicts. We enjoy a world of clean kitchens, scrubbed floors, and smiling landscapes. Who could help loving such rustics? They seem so much alive and so amiable in their rusticity. Yet their *naïveté* is deceptive. They are the brief abstract and chronicle of rationalism. As we follow their thoughts and actions, or listen to their shrewd uneducated talk, we are constantly meeting something familiar—our own theories in politics and ethics, or our own cultured desires. *Adam Bede* exemplifies the

[1] Cf. letters written in 1859; to Miss S. Hennell, 19 Feb.; to Mme Bodichon, 11 Aug.; to d'Albert, 18 Oct.

new social science with its obligations and tests for conduct. Hetty Sorrel and Arthur Donnithorne represent those who try to get more out of society than they contribute. Seth Bede is one of those for whom religion is a refuge from life and a substitute for morality. Obviously he should never marry Dinah Morris. For her, religion is not a refuge but an outlet. She embodies the New Testament spirit of universal love and service. Lay ministry is the only expression for her soul and exercise for her splendid gifts. Adam Bede is the hero of the book. His soul is not limited to religion, it is only that his education has been limited to the Bible. Nevertheless, he is the kind of religionist that Arnold wished to see, the spirit which relies on its own discernment and fortitude. In fact, he is so quick to turn convictions into principles, that he cannot allow for the weakness which errs in spite of foreseen consequences. This severity is cured by his infatuation for Hetty. With the breaking of that idol he learns sympathy and tolerance. Henceforth he approaches the highest stage of social evolution, and his worth is no less influential than Donnithorne's recklessness. Just as Dinah had raised others, so he raises Dinah. The other characters are commentators. George Eliot was sufficiently Thackerayan to insert her own comments but too good an artist to rely solely on her own voice. The common folk—Lisbeth Bede, Mr Poyser, his inimitable wife, Bartle Massey—keep the reader's mind clear and prevent him from drifting into Victorian sentimentality. Mr Irwine, like Dr Kenn in *The Mill on the Floss*, exemplifies what the priests in *Clerical Life* missed. He is the one preacher to whom we are expected to listen, for the simple reason that he does not preach.

Adam Bede was hardly finished before she began to work on *The Mill on the Floss*. On 22 January 1861 she wrote to d'Albert: "To my feeling, there is more thought and a profounder veracity in 'The Mill' than in 'Adam', but 'Adam' is more complete and better balanced." The criticism is admirably true. *Bede* was built up round a single incident—the crisis in poor Hetty's destiny—and the problem was studied from outside. Hence the unity of action and the convincing demonstration that social life is interconnected. She had not told the world half of what she had herself learnt about its duties, especially the newly asserted truth that social responsibilities differ according to temperament and circumstances. She much admired the pronouncement "l'inégalité des talents doit aboutir non à l'inégalité des rétributions mais à l'inégalité des devoirs",[1] and she had yet to show how each individual can adjust the claims of society to the claims of one's own self, and yet discharge both. These searching questions involved a study of lifelong influences and family ties. In fact the novel to suit her purpose would have to contain biographies in arabesque. Thus even at the height of her great success George Eliot must have felt that *Adam Bede* did not leave elbow-room for her philosophy, for her "message" as it was then called. At any rate she intended in *The Mill on the Floss* to penetrate more deeply.

The scene is still placed in the leisurely complacent country-side of the pre-railway era and the stage is peopled with picturesque personalities, naïvely loquacious. But the reader soon perceives that these narrow and unprogressive characters, "these emmet-like Dodsons and Tullivers", are not the protagonists. They are the older generation from whose unenlightenment the children have to free themselves. Both of the miller's children will have a lot to learn from experience if they are to play their part in life, and after the bankruptcy their moral education begins. Tom finds his true scope at once.

It is otherwise with Maggie, the central character, and nothing demonstrates more clearly the inwardness of this novel than the study of a protagonist whose soul is not allowed to find an outlet in action. Maggie must live the life of a lady; she cannot contribute towards the restoration of the house of Tulliver; Tom will see to that. Yet she has what Tom has not: imagination, the passion for pleasure, the need to know and understand things, and above all the need to love; problems more difficult to solve than the family affairs. She has to satisfy these longings without evading the service and self-devotion which society exacts from all its members. To achieve this adjustment between what Comte and Spencer call egoism and altruism, she is thrown back on her own resources, that is to say, on the old-fashioned family ideas of duty and reverence, and on what she can learn from the experiences of her own restricted life.

So she becomes, to a certain degree, the prototype of the mid-Victorian spirit struggling to emancipate itself. She turns first to the few works of literature considered proper for young women; then to her brother's school-books. Then she lights upon Thomas à Kempis and gives her whole soul to the old book of devotions,

[1] To C. Bray, 8 June 1848: "Inequality of talents ought to culminate in inequality of duties, not of rewards."

thinking that she has now found the cure for her restlessness. She must form "plans of self-humiliation and entire devotedness", as if she were living in a convent and not among her old associations where each daily experience irritates her wilfulness and calls her back to her unsatisfied longings, yearning to live her life as if it were a drama.

She has her wish when she falls in love with Philip Wakem. He too had risen above the level of his father, the practical scheming lawyer. His companionship would have given Maggie just the expansion which she needed, while his deformity precluded passion but aroused sympathy and tenderness. He would have drawn her out of herself. Yet Maggie hangs back, urging her duty of self-renunciation, and George Eliot seems to approve because her heroine has not yet discovered herself. She is attracted not by love but by pity and the egoism of self-realisation.

A severer temptation awaits her. Her cousin's lover, Stephen Guest, is attracted by her dark eyes and passionate beauty; and this time Maggie feels the call of the blood bewitching her imagination with a world of beauty and delight such as she has read of in poems and romances. Stephen offers her marriage, even assails her with the offer, urging, in the modern spirit, that true love is reckless and that the individual has the right to fulfil himself at all costs. Again Maggie holds back, urging the ties which ought to restrain them both. "You feel, as I do, that the real tie lies in the feelings and expectations we have raised in other minds. Else all pledges might be broken, when there was no outward penalty. There would be no such thing as faithfulness."[1] She realises that her spirit is a complex of many impulses, of friendly love for others, of the need of their friendship in return, of lifelong reliance on her brother, of loyalty to her family traditions; of all those associations on which such worldlings as Mill and Spencer relied to build up the morality of the future. If she had clutched at her happiness she would (according to George Eliot) have sacrificed the divine presentiment of something higher than mere personal enjoyment, which had created the sacredness of life.

So Maggie Tulliver becomes a saint, not according to the New Testament or Thomas à Kempis, but according to the moralists and ethical writers of the mid-nineteenth century. In fact *The Mill on the Floss* might be described as the only good agnostic novel in our language. It will be noted that the heroine does not renounce

[1] Bk VI, chap. XI.

the world. On the contrary she affirms it; she finds her salvation in embracing it. She has at last discovered that "the world" means or should mean our humanity, our points of contact with our fellow-creatures. Here again George Eliot is illustrating the advanced German philosophy of her age. Schweitzer, when reviewing the consequences of nineteenth-century Christology, concludes: "For the general, for the institutions of society, the rule is: affirmation of the world, in conscious opposition to the view of Jesus, on the ground that the world has affirmed itself. This general affirmation of the world, however, if it is to be Christian, must in the individual spirit be Christianised and transfigured by the personal rejection of the world which is preached in the sayings of Jesus. It is only by the tension thus set up that religious energy can be communicated to our time."[1]

As regards the imaginative interpretation of philosophy, George Eliot did not break fresh ground after the publication of these two books. *Silas Marner* (1861), however charming, contributes nothing to our thesis. The reader will agree that the story "unfolded itself from the merest millet-seed of thought" and that it was nothing new for George Eliot "to set in a strong light the remedial influences of pure, natural, human affection". It was inevitable that a change of canvas should be attempted. On 17 February 1862 she notes in her Journal: "I have lately read again with great delight Mrs Browning's 'Casa Guidi Windows'. It contains amongst other admirable things a very noble expression of what I believe to be the true relation of the religious mind to the past." The Leweses had paid Italy an extensive visit in 1860 and another in 1861 and on both occasions spent much time in Florence, and were charmed with "the evening lights on the Arno, the bridges and the quaint houses".[2] Why should not these surroundings be used to emphasise and interpret the values of life, especially the moral law that a human being wins to release from his own troubles only by helping other people? What a complete and picturesque exemplification of this doctrine would be the history of Savonarola?

So in an evil hour George Eliot set herself to write *Romola*. Not without wisdom she chose one of her own sex for the central character, a girl endowed with immense resources of character but undeveloped and ignorant of the world outside her father's library. She is married to the Greek adventurer, Tito Melema, and dis-

[1] A. Schweitzer, *Von Reimarus zu Wrede*, chap. xx [The Quest of the Historical Jesus]. [2] To C. L. Lewes, 17 May 1861.

covers that she can never realise the good in herself while bound to
this graceless scheming husband. She is not going into a convent;
but she is going to do something just as faithless, according to
Victorian ethics. She is going to break all links with the past, with
her duties and sources of affection, and to turn her back on Florence
and the pleasures of life, and to live somewhere in proud isolation,
given up to a life of labour. There is no need to recall how
Savonarola meets her, discovers her through her disguise and
reveals to her that her duty lies in her native town, devoted to the
service of her fellow-creatures—"to keep alive that flame of un-
selfish emotion by which a life of sadness might still be a life of
active love".[1] Those few words from the Frate saved her, and by
the end of the story, after more disillusionments and moral
truancies, she at last achieves the kind of happiness which consists in
forgetting herself. Her true sphere of activity is found in caring for
the children which her husband begot with the peasant girl Tessa.
So Romola is the character who completely wins to goodness.

The other figures, who influence her progress, are those who
(except Tito) have some touches of virtue but do not go the whole
way. The most significant is Savonarola, who might have reformed
the Roman Catholic Church from within and saved it from Luther.
How was it that he could not persevere to the end and be true to
himself? Why did he at the last have to confess to his own insincerity? Because his egoism was stronger than his altruism; his
passion for ascendency effaces his zeal for God. "No man ever
struggled to retain power over a mixed multitude without suffering
vitiation; his standard must be their lower needs and not his own
best insight",[2] as Carlyle maintained. Thus Romola is more saintly
than he, and this contrast is cleverly brought out, when she begs
him for the reprieve of her godfather.[3]

An enormous amount of labour is lavished on this novel. The
authoress declared that there was "scarcely a phrase, an incident,
an allusion that did not gather its value to me from its supposed
subservience to my main artistic objects".[4] Yet the book is a failure
because it is so decidedly and ambitiously a novel. *Bede*, *Mill* and
Silas were treatises of social morality in which the theory was skil-
fully developed into a web of illustrations, illuminated by genius.
Romola is also full of theories and their illustrations, but it also tries
to be a novel on its own account, to arouse and keep your interest

[1] Chap. XLIV.   [2] Chap. XXVI. For Carlyle, *ante*, p. 131.
[3] Chap. LIX.   [4] To R. H. Hutton, 8 Aug. 1862.

by its literary, artistic and historical associations. And why should it not? Because George Eliot had not really the novelist's peculiar genius. Except when describing the conversation and mannerisms of country folk, she was not interested in life for its own sake, but for its moral significance. This prepossession is fatal in an historical novel. As the authoress wants to exemplify a Victorian doctrine, her carefully acquired antiquarianism does not ring true. She accumulates and recapitulates her psychological explanations till we are quite out of harmony with the medieval setting. Undoubtedly that setting is vividly described; no one who has ever visited Florence can help recalling his impressions at every page; but that sense of familiarity is another proof of failure. The real Florence of Savonarola was not the town we visited with the help of Baedeker and some touring agency, although many of the buildings are still the same.

The disappointment with which we close *Romola* does not lessen with the study of her subsequent books. The authoress felt that she was growing old and complains in her letters and Journal of her failing health, and alludes several times to the approach of death. But that is not the reason for her decline. Her intellectual powers show no sign of weakening and her zest for life increases with her increasing prosperity. Her novels become less interesting because she tried to widen and vary their interest. *Felix Holt* (1866), her avowed approximation to the conventional novel, is the least readable of all her works except *Theophrastus Such*. *Daniel Deronda* (1873) contains a great idea. It is the study of a knight errant of the nineteenth century. It tells how a great and gifted man devotes his genius and his money to help the unfortunates, not only the victims of poverty and crime, but the victims of their defects, for instance Gwendolen Harleth, the victim of her own egoism. Yet the characters become tedious and the varied scenes of social dissipation soon pall.

Middlemarch (1872) is undoubtedly the best novel of this period. It tells again of the revolt of noble aspirations and intellectual ambitions, cramped in the philistinism of Victorian life. Nor are the characters much below George Eliot's best. Dorothea Brooke is another Romola in her purity and singleness of aim, her self-devotion, her need of experience, and her patient willingness to do all that her duty requires of her. Casaubon illustrates brilliantly and bitterly a favourite opinion of hers "that the deepest disgrace is to insist on doing work for which we are unfit—to do work of any sort badly".[1] Another fine piece of work is the way Rosamond

[1] To Mme Bodichon, 6 April 1868.

Vincy, Lydgate's expensive and selfish wife, plays her part as a foil to Dorothea's devotion and altruism. As these and other personages with their many connections must slip into situations which multiply their troubles, test or purify their motives and expose the futility and malevolence of provincial life, we can well pardon the narrative for stretching to an unconscionable length and involving no less than four distinct intrigues—more than Thackeray ventured to elaborate in the longest of his long serials. The novel was more successful than *Adam Bede* and the authoress received, as she records in her Journal, "many deeply affecting assurances of its influence for good on individual minds". Then why does the work seem to us to be heavy and at times even wearisome? Because it is dated. We have (or think we have) outlived those old bad times. So we note that George Eliot is repeating herself.

These last three writers—Mill, Spencer and George Eliot—represent an interesting stage in the progress or regress of Victorian sentiment. None of them was fundamentally influenced by Darwin. The author of *The Synthetic Philosophy* had (as we have seen) planned his system before *The Origin of Species* appeared, at a time when, according to Huxley, he was the only reputable thinker who asserted his belief in evolution. Mill[1] spoke of Darwinism as a counterblast to the doctrine of creative foresight, and concluded that this hypothesis was "not so absurd as it looks", adding: "*Whether it will ever be possible to say more than this, is at present uncertain.*" George Eliot in a letter to Madame Bodichon, 5 December 1859, welcomes *The Origin of Species* as "a step towards brave clearness and honesty", but regrets that "the Development Theory, and all other explanations of processes by which things came to be, produce a feeble impression compared with the mystery that underlies the processes". Thus, all three represent a definitely pre-Darwinian effort to rule and direct one's life by the light of reason, before monism and the mechanistic explanation of the universe had made its deep impression on the public consciousness. In fact their aims had been well formulated at least half a century earlier by Senancour:[2] "Il faut se hâter de prouver aux hommes

---

[1] *Theism*, Pt I: "The Argument from Marks of Design in Nature."

[2] *Obermann*, Lettre XLIV: "Men ought to be convinced as soon as possible that, quite apart from a future life, the belief in justice is a spiritual necessity, that even for the individual there is no happiness without the exercise of reason, and that virtuous conduct is as essential to man in society as are the natural laws which govern the senses."

qu'indépendamment d'une vie future la justice est nécessaire à leurs cœurs; que, pour l'individu même, il n'y a point de bonheur sans la raison, et que les vertus sont des lois de la nature aussi nécessaires à l'homme en société que les lois des besoins des sens."

Yet all these writers now prove to be disappointing. They do not give elbow-room to the mind. Despite the freedom of their thought and the range of their vision, one feels restricted. They explain too much. As Heine[1] had said in 1828 or 1829: "Vielleicht bringt solche Lösung grössere Qual als das Räthsel selbst, und das Herz erschrickt und erstarrt darob, wie beim Anblick der Medusa." It might be urged that such impatience is wilfulness; the truth should not be doubted, because unwelcome; a modern human being should face the difficulties of his position. Yet that is just the point. We do not feel sure that any of them understand what we want to know. They mistake the problem of society for the problem of life. Mill's and Spencer's attitude is such as one would expect; they are controversialists, at war with the romantic tradition, so their view was bound to be partial and restricted. George Eliot is the test case for she aims at humanising science. She brings reason into touch with emotion and idealism. She enjoyed an immense success because, as we have seen, she practised the arts of the great novelists, and because she gave imaginative form to the new philosophy which only a minority had studied, but of which the majority was vaguely conscious. One still admires the clearness and consistency of her character-drawing, the homely shrewdness of her dialogue, the careful construction of her plots and, above all, her genius for literary expression. Yet her novels have not stood the test of time. They suffer from the same defect as Goethe's do— they remind one of a menagerie of tame animals, or rather of performing animals. One would have expected the opposite result. She has rightly summed up her own idea: "that a religion more perfect than any yet prevalent must express less care for personal consolations, and a more deeply awing sense of responsibility to man, springing from sympathy with that which of all things is most certainly known to us, the difficulty of the human lot."[2] She evolves this theory among the deepest human passions none the less significant for their homely setting; her pages are crowded

---

[1] *Italien. Die Bäder von Lucca*, Kap. VII: "Such a solution may, perhaps, bring more grief than did the enigma; and the heart shudders and turns to stone, as if Medusa had looked at it."

[2] To H. B. Stowe, 8 May 1869.

with incident. It is of no importance that her simple folk are unthinkingly orthodox, but it is highly important that their creator is thinkingly unorthodox and yet initiated into the secrets of humanity; all save the biggest, the depth and impulsiveness of developed human beings. Her characters may seem to be free, but her creativeness is circumscribed by her exemplary sentiments. Like Spencer, Mill or Comte, she did not want belief but proof; she staked her sense of reality and of human dignity on the study of cause and effect, and left nothing to the creative spirituality of her readers.

Her attitude should be compared with that of De Quincey. He was not only the "opium eater" describing dreams which he had never experienced. He was in sympathy with the clear-headed and rather positivist mentality of the ancients; he was also a close student of Kant; he wrote hard-headed and yet illuminating essays on political economy. But he still found truth in the romantic idea of man. When writing of the human being's attitude to astronomy, he could say "he trembles at the abyss into which his bodily eyes look down, or look up; not knowing that abyss to be, not always consciously suspecting it to be, but by an instinct written in his prophetic heart feeling it to be, boding it to be, fearing it to be, and sometimes hoping it to be, the mirror to a mightier abyss that will one day be expanded in himself".[1] In a *Postscript* added 1854 he could concede all the inconsistencies, inaccuracies and solecisms of the Bible, because they do not matter. The God of the Bible is a *Revealer*, but not of geology, zoology, history or astronomy, or indeed of anything that man can learn for himself, "but of those things which, were it not through special light from heaven, must eternally remain sealed up in inaccessible darkness". He was as untroubled by the conflict between Rome and Evangelicalism as between science and inspiration. For him religious Truth could not be affected by verbal changes. "It is like lightning, which could not be mutilated, or truncated, or polluted."[2] What does it matter if any particular doctrine is invalidated? The truth and the secret implications of the truth would escape at a thousand points and sow the earth with memorials of their mystery.[3] In the same essay he compares the truth with the sun which is hourly undergoing change, as far as we are concerned, but does not develop imperfec-

---

[1] *System of the Heavens, Tait's Edinburgh Magazine*, Sept. 1846.
[2] *Protestantism, Tait's Edinburgh Magazine*, Nov. and Dec. 1847; Feb. 1848.
[3] *Ibid.*

tion, growth or decay. In another essay,[1] he admits that there is a distinction between worldly ethics talking in terms of vice and virtue, and Christian ethics in terms of sin and holiness; but no antagonism, since religion cannot stimulate unless the social state be healthy.

It is no use discussing whether De Quincey or George Eliot is nearer to the truth. But it is safe to say that De Quincey expounds a less partial view. He links the finite with the infinite, the positive with the mystic; and to that extent his vision seems to be more true to human nature. Neither Spencer's synthetic system nor George Eliot's illustrations of his sociology and psychology reveal, to borrow and apply Hobhouse's phrase, that "niche of organic opportunity".

[1] *Glance at the Works of Macintosh, Tait's Edinburgh Magazine,* July 1846.

CHAPTER XVIII

Darwin, Huxley and Haeckel explain man's relation to the Universe, thereby leaving him to discover his relation to himself.

A man of letters is naturally tempted to underrate those who trust only to logic and observation, for it would seem that he had on his side the whole testimony of the human race. Since the dawn of literature man has been chiefly inspired by what was above and beyond his senses or his comprehension. Yet, despite the foregoing chapters of this book, such an inference would be unjust if applied to the nineteenth century. The study of facts had become creative. As early as 13 February 1829 Goethe had asserted to Eckermann that if a human being uses his highest reason (*Vernunft*) he can attain to God through science; provided always that the quest is pursued among data which are living, not dead. "Sie ist im Werdenden und sich Verwandelnden, aber nicht im Gewordenen und Erstarrten."[1]

That remark is of importance. It shows that men of science not only could, but must follow the lead of facts with imagination. For instance, those who cultivated the principles expounded with so much conviction in Claude Bernard's *Science Expérimentale*, must apply them with vision and other worldliness. A materialist could no longer be a broad-minded and dispassionate seeker after truth. We have just discussed three exponents of nineteenth-century modernism, and many more might have been noticed. But Mill, Spencer and George Eliot were enough to represent this quest of a new romanticism founded on experiment and logic. They expound a religion of progress and development; they advocate, construct or exemplify a system which satisfies the moral instinct and does not leave the imagination altogether cold. Yet all three have betrayed a new limitation. They make us think of ourselves as types, or units of an aggregate, a class, a stratum. They take no account of the labyrinths and abysses of individual consciousness. If science were to reform the world it must produce a man of facts who also created in his readers a sense of personal mystery and spiritual adventure. The more accurately his theories are estab-

---

[1] "Godhead is to be found in growth and change, not in things that have completed their growth and are fixed."

lished, the more they must end in a journey through space and time.

The chances and possibilities of such a development were soon to be tested, and, as often happens in the history of culture, the protagonist was to be the most unlikely man in the world. He was not to be qualified for his task by any personal and domestic trials such as George Eliot underwent, nor was he stamped with a peculiar parentage and education such as Mill and Spencer received. He was a singularly tranquil and fortunate member of the upper middle class who refused to succeed except as a naturalist, who enjoyed unique opportunities in that career, and up to the end of his long life he was content to remain a specialist, almost unconscious of his own wider significance. Moreover, he was to be accused of banishing mystery from the Universe.

Charles Darwin was born in 1809. At Shrewsbury he acquired the habit of reading and experimenting in chemistry. At Christ's College he learnt certain sound methods of argument and deduction from the study of Paley, whose conclusions he was afterwards to refute. His friend and adviser, Professor Henslow, proposed him for the post of naturalist in the *Beagle*'s scientific tour round the world. Despite all kinds of accidents and obstacles he was able at the last minute to embark. On 27 December 1831 the ship started on its three years' voyage, but was absent for five. On its return Darwin's apprenticeship was complete.

It was complete because his imagination and human sympathies had kept pace with his astonishing powers of memory, observation, classification, and scientific proof. Unlike so many of his contemporaries he did not waste energy or spirit on a quarrel with religion. During the voyage he remained an orthodox Anglican, and between 1836 and 1839 gradually lost interest in ecclesiastical dogmas because they could not withstand the methods of scientific induction. "Disbelief crept over me at a very slow rate." In the meantime he had found another religion in geology, to which he remained a devoted adherent for more than half his life.

Assuredly Balzac was too hasty when he asserted in 1831 that Cuvier was the greatest *romancier* of the century.[1] After waiting another three or four years, he should have said Lyell and should have said *poet*, for the English geologist carried the inquirer out of himself into the secrets of the Creator and admitted him to the long-buried history of his primeval ancestors and of those other

[1] *Ante*, p. 214.

less pretentious fellow-creatures, the animals. Astronomy staggered the imagination and confounded the reason, and was ill-served with its inadequate instruments, but this study of the earth required only a specialist's hammer and was as wide as the idea of God in His relations to men. Geology had captured Darwin's imagination in youth; it was his dominant interest till after he published the *Voyage of the "Beagle"* (1842–6); during all these years he considered other studies to be "indulging in idleness". He learnt to combine his imagination so effectively with his deductive powers, that he was able to predict the nature of rocks in each district before arrival, and between 1834 and 1835 he thought out his theory of coral reefs before he had even seen one.

But the vitalising power of geology is even more remarkable in that it carried Darwin's genius beyond his chosen orbit, and like religion led him from things known to things unknown. As soon as he returned to England and had begun to revise his specimens and voluminous note-books, he realised in less than a year how many facts indicated the common descent of species and therefore the tendency for some types to progress and for others to degenerate. So far the new knowledge was only confirming what had often been conjectured and implied. The idea of biological progress, differentiation and reversion was old. Not to mention Aristotle's guesses, Kant (1724–1804), Linnaeus (1707–78), Erasmus Darwin (1731–1802) and Treviranus (1776–1837) had suggested or affirmed the progressiveness and instability of organic life. Philosophers had come to the conclusion that external influences hinder the steady advance of nature. Lucretius[1] pictured the wild life of a forest, each species trying to exterminate the other. Hobbes had recognised the principle of *bellum omnium contra omnes* in society as well as in the animal kingdom. Lamarck (1744–1829) had come to the conclusion that changes in environment breed a spirit of change in the habits of animals, and that these new habits produce new organs. Goethe had realised both the likelihood of an inherent growth-force, and of external causes which hindered its effects. These principles in various degrees had been adopted and developed by Saint-Hilaire (1772–1844), Von Buch (1773–1853), W. C. Wells (1757–1817), J. C. Prichard (1786–1848) and P. Mayhew in his Appendix to *Naval Timber and Arboriculture* (1831). We have already noted how much Chambers and Spencer contributed towards popularising the idea before 1859.

[1] *De Rerum Natura*, v.

It is necessary to bear in mind how completely the way had been prepared for Darwin, as otherwise his originality and influence may be misunderstood. The world was familiar with these ideas, but vaguely; and people were not particularly interested because no one had produced an explanation of the actuating principle, at least not a satisfying explanation. It will be remembered that the study of Spinoza was coming into fashion in the nineteenth century and that the Jewish metaphysician always explained a thing by discovering its cause. He traced all phenomena backwards to their source, resolving each cause into its proximate, till he finds the end of the series, the "cause of itself", which is God.[1] That was the chief reason for the seventeenth-century thinker's influence: he conducted our intellects to an idea worthy of our highest aspirations. Nineteenth-century science up to this point was not thus justifying itself. It revealed conditions which could not be attributed to God without challenging his wisdom or omnipotence. Evolution, as observed through modern knowledge, was too clumsy and wasteful a process to be assigned to the purposeful and world-ordering Intelligence. To deny such an Intelligence was to deny that an explanation could be found. Otherwise the combined intellects of the ancient and modern worlds would already have arrived at a scientific solution. But under the circumstances it was easier and more logical to assume that our data must still be insufficient. Huxley states in 1858[2] that Spencer was the only reputable authority who believed that evolution could be established by proof. Louis Agassiz in his *Essay on Classification* (1858) still believed in a purposeful, almost an anthropomorphic, Creator.

In 1859 Darwin published his explanation in *On the Origin of Species*. It asserted and established a principle which, at first sight, was satisfying only in the sense that it could not be disproved. As is well known the theory was suggested by Malthus's *An Essay on the Principle of Population*, one of the most pessimistic books ever written. This cold, mechanistic reasoner explains that in a modern industrialised community the proletariat multiplies so fast that the workpeople have to compete with one another for the means of subsistence; in their case wages. So they are eager to accept a starvation pittance; the successful ones continue to breed; the unsuccessful starve. Starvation is the one limit to over-population.

[1] *On the Improvement of the Understanding.* See also *ante*, pp. 226–8.

[2] "The Reception of *The Origin of Species*", contributed by T. Huxley to *Life and Letters of Charles Darwin.*

Being an economist, Malthus was chiefly interested to notice that this necessitous and competitive existence would as a sheer matter of cause and effect keep wages down to the barest minimum. The Creator had ordained that men should be fruitful and multiply, therefore labour would always be cheap. But the world was not then resigned to accept the Iron Law of Wages as the Law of God. The theory, if welcomed by capitalists, was indignantly repudiated by Engels, Carlyle, Froude, Marx, Ruskin and Morris, and socialist reformers have since demonstrated that the Iron Law is at its worst only cast-iron. The controversy would probably have been relegated to the arena of politics and humanitarianism, except that in October 1838, in a vacant hour, Darwin happened to peruse Malthus's essay, and being a pure scientist it at once flashed upon him "that under these circumstances favourable variations would tend to be preserved and unfavourable ones to be destroyed. The result would be the formation of new species." Here was an idea which might throw light on his geological researches—his proper subject—and it was only gradually that the intrinsic importance of the theory grew upon him. Meanwhile A. R. Wallace, who also realised that species change rapidly or slowly into each other, but could not understand the cause or process of the change, nor see how the world should be full of well-defined and self-contained species amid this gradual fusion and mergence of forms, happened in 1858 to be suffering from intermittent fever at Ternate and, to while away the time, he also read *Principles of Population*, arrived at the same conclusion in an equally disinterested and for him unusually unhumanitarian spirit and sent his hypothesis to Darwin. The two scientists communicated their theory to the Linnaean Society in 1858. A few months later Darwin had shortened and completed the massive work on which he had intermittently meditated for twenty years, and published it in the form now familiar to us.

Thus two men of science discovered what Wallace described as "the long-sought clue to the effective agent in the evolution of organic species". They had both realised that natural selection depends on the struggle for life. Those survive who can continually adapt their organs and energy to the exigencies of existence. They are the fittest. So the modification goes on, and as the unmodified die out, each new species preserves its definite character. Both scientists had found this explanation ready-made for them and familiar to all who systematically study political economy. Both transferred the principle from the works of man to the works of God; and they were able to do so because they kept their minds free from any religious or anti-religious prepossession. Their attitudes to the theological problems of the time were not even the same. Darwin, as we have seen, became an uncontentious agnostic, indisposed to believe in a creative Intelligence chiefly because he found so much suffering and defectiveness in creation. "The mystery of the beginning of all things is insoluble to us." Wallace, to the end of his days, believed in man's immortal soul, cultivated spiritualism, and in 1870 offended Mill by suggesting that an omnipotent and benevolent Deity was quite thinkable, since what we call evil may be essential to the development of the highest good.[1] Thus sentimental convictions had nothing to do with their deductions; their motives were exclusively scientific; had it been otherwise they would have seen too far or not far enough.

The *Descent of Man* was equally disinterested. As early as 1837 or 1838 Darwin had come to the conclusion that man must have evolved much as other forms of life, but he made only a brief allusion to this conviction in *The Origin of Species*, because he had not collected sufficient data, and besides he was more interested in the fertilisation of orchids, the habits of climbing plants and the domestication of animals. He returned to the subject in 1868 or 1869, partly because he was accused of concealing his views, though he was aware that they would "be denounced by some as highly irreligious". The first edition appeared in 1871, and the second, much improved, in 1873, but thereafter he confined himself to research which did not admit of controversy, such as the suggestive *The Expression of the Emotions in Man and Animals* (1872), and "the curious little book", *The Formation of Vegetable Mould, through the Action of Worms* (1881). As early as 1 November 1837 he had read a paper before the Geological Society "On the Formation of Mould".[2] It was the first of his essays to be published in full. Forty years later he returned to the theme and devoted his immense knowledge to proving the delightful thesis that worms are one of the most ubiquitous influences in changing the surface of the globe and one of the most useful to mankind.

It is often urged that Darwin's subversiveness is more apparent than real; that he did for organic matter what Newton did for

[1] A. R. Wallace, *My Life*, chap. xxxiv.
[2] *Geological Transactions*, vol. v, pp. 505–10.

inorganic—reduced it to law; that he explains the principle on which life spreads, propagates and assumes different forms. In his own words, "we no longer look at an animal as a savage looks at a ship". Thanks to this exposition he was able in Cornot's phrase to *réintégrer l'homme dans la nature*. If that were all, Darwin would still be an influential and memorable figure in the progress of science, but only of secondary importance in the history of literature. In fact, he and his fellow-workers made no other claim. But he and they achieved much more for two reasons. In the first place, because his literary style and inexhaustible wealth of picturesque illustrations have captured every thoughtful reader's imagination, and secondly, because his theories, propounded so attractively at that particular moment, first took the heart out of all but his specialised followers, and then put another stronger heart in its place. He comes before us as the most unspiritual of writers. Yet he renews the spirit. For both these reasons his books circulated rapidly. If they are no longer read it is because their import is now part of the modern habit of mind.

It is essential to distinguish what Darwinism denies and affirms. Let it be granted the theory is, from one point of view, dishearten-ing, all the more because Darwin is not an uncompromising atheist. He did not deny the possibility of progress; in arguing that the fittest survive, he pointed towards the amelioration of living things. For instance, the horse has evolved from a little creature hardly bigger than a cat; a man has evolved from an animal which cannot stand upright and gibbers as you pass; this pitiable quad rumanum has struggled upward in common with other vertebrates from a Palaeozoic amphibian, an aquatic bisexual animal whose brain and heart are almost undeveloped. So far none need be dismayed, except the confirmed fundamentalists, and their position had long ago been shaken. In fact Matthew Arnold dismissed the whole moral significance of Darwinism without any hesitation, and then went on to speak of "the awful sanctions with which this right way for man has, he believes, been invested by the mighty *not ourselves* which surrounds us".[1] That belief is the point at which the paths hopelessly diverge. Darwin's *not ourselves* was a combina-tion of impersonal causes and effects which looked grim enough in the social and industrial sphere, where it can or could be influenced by human idealism, but much more grim in the realm of nature. There is no Robert Owen or William Morris in the cosmic process.

[1] *God and the Bible*, chap. III, §5.

Darwin's picture of the consequences created so deep an impression because his illustrations and examples are unforgettable. Huxley's simile "The individuals of a species are like the crew of a foundered ship, and none but good swimmers have a chance of reaching the land"[1] is an unduly optimistic interpretation of natural selection. The struggle for life renders creation incomplete. One need only quote the sting of the bee which tears out the insect's own viscera;[2] the cuckoo, owing to its strength, its instinct and the shape of its back, ejecting its foster-brothers from the nest so that the rightful inmates die of hunger and cold;[3] the boa-constrictor with rudiments of hind-limbs and of a pelvis.[4] Man, having travelled the farthest along the path of evolution, may be the most complex organism, but for that reason retains the greatest number of imperfections and disablements. These and such-like illustrations sink deep into the mind. But on the other hand Darwinism does not only disillusion. It captures the imagination because it carries our thoughts away over the whole globe into the web of life, binding the species together since the beginning of time, and yet reminding us of the details of our own lives; the peculiarities of our own bodies, the origin of our most intimate and essential institutions. Faust[5] need no longer complain in his study that he had surrounded himself with dead bones and skeletons instead of Living Nature. The Darwinian hypothesis was bound to pervade culture and transform humanism, though it begins in a soulless economic formula and for most readers seems to end in an impression of errancy, purposelessness and unintelligence. The theory was indeed disheartening, but it had the depth and suggestiveness which challenge the older humanism.

What most of his contemporaries did not realise was that this challenge became a tonic and inspiration. When first his theory was propounded, some of the humanists and churchmen, for instance, Kingsley, welcomed it; others, for instance, Adam Sedgwick, the Cambridge professor of geology, who attacked *Culture and Anarchy*, also attacked *The Origin*; others of the old school, for instance, Disraeli and Bishop Wilberforce, waxed facetious. A few years later the most liberal-minded became reconciled to the idea, and the Metaphysical Society, founded in order that ecclesiastics, scholars and scientists might ventilate their differences, "died of

---

[1] *The Times*, 26 Dec. 1859.   [2] *The Origin of Species*, chap. VI.
[3] *Ibid.* chap. VIII.   [4] *Ibid.* chap. XIV.
[5] *Faust*, 1er Theil, 1. Gothisches Zimmer.

too much love". Yet, despite this seeming reconciliation, nothing has been the same since Darwinism has been established. Its triumph meant that we are responsible to nothing and nobody except ourselves and our descendants. Whether this particular induction has at last run truth to earth, or is yet another of the false scents which man has followed since the last ape evolved into the first human being—has yet to be discussed. For the moment it is enough to agree that the hounds had again broken covert, and were giving tongue vociferously. The two most prominent propagandists who realised this significance were Thomas Huxley and Ernst Haeckel.

Huxley must have been by nature one of the most imaginative and penetrating students of facts, for the more he discovered, the more he guessed at what was hidden. For that reason he soon found physiology and biology to be more interesting than the classics. Being a poor man, he started to earn his living as a surgeon, but after his four years' cruise in H.M.S. *Rattlesnake*, during which he studied flora and fauna unknown to most naturalists, he gave up all thoughts of practising, and devoted himself to discovering and disseminating the secrets of science. With the instinct of a philosopher he refused to specialise. By the time that he was thirty, he still counted on several more years of general preparation in histology, morphology, physiology, zoology and geology. By 1860 he expected to be ready for any special pursuit.[1] So here was an erudite, as eager as any of his generation for spiritual progress, but more conscious than most of all the maladjustments, catastrophes, anomalies, and relapses fatally intermixed with human and animal existence; unable to visualise the system by which we are encompassed, but convinced that no free human being could face his life problem in the spirit of a true man unless he also faced the influences which condition his destiny. The alternative was to accept the authority of the Bible as founded on miracles, that is to say, founded on superstitions so jealously guarded that a man's word of honour was rejected in a law court, unless he kissed the book which reported these fables. Assuredly the nineteenth century needed a new religion. So thought Huxley.

Darwin supplied this faith because he adduced "no causes but such as could be proved to be actually at work". By so doing, he had solved the problem of good and evil, or, at any rate, had deprived those influences of the mystery which paralyses human

[1] See *Diary*, entry 1856.

confidence and energy. Creation was not the victim of a Power which aimed at perfection and was thwarted either by the intractability of the material, or by a rival power bent on imperfection; nor was creation the victim of an omnipotent Power whose beneficence often inflicted inexplicable misery. Either explanation was an insult to man's dignity—and to his intellect. Creation was not governed by any Power; it was conditioned by *the struggle for life*; that is to say, by a complex of cause and effect, beyond our control indeed, but not beyond our comprehension. It was an influence which could be reckoned with.

Darwin had been content to regret that his conclusions would be "denounced by some as highly irreligious". Huxley argued that they were not in any true sense of the word irreligious, because they encouraged men to work out their own salvation. Darwinism inspired him with the vision of a superman, infinitely more independent, self-reliant, and godlike because free from fear. We now understood our own resources and the limitations of our antagonist. "The progress of society", he declared in *Evolution and Ethics*, "depends not on imitating the cosmic process, still less in running away from it, but in combating it." Any sin, crime or vice was like a careless mistake; it was a wilful relaxation of vigilance in the face of this adversary, who never overlooked a false move in the game.[1] The recognition of this conflict he felt ought to inaugurate a new stage in the development of human mentality.

Should any individual lose heart in this racial struggle against a mechanical universe, he had only to glance backwards on his human ancestry, as far as the apes from which we had evolved by the virtues inherent in our tissues. That review would explain the defects and anomalies of human nature, reminding us that we are still at a half-way stage. It would also reveal the vast distance that we have already travelled and suggest the yet vaster distance that we may hope to go. For it had been proved that, if man had unlearnt some of the animal's instinctive intuitions and skilfulness, he had acquired an almost limitless capacity for being educated. This "educability" could be transmitted; and the development of its possibilities was henceforth to be the greatest of human inspirations.

Thus science was recognised to be very much more than a disinterested quest for truth; it showed us how to live. It had already, in the previous hundred years, produced all kinds of inventions by

[1] Letter to C. Kingsley, 22 May 1863.

which man had outgrown his old puny ill-used self: spinning jennies, iron-foundries, steamers, railroads, anaesthetics, antiseptics; even a more humane and equitable society, for as early as 1845 Disraeli could observe that "modern science has vindicated the natural equality of man".[1] And now this second Renaissance was bringing the new wisdom of self-knowledge. In revealing our kinship with animals, it taught us how to understand ourselves. In revealing the mechanics of evolution, it taught us to calculate the effects of environment and to regulate our adaptations. The prospect seemed to be almost boundless; but only if we could be worthy of our newly discovered destiny. Huxley's attitude admirably illustrates this phase of thought. One would have expected the specialist, one of the greatest living authorities on anatomy, to confine his energy and erudition to the technique of natural selection. Instead of these academic limitations, he entered the lists not only as a scientific controversialist but as an antitheologian. He learnt Hebrew so as to disprove the authenticity of miracles, he wasted his own and Gladstone's time disputing about the Gadarean swine. He did not refute churchmen; he attacked them. He almost reminds one of Goncourt's exclamation: "Oh! l'intolérance du parti de la tolérance. J'ai pensé au mot de Duclos. Ils finiront par me faire aller à la Messe."[2]

In order to establish Darwinism, Huxley was always encountering dogmas and convictions which to many humanists seemed as real as their consciousness of themselves. For that very reason his polemics were scattered and incidental. If we are to form a comprehensive idea of all this movement meant, we must glance at a more consistent and philosophical controversialist.

Ernst Haeckel was born in 1834 and trained as a medical practitioner. But this was an age in which students expected more from science than the means to a livelihood. So Haeckel studied biology in Italy and Sicily, and read *The Origin of Species*. While almost all German experts turned from the book in anger or derision, Haeckel was one of the first to believe in it. Thenceforward he became absorbed in the science of tracing the genealogies of species and interrelating their families. By 1866 he was able to explain in *Generelle Morphologie der Organismen* how Darwin had reconciled accuracy with imagination, natural science with natural philosophy, and had thereby reduced an indescribable tangle of evidence to a single abstract idea which created a new

[1] *Sybil: or The Two Nations*, Bk IV, chap. v.   [2] *Journal*, 8 Oct. 1867.

attitude to life and learning.[1] By 1877 he had almost completed his philosophy of life in *Die Perigenesis der Plastidule* (1877) with the doctrine that unconscious race-memory inheres in the molecules of protoplasm, and thus the *plastidule* is the primary factor in the origin and development of the soul.

These and many other such ventures into science challenged attention but carried little conviction, though enforced by skilful accumulation of evidence, incessant revision and enlargements and the most attractive and artistic illustrations. He soon realised that Darwinism with all its implications was a religion which would meet with unending opposition till it caught public attention and convinced the public conscience that its message was one of progress and aspiration. Humanists and preachers must be persuaded to acknowledge the men of science. So he delivered a course of popular lectures which appeared in book form in 1868 as *Natürliche Schöpfungsgeschichte*, and he again appealed to the whole educated public in *Anthropogenie* (1874). In both these works and in *Inhalt und Bedeutung der Abstammungslehre* he aimed at limiting our sense of awe and mystery, encouraging his age to study the growth of plants, the reproduction of animals, and the psychology of man in the same disillusioned and critical spirit as they already studied magnetism and electricity, earthquakes and thunderstorms.

But it was not till the turn of the century that he struck to the kernel of his problem. He must convince everybody that a knowledge of evolution would lead to a clearer and nobler standard of ethics, that, moreover, scientific realism did not exclude the highest activity of the spirit nor that sense of background and space which seems necessary to the human soul. With this end in view he chose as the subject for his *Altenburger Vortrag* in 1892 "Der Monismus als Band zwischen Religion und Wissenschaft",[2] arguing that monism was as comfortable and satisfying to the soul as to the intellect. Such also is the object of *Die Welträtsel* (1899).

This work differs from those of the English school for three reasons. In the first place, Haeckel was writing for a nation much more under the influence of Rome and much more exposed not only to the aggressive and antirationalist bulls and encyclica which Pius IX issued between 1854 and 1870; but to the diplomacy which his successor exercised with such skill that Bismarck's and Falk's liberalism was thwarted and that Haeckel could protest against

[1] See especially Kap. IV.
[2] "Monism as bond between science and religion."

the "Schlangenwindungen seiner aalglatten Jesuitenpolitik".[1] In the next place, he was writing for a nation whose higher education was largely metaphysical, who still believed in the dualism which Kant taught in his second phase: that there were two worlds, the world of experience (*mundus sensibilis*) such as our observation can penetrate and the world of spirit (*mundus intelligibilis*) of which we were conscious only through inward intimations, moral consciousness and the categorical imperatives. It was only thanks to these intuitions that we gained some idea of reality. Thirdly, as Haeckel was bent on attacking both the theology of Rome and the immaterialism of Kant, he wrote more systematically than did Huxley and more humanistically than did Darwin.

He rearranged and interpreted all his learning and erudition to convince Europe that reality could be established on a more positivist basis. It was matter in contact with motion, and this combination can be called substance. Thus energised, matter has been evolving (we know not why or how) since the beginning of things. So our whole world arises, multiplying into all we see, hear, feel, think and hope. Even human psychology (*jene Summa von Gehirnfunktionen*) is at long last nothing but vitalised nerve-cells and subject to the same laws. It is an inspiring idea, this vision of man issuing from substance and instinctively seeking to know the causes of things, because thereby his development is advanced and his sentiments are focused on the paths of scientific progress. At the Leibnitz-session of the Berlin Academy in 1880, Bois-Reymond had confessed to seven enigmas in human existence. Haeckel believes that his system will simplify all seven into the problem of man's place in creation.

When this relationship is explained, the riddle of the universe (according to Haeckel) will be solved. Its explanation will satisfy our greatest intellectual need, the knowledge of causes, and our greatest moral need, the knowledge of how to express our best selves, thus reconciling religion to science. We shall know where to find and recognise the True, the Good and the Beautiful; man will reason himself out of both self-contempt and self-idolatry; human effort will culminate (as perhaps Arnold would agree) in the creation of a state which was *nomocratic* not *theocratic*.

The book enjoyed an enormous success; ten thousand copies were sold within a few months; by 1918 three hundred and forty thousand copies of the three original editions had been printed; it

[1] "The snake-like coils of his Jesuistic diplomacy, as slippery as an eel."

was translated into twenty-four languages. It not only provoked hundreds of books, brochures and reviews, but elicited over five thousand private letters, mostly drawing attention to biological points which the author had left unsettled.[1] To fill in these gaps as well as to reiterate his principles in the face of criticism, he published *Lebenswunder* in 1904.

These two books contain no new facts; in that sense they are popular manuals. But they contain moral and ethical implications which amount to a reorganisation of science in relation to philosophy and religion.[2] This import is especially noticeable in *Lebenswunder*. Our author keeps before our eyes the two streams of thought: dualism inaugurated by Plato and Aristotle, reiterated by Descartes, and Kant (in his later period), by the romantic philosophers, especially Hegel, and still upheld by the authority of the Church and State; on the other hand monism, first proclaimed by Democritus, then by Lucretius (Haeckel might have added Epicurus), and implied by Spinoza, and now asserted by Goethe (though the reader may wish to qualify that claim) and at last established by the nineteenth-century men of science, Laplace, Lamarck, Baer, Müller, Cuvier, Lyell, but especially Darwin, Spencer and (at the time of writing) Romanes. Haeckel's monism amounts to the conviction that whatever metaphysical forces there may be (generally styled *god* or *spirit*) are only known to us through matter and motion. Thus matter and motion constitute a single principle actuating all phenomena alike, a principle which must be valued not as a superhuman influence, but as an ascertained truth. Science was a thought-picture or rather a mental structure built out of the knowledge of facts, and of course there were still gaps in the architecture which had to be filled by the imagination. Certainty must be supplemented by hypotheses. But this reparation must no longer be effected through romances which flatter the vanity of the human species, or sanctify their intellectual inactivity, but through disinterested inquiry. Haeckel might have postulated an *illative sense* according to his lights as confidently as did Newman[3] according to his. By such scientific-mindedness, man would acquire complete self-reliance, and learn how to reconstruct his life according to the laws of nature. Haeckel is at his

[1] H. Schmidt, *Der Kampf um die Welträtsel*, 1900.
[2] Cf. E. Adickes, *Kant contra Haeckel; Erkenntnistheorie gegen Naturwissenschaftlichen Dogmatismus*, 1901.
[3] *Ante*, chap. v.

best when explaining how a monistic conception of society will lead to gentler manners and purer laws.

These two efforts at popularisation and propaganda are a masterpiece of lucidity, so their success was assured. In the first place they unified and reaffirmed many reactions against the vested interests of official orthodoxy, what Haeckel himself called *Scheinchristentum*. Even though this freethinker could complain in 1907 that neither Prussia nor Bavaria allowed their priests and schoolmasters to teach the truth, yet the revolt was long overdue. The rise of Garibaldi in 1860 and the fall of France in 1871 had deprived the Curia of its temporal power. Zola's *Lourdes* and *Rome* had rendered infidelity fashionable. Even within the fold, men like Bunsen, Döllinger and Newman had shown where to look for the feet of clay. In attacking the officialdom of Christianity Haeckel was killing a corpse; so all its enemies were in at the kill. In the next place, *Die Welträtsel* and *Lebenswunder* offered a thrice welcome release from this "multitudinousness of life"—all the jangling creeds, contradictory convictions, all the romantic pretensions which troubled nineteenth-century humanism, and led to so many disillusionments. Much had to be renounced, but in return each human being could now control the rudder of his boat. It was an easy way out of the cross-currents.

Besides, if Huxley and Haeckel were right, there was nothing in Darwinism to discourage human aspirations. Even if we could no longer rely on Divine Intelligence to direct our course, we could still conclude that man had evolved an inner purpose of his own; though individuals might disagree as to what that purpose was. Darwin himself had not discussed, much less explained, this purposiveness, because he had something else to do. His task was to establish a principle (hitherto overlooked) which had influenced this purpose. Huxley had been equally indefinite for a similar reason; he was too busy disproving the old teleology to say much about the new. Haeckel, as we have seen, set himself to supply these omissions. His enthusiasm was contagious, but on second thoughts not convincing. One cannot help feeling that this German optimist was childlike in his faith; was too easily pleased; and that so were his readers.

For these various and contrary reasons Darwinism, despite its triumph, produced an effect which was unnecessarily negative and depressing. It need not have been so. In fact more than one thinker was able to face our predicament on this planet with all

Darwin's and Huxley's cool-headedness, and to use all his knowledge to direct human purposiveness, without resorting to Haeckel's
illusions. One of the less familiar is Remy de Gourmont. He could
write "La vie est terrible. Elle a un but qui n'est pas celui que
nous insinuent notre vanité et notre lâcheté";[1] lest we should mis-
understand this ruthlessness he composed *Physique de l'Amour*, a
study of the sexual instinct as nature willed it to be; yet this poet
and novelist developed his own "philosophie du bonheur" and
devoted his talents to show how our conduct and especially our
habits of mind should be readjusted to face the truth.

The most illustrious is Elie Metchnikoff, who was born in Russia
in 1845 and after studying and teaching zoology in Germany went
to the Pasteur Institute in 1888, where he lived and worked like a
medieval anchorite. No man better understood the Darwinian
hypothesis and all its implications. Towards the end of his life he
wrote: "Man is a kind of miscarriage of an ape, endowed with
profound intelligence and capable of great progress. His brain is
the seat of processes that are very complex and much higher than
those of other animals, but these functions are incompatible with
the existence of an immortal soul."[2] Yet this *savant* not only devoted
his life to studying bacteriology and the embryological history of
the lower vertebrates, learning therefrom how to create serums
against chronic disease. He used these highly specialised researches
to heal the human spirit. He ventured to explain that much of our
restlessness, melancholy, and bitterness result, like many of our
illnesses, from disharmony with our environment, from the rapidity
with which we have outgrown our animal ancestors. Nay more,
he suggested how we could use the knowledge of our ignoble and
hybrid origin to heal the discontent which sentimentalists believed
to be divine. For instance, one of the curses of humanity was the
fear of death, yet this science which established the animalism of
man could thereby teach us something (according to Metchnikoff)
beyond the power of religion and philosophy. The study of phago-
cytes would convince us that we were evolved to live twice our
present span, perhaps about 140 years; that the fear of death is
nature's urge to complete this circle; that life can be prolonged
(not by prayers but by antitoxins) to this normal limit; and then,
full of years, we shall be ready to die—like other animals.

[1] *Le Chemin de Velours*, 1902, chap. xi: "Life is terrible. Its purpose is not such
as our vanity and cowardice flatter us into believing."

[2] *La Nature de l'Homme*, 1903, chap. xii. Translated by P. C. Mitchell.

CHAPTER XIX

Darwinism had created a new atmosphere for literature to breathe: individual self-expression and self-realisation without spiritual guidance —Under that influence imaginative authors tend to become neo-realists —The inherent weakness of that school can be appreciated by a glance at the de Goncourts.

What a numerous and energetic party had long wished for was made possible in 1859. In that year it was demonstrated to their satisfaction that man must trust nothing but his own intellect. Such was the only right way of facing the mysteries of human nature, which had otherwise proved to be so disquieting and un-reliable an influence; such was the only right way of helping our-selves and our fellows to attain a freer and therefore a happier manner of life; such was the only right way to conquer disease, waste, injustice and mismanagement.

The subsequent history of civilisation has not definitely dis-credited any of these hopes and pretensions. The human race has passed on to realise and improve its opportunities as never before. The mechanisation and scientification of existence have, of course, brought their own burdens and dangers, which have to be faced; but they need no longer bring despair. In the pre-Darwinian periods (it might be urged) there were good grounds for revolt against material progress, since, quite apart from the obvious abuses of commercialism, the pursuit of prosperity left the spirit behind. It was not a question of dogmas, doctrines, but of culture *versus* civilisation. But now, the new science was beginning to create an immense confidence in man's own resources. We were learning to inquisitorise our human destiny in the quiet aloofness of our laboratories and studies; it was as if we were superior beings superintending the management and mismanagement of a system which we served as animals, but dominated as thinkers. Darwinism (so it then seemed) confirmed and consummated this attitude. If it battered the last trust in pneumatology, it put human difficulties in a new perspective. We advanced firmly, step by step, into the mysteries of life; each humiliating discovery ennobled us by the courage and intelligence with which we achieved it.

Could such a culture satisfy the life of the spirit? That is the

question which we must now answer. At first one is tempted to
reply that there should be no lasting difficulty, only an awkward
period of transition. It will be remembered[1] that the influence of
the spirit can be recognised in literature as often as a man feeds in
his heart on a noble and satisfying conviction and also finds his
idea reflected in the world around him. He verifies his aspirations
in his daily contacts. There was no necessary reason why a
Darwinian should not thus realise his highest self. Modern science,
pursued in collaboration, had become an organised power capable
of transforming religion, philosophy, administration—our most
private and public concerns. Could not the educated man acquire
a reverence, even an enthusiasm for the intellectual creativeness of
his species as mirrored in his own thoughts? Could he not substantiate his consciousness of adaptive power a hundred times over,
in experiment and speculation? Would he not thus be able to
confirm his idealism and keep his spirit alive?

Despite the prospects and promises discussed in the previous
chapter, it seems unlikely. The more man has learnt to venerate
his powers of deduction and construction and scientifically to
impose on life his own sense of form and regularity, the more he
has found that life was neither regular nor formal, nor susceptible
to the laws of construction and deduction; not at least the life of
personal experience. It was an old disillusionment; not a discovery
but a rediscovery. Darwin and his followers had merely intensified
the shock by asserting the effectiveness of the scientific mind and
by eliminating other compensations and encouragements; for instance, trust in our divine origin. Such, it appears, is our present
dilemma; and the history of its development is to be traced in the
history of the novel.

The older Victorians (as we have seen) had gradually ceased to
believe in themselves, though they refused to believe in Darwin.
But it need not be added that many younger men were still prepared to grapple with the complexities of the life among which
they were learning to feel their powers, and that the more they
examined and even enjoyed the paradoxes of the new civilisation,
the more they were constrained to express their reactions. The
novel exactly suited this new spirit of experiment. It was not a
highly developed type; it was still an embryo, a plaything. It was
not pledged to any school of sentiment or thought. Mrs Radcliffe,
Miss Austen, Disraeli and Dickens had put its narrative form to

[1] *Ante*, chap. i, pp. 3–5.

so many unexpected uses, that by 1860 it was a vessel ready for any content—*un genre qui se prête à tout* as Sainte-Beuve remarked.[1] Its one essential quality was the pedestrian, commonplace range of its interests. Since Thackeray made his name, it had become earth-bound; an escape from the flights of poetry and of metaphysics. Obviously the novel must become the organ of this mechanised science-burdened age. It was Jules de Goncourt who formulated these possibilities. When in 1856 he closed one of Poe's volumes it dawned on him that he held in his hand the literature of the twentieth century called into existence to describe a world in which things are more important than personalities—"Le roman de l'avenir appelé à faire plus l'histoire des choses qui se passent dans la cervelle de l'humanité que des choses qui se passent dans son cœur."[2]

Once such interests were associated with the arts of narrative, it was bound to become the prevailing literature of modern times. It was able to assimilate all that was least pretentious and most intimate in the older types of literature, especially the prose essay and verse satire; and at the same time its expressiveness was better adapted to the works of man than to the works of God. Besides it gave full scope to the newborn taste for scientific courage and accuracy of impression. The author now had his chance to catch and perpetuate the characteristic phrase, gesture, or peculiarity of dress which revealed in a flash the elemental human being reshaped into some social type. In fact, the novel could be created out of documents written by nature as history out of documents written by man. Nor did this truthfulness exclude the play of the imagination. The novelist, and by the same token the reader, could multiply his personality again and again; however closely bound to his verifications he could choose anybody else's character through which to study and enjoy his own contacts. Each impersonation made realism more romantic. And lastly, in this age of universal education and multiplied printing houses, the novel was likely to attract the largest reading public.

Thus the time, the place and the material were to hand, and neo-realism entered upon its career. The reader will forgive a reminder that this type of novel was then a specialised and hitherto unattempted experiment in truthfulness. Realism of another kind

[1] *Journal des Goncourt*, 1861.
[2] *Journal*, 16 juillet 1856: "The novel of the future summoned to record what passes in the human brain rather than in the heart."

is probably as old as good literature, and some of its best examples are to be found in the *Iliad*. Most of those and other such vivid descriptions represent what is painful or dangerous, but from the time when Homer portrayed the horrors and disasters of battle to the time when Shelley created the desolation in the garden of the sensitive plant, the realists (if so they may be styled) were guided and inspired by some ideal of what human beings were or ought to be. Even Crabbe, whom Hardy[1] honoured as an early apostle of realism, was bent on awakening the virtue of charity. They all wrote with an *arrière-pensée*; they used their vivid descriptiveness to reflect or at least suggest their own spiritual content; they aimed at reality more than at realism.

The Cloister and the Hearth is one of the latest examples of this old-world realism. It started as *The Good Fight* in *Once a Week*. The editor tampered with the text, so Reade terminated the story after a few numbers and then set himself to recreate and enlarge the theme into a four-volume novel. He lavished on it all the resources of historical research; he employed undergraduates to devil for him at the Bodleian; he almost buried himself beneath the heaps of sifted facts; at times he despaired of producing anything worth all this labour and resolved never again to attempt an historical novel. He had his reward. The book appeared in October 1861; its medievalism was at once recognised as breathing the very spirit of that time; when *Romola* was published two years later, George Eliot's romance was revealed by comparison to be Victorian tinsel.[2] Yet *The Cloister and the Hearth* is one of the most expansive and elevating books of the century. If it recreates a vanished age, it does so through the modern sense for practical details; while satisfying the most meticulous passion for accuracy, it exhilarates and ennobles with its visions of human perfection. Reade has measured the Middle Ages by his own highest standards, and has found after thorough research that they can stand the test.

The older realists studied their actuality by the light of their ideals, but neo-realism was to be purged of such prepossessions. Its principle was to be the scientific mastery of human conduct; the impersonality of research even among the social sentiments; intellectual impartiality in the world of daily experience. Jules de Goncourt had first visualised these possibilities; he and his brother Edmond are the most typical exponents, even if not the most talented.

[1] F. E. Hardy, *The Later Years of Thomas Hardy*, 1930, chap. VIII.
[2] M. Elwin, *Charles Reade*, 1931, chap. VII, § 1.

Edmond who wrote most of the novels and Jules who shaped his brother's mind and composed, before his death, the two first and best volumes of the immortal *Journal*, were of aristocratic descent and sensitive even for Frenchmen of the Third Empire. They gave up years to studying the eighteenth century, read thousands of pamphlets, journals, diaries, examined hundreds of prints, engravings and sculptures; never rested till they had mastered the significance of every gesture of the *ancien régime*. Thereby they not only soothed their anti-modernism with the refinement and repose of a vanished culture, but they learnt how to revive the past out of its surface hints, poses, and reminiscences. They cultivated the art of fixing what is fugitive. Such interests might seem opposed to the study of modern vulgarity. And yet, having acquired and exercised these talents, it was impossible that they should remain antiquarian scholars, limited to intellectual reconstruction. They were much too perceptive and artistic, too restlessly imaginative, and responsive to the living interests around them, and at the same time they were utterly unpreoccupied by any devotion which might give an unworldly direction to their spirit. So it was almost inevitable that they should do for the Paris of Napoleon III what they had done for the Paris of Louis XV.

Under the influence of their age they were starting to record their experiences with the hand of an artist and the head of a man of science. But they did not tell the whole truth, only that part which stank of poverty, perversion or crime. They burrowed into slums, brothels, prisons; they practised the *métier* of the *mouchard* and the *agent de police*; they lived in imagination the lives of prostitutes, perverts, paupers, lunatics and murderers. If asked why they had left the polite *salons* of the eighteenth century for the sewers of the nineteenth, they would have replied that they sought creative inspiration, that if they wanted those raw, intensified individualities which give life to a book they must look for them where civilisation was almost effaced; that, moreover, being aristocrats, the *canaille* had for them the roominess and adventure of an undiscovered country. Only these sour, drab, crude specimens had the property of glowing red-hot in contact with the imagination.

Why should the neo-realist feel that his inventiveness required such pungently seasoned food? Because he had tried to clear his mind of all spiritual prepossessions such as Balzac, or Victor Hugo might have cherished. He wanted to note, mark and report in the new spirit. But a man of letters cannot record his impressions as if

he were a man of science. He cannot be detached as well as subjective, the interests which he creates in his reader's mind must be
of the same sort as those he feels when identified with the business
of living and dying. He must mix his ideology with what he creates.
But what had the neo-realist within his spirit on which to draw?
No saving sense of grandeur or beauty, no ideal or even idea such
as satisfy oneself and can be suggested in a hundred inventions,
founded on experience. He was thrown back on his natural disposition, that is to say, the unsatisfied hopes, ambitions and
expectations of life, the outraged sensibilities, the yet more outraged humanitarianism, all the individual's immemorial quarrel
with destiny embittered by the artist's quarrel with the perfection
which he cannot achieve. He must handle material which will
rouse this nest of wasps.

Such is the attitude of the neo-realist, whatever his nationality or
social position. For instance, Flaubert consecrated his genius not
to the study of human nature but of human stupidity; and pro-
secuted his researches with such penetrating resentfulness that he
has discovered a new mental abnormality in our human pathology:
Bovaryism,[1] the mania for misconceiving oneself. But just as the
de Goncourts are the most uncompromising example of the aptitudes
of the school, so they are the best illustration of its disabilities,
thanks to their *Journal*. They tell us that the strain of their researches
into human misery was almost unbearable. They worked not only
with their brains but with their sensibilities—"Les premiers nous
avons été des écrivains des nerfs."[2] Such was literally the case. In
order to discover something new in what was familiar and something attractive in what was sordid, they were constantly projecting
themselves into imaginary situations, and then anatomising the
sensations and susceptibilities which ought to result. Thus their
documentations were galvanised into artistic effect, but this continual self-examination—this *autopsie perpétuelle et journalière de son
être*—ended by laying bare the most sensitive nerves, till moral
irritability perverted their outlook. When they heard talk of an
operation, they called God a *bourreau* for necessitating surgeons, or
an *empoisonneur*,[3] because He filled the tropical paradises with
insects, fevers, and wild beasts. They declared that birth, life and
death were chemical actions, that animal movement resolves itself
into the fermentation of a dung heap;[4] that any touch of charm or

---

[1] Cf. J. de Gaultier, *Le Bovarysme*.   [2] 22 Déc. 1868; cf. 5 Mai 1869.
[3] 18 Déc. 1860.   [4] Jeudi, Jan. 1861.

glory in this *misère de la matière* was due to the imagination of man. They defined life as *l'usufruit d'une agrégation de molécules*.[1]

The de Goncourts are, no doubt, an extreme case, but their state of mind seems, then, to have been more or less inevitable as soon as a novelist studied human nature by the light of experience, especially his own. Zola was making a curious attempt to recover width and steadiness of vision. He told Edmond[2] that he intended to write the natural and social history of a family, examining the temperaments, characters, vices and virtues developed by environment —like a garden varied by cloud and sunshine. Yet he succeeded only in portraying the vices, the shadows. Like the others, he fell a victim to cynicism. Could it have been otherwise? Jules laid his finger on the fundamental disability when he noted "Le tourment de l'homme de pensée est d'aspirer au Beau, sans avoir jamais une conscience fixe et certaine du Beau".[3]

It may be objected that this pessimism and perversity were due to the French temperament and mode of life. But we shall find that the same conditions produced the same consequences in our literature, though not to the same degree. English writers did not so readily form schools and encourage each other to go to extremes —not at that period. Besides, the taste of the preading public was still supposed to be sentimental, and authors therefore tried to create an interest outside photography. Nevertheless, it remains true that the man who undertook the interpretation of life without preconceived hopes fell a prey to his worst fears. So it came about that English neo-realism which ought to have resounded like a battle-cry for courageous truth, began to play on the aggressiveness prompted by craven thoughts. Even those who were also in revolt against Victorian foppishness and affectation became too destructive. In their readiness to jettison sentimentality they threw overboard the worth of life.

Contrary to a widespread impression, the English are optimistic and many attempts were made to dissipate this atmosphere of gloom—to probe the truth without losing heart, to know the world and yet know more than human nature at its worst. We must now see whether these efforts enjoyed any measure of success. There is no need, nor enough space to discuss all. The failure of Gissing, Meredith and Hardy will be more than enough.

[1] 23 Août, 1862.   [2] 27 Août, 1870.
[3] 23 Août, 1862: "It is the curse of an intellectual to aspire towards the Beautiful, without ever having a certain and consistent conception of what it is."

CHAPTER XX

Gissing and Meredith set themselves to describe life as it is—Neo-realism gives them no other standard than their own inhibitions and disappointments.

It was suggested in the previous chapter that the scientific spirit of the age had jaundiced the eyes of imaginative writers and that novelists were almost doomed to describe the worst aspects of modern life, because they had lost affinity with the better. Whoever looked for too much of the naked truth found his undressed self. Consequently our most talented authors failed to make the best of their art. The three most conspicuous examples must now be discussed.

The first and most conspicuous case is George Gissing (1857–1903). Fate had specially appointed him to enlarge and ennoble the scope of realism. Though the son of a Wakefield chemist, he enjoyed a University education, and acquired a very genuine talent for humanism, especially an enthusiasm for the classical attitude of mind, its reasoned ideals, its dignity, and resignation. "With leisure and tranquillity of mind I should have amassed learning. Within the walls of a college I should have lived so happily, so harmlessly, my mind ever busy with the old world."[1] Such ought to have been his lot, but by the time he was nineteen years old he had thrown away every chance except that of living by his pen. After a visit to America and Germany, he returned to London penniless and saddled with a wife. He settled down in slum lodgings (once in a cellar with an area grating) and subsisted on pennyworths of pease-pudding sold round the corner, till he should make a decent living out of neo-realism.

He had, one would say, every qualification. The new movement was in the air; it was the cry of the progressive novelists; it required just that material which Gissing was in a position to exploit. No other author was serving so appropriate an apprenticeship. By experience and opportunity he was easily an unenviable first. Nor was he without his spiritual standard, for he had saturated his mind in classical literature. In 1884 he wrote to Mrs Frederic Harrison: "The conditions of my life are prepos-

[1] *The Private Papers of Henry Ryecroft*, 1903.

terous. There is only one consolation, that, if I live through it, I shall have materials for a darker and stronger work than any our time has seen." In other words, his purpose was to apply the Greek idea of tragedy to the miseries of London poverty.

He nearly achieved the feat. He realised—no one better—that in his day "Destiny" sat at the tables of the money-changers, that the cash-nexus was the means to self-fulfilment. Personally he hated commerce and business; he even hated science, which seemed to be arming humanity with appalling powers of destruction and would one day threaten the future of our race. Yet he realised that this civilisation had created a world in which it was possible for some individuals to grow in grace, and leisurely to mature the noblest qualities granted to mankind. The sweating, toiling millions, the clanging factories and steam-driven, smoke-sullied monsters of mechanical transport bestowed on some few fortunates a life of dignified and cleanly activity, personal refinement, intellectual pursuits and contact with feminine charm. Nature and education (itself one of the most expensive privileges) prepared the human being for this destiny; money did the rest. Failing this claim on human labour, the modern man will be devoured by a passionate longing which he can never satisfy, and all this time he will be sinking lower and lower among the mutilated, thwarted millions who lose their own lives to give ease and prosperity to the few. Such were the hopes and fears which possessed Gissing's soul and came to life in his novels.

Not that he was really one of the victims. On the contrary he was a scholar. If we are to believe his letters he had read all ancient and medieval history, all ancient and modern philosophy, beginning with Plato and Aristotle, all Greek poetry and the best of medieval and modern verse. He made several trips to Italy, Germany and France. Once he visited Greece. In the spring of 1890 he decided that London was too lonely and he went off to live at Exeter and there wrote *New Grub Street* and *Born in Exile*. But he was always in danger of being overwhelmed. His improvidence kept him poor, his imprudent marriages impaired his social position and poisoned his domestic life. Thus, partly through his own fault, partly through the accidents of his birth and his broken career, he was uniquely qualified to visualise and appreciate the more than human influences which surround us. Just as Herodotus revealed the deceptiveness and irony of the gods, so Gissing could reveal the insidiousness peculiar to industrialised

society. He does not, of course, anywhere claim to be continuing
the classical tradition. Nevertheless, his themes are akin to those
of Sophocles: the strong man struggling against the Fate which
he has not fully deserved and cannot clearly trace to its source.

So Gissing tried to endue neo-realism with the seriousness of
great literature

> As when some greater painter dips
> His pencil in the gloom of earthquake and eclipse.

He haunted police-courts, factories, soup-kitchens, attics, base-
ments, public-houses, coffee-houses. He watched the glimmering
streets filled by workers before the dawn and filled again at the
unyoking hour; he listened to barrel-organs and to the rough east
wind whispering in the autumn its first presage of bronchitis and
nasal catarrh. He celebrated the working-man's bank holiday at
the Crystal Palace and all the boredom of his ordinary Sunday
afternoon in the slum. But wherever he went, he was conscious of
the destiny from which he himself was fleeing—self-fulfilment
thwarted by poverty. It is not true that Harold Biffen in *New
Grub Street* was speaking for his creator when he declared his theme
to be the "ignobly decent life". Gissing's spokesman is the Waymark of *The Unclassed*: "...the novel of everyday life is getting
worn out. We must dig deeper yet to untouched strata." Yet he
did not reach them, he only appeared to do so. Here is another
latter-day novelist practising the scientific methods of realism, his
mind broadened by the depersonalising sympathies of all the
great literatures—every inducement to be detached and universal
—yet he cannot "dig deeper" than his own fears and hopes. He
lacks the spiritual standards of the masters. He cares only to find
his own problem multiplied and intensified in every scene of
misery and shabbiness, he places himself in the other person's shoes,
then fills in every detail from faithful and minute observation,
inspired by hatred of these disgusting conditions.

It is true that the scope and range of neo-realism mitigate and to
a certain extent conceal this continual repetition of self. Just as
Zola disguised his formula for novel-construction by varying the
scene, conducting his admirers from one phase of modern activity
to another, from coal-mines to La Bourse, from the meat-market
to Lourdes, from a biologist's laboratory to the French army at
Sedan, so Gissing was able to diversify his tragic theme by changing
his backgrounds till the reader feels that all the secrets of London

suffering have been disclosed to him. Nor can it be denied that these revelations to a certain extent justify themselves. They satisfy a legitimate curiosity in the reverse side of industrialism. But Gissing is not writing as a humanitarian, but as a humanist. He is drawing on his experiences and expectations to create tragedy in the form of a novel, and in this higher sphere his work has surely failed.

His heart was not big enough for his arduous enterprise. Early in life it looked as if he would succeed. After the immature *Workers in the Dawn* (1880) he produced his first masterpiece, *The Unclassed* (1884). It is as pessimistic as any of his later novels, yet the book is permeated by the young man's love, or rather his expectation, of London: the conviction that below the drab, preoccupied surface—behind that lighted window blind, or inside this open shop, apparently monopolised by its insignificant traffickings—there lurk not only romance but heroism and aspiration. For instance, we find a prostitute, Ida Starr, who has been left to face the world in her 'teens. Her decline is studied as realistically as in *The Harlot's Progress*. The novelist does not spare you a single unpleasant truth, yet he leaves his heroine at the end unsullied in thought, even noble. Waymark, the underpaid schoolmaster and scribbler, becomes attached to her; and so this woman who lives by immorality and this man who has never pretended to be moral are drawn into a perfectly pure alliance through kinship of spirit. In fact what Gissing finds beneath the surface of London are the people who will not be enslaved by life, who "refuse the statistic badge", and decline to be classed and done with—the "unclassed" who suffer the "ostracism of an intellect without an income" and stoop to all kinds of sordid trades, yet live a second life, intent on their ideal of happiness, and always recognise each other by some secret sign or token.

Gissing afterwards alluded to this novel rather contemptuously as "the work of a very young man who dealt in a romantic spirit with the gloomier facts of life". The novel is certainly immature, in places devoid of all verisimilitude, but it is not so much romantic as fraught with an idea, a part of himself made true of others. With the passing of his youth the idea passed also. Gissing gradually became so careworn with his own inhibitions and frustrations that he failed to see more in other people than he himself was suffering; he lost the Sophoclean vision of what the victim gains and misses. His characters become as uninteresting as their surroundings.

There is still something of his earlier sense of potentialities in *Thyrza* (1887), his favourite novel. Gilbert Grail, the soap and candle factory-hand devoured with a passion for humanism, is a truly tragic figure. The prospect of the poor man's library, which will bring all heaven into his dreary, ignoble life, has just that glamour of prosaic idealism which our industry-ridden age requires. But he and Thyrza soon sink back into the commonplace and there is left the *mise en scène*, interesting only to those who are unfamiliar with its realities. So with *The Nether World* (1889). Gissing crowds all the dirt, wickedness and stupidity of all the slums into its pages. He picks out two characters; Sid Kirkwood the skilful, unencumbered mechanic, and Jane Snowden, the penniless orphan, the drudge tolerated out of a show of charity. These are two beings of a different order, and he puts a fortune within their reach, one which they are to devote to the relief of poverty. There are boundless possibilities in the theme; not of course as an old-fashioned study of alms-giving; but for two personalities uprooted from the rank soil in which they have grown, enlivened by new activities, exposed to new temptations, while the discharge of their mission would have brought the reader into touch with all the graft, misery, heroism and imposture of industrial London. But the author is by now overwhelmed with his own disappointments and heaps them upon his characters, worthy of a less savage fate. They remain as good as human beings can be —perhaps better—but they do not achieve the words and gestures which would reveal their goodness. Instead of such discerning interpretations, we are given some powerful studies of the frustration which brutalises or stupefies its victims, for instance, Bob Hewett, Clem, Scawthorne and Pennyloaf Candy, and some unforgettable glimpses of London streets and manners in all their monotonous beastliness.

It is significant that for his next great work, *New Grub Street*, he chose a subject which was bound to delight a misanthrope, the careers of professional writers. Whatever his failures, Gissing knew by now that he was master of an uncommon talent, and he might very well have portrayed the labours and struggles he understood so well and yet, without sentimentality or unfaithfulness, have added that touch of more than worldly achievement and self-fulfilment which he always felt that he had missed: he could, in this way, have made much of Reardon or Marian Yule. But his men and women enter the kingdom of ink and paper, and find themselves caught in a web and sucked dry of their life-blood. The character of Jasper Milvain is very noteworthy. Gissing had already attempted in *The Unclassed* to create the portrait of the intellectual without money who hankers after the good things of this life and means to buy them with the help of journalism. But whereas he allowed Waymark some idealism, he has now convinced himself that Milvain should be superficially affable and utterly mean and unscrupulous at heart. Yet this novel is admirably written, even the author was pleased with his work.[1]

Gissing wrote nine more novels and many short stories, especially after Morley Roberts had convinced him that the United States offered a better market for such wares. They lack the pointed bitterness of his earlier work, not because the author had become reconciled to life, but because he was losing power, all except *Born in Exile* (1892).

This novel, his most introspective and broad-minded effort, has often been discussed by critics, for instance, J. W. Cunliffe and H. Williams.[2] So it is enough to remind the reader that *Born in Exile* is another and much deeper study of *The Unclassed*. Godwin Peak is a self-made man of intellect who cannot find his proper place in the world, because he lacks money, social opportunities, and above all, breeding. The resemblance between this type and Gissing has been over-emphasised. Ever since the publication of *Demos*, if not before, our author had been recognised by the aristocracy of the intellect. By the time that *Born in Exile* was written he knew Meredith, Hardy, F. Harrison, Morley Roberts, W. H. Hudson and H. G. Wells. He used to receive invitations to dinner, to week-ends in the country, even to tennis parties. Of course he nearly always declined,[3] and if he sometimes went for weeks or months without speaking to anyone except his landlady it was because his intellectual confidence was only equalled by his personal diffidence. Nor was his taste in women as exigent as Peak's, otherwise his domestic life would have been less lonely and more tranquil. But in another more subtle connection Peak is the impersonation of his creator. Gissing was one of those characters explained and classified by Maurice Barrès in *Les Déracinés* (1897), that is to say, students belonging to the age of science and analysis

---

[1] To his brother, 19 Feb. 1891.

[2] *English Literature during the last Half Century*, 2nd ed., 1923. *Modern English Writers*, 1918.

[3] A. and E. Gissing, *Letters of George Gissing to His Family*, 1927.

who create their moral and spiritual atmosphere out of their own intellects, and being free to play with the materials of culture, make free with everything else. This new generation lose touch with the traditions of their class and consequently they lose touch with their inner selves.[1] Godwin Peak is one of these; he does not possess himself. Gissing, in one of his best prose passages,[2] describes how his hero once lost all sense of personality when he let his thoughts stray along the lines of scientific research. Thus isolated among the medley of ideas which constitutes the universe as we know it, he becomes inconsistent and irresponsible. When posing as an orthodox Christian at the Warricombes' house he feels that he is in a dream. "A tormenting metaphysical doubt of his own identity strangely beset him. With an involuntary attempt to recover the familiar self he grasped his own wrist."[3] Barrès and Paul Bourget (beginning with *Le Disciple*) have thrown out ominous warnings that this impersonality and rootlessness may lead to crime. Gissing shows how it may lead to dishonour.

Born in Exile is all the more revealing because Gissing had not set himself the task of demonstrating such possibilities. But the truth slips out. For instance, in one of those interesting conversations in which the novel abounds, Malkin at the end of a tirade exclaims,

"'Do you seriously believe that happiness can be obtained by ignoring one's convictions?...'

'But what if you have no convictions?' asked Peak.

'Then you are incapable of happiness in any worthy sense! You may graze but you will never feast.'"[4]

For such people the only reality in life is the *culte du moi*; they must multiply their self-consciousness by studying their reactions to experience. We shall watch this tendency develop unexpectedly in the twentieth century, but it is no less significant to find that such was also Gissing's attitude. One of his last publications, *The Private Papers of Henry Ryecroft* (1903), is almost exclusively a self-portrait, and it was the favourite work of his middle age as was *Thyrza* of his youth. He writes to Miss Colleton 24 December 1902: "On the whole I suspect it is the best thing I have done, or am likely to do; the thing most likely to last when all my other futile work has followed my futile life." Gissing's work was not so futile as he appeared to imagine. It would have been less so if he

[1] *Ante*, pp. 188-9.   [2] Pt I, chap. III.
[3] Pt III, chap. IV.   [4] Pt III, chap. I.

had discovered in his poverty-stricken scenes something more than a reflection of his wounded egoism. Without making the least little concession to sentiment, much less to sentimentality, he might have found a broader, brighter, or at least less savage, standard by which to measure the grimmest of truths. But the tastes and persuasions of his day led him to neo-realism and he could not register facts without registering his personal grievances.

Meanwhile, another author, a poet as well as a novelist, with far more initiative, experience and adaptability than Gissing, was nevertheless labouring under the same influences. Meredith's life (1828–1909) is now too well known to need recounting. It is enough to remember that he was the descendant of a tradesman whom none could forget; that his three aunts gave him a gentleman's education and training but not a gentleman's private fortune; that he availed himself of these incomplete advantages and of his own superb talents to make himself a position through authorship; that his marriage with a widow and a mother (T. L. Peacock's daughter) was a tragic mistake and brought to the surface all that was intolerant, passionate and vindictive in his character; that at the end of his first thirty years of life (1858) he found himself a deserted husband, an unrecognised author, and a gentleman so poor that he hardly knew where to turn for his next meal.

It must also be remembered that Meredith's career was arranged for him among the upper middle-class and the landed gentry. Well-to-do people, especially in the south of England, were becoming acutely conscious that business was crude, that democracy was vulgar and that "the grand old name of gentleman" was the one compensation—and incidentally the best excuse—for spending their money. So they cultivated the type as a moral and social distinction, embroidering the ideal with a ritual of refinements, observances and exalted sentiments. Newcomers and aspirants (for example the grandson of Melchizedec Meredith the naval outfitter of Portsmouth) were of course exceptionally sensitive to these exigencies and became more critical, exquisite and aristocratic than the bluest-blooded Norfolk Howard. Our author's exigence afterwards shifted from gentility to wit, but as a young man he embraced this discipline and sentimentality with the ardour of a fanatic more than an amateur, forgetting that the cult was appointed for those who do not feel the pinch of poverty or the sharper pinch of wounded vanity. It flattered one's sense of dignity and moral worth, but it did not bring peace to a man at war with himself and his fortunes. It repressed the inner man. For all these reasons, domestic and social, Meredith became so wrong-headed, resentful and sensitive to his many disadvantages, that he would not reveal the place of his birth, nor cultivate the arts by which an author should help his public to understand his ideas, nor even forgive his wife till she had died.

In other words, Meredith seems to have lost his soul and we should probably have heard no more of him, except that, like Tennyson,[1] he had the talent and the tenacity to go in search of it, and thereby made a living and a reputation.

Did he find it? That is to say, did he rede his own riddle so as to help us to the solution of ours? To a certain extent, but not so much as we have a right to expect from a man of his intellectual penetration and spiritual experiences. For we must now consider whether or not Meredith elaborated a deep and discerning philosophy of life, but failed like too many other Victorians to substantiate what he believed.

Like the previous generation, he served his apprenticeship in romantic philosophy. While still a young boy he found out that he was a ward in chancery and that a sum of money was available for his education, so in 1842 he took himself off to school at the Herrenhütte in Neuwied, where the Moravian monks taught him, at that impressionable age, to believe in the universal spirit which pervades all creation and unites all living things with God. He never forgot this pantheism, but he gradually adapted it to his own individuality and experience.

In the first place, he enjoyed abundant health and physical energy, which kept him a child of nature. He could rely on exercise and the open air to enjoy the consolations which some sedentary people are obliged to seek in church services. This sense of vitality was in him so strong that it coloured his poetic sensibilities. He could even realise the teleology of life when in contact with the wastefulness and mortality of nature. In the next place his intellect was so keen that he could detect the inadequacy of our own little human theories and explanations in the face of these cosmic mysteries. He could see that the average individual, at any rate since the Renaissance, expected nature to be man on a larger scale. In modern civilisation human affairs never worked well unless administered according to the laws of logic and method, one single

[1] *Ante*, pp. 77 ff.

end in view, every detail conforming to the preconceived design.
So we had persuaded ourselves that the same is true of the universe;
it is like an effort of human economy; organisation and efficiency
are the decisive virtue in the works of God as of man, even in the
fluctuations of thought and impulse, and the apparent inconsistencies of growth and decay. But whoever came to nature with the
intuitions of a poet and an athlete—the nature within him and
without—he would find that organisation was a purely man-made
idea, that the elements acted and reacted in a very different
manner, by the interplay of equilibrium and compensation (to
relapse into the terminology of reason)—opposing forces balancing
each other's excesses, each hazard correcting the other.

This interpretation, implied by Darwinism, has often been
mooted in the twentieth century and has recently been expounded
in popular form by a man of science.[1] Meredith seems to have
guessed the truth at least fifty years earlier. But as he was a poet,
and had, moreover, arrived at this conclusion through his own
searchings of heart, he propounded his philosophy in a more
pictorial way and with a view to conduct. What chiefly impressed
him was the conviction that the brain could play its proper part
only if it accommodated and even fused itself with the other
elements of our nature, with the sheer animal instincts, and with
those other impulses and aspirations which may perhaps originate
in the humours of our bodies and yet seem to leave the intellect
far below on its pedestrian level. They must compensate not exclude each other. Such was his well-known doctrine of *the triad*—
the balancement of blood, brain, and spirit—and this equilibrium
would not have been so difficult to make and so easy to mar, except
that the intellect is a treacherous member of the triumvirate. It
pretends to have absolute power, to be an illumination by which
the human being rises above his common self, and under the spell
of this flattery the modern man, especially the modern gentleman,
forgets that the projections of his brain cannot be directed to the
best advantage, unless its momentum is blended with the other
energies of the human system.

So man becomes possessed of an artificial idea of himself, and
this intellectual one-sidedness does not only cripple his understanding of himself and (by the same token) of other people; it
misrepresents his place in the bigger scheme of nature. Whoever
cannot believe that his soul rests on the interplay of mind with

[1] C. Nicolle, *La Nature. Conception et morale biologiques*, 1934

body, cannot reconcile himself to the fact that all life is a wasteful and oscillating plexus of reciprocities, an unending and unsystematised interchange of growth and decay in which he, like all other mortals, must play his petty part. Living things are shadows, only life is grand in its multitudinous continuity and collaboration.

Meredith elaborated this philosophy in verse which is difficult to read. The obscurity may partly be due to the subject. This triadism would eventually become a mere formula of the intellect, an embellishment on Darwinism, unless its mystery were suggested by mysterious imagery. The reader must be made to guess riddles and think in figures before the web of creation can be intuited and man's egoism be shamed into awe. Besides, as some twentieth-century poets were to believe, oracular ambiguity sifts the genuine from the disingenuous inquirer. But whatever the explanation, Meredith's philosophical poems, for all their vivid symbolism and haunting rhythms, are unsatisfactory. In fact, here again we meet this Victorian incompleteness, the promise of more than is performed. Meredith's tone is not only mystic but monitory, almost menacing. He has the severity of a schoolmaster, schooling himself and therefore impatient with his pupils. There is a more fundamental defect. Moral truths are not true for the human mind unless they turn the thoughts towards conduct, as Goethe, Browning and Arnold had insisted. A theory is only a glimpse of what ought to be, unless it can be put into practice. Otherwise the man who could find his soul only in the Woods of Westermain, would lose it a second time, as soon as he returned to the town and the country houses.

Besides, Meredith had to earn his living as a novelist, so he could not remain within his own orbit. He must wander among the thoughts of other people. It is, moreover, a proof of sincerity that he should, as if by instinct, turn his eyes to the classes of society in which he had suffered keenly and often doubted of himself. He learnt that the disequilibrium of the triad was most worth studying where one would least suspect it, that is to say, among the well-educated or at least the well-mannered classes. So Meredith sought the material for his novels among the sentiments, affectations, conventionalities and luxuries of the Victorian governing class. In this field he would have ample opportunity to test his ideas and give them the living forms which have power over other men. It only remained to season his inventiveness with accurate observation, and to that extent his long series of novels are as neo-realistic as those of the Goncourts, Zola, Gissing and George Moore. At the same time he would rise above them all, if he could illumine this registration of facts with the sense of a higher more spiritualised order of things. Could he arouse an idea of perfection, by illustrating its absence? He believed that he could. His purpose was to be achieved by writing as if his readers were themselves whole and needed not the physician.

As soon as the average intelligent man meets with his own faults, either in his friends or in a book, he is roused to fury. He cannot easily pardon a fellow-creature for giving way to a temptation which he resists with difficulty, if at all. Satirists have usually appealed to this natural resentment. Meredith did just the opposite. He presented one-sided people, obsessed, deluded or undisciplined, for the perusal of those whose blood, brain and spirit were harmoniously balanced. These "*triadists*" would harbour no resentment against the incomplete. But on the other hand, being at peace with themselves, their minds worked freely, their vision was clear, and they had a just sense of fitness. They would at once detect what was incongruous or illogical in their less disciplined fellow-creatures. The novelist had only to address his realism, not to their indignation, since they felt none, but to their serene judgment. The perception of other people's inferiority would (as Bergson was afterwards to argue) induce laughter—not the *rigidi censura cachinni*, but the relaxation of an intellect which sees things in their true perspectives. Such, in Meredith's terminology, was the exercise of the *comic spirit*.

The men and women graced by humour and goodwill should have gathered round Meredith's novels; each volume would be like a password and pass-grip to a fraternity. Our author illustrated the futility of those who have the education and the money to humour themselves. The initiated would perceive this futility and would thereby understand more clearly their own place within the scheme of nature, and within that extension of nature which is, or ought to be, society.

This philosophy of life was not new, but was put in a new way, adapted to contemporary culture, but we cannot measure its value because Meredith did not do it justice. How could he, since he was not a member of the fraternity which he hoped to gather round him? The human imperfections which he portrayed arose from the consciousness of his own one-sidedness. They were conceived with all the sensitiveness, the irritability of wounded vanity and self-reproach. He so far mastered himself that he raised these painful themes into an atmosphere of disinterested and intellectual criticism; "a supreme ironic procession with laughter of gods in the background. Why not laughter of mortals also?"[1] A notable achievement. But such figures could not be made to imply or suggest (even by contrast) all that their creator needed. He was too uncertain of his victory to record it with the serenity and insight which he expected of his readers. He could not linger and sympathise with his characters till our knowledge of their peculiarities grows into a knowledge of life's possibilities. Meredith merely leads his men and women unsuspectingly along their downward paths, consoling himself with his flashes of wit, until a situation is formed in which their wrong-headedness or imbecility collapses amid roars of laughter. The characters are so charged with energy that any conflict within themselves will work havoc. Their only chance is to find a life-purpose on which the three sides of their being can be unified. Such harmonious concentration is not vouchsafed to Meredith's world.

Such is the culmination of Meredith's career, but, as we have noticed in so many other cases, such was not his initial idea. He set out to demonstrate that humanity is greater than its limitations. Take Richard Feverel. To the average Victorian onlooker from the outside, this heir to Raynham Abbey would appear to be a reckless young man who marries a farmer's niece, fights a duel and breaks his wife's heart, in fact a disgrace to his father. Yet we are enabled to perceive that he "has a character of a bullet with a treble charge of powder behind it" (as that wise youth, Adrian Harley, observes) and that it is this same devoted father who perverts his nature, because Sir Austen Feverel will insist upon reading other people by his own book. Evan Harrington appears to others as a snob and a climber, almost as an impostor, certainly as disingenuous, but we are privileged to know that he is struggling to sustain his self-respect without the respect of others who are socially superior to him. Emilia, as she appears in England, is a foreigner possessing only a divine voice and likely to lose this, her sole possession, because she is foolishly in love. We learn that her true virtue is "a noble strength on fire"; that she is simply fulfilling her nature; that she ends by finding her bent, "that oneness of feeling which is the truthful impulse". In *Vittoria*, the sequel which passes amid the fierce and sometimes melodramatic scenes of the *Risorgimento*,

[1] *Ordeal of Richard Feverel*, 1859, chap. i.

this power becomes mature, "an unspoken depth in her, distinct from her visible nature". *Rhoda Fleming*, again, contains the ordinary rubbishing theme, true enough to life but falsely retold in a hundred trashy novels. There is a country girl, Dahlia, who goes to town, is seduced by a rich young man; they become estranged and repent too late; her honest yeoman family cannot bear up under the disgrace. Yet Meredith shows how Dahlia and Edward are really drawn together by the mutual attraction of love and youth, and are kept apart by the prejudices of society and religion.

These are examples from among the earlier novels in which the structure is far from perfect, the plots often artificial, but nature still celebrates her triumphs. In *Beauchamp's Career* (1876) Meredith has perfected his manner and at last acquired his peculiar art of suggestiveness. He does indeed set in motion "the clockwork of the brain" and appeal to "the conscience residing in thoughtfulness". But he no longer appeals to our idealism. Nevil is his best character. He has talent, strength, the family adoration for women, and the refined manliness which in Meredith's novels attracts women. Such is his love for England that he flings himself into social reform, as anyone might do in the 'sixties, especially after reading Carlyle. Yet our author subjects him to every influence which would irritate his faults and betray him through his weaknesses, whether the "cold Tory exclusiveness and inaccessibility" of his uncle or the elongated "theory-tailor", Dr Shrapnel, who "takes his honesty for a virtue and that entitles him to believe in himself". So the novelist overwhelms his hero beneath his own pig-headedness and imaginative enthusiasms. What does he leave for the spirit to feed on? Only the incomplete portrait of Renée de Croisnel, who could speak fluently with a smile on her mouth and whose personality was like "the peep into the dewy woodland onto dark water". Three years later, in 1879, Meredith published *The Egoist*, perhaps his wittiest and most humorous novel, but the ideals which might have been developed out of Clara Middleton and Vernon Whitford are lost in this study of the self-centred man. The egoism of a single human being seems to encompass and enervate the souls which fall into its soft, clinging embraces. In revenge he brings out into the clear light of the intellect a portrait of what this type really is: a spiritual beggar whom the author places in possession of vast wealth and social eminence, so as to enhance the irony of his humiliation.

At a later period Meredith recovered somewhat of his youthful optimism. *Diana of the Crossways* (1885) is a realist's attempt to show the best that can be hoped for our species. He portrays a more or less representative assemblage of human beings, all, as befit their nature, to some degree egoistic, animal and unintelligent, but of whom the best have a *growing soul*, that is to say, some quality which enables them to make a fresh start, "a finer shoot of the tree stoutly planted in good gross earth". Being such, we need an elastic and tolerant society in which to grow, and Meredith enforces his Rousseauism by creating the character of a woman (more or less modelled on Mrs Norton) with the accomplishments which suit her own age and the spiritual vitality which qualifies her for a much better age. Then, taking hints from contemporary events, he manœuvres her into all the situations which would play upon her inevitable weaknesses, and discredit her position in the eyes of the world. So this brilliant imperfect being is like a bird fluttering in a cage. We catch glimpses of what she might have become in her sublime friendship with Lady Dunstane and in the disinterested and noble love which she cherishes for Redworth, and finally awakens in him.

Thus Meredith's conclusions are not entirely negative. He is the humorist of his generation, the man who uses his intellect to see things in their true perspective, especially the things most difficult to rationalise, that is, the traditions and ideals of the upper class. He tests them by their influence on the human spirit. But he could not apply his standards of judgment in all their fullness because the application was too painful; he was compelled so often to judge himself. So he took refuge in laughter, in the multiplication of comic scenes, sometimes irrelevant to his purpose—human nature crawling on the ground, because unable to concentrate its efforts to fly.

CHAPTER XXI

Hardy sets himself to reveal the inadequacy of life and reveals the inadequacy of culture.

Meredith did not only contribute novels and poems which have served their turn and are now nearly forgotten. In 1867 he was appointed reader to Chapman and Hall, and in 1869 and 1870 he helped to usher Hardy into the unfraternal fraternity of authors.

If appearances count for anything, Thomas Hardy (1840–1928) was one of those mortals born to be happy. Both parents displayed the uttermost care for their son's health, and sympathy with his literary tastes and artistic aptitudes. When in 1856 it was necessary for him to think of earning money, he fell into a profession and a place in which his mind could grow. By the time he was a full-fledged architect in 1862 he had found the energy and the time to learn Greek, partly in order to interpret the New Testament, but even more to read Aeschylus and Sophocles, who never afterwards lost their hold on his mind. Thanks to the Hardys' reputation as string-bandsmen, he (often with his father and uncle) was invited to perform at rustic weddings, christenings and Christmas parties. Thus he led a triple existence—"a life twisted of three strands", as he put it—each contact supplementing the others.[1]

In 1862 he went to London to seek his fortune as an architect, and he had the luck to be associated with some of the leading men in his profession. For the next ten years or more he lived in the metropolis, and had ample opportunity to shed his provinciality and to become if not a man about town, at any rate, a man of the world. At the same time he was succeeding in a profession which promised great things. So much so that in 1872 his chief (at that time Professor R. Smith) offered him a permanent engagement with an increased salary.

He refused, because he had been drawn, almost against his will, to another vocation; novel-writing. Of course he made mistakes, and endured disappointments, but his very first novel found a publisher, though Meredith persuaded him not to publish. His third, *Under the Greenwood Tree* (1872), was an artistic success; his

---

[1] F. E. Hardy, *The Early Life of Thomas Hardy*, 1840–1891, 1928.

fourth, *A Pair of Blue Eyes* (1873), established his position in the literary world; his fifth, *Far from the Madding Crowd* (1874), made good his financial position and he was able to marry Miss Emma Gifford without giving to Fortune more than the inevitable hostages. In his dealings with publishers he showed business ability and a knowledge of the law. Our author was not one of those who add to the burden of life by improvidence or carelessness.

So Hardy rose to fame with far less trouble than did Trollope or Meredith. In the following half century he had one serious illness and the worries and anxieties which beset any energetic and sincere man in any occupation. But he enjoyed the pleasures of a growing reputation, and the more subtle pleasures of realising that he was becoming (with a few lapses) every year more and more the master of an art which he had made peculiarly his own. He enjoyed also the pleasures of society. He and his wife nearly always visited London for the "season". It was only during the pleasant months that he lived at Max Gate and enjoyed Dorset and Wiltshire, often on the newly invented safety-bicycle. He prospered so well that by 1895 this novelist could afford to "retire" and devote the rest of his long active life to his first love, poetry.

He began life as a village boy. He devoted the mature years of his life to the profession of literature. He won enough money to live in comfort; and he died full of years and honour.

Despite this prosperous career, Hardy has proved himself to be the most confirmed pessimist of his age (though he disclaimed the imputation). Moreover, his pessimism strikes deeper than Carlyle's, Arnold's, Housman's, George Moore's or Galsworthy's. We have now to consider its significance in the spiritual history of our time.

He appears to have approached the experiences of life in the spirit of mid-Victorian rationalism, as modern as his most modern contemporaries, resolved to take nothing on faith; confident in the resources of the intellect, prepared for any surprises. In the 'sixties he knew Mill's *On Liberty* almost by heart. He was among the first to acclaim *The Origin of Species*.[1] When all England was wondering at the periodical publication of Newman's *Apologia*, he was sufficiently a sceptic to detect at once that there was "no first link in its excellent chain of reasoning".[2] Like many others of his contemporaries and predecessors, he was attracted by the hypothesis of the Finite God[3] who planned a perfect world and could not con-

[1] F. E. Hardy, *op. cit.* chap. XII.   [2] *Ibid.* chap. VII; Diary, 2 July 1865.
[3] *Ante*, pp. 223–4.

summate his purpose, and when he found the idea expounded in McTaggart's *Some Dogmas of Religion*, he sought the friendship of its author. Of course he allowed himself his flights of imagination: he loved to evoke the past; but only as authorised by antiquarians and palaeographists. The company of ghosts seems to have restored the sense of continuity and racial permanence, which sceptics are always liable to sacrifice.

In all these respects, Hardy comes before us as a man of remarkably adaptable intelligence who chose of his own accord to be a freethinker. He differs from his more progressive and independent contemporaries only in so far as he was more depressed and discouraged, though few men had less reason to be so. If we would find the explanation, we must begin by considering his verse. There is more autobiographical interest in his poetry than in all his novels, as he once told Clive Holland.[1]

This large body of occasional poems, some of it written as early as the 'sixties, is in the first place an experiment with the culture which he embraced so eagerly. Hardy's mind had received the imprint of his time all the more readily because he was almost self-taught, a newcomer into the educated world. But the theories and doctrines of the late nineteenth century were generally propounded as crystallised abstractions, in this or that dissertation, which sums up the subject and claims to represent it. For most people, especially beginners, modernism was a collection of neat and expressive phrases, mere mnemonic acquisitions, unconnected with realities. Hardy experiments in that he brings these abstract notions to the test of poetry. He transfers them from his intellect, brings them into contact with his senses, tries to see, hear, feel, and dream of them, and create the highest of pleasures by clothing them in flesh and blood. At first his themes seem to arise out of some casual impression, some chance observation or fancy; but it will soon be noticed that for the most part they illustrate or exemplify the kind of thoughts which were circulating in the progressive books of the time. Hardy, having no religion in the ordinary sense, is using all this cerebration as a substitute; he is mixing it with his emotions; visualising it in contact with the instincts and impulses of human nature; expressing it in terms of elemental experience; testing it to see how far it satisfies the call of the blood. His resourcefulness is astonishing; one hardly knows whether to admire most his sense of form or his ingenuity in devising epigrammatic situations.

[1] C. Holland, *Thomas Hardy, O.M.*, 1933, chap. VI.

This talent for dramatic externalisation delights the reader and the author, so neither is inclined to confess that Hardy is unfortunate in his inspiration. After a dozen poems have been read, one begins to realise that he is not at home in his acquired culture. He cannot mix his best self with his material, however artistic the execution. The resilience, expansiveness and vitality of human nature find no outlet. What he writes does not serve the highest emotional experiences which imply self-fulfilment. That is to say, modern culture will not serve as this artist's religion.

Culture leaves him to the religion of humanitarianism; and the sincerity of his verse is proved by the almost constant emergence of this only possible sentiment. He gives his spirit its one outlet by translating his disillusionment into protest and fellow-feeling. He defined art as "the changing of the actual proportion and order of things so as to bring out forcibly that feature which appeals to the idiosyncrasy of the artist".[1] So he does. He looks everywhere for what will express this mood. To judge by appearance, there is no advocacy on the part of the poet; he is leaving facts (albeit poetised) to speak for themselves. But all the time he is rearranging the elements of life according to the refinements, conjectures and susceptibilities of modern culture. So on the one hand we have those tales of sudden crime (amongst them *The Tranter's Wife*, which he considered to be his finest piece), or those many situations in which human beings unwittingly ruin each other's happiness, or such poems as *On a Fine Morning* and *In a Wood*,[2] revealing how scientific curiosity impoverishes spiritual experience, or again those wry-mouthed burlesques on the idea of God. In all these glimpses, visions and studies man is represented as driven by a passion for happiness and acquiring in his fruitless search a sensitiveness which rouses our helpless indignation, but weakens every other sentiment or impulse except commiseration. His poetry might be epitomised as paradox leading to pity.

Thus, Hardy is yet another of these neo-realists who rely on their own sense of unfulfilment to interpret life and in consequence he relinquishes that classical energy and resolution which Goethe celebrated and which the earlier Victorian poets tried to revive. On the other hand, he is not out of sympathy with twentieth-century taste. For instance, T. S. Eliot has declared "to write poetry which should be essentially poetry, with nothing 'poetic'

[1] F. E. Hardy, *The Early Life*, chap. xviii.
[2] *Poems of the Past and Present*, 1902. *Wessex Poems*, 1898.

about it, poetry standing in its bare bones, or poetry so transparent that in reading it we are intent on what the poem *points out*, and not on the poetry, this seems to me the thing to try for". He is writing on D. H. Lawrence, one neo-Georgian on another, but every word applies to Hardy. And what is the kind of significance which Eliot would intuit? Again in his own words "the struggle— which alone constitutes life for a poet—to transmute his personal and private agonies into something rich and strange, something universal and impersonal". So Hardy was always trying to do, and he recorded in 1891 "the highest flights of the pen are mostly the excursions and revelations of souls unreconciled to life".[1]

This attitude of mind is all the more interesting because it results from two influences predominant in late Victorian culture, and in our own; in the first place, an urge towards self-expression, partly the fruit of liberalism (as we have seen) and partly the fruit of easy circumstances, mechanical conveniences, and the expectation of progress. In the second place, a lack of any great and penetrating ideas which could vitalise our deepest yearnings and hitherto unrealised aptitudes and raise them to the surface of intellectual consciousness—complete the man's conception of himself, inspire a sense of racial and individual purpose. Hardy's identity was divided between his civilised interests and all that civilisation could not satisfy; between his life as a function and his would-be life as a self-hood.

As other resources failed him, he was always trying to find something strange in what was familiar. He notes on 19 April 1885 that "the business of the poet and novelist is to show the sorriness underlying the grandest things, and the grandeur underlying the sorriest things".[2] On 5 August 1888 he believes that "to find beauty in ugliness is the province of the poet". As has been suggested, he often missed the deeper values for which he was searching, and his partial failure is illustrated by his readiness to indulge in what Remy de Gourmont has called *la dissociation des idées*.[3] That is to say, Hardy is fond of separating images or thoughts which generally go together (for instance, a dog and fidelity; God and omnipotence; a grove of trees and restfulness) and working them over and rearranging them in new combinations which startle the reader and arrest his thoughts. But in many cases they do no more; they prove to be mere exercises in humanism and

[1] F. E. Hardy, *op. cit.* chap. xix.   [2] *Ibid.* chap. xi.
[3] In *La Culture des Idées*.

humanitarianism. What really delights us is the technique. We admire the skilful penetration; above all, we enjoy the poet's irony —the classic restraint which leaves the reader to supply the missing note of indignation or regret. But one cannot help suspecting that he is partial to depressing themes because they suit his art even more than his convictions, as if his true object were the subtle mastery of effects, the delicacy and sureness with which he could play on a single sentiment—in a word, the cult of the aesthetic thrill.

However, Hardy was not to devote his genius to this pastime. As has been recorded, he took to novel-writing in order to make money. Commercial literature has often proved to be truer and greater than art for art's sake, principally because the man who would beguile others of their pennies must at the same time beguile them of their secrets. So it is not surprising that Hardy's novels mean more to most readers than does his occasional verse.

In this enterprise, a temperamental peculiarity stood him in good stead. When he first meditated fiction, in the late 'sixties, Thackeray, Dickens and Trollope were, or seemed to be, at the height of their influence. These were the commentators on the upper classes. So Hardy first tried his hand at the same kind of theme. Fortunately, he was quite inept. Like many other successful novelists he found himself unable to portray the gentry, like very few he found himself unable to take any genuine interest in them. Like Ethelberta, he probably felt himself to be in some sort an intruder in such circles and a renegade to his own class.[1] Eventually, he came to speak with contempt of novelists who "treat social conventions and contrivances—the artificial forms of living—as if they were cardinal facts of life",[2] and of London as "that *hot-plate* of humanity, on which we first sing, then simmer, then boil, then dry away to dust".[3] Thus he was saved from committing his inventiveness to backgrounds and foregrounds which then seemed to be in the highest favour but were soon to become too familiar. Instead of such conventionality, he dared to be original, to attract the reading public by something which it did not know, and of which he alone possessed the secret.

Novelty was to be created, in the first place, by the setting of his stories; and this environing atmosphere will always constitute the abiding charm of his prose, and perhaps ensure its immortality. But the scenery is much more than an embellishment; it is subtly

[1] See *The Hand of Ethelberta*, chaps. xxxiii, xxxvi.
[2] Diary, 21 Aug. 1888. [3] *Ibid.* 16 April 1892.

interwoven with the texture of each story, and though nearly always Wessex, it varies essentially with the essence of each plot. To quote only three examples: *The Mayor of Casterbridge* (1886) does not only reveal the market town of Dorchester, where shrewd men make money and fools lose it. It was once a Roman encampment; there are prehistoric earthworks in the neighbourhood, and the brutal passions and rivalries of the Heroic Age seem still to haunt the place. So the reckless, war-ridden past seems to blend with the busy, chaffering present. In January 1887 Hardy noted in his Journal, "I feel that nature is played out as a Beauty but not as a mystery". Later in the same year be brought out *The Woodlanders* which is filled with the whispering of trees, the breathing of their leaves, the play of light and darkness beneath their shade, the growth and decay which follow the recurring seasons, and the animals which make their home among the trunks and branches. In *Tess of the D'Urbervilles* (1891) there is also a mystery, but this time it is the ghosts of feudalism haunting the ancient streets and chases and churches, invisible even to the most imaginative eye, but always felt; especially in the instincts and impulses of their unsuspecting descendants.

These, with *The Return of the Native* and *Jude the Obscure*, are the tales in which the backgrounds are the most memorable, and it will at once be noticed that these are also the stories in which the characters have most fire and individuality. Such was the other novelty which Hardy introduced. He created men and women who breathe the strangeness of their environment, and embody its spirit.

So Hardy was well on the way towards creating a new type of human being—new, of course, to the minds of the educated reading public, new to the history of culture. The characters of the older novels are absorbed in some conventional pursuit, external to themselves; an artificial and imposed activity, which shapes or misshapes their minds, for instance, the pursuit of wealth, reputation or revenge. Hardy's great characters depend only on themselves. The novel gave him the chance of rejuvenating humanity, not by relieving it of our burden of sin and suffering, but of our burden of artificiality. His scheme cuts across all social assessments and educational influences, in fact, as he told the editors of *L'Hermitage* in August 1893, he would like to base the social system on individual spontaneity and divide the community "into groups of temperament, with a different code of observances for each group".

If Hardy had been the contemporary of Virginia Woolf or even of Marcel Proust, he would probably have produced studies of character rather than stories. But in his day the reading public expected that a career should be designed for any figure which appeared in a novel. However interesting his children of nature might be, they must be set in motion among the adventures which make up life, and Hardy had spent much time thinking how plots should be managed. He liked to feel that in devising a novel he was tracing a single pattern in the scheme of things, much as one might follow some particular colour in the design of a carpet. But if the plot was to be true to his idea, the incidents like the characters must be spun out of nature, that is, out of that mysteriously cruel and inhuman power which J. S. Mill[1] had recently revealed to the world. Darwin was demonstrating that seeds, insects and animals lead precarious lives at the mercy of accidents, so also must man take his chance like any other creature in this inhospitable existence. Being a higher animal, he does not run the same risks; for instance, even the humblest can more or less control the physical dangers which beset life. But in the course of his adaptation he has evolved another sort of vulnerability peculiar to his development: an insatiable appetite for happiness (the old call of nature individualised and rendered acutely conscious), generally expressed as a passion for mutual understanding and intimacy which is always being thwarted by flukes, accidents, sometimes literally by a cast of the die.[2] His definition of tragedy (November 1885) is a state of things which converts some natural aim or desire into a catastrophe.

To render this hazard all the more acute and the consequences more fatal, Hardy does not take ordinary peasants to be his subject. There are plenty of normal characters in his books, but they are supernumeraries, they lend themselves to his humour, but not to his philosophy. His protagonists lead self-conscious, insulated lives. As early as 1866 he notes: "A certain man: he creeps away to a meeting with his own sensations." In 1884 he considers "the intense interests, passions and strategy that throb through the commonest lives" to be an ample theme. By the time he wrote *The Woodlanders* in 1887 he is thinking of a personage "charged with emotive fluid as a Leyden jar with electric".

---

[1] *Nature*, in *Three Essays on Religion*, 1873. See *ante*, p. 241.
[2] From *The Return of the Native*; cf. *The Problem* (*Poems of Past and Present*) and *Hap* (*Wessex Poems*).

Thus he was almost constrained by the exigencies of his art, by the backgrounds and the need of a progressive story, to make his novels more gloomy than they need be; to pick out a tortuous and blood-stained pattern in the carpet of life, and as every author must put something of himself into his creations, we find him projecting his own susceptibilities and unsatisfied longings into these figures, giving them life from his own supersensitive store, picturing himself as no less inarticulate and unfortunate than they, and then imagining how he would suffer and revolt. Nor was this overcharged pessimism altogether unbusinesslike. It appealed to two tendencies of the time: the disillusionment of the intellectuals, and the sentimentality of the real or affected humanists—the cult of melancholy as the note of refinement.

But if Hardy's novels are to be judged by the highest standards, we must ask a more searching question: does this portraiture enlarge or restrict our sense of life and purpose? It matters not that he is at such pains to interest us in misfortune: but does he present failure so as to render existence more mysterious, more rich or at any rate more worth while? He says himself in *Two on a Tower* that "unexpectedly grand fruits are sometimes forced forth by harsh pruning". What fruits do his characters bear?

To answer that question he must be compared with the Greek classics who profoundly influenced his imagination from adolescence onward, who are just as disillusioned as he is, and yet satisfy the modern spirit. To quote only three characteristic utterances. The first and greatest of all poets makes the King of the Gods declare that of all creatures which breathe and crawl, man is the most to be pitied,[1] and the two greatest of the age of Pericles, Sophocles and Euripides, both confess that death is preferable to life.[2] Hardy himself seems to have been at one with them. On a holiday, at the height of his fame as a novelist, he confided to Clive Holland that he would rather not have been born,[3] and one certainly feels that the best characters in his novels had overwhelmingly good reasons to agree with their author and with the ancient Greeks. His art seems to aim at demonstrating that man is too highly developed to inhabit this world. Thus Hardy can claim that his novels continue a tradition consecrated in two literatures

[1] *Iliad*, xvii, 446–7.
[2] Sophocles, *Oedipus Coloneus*, 1225 ff.; Euripides, *Fragment* 900 (Nauck).
[3] C. Holland, *Thomas Hardy, O.M.*, 1933, Preface.

which have not yet lost their power to elevate and inspire the imagination. Our modern author is at his artistic best when he follows their lead, so one is tempted to conclude that his melancholy should have the same kind of significance.

But despite resemblances of sentiment, Hardy cannot lay claim to the classical broad-mindedness and vision. The great hellenic poets and historians were indeed impressed by the briefness of individual lives and the insecurity of mortal happiness, but they were judging heroes, who played for the grand stakes in life. The mighty figures in Homer, Herodotus, the Athenian drama or Virgil, are not actuated only by a vague instinct for joy, like the humble folk of Wessex. These legendary heroes just miss the happiness which might have been theirs; generally they invite misfortune through ignorance, inadvertence, or vanity; and yet the onlooker's pity is tempered with admiration. Great deeds dispose the reader to think greatly. One feels that even their errors proceed from a certain unguarded magnanimity and that they would have suffered less if they had been smaller. The disaster brings to the surface what Sophocles called reverence (εὐσέβεια) and Euripides high courage (εὐψυχία). It is even more noteworthy that their downfall culminates in enlightenment. The classical humanists recognised that human disasters were fated, sometimes contrived, by an unhuman power, and could not be averted, but at the same time they convinced themselves that this unfriendly providence was compact of wisdom and justice—"The Eternal Laws which dwell in Heaven and wax not old."[1] It was not suggested that a puny mortal, "the shadow of a dream" as Pindar called him, could derange the scheme of Divine Destiny, but rather that the trespass implied moral insensibility and obtuseness; a lack of insight which was often to be recovered in suffering. Oedipus saw further and deeper when a blind beggar than as king of Thebes. We moderns find it difficult to follow this reading of the mystery but yet its expositors speak with such conviction and vividness that they suspend our unbelief. By some means or other the hellenic and hellenised poets make us feel that they and their fellow-countrymen were indeed governed by Powers above them but that their own will was nevertheless free to co-operate, and moreover that there was hidden in man's reason a spark of intuition which through calamity achieved clairvoyance. So if to be born were a curse, it led, nevertheless, to courage through wisdom. No

[1] Sophocles, *Oedipus Tyrannus*, ll. 863–71.

Greek has asserted this gospel of moral harmony and enlightened resignation with more conviction than Sophocles.

Hardy had trained his mind on Greek literature, and, to judge by his allusions, for instance in *The Woodlanders* and *The Dynasts*, he was especially impressed by Sophocles, and on 24 October 1892 he notes that the highest tragedy "is that of the Worthy encompassed by the Inevitable". Yet his tragedies are not Sophoclean. They lack the Athenian's calmness and enlightenment. If he must be compared to any of the Ancients he is more like the Persian who burst into tears at Attaginos's banquet and declared that "the most hateful of all human griefs is this, to have knowledge of the truth but no power over the event"[1]—to watch human beings wrecking their lives, to see how it all comes about, and yet to go with the rest oneself, "being bound in the bonds of necessity". That is to say, Hardy knew too much. He has outgrown the old Greek anti-pessimism. He has chosen the classics for his guide and then refused to put their morality into practice and so lost their virtue. He no longer believes that mortals through suffering learn wisdom or gain anything at all. He appreciates our follies and misfortunes as deeply as they do, but he has unlearnt their reasoned confidence.

It may be answered that the modern novelist was right, for he has helped us to leave a fool's paradise, and come out into the open country, face to face with the truth. But what we seek in literature is not so much the truth about zoology or social evolution, as the truth about man's mental resilience and emotional power in the world which he creates for himself within the limitations of science. Hardy does not help us towards such self-expression. His characters enter their story endowed with a quiet and simple grandeur which is almost a revelation, but they gradually lose their dignity through the aimlessness of their fate—belittled by their destiny. Thus he leaves us to the conclusion that the best in man is an attitude of pity and resignation. This fellow-feeling is the most satisfying virtue that he can find in life up to about 1895, and it might be urged that no more was to be expected within the prescribed limits of his art. In his desire to tell a story "worth the telling", he had kept to the things which his readers did not know —secluded lives in unfamiliar scenery. The world of agricultural Wessex was not a world but a province, and even in this selected and artificially concentrated field, he dwells only on the eccentrics

[1] *Herodotus*, Bk ix, chap. 16.

and originals. If our novelist-poet were to speak the mind of his age, he must extend his range, and embrace the big world of action.

Fortunately, he had both the leisure and the material. Having probably exhausted the aspects under which Wessex could be called to life, and having certainly exhausted his patience with editors who required him to temper his realism to the prudery of family fiction, he gave himself up to his hobby, poetry, and to his other hobby, the Napoleonic wars. He had been constantly turning the subject over in his mind since May 1875.[1] The chief difficulty was to create an artistic form capable of embracing such big issues in the spirit of modern culture, for he had to combine the far-sightedness of the philosopher with the microscopic vision of the realist. The shape in which he eventually cast his drama would seem to fulfil these conditions as far as it might be possible. There were the actual fragments of dialogue and the stage directions, which should give prominence to the realism which we might call human nature in miniature; there were the dumb-shows and bird's-eye views, which revealed almost for the first time the whole vastness and impersonality of concerted human movements; and there was an elaborate chorus, the over-world of spirits, to express how this almost immeasurable pageant is reflected in the thoughts and sensibilities of man. So the scheme seems as perfect as it can be.

As a consequence the drama is far more artistically expressive than the novels; it reveals an incomparably bigger stage; but the lighting is the same. His presentment of battles, especially of Waterloo, is unforgettably vivid, but only as a succession of intensely vitalised plans and diagrams. His glimpses of citizens and of common soldiers are accomplished with admirable insight, but not their heroism or fortitude. Hardy portrays them chattering, or singing, or suffering and is unquestionably at his best when they suffer. No one could forget the Dantesque description of the men frozen round the bivouac fire,[2] or the cockpit of the *Victory*, the atmosphere "heavy with the fumes of gunpowder and candle grease, the odour of drugs and cordials, and the smell of abdominal wounds".[3] There are plenty of great men; statesmen, generals and kings roused to play the role of heroes, pitting themselves against the problems of life, making history. Yet Hardy's genius seems to be free only when they are caught in moments of irresolution,

[1] F. A. Hardy, *op. cit.* chap. VII.   [2] *The Dynasts*, Pt III, Act I, Sc. 2.
[3] *Ibid.* Pt I, Act v, Sc. 4.

anxiety or despair, as when Mack makes his fatal decision at Ulm;[1] Villeneuf commits suicide at Rennes,[2] the Emperor Josef watches the disaster of Wagram from Wolkersdorf,[3] or Napoleon faces himself after Waterloo.[4] Thus even in the highest circles it seems that the greatest figures are no greater than the rustics; only the setting is bigger. As Mill and Meredith had already explained, we are mighty only in the mass, because there are so many of us. Even an army of ants would end in crossing a river if there were enough of them.

Hardy often protested that he was not a philosopher but an artist and that he never pretended to do more than interpret life through the fancies and figments which caught his imagination. In fact in 1882 he had already confessed that as nothing bears out in practice what it promises incipiently and as development according to perfect reason is limited to mathematics, he had relinquished theories and was reduced to "tentativeness from day to day". But no one can read his diaries and journals without realising that he had a deep and subtle mind, a talent for metaphysics, and a marked capacity for assimilating ideas; only he preferred, as often as possible, to think in figures, situations, and symbols. As early as 4 March 1886 he notes in his Diary that the abstractions of the analytical schools of thought could be rendered "as visible essences, spectres, etc." He may be more of an allegorist than one would suppose, and, if so, it may be a misreading of *The Dynasts* to expect from its pages the portraiture of earth-bound heroes. We ought rather to look to this "Overworld"; it represents the moods in which the human drama should be contemplated. Is such the virtual hero of *The Dynasts*—not Wellington, nor Napoleon, but the modern consciousness, at one and the same time perceptive and positivist—pity, irony, historical interpretation and mysticism—a small part indeed of the present nexus and plexus, but so intellectually and emotionally responsive to the events of this world, that it can be represented only by different groups of spectres? In that case, *The Dynasts* ought really to be offering its readers a revaluation such as would render us more intellectually and spiritually alive.

The Dynasts certainly enlivens the intellect; it can hardly be claimed that it enlivens the spirit. The phantoms carry us no further than their creator's old conviction, "the view of life as a

---

[1] *The Dynasts*, Pt I, Act IV, Sc. 3.   [2] *Ibid.* Pt I, Act V, Sc. 6.
[3] *Ibid.* Pt II, Act IV, Sc. 3.   [4] *Ibid.* Pt III, Act VII, Sc. 9.

thing to be put up with, replacing the zest for existence which was so intense in early civilisations".[1] We are taught stoic resignation without stoic serenity. Nor does Hardy seem to have derived much inspiration from his own idea. The recitatives and odes of these spirits are amongst his least felicitous efforts. The best is the lament over the tiny animals before the Battle of Waterloo.[2] Yet he claimed that he had a religion, the belief in the Immanent Will. As early as 16 February 1882 he notes in his Diary, "write a history of human automatism or impulsion—viz., an account of human action in spite of human knowledge, showing how very far conduct lags behind the knowledge that should really guide it". Twenty-five years later, when replying to E. Wright's letter on the philosophy of *The Dynasts*, he writes on 2 June 1907 that this "Will of the Universe" might one day become aware of itself, was already self-conscious in a fraction of the whole, and would eventually work out its purpose with a more sympathetic adjustment, thus solving the conflict between free-will and necessity.

If Hardy could have convinced his readers that this development was not only possible but probable, he would have made a notable contribution to the spiritual history of his time. But he did not even convince himself. His epic-drama, so artistically effective, does not give effect to his theory of determinism; nor would the heroes of *The Dynasts* have continued to be heroes if they had held his profession of faith. Nelson did not believe in the Immanent Will when he faced death at Trafalgar. Ten years later, when Alfred Noyes in his lecture on *Poetry and Religion* taxed Hardy with describing the Power behind the Universe as "an imbecile jester", our author on 19 December 1920 replied that he believed in a First Cause which was neither moral nor immoral but un-moral, "loveless and hateless". Thus in the end he had not advanced beyond the agnostic position of the mid-century, for instance Herbert Spencer's theory of evolution already foreshadowed in Adam Smith's idea of economic society. In fact four days after answering Noyes's criticism he was content in a letter to *The New York World* to claim that his idea of causation was "sufficiently probable for imaginative writing".

Thus Hardy ended as he began, protesting against the maladjustment of man to his environment. Even this life conviction was a quite familiar idea. As a philosopher, he differed from many of

---

[1] *The Return of the Native.*
[2] *The Dynasts*, Pt III, Act vi, Sc. 8.

his contemporaries in that he based his grievance on the belief that the resources of the human *psyche* were infinite. He has not explained, much less justified, this belief, but it radiates through all that he has written. Such is his value to us at the present time, at least for those who expect more from literature than the pleasures of the imagination and of expressiveness.

CHAPTER XXII

George Romanes shows that even a man of science could believe in theism, if he cultivated the inclination or rather the necessity to believe —Yet the late Victorians and the Edwardians lacked the will; the progress of culture and civilisation bred other affinities—The men of imagination became more spiritually self-sufficient and infidel than the men of science, as Henry James, Conrad and George Moore will show.

It has been argued in the last three chapters that science, and particularly Darwinism, created distrust in the convictions and ideals which men used to cherish in their hearts and substantiate in experience; that the neo-realists began to interpret and criticise the world without the guidance of these spiritual standards, now discredited; that consequently this school of writers had to describe their impressions by the light of their own moods and mental habits; that lacking any other illumination they have shown themselves to be thoroughly miserable. It was this unhappiness of atheism which so much impressed Pascal,[1] and which helped to convince one of Darwin's greatest disciples that God was the cause and consummation of human life.

George Romanes (1848–94) went up to Cambridge in 1867 and was so far under the influence of evangelicalism that in 1873 he won the Burney Prize with an unexceptionably orthodox essay on *Christian Prayer and General Laws*. But his proper subject was science, especially the more philosophical aspects of biology, and above all, instinct and animal intelligence. As his studies accustomed him to rely solely on his intellect, he set himself to investigate his religious beliefs as he would investigate a biological hypothesis. The upshot was *A Candid Examination of Theism by Physicus* (1878), in which he argues against his most cherished convictions, while lamenting the sacrifice which he thereby has to make to truth. By 1890 he began to realise that the sacrifice need not have been made. In 1894, while sinking into his last illness, he started making notes for a counterblast to his own *Candid Examination*. This draft has been edited by Charles Gore as *Thoughts on Religion* (1895).[2]

---

[1] *Pensées*, Article I.
[2] *The Life and Letters of George John Romanes*. Written and edited by his Wife, 1896.

Romanes is of great significance in this inquiry because, himself a scientist, he recognised the subordination of science to the claims of the spirit. He admitted that the intellect explains phenomena by adducing their causes, but only their proximate causes; not the *causa causarum*. For instance, "the far-reaching thought of Mr Herbert Spencer" can work backwards to Force as the *primum mobile* of our composite, articulated system, but he is no nearer to explaining the ubiquitous and eternal direction of Force, how it comes to compose and articulate this system in this particular way. He may have mastered the facts of causality but not the cosmos in which they occur. The construction and maintenance of the universal order must be due to one first integrating principle, probably of the nature of mind. So said Thomas Aquinas, so says George Romanes. Modern science, dealing in sense perceptions, can form no idea of this constructive and creative Power or Personality. Step by step science has disproved the evidence of design, till we are left with the sole fact that nature as a whole is a cosmos. Thus science ends in agnosticism; but a false agnosticism. It does not merely deny that we know, it affirms that we cannot know.

This position is false because there is one thing that science has never established: that any living thing ever has an instinct without its purpose and object. Now the greatest of all is the human instinct for morality and religion, admitted to be a higher propensity even than the intellect. This instinct grows stronger with the ripening experience of life, becomes an aspiration, absorbs the imaginative, artistic, and sentimental faculties, becomes the most fundamental and representative urge of our organism. If it is an instinct, since it is an instinct, it must have an object as essential as itself but far greater, for it is contrary to all laws of scientific reasoning to argue that the created or evolved mind is greater than the superhuman mind which it recognises as its creator and model. This dominating influence cannot be seen as it really is, but only through our religious consciousness, and if so, Christianity is the ideal exercise.

Such an assurance rests on belief, which requires the co-operation of the intellect, the affections and the will; especially the will. That is to say, the truth is to be reached in this, as in all other matters, by the united effort of the whole being. Mere demonstration never was enough, except in cases of sense perception. The inquirer must have the disposition, the desire and the temperament to direct his intellect aright. Thus George Romanes, the disciple

of Darwin, learns with the help of Thomas Aquinas, Pascal and
Spinoza to cultivate the *illative sense* such as Newman had proclaimed in *The Grammar of Assent*.[1] Even his line of thought
occasionally resembles that of the Roman Catholic. Romanes
writes: "Even in human relations there is a wide difference between 'belief' in a scientific theory and 'faith' in a personal
character. And the difference is in the latter comprising a moral
element." Newman writes to H. Wilberforce in August 1866:
"Does not nature, duty and affection teach us that a difference is
to be made between things and persons? Ought I to be as open to
listen to objections brought to me against the honour, fidelity and
love towards me of a friend, as against the received belief that the
earth is ninety-five million miles from the sun?"

Thus, the biologist and the ecclesiastic agree that a man of pure
intellect is half blind. His mental vision must be widened with a
certain willingness, expectancy, and intuitive understanding before
he becomes clear-sighted enough to perceive the whole truth.
Logic must be energised by an affinity for the supernatural. No
doubt this affirmation was of great help in various individual cases,
but as regards the trend of progressive and constructive thought
we must now note that the age was not inclined to take this
course, though quite acceptable to the scientific mind. It may be
said that the contemporaries of Romanes had no leanings towards
any intelligent power greater than themselves. We are thinking of
the generation which entered upon manhood round about the
'eighties and the 'nineties and predominated more or less till the
outbreak of the war. These libertarians valued intellectual independence more than spiritual happiness. The older generation had
tried to maintain contact with eternal verities, and its successors
were not impressed by the result. They were resolved to trust their
own chances in life. Most of them had ripened in an atmosphere
of freethought; they did not have to overcome the scruples and
regrets with which their fathers had been troubled; they could
start where their elders left off.

At first the omens seemed to be most favourable. The late
Victorian and Edwardian eras promised another renaissance. The
accumulated wealth and prosperity of the last hundred years
seemed to be developing into a more enlightened and inventive
civilisation.. Of course the political situation was clouded—as
always; nor was England's commercial supremacy unchallenged;

[1] *Ante*, chap. v, p. 71.

but humanists and humanitarians were not greatly troubled about the future. It was enough that all the resources and energies of the world were gradually coming within our power, and that culture was revealing new possibilities in their application.[1] Now was the time for the upper-classes to make a success of their adventure on earth.

The responsibilities of their position were a moral education. Quite apart from any social obligations, power and prosperity had conferred privileges of which the beneficiaries had to prove themselves to be worthy. Industrialism might be the curse of those who were poor and consequently uneducated; it was a test and trial for the fortunates; it stimulated new virtues and vices and thus exacted a deeper self-knowledge. For instance, the well-to-do enjoyed leisure for cultivating good manners, and an interest in art, history and humanity. But the money which brought them these good things did not also bring them the requisite aptitudes. On the contrary, possessions led to possessiveness rather than to self-expression. Every member of the upper-classes had to discover what he had in him to express—the men and especially the women. For industrialism had filled their comfortable homes with the commodities and conveniences for which the housewife and her daughters were once responsible. Consequently, the women now lost in importance what they gained in leisure, and had to create for themselves a new position in society. Thus, both sexes found themselves born into a life of many vistas. These opportunities required a more responsive and imaginative habit of mind, but they also required more money, and many a young person ran the risk of sacrificing the ends to the means, of schooling himself to earn an adequate income, till he had no soul left with which to spend it wisely. Altogether, the refinements and amenities of modern civilisation brought endless possibilities both for good and evil.

The perception of these difficulties was in itself a sign of progress, and no student of literature will regret a vigorous tone of criticism, even if it amounts to protest. Such is always the consequence when literary men turn moralists. If we were to believe such pamphleteers and censors as Ascham, Stubbes, Harman, Scot, Greene and Dekker, we should conclude that the Renaissance was England's darkest hour. And so with the late Victorians. There would not have been so many critics, nor would their criticisms

[1] H. V. Routh, *Money, Morals and Manners*, 1935, chaps. x–xii.

have been so searching, unless the age was a Prometheus already breaking his chains. This restlessness was not, of course, confined to England. Instead of discussing Gissing, Meredith and Hardy, we might just as well have examined Daudet, Barrès, Bourget, Björnson, Strindberg and especially Ibsen, "a torpedo under the ark". All over Europe, iconoclasm ought to have heralded a new enthusiasm and expansiveness.

And yet, while reading these authors, one feels that they have not made the most of their opportunity; they are more in earnest about what is bad than what might be better. In reading some others, their contemporaries or very immediate successors, one feels that the satire is often no more than an artistic diversion; that the poem or novel lacks the moral aim of earlier literature. It has become a mere exercise and experience for the reader; less pretentious but also less intimate and significant. The talent of the authors is unquestionable, and yet their literature has fallen to a lower level; they seem to be on their guard against their readers, or to have nothing to share with them but their cleverness. Those who have drawn a curtain over their spiritual backgrounds seem also to have surrendered a claim on their readers' confidence. Perhaps, after all, there was more than one supposed in the "high seriousness" which Matthew Arnold emphasised. Without its inspiration, writers and readers seem to be too much afraid of violating each other's privacy. A glance at a few more or less representative figures will perhaps confirm this impression, before, in the last two chapters we guess at what may be the outcome.

Henry James is a notable example. He came of an English stock; he acquired the tastes and aptitudes of old-world culture; he revolted against the commercialism and provinciality of the United States, and he migrated to Europe in search of a spiritual home. He tried Italy and Paris and finally, perhaps responding to a call of the blood, he settled in England in 1876. As he had, apparently, found the ideal which he sought, one would have expected this gifted novelist to show the rest of us how to find it. Yet all he reveals is that there is nothing to find. He chose as his special province what he was specially qualified to portray: the highly refined middle-class, the people born to affluence and the arts of leisure, who have no other duty than to make the best of life—their own and other people's. The theme offered endless possibilities to an author who understood what human nature was ready to become. Nor would such an author as James have chosen this world unless he felt equal to his argument. He certainly lacked neither insight nor imagination; one sometimes catches rare glimpses into mysteries which look like platitudes; but too often he has lost his vision among subtle experiments, what the Misses Pole termed "the finer shades". "Why is nothing ever accomplished?" exclaims George Moore.[1] "In real life, murder, adultery and suicide are of common occurrence; but Mr James's people live in a calm, sad, very polite twilight of volition." In fact our pragmatist has invented fascinating and ingenious hypotheses; problems of upper-class ethics and psychology, which he then sits down to solve as if he were illustrating an idea extracted from one of his brother William's philosophical treatises. No situation seems to him to be too subtle, provided that it reveals an unexpected aspect of the Victorian lady and gentleman. So his complex and labyrinthine novels attract those interested in the manners of the vanished, if not imaginary class, or in the arts of transforming experience into moral speculation. But in either case the interest generally ends with the technics of the intellect.

Joseph Conrad is an even more striking example. One would have said that he was specially qualified to give the new generation its lead. His outlook was purged of those class-restrictions which hampered so many English writers. On the other hand, his cosmopolitanism was not of that easy and superficial kind which one notes and suspects in Ruskin, Arnold and the æsthetes. His favourite reading was French and Russian,[2] but his ideas of life were drawn from men of action, beginning with his father who sacrificed everything to the cause of Poland, and ending with those who sacrifice everything to a spirit, not so much of adventure, as of self-reliance and self-fulfilment consummated in danger. Conrad's material was human nature simplified of its sedentary accretions and civilised atrophies, the very best starting-point (one would think) for an inventive genius which, having once found the naked truth, could reclothe it in forms to reach his readers' sympathies. And lest this traveller of many seas should be tempted, as Longinus thinks that the author of the *Odyssey* was tempted, to dally with romance, fate had placed one restriction on his experiences. He had studied life in contact with the biggest and most industrialised machines of the age—in steamers which serve the money-market and impose a servitude as rigorous as that of any factory; or else

[1] *Confessions of a Young Man*, 1888.
[2] R. Curle, *The Last Twelve Years of Joseph Conrad*, 1928, chap. VI.

among ports and islands where the most eccentric individual is either engaged in a prosaic struggle for existence, or else dies an outcast. So whatever the appeal of his fiction, it would depend on realism.

Seldom has a realist enjoyed a better opportunity. Conrad's own experiences embraced the epic of modern times; not, of course, the old-fashioned exploits of pirates, and trackers, nor the old-fashioned disasters in maelstroms and burning wrecks, but the more or less peaceful penetration of half-settled or savage countries, in search of raw materials and the wealth out of which civilisation must continue to evolve. Modern life subsists on discoveries, inventions, and the circulation of money; hence neo-commercialism with its search for foreign markets, spheres of influence, commercial treaties, and the trade which follows the British flag. Undoubtedly we are entering on a new era of adventure and action, urged partly by the pressure of over-population and the hope of domesticating natural power—a new "Heroic Age", and the explorers, traders and prospectors are the heroes. Conrad had the knowledge to make them live in literature.

One would add that he also had the insight. After twenty years of contact with mariners, adventurers, and globe-trotters of every race and colour, he knew all that need be known of danger on the high seas, and those other dangers of decivilisation in eastern ports and southern lands, and he had formed a clear notion of the manhood requisite to conquer them. These qualities, the special mark of the modern hero, were suggested to him by his own professional sense of the "ship-shape",[1] and might be described as the virtues of responsibility, self-control, self-adaptation, and recognition of what is due to justice, humanity and one's personal dignity. His vivid and convincing backgrounds might have served to throw into relief this prosaic and business-like heroism, to make it live in the reader's imagination, but, of course, these qualities were not only needed on stormy seas and tropical forests; they were just as essential to the merest city clerk or country labourer. To that extent Conrad was a moralist as well as an artist.

This philosophy of life could easily be formulated, and Conrad often inculcates or implies his view either by the arrangement of events or through the personage of Marlow. But to work his ideal into the soul of his story, to vitalise it in the characters, to create the sense of moral inevitability is quite another matter. This

[1] Ford Maddox Ford, *Joseph Conrad: a Personal Remembrance*, 1924.

spiritualisation requires in the author more than imagination and mastery of language. He must be possessed by enthusiasm for human accomplishment and development, and must also be confident that the reading public will welcome his idea. Conrad's greatness is not to be found in these qualities. On the contrary, he is at his best when studying aberrations from the perfect type. One should not infer too much from his earlier efforts, *Almayer's Folly* (1895), *An Outcast of the Islands* (1896) and *Tales of Unrest* (1898). These are stories of degenerates who waste their lives among unforgettable scenery—human beings vitiated by some taint of blood or obsessed by some megalomaniac dream. Perhaps he was venting his spleen against all that insults his ideal before he passed on to develop it, or perhaps, under the influence of the neo-realists, he was portraying the ignoble in order to reveal the skill of the portraitist. On this lower plane, his first books were full of promise.

This phase is followed by his best works: *The Nigger of the Narcissus* (1897), *Lord Jim* (1900), *Youth* (1902), *Typhoon* (1903), *Nostromo* (1904). The stories in which the men seem to be heroes. All the more so, because they are not made of iron, like some of Kipling's Englishmen or Hugo's Frenchmen. They are sensitive, in fact hypersensitive; men of imagination as well as of action (except the immortal McWhirr of *Typhoon*); self-conscious and sub-conscious at the same time. Jim has once incurred disgrace and till the end of his life is haunted with the nightmare of an exposure. The nameless heroes of *The Narcissus*, who work their ship round the perils of the Horn, are nevertheless afraid and divert their fears into an almost idiotic anxiety lest that consumptive nigger should die. Nostromo loses his moral character as soon as he loses pride in his subordinate position. In fact, Conrad achieved a remarkable feat in that he revealed the modern mind working at the primeval game.

Yet a careful study of these and the subsequent novels will convince that our author is not really interested in the most that his fellow-creatures can do. His ideal of the modern hero is, indeed, the standard at the back of his mind, but he does not give it effect. Two of his favourite authors were Turgenev and Dostoevski, of whom the first studied "lamed souls" and the second perfected the technique for portraying criminals, double-types and the significance of the Unknown.[1] Conrad never escaped their influence; nor (it seems) did he wish to do so. His genius was more

[1] Cf. H. Bennewitz, *Die Charaktere in den Romanen Joseph Conrads*, 1933.

at home with inverts and perverts. As a consequence, the adventures of his characters may be interesting, but their author's irony is more interesting still. He loves to start his hero on a career of high ambition and pure motives and then, if possible, to throw in his way some bait to his vanity or timorousness, and tempt his unwitting victim out of his course, while we and he look on. This satirically dispassionate attitude, even to such figures as Mitchell, Heyst and Lingard, is its own justification; Conrad has more than fulfilled the promise of *Almayer*; but especially, in the narrowness of his vision. He experiments with the strangeness, often the ignoble strangeness, of real life; at the same time he refines his irony; and, since he can create no deeper interest, this Olympian aloofness ends in the posing of psychological puzzles, and experiments in the probabilities of human volition. If we have no right to say that Conrad is untrue to life, it is because his characters are such as we have never encountered. Moreover, we are beguiled into acquiescence, because he has created and embroidered a background both new and convincing—adventures on wild seas and in savage lands, with modern inventions for the instruments and accessories.

However, Conrad is not by any means the most complete or representative example of English neo-realism. He is significant as a foreigner, laden with exotic influences, who ventured into that atmosphere because it seemed to promise more to the artist than it took from the moralist. If we are to consider the most wholehearted, consistent and comprehensive experiments made in our language we must turn to another alien, George Moore.

This Irishman (1853–1933) was by nature an egoist with a very considerable talent for literature, who had private and family reasons for hating his own country with its religion. Like so many of his generation, all over Europe, he broke all the bonds of nurture and place and went abroad in search of that sense of continuity and purposiveness, without which human beings do not often feel happy and rarely if ever become artists.

Like Henry James he looked for his lost self among the artistic and literary circles of Paris; and at first seemed to be more successful; perhaps because he was more expert in the arts of spending money. He learnt that there is much more to be developed than the reason and the intellect; there are vital impulses, subconscious resolutions, "brain instincts" stimulated by the caprices of the flesh, and if a man is to become a personality, these must be roused—and ruled. These intimations swarm within us, indistinct and inarticulate. What Moore missed and sought was some connection between his own esoteric impulses and the outside world of the 'seventies. That world had discarded its hereditary beliefs (at any rate in Paris) and was not likely to find new convictions among its mechanical complexities and commercial interrelationships. So even at its best the prospect was not encouraging, and Moore intensified his difficulties by seeking inspiration among the over-moneyed or the over-cerebrated, that is to say, among those who artificialise both life and thought, and look no further.

Consequently, he was thrown more than ever upon his own resources, and that is why he learnt so much first from Gautier, then from Balzac, then from Zola and the de Goncourts, then again from Balzac, and finally from Pater. Under these successive influences he learnt as the other neo-realists had learnt, how to develop his impressions so as to become acutely conscious of his own mind; how to observe manners, gestures, words, appearances which epitomise an emotion or an idea; how to take any hint which might set the powers of his own being in motion. The realism of these masters appealed to him as "the idea of a new art based upon science, in opposition to the art of the old world that was based on imagination, an art that should explain all things and embrace modern life in its entirety, in its endless ramifications".[1] Thus what really fascinated him in the new school was its platitudinous suggestiveness—to feel the burning influence of art while thinking of the commonest, coarsest things. Such were the effects which he intended to cultivate, and so strong was the call towards self-expression that he left Paris, and turned his back for ever on that bohemian life centering in *la nouvelle Athènes* where he had learnt so much, because otherwise he would lose the artistic mastery of English.

So George Moore comes before us as the most sincere or at least the most self-conscious of the neo-realists. He was to cultivate his talent with his eyes bent on the sorrow, vulgarity, hardness, or stupidity of life. In his hands the novel was not intended to reveal the height and depth of human nature in unexpected places; nor to photograph aspects of contemporary life unfamiliar to the people who buy the volumes. His novels were written to convey a sense within the sense; a tacit revelation of the author's personality, while the thin pageant of the story unrolled itself. We are expected

[1] *Confessions of a Young Man*, 1888, chap. VIII.

to watch it pass us by, without bias or partisanship, interested chiefly in the creator's sense of aesthetic completeness, thus sharing in his artistic vitality.

It is hardly necessary to add that Moore has not realised his ideal. In order to assert the integrity of his essential genius he has had to strip himself bare, and very few of us since Adam have been able to stand naked and unashamed. Disdaining all garments borrowed from the false culture of the period (like so many others from Byron to Swinburne and Hardy) he has to trick himself in the insignia of "the blithe modern pagan". Like Nietzsche he discards pity, because it is a concession to weakness and un-development. Hence his insensibility to the misfortunes of his characters, his sometimes unnecessary insistence on physical pain, and his avoidance of any sentiment associated with "the pale socialist of Galilee". As a boy he had shrunk from the repressive-ness of Irish Catholicism; so in exchange he cultivates the pagan sensuousness, which in the first place he had learnt from *Mademoi-selle de Maupin*, and dwells more than is necessary on the physical aspects of sex immorality. These and such like studied effects are cultivated in order to ensure intellectual independence and self-realisation, but having only himself to realise, his vigorously con-structed novels, for all their descriptiveness, exhale a sense of spiritual incompleteness, almost a confession that the author is trying to pose as the superman who is beyond his reach. Despite his glimpses of cruelty and violence, there is nothing virile about his novels; he has an inexhaustible curiosity in women—in their sexual appetencies and religious instincts. He does not miss an opportunity of shutting them up in convents in order to see how they will react. On the other hand, though he can create the impression of a man's presence with admirable felicity, he does not understand more of male characters than the ordinary routine habits, unless they are themselves half-women. Yet an atmosphere of intellectual impartiality pervades his work, especially when tracing human instinct and its maladjustment to the varied forms of man-made culture.

Can the study of this tension produce great work? Moore, at his best, has hardly succeeded; certainly not while he was "a student only of ballrooms, bar-rooms, streets and alcoves". The cold veracity of *A Modern Lover* (1883), *A Mummer's Wife* (1885) and *A Drama in Muslin* (1886), though daring and provocative in their day, are not worth discussing from our point of view. *Esther*

Waters (1894) is an artistic triumph. The serving maid has to spend a life labouring at everything for everybody; she goes through the under-world and the upper-world; and she ends where she began. Her dissenter's faith is worth nothing to her; her convictions are worth less, for she has none; her only religion is a mother's fight for the life of her child against society. George Moore constructs the story with admirable selection, and yet crowds his pages with fascinating glimpses of social types. He holds us enthralled, while we read. But at the end there is nothing to remember and meditate.

Evelyn Innes (1898) and *Sister Teresa* (1901) penetrate deeper. Both study the psychology of a woman of great gifts who resolved to realise herself. At first she tries the life of the flesh. Having the voice of a *prima donna*, she becomes the mistress of a dilettante millionaire, is trained to sing by the best masters, and makes a European reputation and a fortune. So she lives in the present. Yet at moments the world with all its pleasures and triumphs sinks beneath her like a wave, and she seems to be drifting like a piece of seaweed. She becomes conscious of an infinity around her and of her own littleness. To some extent this loneliness and sense of futility are due to the sacrifices she has made for her art; she ought to have accepted the life of the flesh wholly and have borne children. But her despondency is due even more to an unsatisfied instinct for religion. She cannot stifle a yearning for the life of the soul. She meets a second lover who has beliefs, but he only intensifies her sense of aimlessness. At the height of her career she leaves wealth, fame, and love for a life of obscurity among the nuns. As Sister Teresa she does not find what she seeks. She had gone to the convent at Dulwich in quest of herself and had found a refuge from one half of herself and a group of women who thought as she did. But the empty-headedness and superficiality of the young ones tire her, and in the older women, who had lived in the world and suffered, she finds the same kind of void as in herself. Thus the story ends, or rather, it leaves off.

So George Moore has worked a distinct philosophy into his clear narrative, as sculptured as a frieze. He has outlined the mysteriousness and labyrinthine energy of human instincts, has shown how they grow in appetency and aspiration with the development of the intelligence, till at the present time neither civilisation nor religion is equal to their aims. Man seems to be greater than the culture which his fathers prepared for him. As if to prove his case, he turned his hand to the most famous records of old time, apparently bringing realism. into the 'historical novel (after the manner of *Salammbô* and *The Cloister and the Hearth*). It may be accident or design, but it is significant that in this last phase he utterly ignores the associations wound round the well-known facts by culture, and reinterprets them in the light of modern consciousness.

The most remarkable is *The Brook Kerith* (1916), in which all mystery and majesty are stripped from the story of the four gospels in order to give artistic effect to a deeper human value. With the help of K. H. Venturini's *Natürliche Geschichte des grossen Propheten von Nazareth* (1800–2) and E. Renan's *Vie de Jésus* (1863), our novelist reconstructs the facts and implications of Christ's career into a man's quest of his own personality among the delusions and cross purposes, which every age throws in the way of its men of genius. Jesus was the greatest shepherd that Judaea had ever produced, with a winning manner and a gift for meditation. He was hypnotised by John's preaching and started himself to preach, and to interpret the Scriptures, thus trying to make others like himself. Opposition bred harshness in him, and applause bred pride, till he really believed that he was the Messiah. When crucified, he did not die but swooned, and Joseph of Arimathea, a *candida anima* if ever there were one, and the one Jew whom Pilate called friend, procured the body and nursed it back to life. For another twenty years Jesus was again a shepherd and underneath the heavens he came to realise that "quires and scrolls lead men from God" and that we find Him as soon as we open our eyes and ears, even in the breeze or the flowers.[1] We find moreover that a sense of good and evil is implanted in our hearts, but only to enable us to fulfil ourselves as we were created. To do otherwise is to alter the work of God, for He shaped each one of us out of a design and therefore we cannot reshape ourselves, much less other people. Thus Moore tells his story so that we become intensely conscious of ourselves while gazing on old friends in a new light. Take, for instance, the climax of the long narrative, the meeting of the two founders of Christianity. Its essence is the pleasure of recognising in Jesus a character so simple and even-tempered that he does not trouble to contradict Paul, and of recognising in Paul (just newly come from preaching Jesus' death) a fanatic with bushy eyebrows and gleaming eyes, bald-headed and bearded to

[1] Chap. XXIX.

the ears, obsessed with his dream of enlightenment from Heaven—
a self-imagined minister of an oriental God.[1]

Compared with this experiment, *Héloïse and Abelard* (1921) seems
almost narrow in scope. Moore does not attempt to revive the
early twelfth century as a realist must imagine it to have been,
with all its primitive roughness and brutality, though he is at
great pains to suggest a background, in which the reader's
imagination can play at will. The novelist is chiefly concerned
with the tendency of culture—the birth of scholasticism, the temporal power of the Church, the premature renaissance of the pagan
classics, Plato as well as the Roman poets. In fact he over-reaches
his realism, for surely the scholars of Notre-Dame were not so
well-equipped or so humanistically minded in those pre-university
days. His purpose is to recreate this atmosphere not for the sake
of its antiquarianism, but as so many picturesque disguises in
which human nature may burn with more than twentieth-century
strangeness and vigour. So we watch Abelard, that sprite of many
geniuses, zigzagging through medieval civilisation, the friend of
troubadours, the fear of churchmen, seeking everywhere an outlet
for his impetuous and many-sided nature, till he meets his convent
pupil, Héloïse the learned and the wise (*la très sage*), and the call
of the blood infuses and completes the call of the intellect.

Thus George Moore had a distinct philosophy to teach, though
he claimed no more for his novels than a new art of telling an old
story. He taught his readers to employ culture so as to forget it,
and to remember the unexplored labyrinths of themselves. Nor is
this teaching to be ignored. It does not, indeed, reveal a new light,
but prepares for its reception. His narratives keep the mind so
keen and polished that it ought to be able to reflect the light, when
the day dawns. He exercises us in vigilance and intentness. He is
doing the best thing, during the interval of twilight.

This rationalising, inductive, critical spirit, which penetrated
the world of the imagination, was not likely to close its eyes with
holy dread before the monuments of humanism. We have already
noticed how the cult of the classics[2] helped mid-Victorians to
recover what their own age denied them. But after Darwin's
example began to spread, it dawned on scholars that they could
anatomise the ancient world, much as novelists were anatomising

[1] Chap. XXXI ff. The whole episode revised and retold in *The Passing of the
Essenes. A Drama in Three Acts*, 1930; new and revised ed., 1931.
[2] *Ante*, chap. XIV, pp 230–2.

their contemporaries. Since Schliemann started to look for Mycenean tombs and Frazer to look for the Golden Bough, antiquarians, folklorists and philologians have set themselves to trace our fallible humanity among the most precious relics of art and architecture, such as only experts can explain. So the humanities have begun to enter upon yet another phase, less dominated by the grand style, more in sympathy with our daily problems, rich in imaginative and ingenious guesses, free from idealism, sustained by the inspiration of disillusionment. The study of English literature has kept pace. Since Lee analysed *Love's Labour's Lost*, we have gradually learnt to think of Shakespeare as a man at war with piratical printers, an artist experimenting in stage effects, a caricaturist of contemporaries whom it is fascinating to identify. Milton's "God-gifted organ voice" no longer rings quite true to our sophisticated ears, and we picture him as a dogmatist intent on believing what he professes. We even find Wordsworth's private vagaries as interesting as the *Prelude* in which they are not revealed.

Yet somehow, all through the nineteenth century, this sharpening of the intellect seems to blunt it towards the perfectibility or even greatness of human nature.

CHAPTER XXIII

Three philosophers who adapted science to humanism, though freed from the humanistic tradition: Samuel Butler, Nietzsche, Bergson—Twentieth-century literature has profited by their hints.

Victorian literature might be described as a magnificent failure, not for lack of genius or idealism, but because the spirit always rears its fabric on intellectual foundations; and these in the nineteenth century crumbled. The foundations had crumbled because man is bound to seek an enlargement of power and in this case had found it in science—both a new direction of himself and a new control of his circumstances—but had not found an adequate recognition and expression of this victory in religion and culture. The consciousness of power had stopped short at the intellect. So the first problem of the twentieth century would necessarily be the creation of ideas and ideals to serve a spiritual revival: to restore our zest in life, our confidence in our species and consequently in our intimate selves, without sacrificing intellectual truth.

It remains to inquire whether any steps have already been made in that direction. To answer such a question we must look backwards to a personality which passed almost unnoticed in the nineteenth century and died at the dawn of the twentieth.

Samuel Butler (1835–1902) had his full share of the aesthete's and neo-realist's consciousness of self. Like them he had a horror of routine, a fear of losing his identity among the conventions of modern society and the experiences which our crowded mechanised civilisation repeats till they become habits. Like them, he was determined to assert his artistic and intellectual personality. As he was descended from a line of clergymen, and was expected, in the 'fifties, to take Holy Orders, it was inevitable that he should examine the forms and formularies of his religion with the utmost care, and should test them by the learning and experience which he had acquired for his own development. It was equally inevitable that he should end by renouncing the Church and all else which seemed to him to be more customary than rational. His stumbling-block was the efficacy of infant baptism. So in 1859 he emigrated to New Zealand and discontinued saying his prayers.[1]

[1] *The Note-Books of Samuel Butler.* Edited by H. Festing Jones, 1930. XIII. "Unprofessional Sermons: Prayer."

In the colony he won financial independence through sheep-farming, and intellectual independence through contact with elemental life and the intermittent study of the new biology, and having invested his fortune of £8000 in New Zealand securities at 10 per cent. he returned to England in 1864. His intention was to live the life of an artist and a composer, and he turned his hand to writing only when ethical or moral ideas clamoured for expression, or the follies of his contemporaries provoked his satire. Something more was added to this education and these opportunities. Not being content with his income of £800 he transferred his small fortune to investments which promised to double or treble the yield, but ended by swallowing the principal. So he learnt the meaning of poverty and consequently the value of money. His father's death restored him to comparative affluence, but he never forgot his lesson. Henceforth, he understood that cheque-books and share-certificates have been evolved, like antennae, to keep the human animal in touch with the resources of his environment.

Butler would probably have remained an amateur of art and music, if he had not also been quite consciously a moralist, anxious to know how industrial civilisation (including the investment of capital) could be adjusted to our spiritual needs. Having discarded theology and cultivated science he realised that he must first form some idea of the universal principle of life. Otherwise he would not understand what human existence involves, nor our chances of fitting into the scheme of creation.

To judge by *Darwin on the Origin of Species* (1862), *Darwin among the Machines* (1863), *Lucubratio Ebria*[1] (1865), *Erewhon or Over the Range* (1872), his first important work, and *The Fair Haven* (1873), he had already formulated his philosophy of life by the time he was thirty-six years old.

This philosophy consisted in completing and readjusting Darwinism. The biologists had more or less disproved the older idea of divine supervision and had left man to find his own way through life on this earth, thus revealing our immense responsibility to ourselves. Thereby, they had also left a glimpse of what the superman might become. If we had evolved all the way from apes, in fact from the embryonic cell, we could and must evolve incredibly further still. Nay more, we had already evolved with the help of

[1] Reprinted in *The Note-Books of Samuel Butler*. Edited by H. Festing Jones, 1912. III. "The Germs of *Erewhon* and of *Life and Habit*."

machines; we had created a new physical and mechanical environment. It remained to improve these yet further and also to create an intellectual, moral, and spiritual environment, in adaptation to which we could far outstrip the present generation. Having formed a scientific and unprejudiced conception of man's nature, we must redirect culture and civilisation with a view to his potentialities. Such was Butler's moral philosophy.

Butler's problem was to adopt or invent an artistic medium, such as would give true effect to these convictions. He was not successful. One might almost say that he missed his proper place through weakness in authorship. As he wrote only when ideas clamoured for expression, he lacked the first quality of a great writer: the determination at all costs to be read. Butler missed this urge which is the first salvation, not "the last infirmity", of genius. He could not or would not learn how to persuade or surprise others into thinking his thoughts. *Erewhon*, his first sustained effort, was the most successful. It took the form of an imaginary state and he very cleverly exposed the falsities and inconsistencies of British civilisation as it is—all that in his day thwarted the progress of man. As a satire the fantasy is not profound, for after all he only ridicules what every enlightened contemporary knew to be wrong. Yet the book exercises a fascination because of its irony and insinuations which make the reader co-operate with the author, and substantiate the accusations. We enjoy the illusion of being ourselves the satirist. Thanks to this quality *Erewhon* attracted attention. It was translated into Dutch in 1873 and into German in 1879, and despite the posthumous appearance of *The Way of All Flesh*, the author's name is still associated with the earlier work. Yet this parable, in the highest sense, is a failure because there is too much of Moropolis and too little of Utopia in *Erewhon*. Butler did not give full effect to the original and creative ideas with which it abounds. He resorted to the Platonic myth. But whereas Plato rises into an allegory only as the consummation or supplement of his argument, Butler introduces it without any such preparation. As we see from the *Note-Books*, he was fond of pushing his theories to the logical extreme, to the last and most paradoxical combination of consequences. But in *Erewhon* he starts with his whimsical conclusions and leaves the reader to work backwards to the theory. For instance, his fable of the "World of the Unborn",[1] has been

[1] Chaps. xviii–xx.

admired as a fantasy and compared to Lamb's "Dream Children",[1] but really implies his whole vitalistic doctrine, and furthermore his theory of our reactions between luck and cunning. The reader must indeed be a student of unusual insight and imagination if he can grasp the full implication from the hint. Most of Butler's admirers closed the volume with full recognition of its author's provocative and stimulating genius, and hoped that his following books would answer their questions and mature the ideas which he had planted in germ. At any rate Butler had created his opportunity.

But he did not know how to follow up his success. In fact seven years later his publisher, Trübner, was still speaking of him as a "one-book man"[2] though his aims had become more constructive. He was now intending to expound what he had so far only prefigured, to extricate from Darwinism the neglected Nietzschean element of the *superman*: that power of self-determination which must be immanent in all life, and which we human beings should tend, cultivate and worship as God, if we must worship something. Darwin, as has been noted, had not disproved this neoteleology, he had merely diverted attention to the influence of environment. His principle worked so well that scientists lost interest in the other aspects. They thought more of natural selection than of human self-determination. Butler, though not of their fraternity, was original enough to appreciate what they ignored—the latent energy and purposiveness without which the surviving species would not have mastered their destinies. He realised that Darwinism held the secret of life, and he might have produced a really great work if he had a great writer's sense of other people's minds. But there was too much aggressiveness and solipsism mixed with his intellect and generosity. While casting about for a suitable approach, he found to his surprise that the teleological principle had already been propounded by the pre-Darwinian evolutionists, and he jumped to the conclusion that they, the holders of truth, were now being superseded in order that their successors might enjoy more than their due. The temptation was too great. Not having yet given shape to his thoughts, he turned them into a protest. Thus, instead of spiritualising evolution and opening its vistas till they illuminated morality, he weakened his purpose by lapsing into controversy.

[1] O. Elton, *A Survey of English Literature*, 1830–80, chap. XII, § III.
[2] *Note-Books*, X.

Even a hurried glance at his scientific polemics will show what we have lost. *Life and Habit* (1877), the first and best, peers into the mysterious sources whence we derive our power of resisting death, and the author finds that each member of each species shares its vitality with all its predecessors, nay, with the one primal and universal energy, a sort of racial purpose created out of the immemorial desire to survive; a continuous hereditary memory of all the difficulties each species has overcome since its origin, of all the needs which it has supplied. Thus we live in our remotest ancestors and in our most distant descendants, participating in one composite, surviving personality which underlies the transitory thoughts and impulses by which we think that we recognise ourselves.

Evolution, Old and New (1879) is an effort to return thanks for this illumination where they are due. As in private duty bound he must first dispose of the older pre-scientific teleologists, especially Paley and his watch found on Robinson Crusoe's island; and then, having refuted what is now termed "interventional teleology", he passes on to the natural philosophers who taught that the species are not manufactured but grow. Again he touches on the same profound idea, though in a different aspect. If an animal feels any given want it will gradually develop the structure to meet that want. Consequently, evolution must imply design as necessarily and more intelligibly than the theological view of creation; but the designers are ourselves or rather the vital urge of which we are the momentary expression. Would that his readers had been told more of this myriad-handed and myriad-lived artisan who labours at constructing himself, till at last his own plan develops into thought and an omnipresent instinct becomes omnipresence of mind. But Butler devotes most of his space to a brilliant exposition of Buffon, Erasmus Darwin and Lamarck, at the expense of Charles Darwin.

He made amends in the papers which he contributed in 1879 to *The Examiner*, from May to July, and published in book-form as *God the Known and God the Unknown*.[1] In this slim volume he discusses the spirit which creates, governs and upholds all living things, what we might call the parent from which all species have sprung, a comprehensive but incomprehensible essence; as it were many animals infinitely varied, yet parts of one and the same

[1] Cf. *Erewhon Revisited*, chap. xv: "The Words of the Sun Child about God and Man."

animal, which comprises them as a tree comprises all its buds. This infinity in unity, this polytypism leading to monotypism, is our only true God. "If man is a microcosm then kosmos is a megalanthrope and that is how we come to anthropomorphise the deity", he afterwards wrote.[1] Whereas man is only a few end-links in an endless chain and God can be conceived only as the continuity which vitalises it. We worship God as often as we love the beauty of animals, birds and insects, or love our own normal healthy bodies, or rejoice to serve the Creative Power which flashes into each being a ray from its heat. Nor does Butler ignore the mystery which encompasses our self-knowledge. This million-bodied deity (God the Known) is only quasi-omnipotent, being finite in space and time, and must itself be the product of a yet vaster and more composite personality (God the Unknown). So if we have eyes to study the visible expressions of the World Spirit we shall penetrate to the boundary beyond which human sympathies are lost in metaphysical speculation.

In one sense this theory is not new, in fact it gains in significance because it is old; because this man's intellect, all compact of modern art and scientific knowledge, nevertheless reverts to it. On the other hand, the theory is new in the sense that it is tested by new standards. Pantheism is being reinterpreted as panzoism. Such an interpretation, however, must be founded on imagination, intuition, and intellectual instinct—something similar to Newman's *illative sense*[2]—not only on the mastery of facts, and Butler could not rise to the height of his argument. He hints at what his religion ought to mean for others, but instead of simplifying our motives and straightening our actions, he relapses into controversy for which he was not equipped and the old gladiatorialism of assaulting reputations. Nor did he yet lay down his arms. In 1880 he published *Unconscious Memory* to corroborate his theory by quotations from Von Hartmann and especially from Ewald Hering, though he confesses in his Note-books[3] that "I forced my view on him, as it were, by taking hold of a sentence or two in his lecture". In 1887 he produced *Luck or Cunning as the main means of Organic Modification* to assert once more that the differentiation of species was caused by the organism's intelligent striving.

Thus Butler, like so many others then and since, fell a victim to the spirit of debate which John Mill did so much to enthrone.[4]

---

[1] *Note-Books*, X. "First Principles." [2] *Ante*, pp. 71; 332–3.
[3] V. "Vibrations." [4] *Ante*, pp. 13; 239–40.

The author of *On Liberty* was at heart a simple soul and believed that when all men were free to advocate all opinions our culture would acquire the inventiveness, vision, and sympathy that we find mirrored in Plato's leisurely and creative dialogues. He probably did not realise that in protesting so effectively against the restrictions of public opinion and in releasing the powers of research and speculation, he also released other and less amiable energies. Unfettered discussion (however salutary) led to the establishment of one's own opinions at the expense of other people's; it became almost a habit to create by means of demolition; and though much rubbish has thereby been cleared away, the edifice reared in its place is inhospitable, built with destructive tools. It is easier to discredit a fallacy than to vitalise a truth. Such is the price we pay for the progress that he exemplifies and in one sense inaugurated. Butler, not having found his special vein of creativeness, fell an easy victim to the mode.

This consequence was all the more deplorable, because our author had been drawing valuable conclusions from his principles. As will readily be granted, he was not a materialist. He believed in an unseen world; he notes how things come up from it into the visible world and then go down again into the invisible. He is convinced that this abstraction is utterly beyond our comprehension, and that we nevertheless move and think in its energy every day of our lives. We feel its influence whenever the cells of our body listen to the memoried instincts of all previous generations and carry on the work of adaptation. Our destiny is to follow its promptings, to merge our petty intellectualised will in the universal natural will; to convert purposiveness into purpose. Nor was Butler really an iconoclast. He broke only idols of clay. This panzoist distrusts indoctrination and ideology simply because the springs of our nature lie deeper than thought. The subconscious self directs the conscious self, and so our progress must be experimental and individualistic, each human being solving his own problem. Preaching and teaching are sure to imply a priggish assumption of more than human wisdom. That is the only reason why he disliked Virgil, Dante and Pope so intensely and confessed that as far as he was an author he was one of the damned.[1] But that is also why he valued so intensely Homer, Holbein, Bellini, Shakespeare, Rembrandt and Handel—"those who do actually live in us, and move us to higher achievements though they be long

[1] *Life and Habit*, chap. II.

dead, whose life thrusts out our own and overrides it."[1] Again, he seems to be an iconoclast because he cut across social classifications even more thoroughly than did Hardy, and instanced the Italian peasant, or the Breton, Norman and English fisherman as about the best types of men that nature could produce. Such preferences appear in their proper light when we remember that Butler valued human beings according to their adjustments. In fact he had much to say for the grace, gentleness and health which were, or could be, cultivated by the "swells". Nor need we complain that he protested against the tyranny of nineteenth-century culture. Since the truth lies hidden in the vital urge transmitted through our tissues, only known to us as the effort to make the best of our circumstances, it is dangerous to seek for spiritual certainty and guidance among man-made theories. Even words fail us when we use them as accurate instruments of thought, for ideas "are like shadows—substantial enough till we try to grasp them".[2] So he held that common sense and good feeling were our safest guides, and moreover insisted that the more we could preserve of tradition and continuity the less we should suffer from friction in our daily work of readaptation. New ideas should be grafted onto old forms. As he wrote in *Alps and Sanctuaries* (1882): "The power of adaptation is mainly dependent on the power of mistaking the new for the old."

Butler had certainly himself accomplished a delicate adjustment of ideas and he believed that his contributions to scientific thought would eventually ensure his immortality. But one cannot be surprised that his apotheosis was long delayed and never completed. As his years multiplied, his reputation dwindled and he became more whimsical, petulant and aggressive, wasting time and temper on digressions into the bibliography of *The Sonnets* and the authorship of the *Odyssey*. Apart from these intellectual dissipations, he wrote on his love of travel and music and late in life he returned to his idea of *Erewhon* and revisited that land of dreams, in which British eccentricity ran riot. Once again, his bitterness confines his imagination. He is too oppressed by his own caricatures of our national hypocrisy and disingenuousness to create more than a sketch of the perfect man of the future, his own and Arowhena's son, whom the father loves, admires and would feign imitate. There were immense possibilities in the meeting of those two.

This failure need not have mattered. Since the 'seventies Butler

---

[1] *How to make the Best of Life*, 1895. [2] *Note-Books*, VII.

had been engaged on a work which should explain the ethics of panzoism and trace "the way of all flesh" among the morals and manners which the humanist could observe for himself. That book should have been the consummation of Butler's career, for it looked as if he had at last created the outline which would give full effect to his idea. He visualised a family with strong hereditary characteristics—moral, artistic and acquisitive—which had found free play in the artisan class of the late eighteenth century and gradually rose in the social scale till the now black-coated descendants of old Edward Pontifex found their natural aptitudes entangled among the money values, sectarianism and pseudo-culture of the educated Victorians; the three generations slowly and successively emerging out of business into the Church, and out of the Church into the free air of creativeness and self-determinism. The difficulties and readjustments involved in this progress were to be the true theme of the book. It was a most felicitous idea and *The Way of All Flesh* ought to have joined *Euphues* and *Wilhelm Meister* (not without a touch of *Tom Jones*), one of those rare studies in self-education, a new stage in the history of the modern individual seeking his proper place in the scheme of things. Butler seems to have realised his opportunity; he kept the book by him for more than a quarter of a century; he died before he was satisfied to publish it.

He might well be dissatisfied; even at the age of sixty he had not learnt to develop his ideas without developing his resentments, and the more he drew on his personal experiences and observations to give life to his theory, the more he gave life to his personal grievances. So this brilliant attempt at a philosophico-scientific novel was narrowed into a satire on Victorian domesticity, education and worship, in which Anglicanism has become a congenial refuge to vulgar or servile natures, the Rev. Theobald Pontifex grows into a monster of unctuous inhumanity, Christina becomes a figure of fun, and Overton and Ernest join characters to represent the author's idea of himself. So Butler's name must be added to the long list of Victorian failures.

Yet he is a post-Victorian success. He awoke after death to a career which is not yet ended. His posthumous influence is, in the first place, due to the very qualities which hindered his progress when alive—restlessness, resentment and irony. His impatience with philistinism and stupidity was a sure passport to the next generation, and no sooner were his younger readers in sympathy with his mood than they found themselves in sympathy with his theories. They met him half-way, forgave his pedestrian manner, let him make up their minds for them and then discovered that he was already in possession of their favourite ideas. They were particularly interested to find him explaining that the human mind is not a clean wax tablet waiting for the selected inscription, but a palimpsest on which layers of impressions had been superimposed since the dawn of the animal creation; that our only chance of self-fulfilment and consequently of happiness depends on fusing these layers and adjusting the fusion to an ever-changing environment; that the more we study each his own nature, instead of poetic sentiments, the deeper we shall penetrate to an unexpected and fundamental self and the less we shall talk about righteousness and evil as two conflicting powers within the breast of man. Thus, he helped to prepare his successors for the experience best epitomised by Paul Claudel:

> J'ai fui partout; partout j'ai retrouvé la loi—
> Quelque chose en moi qui soit plus moi-même que moi.

At the same time he advanced a faith which others have since reached by other paths, that tension which S. Alexander in the Gifford Lectures of 1916–18[1] designated as "the *nisus* towards deity", and which in the Gifford Lectures of 1922 was so convincingly developed by C. Lloyd Morgan as *Emergent Evolution*. In both these respects Butler marks the beginning of the twentieth century.

This passion for self-knowledge was a ferment produced by the daring and contradictory speculations of the nineteenth century. But so many guesses and doctrines would not have converged into a generation's habit of mind, nor would Butler have been so readily exhumed as one of its prophets, unless other thinkers had captured the spirit of inquiry and had directed it with much more assurance and imagination. Two authorities, in particular, were digging channels into which the cross-currents might flow and assume the course of definite ideas. Both of them, like Butler, had stamped their meditations with the precision of a formula which, if elusive, is at any rate stimulating, and helps the stream of contemporary thought to divide again into theories and imaginings. It took time for their influence to sink into the consciousness of the educated world, but their principles were established by the end of last century.

[1] Reprinted, *Space, Time, and Deity*, 1920.

The first was Friedrich Nietzsche who, born in 1844, was old enough to feel the weight of religious sectarianism. Having shaken off that burden, and started in search of his own philosophy of life in 1865, he discovered Schopenhauer, then almost unknown, and eagerly studied *Die Welt als Wille und Vorstellung*[1] because its author faced the picture of life as a whole, not satisfied with technical and subsidiary interests, such as the texture of the canvas or the mixture of the pigments, but examining the intention of the artist. Under this influence Nietzsche set himself to seek the principle of life, and, like his master, he turned his eyes inward, to the only place where phenomena can be observed in their naked truth, that is to say, in our own subjective selves. Here he found neither the pure ethereal presence of the Holy Spirit, nor the clear light of the intellect, but a chaos of energies and urges, as in the Universe outside, each impulse striving blindly for power, until the human being can unite them in some creative purpose. Thus by 1870 Nietzsche's faith was in some respects in sympathy with Butler's. Both held to vitalism, but the German insisted much more confidently on vitalism rendered self-conscious and self-expressive, that is to say, husbanded by the intellect which was otherwise a mere efflorescence of intuition and instinct. Once convinced of this interdependence, it was easy to insist that culture must play a more restricted but vital part in man's progress. It was not a decoration of life, but a new and better *physis*, a completion and rectification of nature.

These ideas came to a head in *Die Geburt der Tragödie aus dem Geiste der Musik* (1872),[2] in which he explained that ancient Greece recognised two strains in man: one controlled by the reason, with thought and conduct adjusted to the cult of virtue, an intellectualisation exemplified by the serene Apollo; the other a strain of wildness and mystery, subconscious and elemental, a ferment of orgiastic forces symbolised by the nature-god Dionysus. At certain stages of Greek culture the Apollonian and Dionysian moods had united, notably in the passion and lyrical enchantment of Athenian drama, and Nietzsche was convinced that the men and women of his time might also, like the Greeks, learn how to liberate and ennoble the animal spirits of human nature. So other essays

[1] *Ante*, pp. 228–30.
[2] *The Birth of Tragedy out of the Spirit of Music.* See also W. McDougall, "The Apollonian and the Dionysian Theories of Man", *The Journal of Philosophy.* Reprinted, *Religion and the Sciences of Life*, 1934.

followed in which he revolted, like Butler, against standardised culture, especially the disposition to magnify and reimpose the humanism which history preserves, instead of deriving therefrom just enough inspiration for to-day's enthusiasm and leaving the rest to the pedant (*Bildungsphilister*). For the same reason he discovered a new value in mythology which allegorised a nation's noblest aspirations and established the continuity of human virtue amid perpetual change.

These ideals were propounded in the series *Unzeitgemässe Betrachtungen* (1873–6) and had already led to his friendship with Wagner, who seemed to fulfil his dream of Dionysian music blended with German legends. When the opening of the Bayreuth opera house in 1876 had shattered this illusion, Nietzsche was still as far as ever from renouncing his principles, but he now began to realise that the man of the future must rediscover his richer Dionysian self in his daily life. We must learn the needs of the spirit from experience, not from art, philosophy or science. In these next two phases, beginning with *Menschliches, Allzumenschliches* (1878) and ending with *Fröhliche Wissenschaft* (1882), he continued to protest against systems of thought, against the dominance of the Apollonian ethics, and to insist that the human race will never rise to its full stature till we have developed the strength and insight to prove our hidden Dionysian nature, to catch it in pregnant movements, and bring to the surface our profoundest instincts in all their freedom and intensity. The secret of a fruitful life was to live dangerously (*gefährlich leben*).[1] Thus, for the future moralist, existence would not be a question of duty, destiny, or disillusion, still less an opportunity for happiness, but *an experiment in self-discovery* (*ein Experiment des Erkennenden*) leading to courage and joyfulness.[2]

Ill-health had necessitated the resignation of his University appointments in 1879 and Nietzsche was wandering in Italy and Switzerland. Between the Engadin and the Riviera he composed the sequence *Also sprach Zarathustra* (1883–5) in which he reaffirmed his Dionysian aspirations as a portrait of the *Uebermensch*. This superman of the future would ruthlessly repudiate any creed, tradition or allegiance which counsels caution, self-contempt or repression; one imagines that he would utterly have scorned his contemporary Mark Rutherford's searchings of heart; he would live to search for imaginative and spiritual treasures. Yet he was not to be a super-egoist, such as Stendhal might have described

---

[1] *Die Fröhliche Wissenschaft*, § 283.   [2] *Ibid.* § 324.

half a century earlier. If he gathered to himself all the joys of life, it was partly for the Dionysian pleasure of sharing his heightened humanity with others. Moreover, he was living for those who came after him, and was prepared to ruin himself if thereby he could ensure the freedom of posterity. He destroyed in order to create, for without graves there could be no resurrection. It must particularly be noted that he also destroyed for another reason: he could not otherwise satisfy his instinct for power. If the man of the future is to escape from the confinement of nineteenth-century civilisation, if he is fully to realise the urges of his nature, he must overflow with aspirations and impulses, and these manifold energies cannot find scope unless he is always bending environment to his will, always changing his world as often as he changes himself. "And this secret did Life tell unto me: 'Lo', it said, 'I am that which must ever overcome itself'."[1] It is also important for our inquiry to remember that Nietzsche's superman was a supermonist. He believed that our basest and most bestial instincts are a part of our strength, that the higher the branches of a tree wave, the deeper its roots strike into darkness and dirt.[2] So the man of the future will not wish to be good but to be noble, for by nobility the philosopher meant the disposition which will not endure waste or futility in oneself, and aims too high to need repression.

Nietzsche was already engaged on a final and yet more comprehensive work, the consummation of his career, when he died in 1900. *Der Wille zur Macht* reaffirms what he had already proclaimed, notably his doctrine of creation as so many centres of impulse, each competing with the rest to become masters of space. Such is the physical universe, such also is man, a mere incident on this single planet of ours, but free, like the other centres of impulse, to assert his will to power. So the test of moral health and progress was the instinct to say *Yes* to all that is strong, *No* to all that is weak. For this reason he again denounces Christianity as the religion of mean-spirited folk, unable to master life; he denounces moral laws because they standardise the virtues, as if all men were spiritually alike and could be catalogued; he attacked Darwinism because it exaggerated the influence of environment at the expense of "that stupendous formative power which creates from within" (*die ungeheure gestaltende, von innen her formenschaffende Gewalt*) and he warns his readers against the emasculating influence of the herd-instinct, which leads to the cult of incompetence and mediocrity—especially

---

[1] *Von der Selbst-Überwindung.*   [2] *Vom Baum am Berge.*

socialism, the refuge of the many, who being themselves weak fear the strength of the few; and fear yet more the leadership of nature's aristocracy.

The reception of these doctrines—or of the name of their author —provides an illuminating side-light on the age. During his own lifetime, his assertions and asseverations aroused the inevitable opposition, even in his own country. Yet by 1897 F. Toennies could write *Der Nietzsche Kultus*, and in 1904 W. Hauff, *Die Ueberwindung des Schopenhauerischen Pessimismus durch F. Nietzsche*. In England two publishing ventures on a series of translations failed, and by 1901 there had appeared only an essay by H. Havelock Ellis in *Affirmations* (1898), a Cornell University Study, and Grant Richard's volume of extracts. Yet in 1903 Bernard Shaw in *Man and Superman* loudly praised Nietzsche and alludes to his vogue and on 7 March in the same year *The Athenaeum* writes: "No contemporary foreign name is more frequently met with than the name of Nietzsche."

It seems that very few people had read the philosopher carefully, but many had caught some idea of his doctrines, and had gradually been prepared for their influence by Meredith, Swinburne (especially in *Herda*) and Oscar Wilde. Young men in revolt against the old order were attracted by the cry for self-determinism through self-adjustment, the plea for the sublimation, not the repression, of our lower nature, the protest against the mediocrity, the spiritual incompetence and the domination of the masses. So even quite second-rate authors played no small part in popularising Nietzsche's name. For instance, Thomas Common, who had abjured Christianity, while studying for the ministry in Edinburgh, was seeking his own explanation of life in the 'nineties and found it convincingly expounded by the German. Henceforth, he dedicated his life to the cult of the philosopher, and in that cause he brought out from 1903 to 1915 his rather attractively naïve but sincere biennial *The Good European*. A. R. Orage wrote with more enthusiasm than judgment on the same theme in 1906–7, and A. M. Ludovici in 1908–11. H. L. Mencken published *The Philosophy of Nietzsche* in 1908, J. M. Kennedy *The Quintessence of Nietzsche* in 1909 and G. C. Hill *The Philosophy of Nietzsche* in 1912. Meanwhile A. Tille had been superintending an English translation of the German's works since 1896 and finally, 1909–13, O. Levy edited *The Works of Nietzsche: The First Complete and Authorised English Translation*. In 1915 his doctrines of "The Will to Power" and "The Superman" were attacked by W. Archer and W. Cross as manifestations of German war policy, and in the same year, partly as a counterblast to such misunderstandings, A. Wolf delivered at University College, London, the first scholarly and scientific exposition of his philosophy.

At the present time some of his ideas and even phrases are household words among people who read no foreign language. What surprises one most is his unconscious agreement with Butler, especially in his distrust of nineteenth-century culture, his trust in the newly realised sense of life, and his insistence on self-expression as more essential than thought. Both these philosophers, however, seem to be unreliable because they are too contentious, yet wistful, even imaginative: the age needed help from the dispassionate insight of science and critical judgment. So it is important to note that Henri Bergson was affirming a similar philosophy by logic and observation and was using science to release his age not from its guidance but from its tyranny.

In *Essai sur les Données Immédiates de la Conscience* (1889) he discussed the most intimate of our notions, a concept which often becomes a sentiment, the idea of time, and he demonstrated that scientists and teachers who talk by the book had accustomed us to think of time as if it were spatial—to divide a period into equidistant lengths of minutes, hours, days or centuries much as one can divide a mile into inches, feet, yards. Such a method helped to establish scientific laws and to that extent was justifiable, but meanwhile it stultified our knowledge of ourselves. It prevented us from realising that deep down in our essential *psyche* we have no past in the sense of periods divided from the present. Time is not like the successive taps of a blind man feeling his way along a stretch of pavement, but like a melody in which all the notes weave themselves into a pattern, the first as living and present as the last. If we look into the recollected experiences which make up our consciousness of ourselves, we shall find an assemblage of influences all active within the mind (even if some be temporarily overlooked). Any object which has any interest for us, may have started by existing in the so-called past, but as long as it endures and engages our attention, it also gathers our thoughts round it, works its way into our minds, progresses with our progress. Each moment of its duration alters its configuration. Thus time is an illusion. The longer a thing lasts the more it mixes with our growing volume of consciousness.

If *Essai* shook our confidence in the all-sufficiency of science, *Matière et Mémoire, Essai sur la Relation du Corps à l'Esprit* (1896) completed the disillusionment by limiting the functions of human intelligence. The philosopher begins by establishing that the organs of sense were not evolved to discover abstract truth. For instance, the eye of an animal does not reveal the reality of things; it only guides its possessor among them. So with the eye of the Mind. We have developed our intelligence not in order to understand nou-mena (which is impossible) but to make the best use of phenomena. Even science and philosophy are justified only as far as they are practical—as means to action, not as means to knowledge for its own sake. They do not explain reality but make it serve our needs. Knowledge, in fact, was power, and Bergson was anticipating Nietzsche's definition of scientific learning as "Nature converted into concepts in order to rule her".[1]

These paradoxes, published as theses in philosophy, would probably not have penetrated far beyond their native academic circle, if they had not cumulated in *L'Évolution Créatrice* (1907). In this stimulating essay Bergson follows up his previous train of reasoning to see how far his conclusions will help towards under-standing the laws of self-fulfilment. If his former inductions were right, if we become conscious of our past only as an urge which swells the present and moves it forward, then such must be our only true idea of reality, and existence is for us a continual trans-formation—the emergence of a force which we call life. It may be desirable for the intellect to represent this force in more precise terms, but when it is studied through the knowledge of our con-scious and unconscious selves, we perceive that evolution does not work on a plan. The life which moves through us is "un jaillisse-ment ininterrompu de nouveautés",[2] an unbroken energy infused into the accretions which obstruct its course, a jet of steam struggling against condensation; not a bullet describing a single trajectory, but a shell bursting into fragments, each fragment destined to become a shell. Only now and then can we get a glimpse of this penetrating *élan vital* in its single simple purity; for instance, in maternal love.

As long as this diversification is easy and effective, and the vital jet strikes through its outlets to its purpose, life is unconscious of

[1] *Der Wille zur Macht*, §610: "Umwandlung der Natur in Begriffe zum Zweck der Beherrschung der Natur."

[2] "A continuous and eruptive urgency full of surprises."

itself and is known to us only as instinct. When the purpose is inadequately fulfilled, when it is checked by circumstances, and the being is compelled to hesitate between impulse and act, to choose between different conditions, sometimes even to experiment, select, fabricate and organise, then life becomes conscious and finally expresses itself as intellect. In these speculations he was completing Nietzsche's suggestion that "life is only a *means* to something; it is the expression of Power growing into form".[1] But he went further and explained how man thereby develops the faculty of noting differences, of classifying objects according to their help and hindrance; so also acquires the habit of systematising living phenomena; dividing them into qualities and attributes as if they were really so divisible, as if they constituted an assemblage interrelated like a machine, not an energy which finds expression in continuity and reciprocal interpenetration.

Bergson is far from denying the value of the intellect which has created so many instruments, material and immaterial, wherewith to refashion matter to our purposes. But he insists that the intelligence views things from the outside, sees only the connections between material objects. Instinct thinks and feels from within. So our reason must turn its eyes inward and reawaken and develop instinct. Thus unified and materialised the mind will attain to the insight which we call intuition, or, in the French phrase, *sympathie divinatrice* (sympathy which places itself inside the object) and will penetrate to the secrets of life. Such, for instance, is the disinterested perceptiveness of the artist.

The ideas in *Évolution Créatrice* were bound to spread and to cause searchings of heart. If Bergson was right, then our usual idea of personality was wrong. Having acquired the habit of valuing our psychological life as a series of separable memories, we had invented an indistinct yet static ego (*un moi amorphe, indifférent, immuable*) to connect all our impressions as a string connects pearls. Whereas, instead of extending our self-hood over such isolated, imaginary stages, we should have merged it in the continuous drive of will-power which evolves consciousness. Again, having accustomed ourselves to judge all phenomena by the geometrical methods of the intellect, we had come to expect the same kind of economised order in the vital jet as we found in mathematics or municipal administration. But now it was clear that

[1] *Der Wille zur Macht*, §706: "Das Leben ist nur Mittel zu etwas; es ist der Ausdruck von Wachstumsformen der Macht."

nature moved on a plane independent of those standards, and what we believed to be disorder was only our own disappointment at not finding what we expected; as if a man seeking a volume of poetry in his library might say of a book "this is not verse" instead of "this is prose". And lastly, we had not trusted enough to intuition which moves along the same line as evolution and sheds a flickering light on all that our intellect cannot penetrate: on our personality, origin and destiny. Assuredly we have undiscovered depths within ourselves which science can indicate, imply and suggest but cannot explore. If we are to be conscious of our own significance we must cultivate sensations and cultivate new literary techniques and nomenclatures to bring them within the restricted range of the intelligence.

These three philosophical humanists were worth a careful review, because their teaching contains much that is familiar to any student of contemporary literature. So at first one is tempted to conclude that we have found the answer to our question posed at the beginning of this chapter. The twentieth century has listened to Butler, Nietzsche and Bergson, and having turned its back on the past, is starting on the exploration of its subconscious, vital or Dionysian self, under their impulse, if not leadership. These three either inspire, register or illustrate the modernism of culture, the insistence on what Henri Bataille calls *les vérités intérieures*, the triumph of will-power over intellect. But on second thoughts, it begins to appear that many of their conclusions had already been guessed and implied by the great Victorians. For instance, Carlyle and Tennyson well understood that they must look much deeper than their intellectually conscious selves if they wanted to discover the urge and drive of human nature within them; Ruskin perceived that reality for us is an immense body of impressions hoarded and assimilated by our personality; Browning has a hundred times pictured that wealth of remembered experiences telescoped into the last phase of the human being's character; Arnold has again and again insisted that culture is not an ornament, but the rectification and completion of imperfect human nature; Meredith was well aware of the antithesis between the Apollonian and Dionysian strain, though he called it the Triad; Hardy perceived that human beings inherit and transmit tremendous powers of adaptation to certain qualities of environment, and that their self-fulfilment depends on recognising and satisfying these peculiar appetencies. Even Oscar Wilde proclaimed that the art of life was the vindication, not the suppression, of our lower selves in a sense of beauty. All were conscious of a continuous vital energy permeating the progressive ramifications of life, and rising into consciousness as self-expression. So perhaps after all these philosophers were not so significant as was supposed; they have merely inculcated what the artists had already portrayed.

Then why should the younger generation be so much influenced by these indoctrinations and welcome them as truths newly revealed? Because the older artists had not driven their lessons home. Their insight into human nature was often profound, but, as we have seen, they were bent on disguising their wisdom in the rather modish garbs of Victorian culture. Their philosophy had to wait on the literary, historical or aesthetic professions of the authors; it had to be substantiated in antiquarian monologues, yoked to Anglican or Catholic convictions, enveloped in emotional narratives, or sentimentalised in the preciosities of elegiac poetry. As Victorian culture gradually lost its magic, this underlying wisdom also grew dim. For the soul of man, as we have seen a hundred times, cannot spiritualise an idea without giving it form among the visions and experiences of life. So the new elements of racial and individual self-knowledge might have relapsed into scientific platitudes, unless Butler, Nietzsche and Bergson had again endued them with human significance, and given them back to the world as wisdom which can keep pace with science and can at the same time be tested by our post-Victorian sense of life.

So literature in the twentieth century is to a certain limited degree unique in its material, but chiefly unique in the imaginative forms under which that material shall be presented. There are, of course, many novelists, playwrights, and even poets—some eminent —who prefer the old-fashioned realism of the surface world and have met with their full measure of success. But the significant feature of the age is the number of talented authors who turn their eyes inward, who explore the resources of our *psyche*, especially the reasons which the reason cannot understand, not as speculative psychologists, but in order to discover new springs of thought and action, and thereby create a new interest in conduct. These more experimental writers seem to find that the older forms of artistic expression are useless for their purpose. That is their originality. For instance, free verse asserts its independence of the English poetic tradition. Yet this style of poetry at its best is nothing less than an attempt to give intellectual expression to the vitality which eludes the intellect, and for that reason the practitioners try to convey more by the sound and rhythm of words than by their meaning and to suggest the inward aspiration by fleeting glimpses and apparently irrelevant allusions. For the most part, the new schools seem to be convinced that the spirit has no need of borrowed aspirations and can always create its enthusiasm out of the mysteries of life. T. S. Eliot used to strip his ideas of all their familiar associations, especially the adventitious glamour of literary rhetoric, and present them in such strange and provocative terms that his readers cannot fling the book aside and yet cannot understand it without joining in the author's creative effort; stripping our thoughts to the sinews, so that we can feel the motor nerves at work. Benedetto Croce has argued with all the seriousness of a logical aesthetician that lyricism is nothing else than the act of creating, not the thing created; the passion not its consummation; the flight of the arrow, not the hitting of the mark. D. H. Lawrence seemed to be searching in the depths of his consciousness for something even more fundamental than his inherited instincts, for some primitive and almost cosmic urge too deep for his thinking life, which comes within the range of intellectual observation only when its current is thwarted by some special circumstance in the individual's life. Lawrence made it his business to create such evocative situations. Nor do such neotechnics seem extravagant when we consider where some intuitionists look for their satisfying sense of reality. Marcel Proust and Virginia Woolf are as psychological as Bergson. They demonstrate that in all our daily contacts we rely on an accumulation of anterior experiences; that each person becomes aware of his or her personality by gathering up our previous memories and fusing them with the impressions of the moment, carrying forward an ever-increasing volume of mentality. Proust even called the quest of his spiritual identity "the quest of lost time". E. M. Forster leads one to think that the spirit springs into conscious life only when it meets a kindred spirit, and if so, then the vitality of the soul depends on establishing affinities.

These few names are quoted merely as examples likely to be familiar to the reader. Obviously, no attempt can yet be made to assess or summarise with any chance of accuracy. The literary business is suffering from over-production, like most other industries, and needs restriction of sales, no less than do tea, coffee and whale-products. Until time has enforced elimination, we must be content with guesses. Nevertheless, it seems extremely probable that the creative author of our time is seeking not (as it appears) a new significance in man but new and more convincing illustrations. It also appears that he is astonishingly adventurous, but that up to the present he has not found what he seeks. His failure is so manifest that it often seems as if he were only trying to advertise himself; having missed fame he may at least hit its counterfeit, prominence. Such a conclusion is justified in the sense that every author wishes to be read, and stands a poor chance, unless he is also talked about. But he does not generally stay in the conversation much less the memory of his contemporaries unless he handles something which is passing in their minds. Now these experimental writers are prominent because they handle those thoughts of their readers which are obscure, often inarticulate, and play the dangerous game of making other people feel that they need to be taught. Even when catching the veering wind of public attention, they merit Nietzsche's admiration for the man who risks downfall in order to prepare the way for posterity. Such is their venture. They are trying to direct the undercurrents of educated opinion before literature has established the canals which could contain the stream. So it is premature to compare talents or talk of immortality. They are explorers who have not yet found the promised land, and so their bones will probably whiten the track over which a more experienced caravan will pass.

Having traced the progress or regress of culture up to this point, it would seem that *Towards the Twentieth Century* has now reached its end. Yet not altogether so. The purpose of this volume is to retrace the steps of the last century in the hope of discovering its influence on the consciousness of our own era. So it yet remains to inquire whether we have also gathered from the failures and successes of the past some indications which may help us in choosing our own paths.

CHAPTER XXIV

Review of our conclusions—Can we look on scientific and industrial civilisation with the same eyes as we look on our ideals?—Can we contemplate life in the spirit though not in the style of great literature?— J. S. Haldane, J. Romains, and T. Mann help us towards an answer.

In the preceding chapter we came to the conclusion that present-day writers do not easily satisfy the spiritual needs of their contemporaries—do not fill the imagination with thoughts which revive our confidence in ourselves and our joy in the life around us. Why is the twentieth century so hard to please? To answer that question let us recall our present hopes and fears as they had grown upon us out of our spiritual past.

Our attitude to life may, perhaps, be summarised as follows. Man realises that he is by extraction an animal, and, what is worse, the descendant of beasts of prey; that these prehuman ancestors hunted all that were weaker than themselves, fled from all that were stronger, suffered every misery except the consciousness of their desperate plight and were possessed only by that mysterious energy termed life, that is, the will to multiply and propagate their kind, the most perishable and defenceless being generally the most wastefully prolific. Man differs from these ancestors, amongst other points, chiefly in his ability to be conscious of this destiny, to investigate, explain and allegorise its causes, and to devise remedies for both body and mind. The nineteenth century promised fair to carry forward this process of self-determination to undreamt of lengths, but modern science, so potent to mitigate our physical evils, has intensified our moral perplexity. It has confirmed the desolating suspicion that the spirit of that wild animal life still lurks under the elaborate organisation of society. We are still beasts of prey (at any rate by instinct) living on each other, and propagating our species. In fact, modern civilisation, in concealing the struggle for life among its thousand newly evolved activities, has intensified our opportunities. The richer the world, the more the inducements to live at our neighbour's expense.

And yet, despite this scientific animalism, the tradition persists, as confidently as ever, that man has somehow and somewhere a second superhuman, or at least deanimalised nature, capable of infinite development; and he has looked to culture, earnestly and eagerly, to render this potential self a reality. Just like the poets and humanists of the romantic movement, he has concentrated on self-examination, though under the cold light of science his introspection has recently become self-analysis. If there is any truth in the foregoing chapters he has been disappointed in his trust. Nineteenth-century culture has not moved with the times.

We have again and again discussed the causes. They might be summarised by saying that in the nineteenth century writers and readers mistook education for culture. Both classes came to the experiences of life with their minds made up for them. Instead of being prepared for all the surprises and wonders of a changing world, they expected what they had been taught to expect: either the worldly contentment promised by the Victorian religions; or the stage effects which can always be enjoyed in the pardonable enthusiasms of historical and humanistic study; or again, growing dependent on the organisations of the modern state, they expected evolution to manage their private affairs as efficiently and economically as a business office. They convinced themselves that life, like a railway train, must have a destination as well as a destiny. Not finding what was sought, both writers and readers lost sympathy in their own civilisation. Some of our finest geniuses sought inspiration from the past purged of its realism, or criticised the present in the spirit of some bygone moralist. If Newman, Tennyson, Browning, Carlyle, Froude, Arnold, Ruskin, Pater, Hardy or even Meredith were asked to justify their attitude, they would reply that human ideals must indeed thrive on actions, but cannot thrive on the activities conditioned by modern industrialism. Our mechanical, commercial age narrows and represses humanity, intensifies our animal egoisms and makes us despise the spiritual values which our fathers bequeathed us.

So literature became a refuge from life rather than a lamp to illumine its ways, all the more because the seclusion of a library suggested continuity with the Good Old Times. Thanks to the modern abundance of cheap teachers and cheaper text-books, this communion with the living dead has now been pushed so far that nigh every university has a faculty for the study and appreciation of its national literature. An immense number of young people (mostly women) receive every year a degree for knowing "the best that has been thought and written", and yet the vast majority acquire no interest in the world around them, nor apparently any sense of life at all. They are content to look at the history of the mind through academic spectacles. In fact, the study of literature is generally so completely divorced from its creativeness that the more experimental and imaginative writers seem to turn away, almost in contempt, from this tradition which converts quite harmlessly commonplace people into prigs and pedants. Yet, as we have seen, the revolutionaries and originals have not recovered the place which their Victorian predecessors have gradually lost.

Such seems to be the position of the modern man of culture. Having resigned his traditional religion under the influence of science, and then having discarded the materialism of science under the influence of experience (especially inward experience), he is now looking for a new spirituality which must be authorised by science and yet contain a religious value. This ideal is still a shadowy ghost because literature has not discovered how to give it the clear outline of a living form.

We have also learnt from the past that literature still suffers from isolation; shrinks from contact with the world and with science which does or did so much to despiritualise the world. As we are now looking to the future, it is instructive to note that one of these estrangements may well be healed. J. S. Haldane's *The Philosophy of a Biologist* (1935) marks an important step in the reconciliation of these two jealous rivals, all the more welcome since the humanism of the future will surely need to recognise, and in some respects reverence, the lore of the laboratory and the telescope.

A glance at his philosophy is well within our special scope, for the professor epitomises and to some extent consummates the nineteenth century quest for truth. He began by trusting in the thinkers from Descartes onward who sacrificed religion to science and developed philosophy as a compensation. He found them all unsatisfying, even Kant and Hegel, because no one shows how the idea of God can be allied to human consciousness. With this question in his mind, he turned to science which has dominated European thought from the mid-century onwards. Here he found everywhere the mystery of co-ordinated activity. Physics teaches that the elemental phenomena, space, time and motion, depend on one another and imply an all-embracing unity. Biology carries the inquirer a step further and proves that organisms also combine and co-ordinate all their activities so as to conserve the single vital principle by which they resist or control their environment. In psychology, this relativity becomes the conscious projection of oneself into one's environment, the marshalling of hopes and fears as motives for conduct, the concentration of thought on the exigencies of life—in a word, as personality. And now it is discovered that this more complex relationship is no longer complete within itself. The human being is not fully conscious of his personality till he co-operates with his fellow-creatures, serving the claims of family and society, joining forces with others in order to sustain himself. Up to the present we have studied these units, each battling for himself in a world of chaos and death. When we pass from science to art we perceive a yet higher and wider co-ordination. We find that the human being at his final development is haunted by a certain religious sense which, when stripped of its theological accretions, amounts to an aspiration towards Beauty, Truth, Righteousness. This aptitude is just as demonstrable as any other scientific fact, but it differs, in one respect, from the lower human attributes: it cannot be realised as long as the human being stays within his single self. The religious sense is a creative energy uniting individual personalities with each other and merging them into an all-embracing composite personality, which is God. The deity of science is in no way akin to the old anthropomorphic creator, who ought to have made a better world. It is the will to perfection, evoked in opposition to sorrow and sin, roused to action by the resistance of brute matter and human perversity. Thus evolution culminates in the highest of all co-ordinations: the assimilation of mortals to a cosmic influence, itself immortal.

This necessarily inadequate summary gives no idea of the depth and width of Haldane's slim volume, hardly bigger than a pamphlet. The author is anything but a dreamer. He trusts to his immense resources of scientific observation and philosophic insight to visualise personality evolving out of co-ordination—personality both human and divine. It should also be remembered that Haldane does not, like Romanes,[1] half apologise for his life of research, leaving it as soon as he can to assert the intimations of his inward self. This ultra-modern biologist stakes the peace of his soul on philosophical treatises and the experiments of the laboratory. Yet in his hands science almost develops into art—intuition substantiated by the intellect—and he ends his long career by establishing the spiritual harmony which the ancient world maintained. "The philosopher listens in his own soul for an echo of the world's unison, and then proclaims it as a theory which others

[1] *Ante*, pp. 331-3.

can understand." Those words admirably summarise the impression which *The Philosophy* leaves behind it, yet originally they were applied to Thales[1] who taught 2500 years ago that water is the source and substance of all created things, using that figure to symbolise (quite inadequately) the unity underlying phenomena, the thesis that *All is One*. So the modern Englishman and the ancient Greek both use their special studies to fulfil the purpose of culture: to concentrate all our instincts and experiences in an idea or figure such as the intellect can interpret, and the spirit can idealise. Assuredly, it would seem that the Englishman had bridged the gulf between literature and science.

Or rather, he had shown that the gulf could and can be bridged, but no more. There must surely be a feeling among many who have admired the book that Haldane has not given us all we want; and as soon as *The Philosophy of a Biologist* is viewed in relation to nineteenth-century tendencies and twentieth-century needs, its one defect is manifest. Like Victorian culture it is too remote and academic. If Haldane has found the truth, we are our spiritual selves only at Beethoven concerts, on mountain glaciers, or by the lake under a starlit sky; perhaps in college rooms when midnight conversation renders sleep impossible. It is not suggested that such are the necessary implications of his religion, but such are the only conditions under which it becomes real to this able exponent. Wisdom may cry without and utter her voice in the streets, but our philosopher hears her in moments of self-escape and self-recovery amid the refined distractions of an erudite profession. This was the temptation to which the romantic schools succumbed, and which has been handed on ever since. But man's whole nature cries out against such restrictions. If the spirit really does rise to conscious self-fulfilment in this interrelationship wide as creation, we must be able to feel its presence in our daily lives; not of course in every action, but in every motive and proclivity. Such an interpretation cannot be left to a theorist. Literature must absorb his wisdom, make it effective in our civilisation, prove it by our usual experiences.

Curiously enough a novelist of note has come near to grasping these possibilities. In *Mort de quelqu'un* (1911) Jules Romains demonstrated that a lonely and inconspicuous person, of no interest

---

[1] F. Nietzsche, *Die Philosophie im tragischen Zeitalter der Griechen*, § 3: "Der Philosoph sucht den Gesamtklang der Welt in sich nachtönen zu lassen und ihn aus sich herauszustellen in Begriffen."

to the world whatever, cannot die without starting endless ripples of cause and effect, which ramify through the community on a network of fleeting thoughts. This idea of social unanimism, of *solidarité universelle*, is being developed and exemplified in quite surprising ways in the series *Les Hommes de Bonne Volonté*, and offers a splendid opportunity for rehabilitating civilisation. Romains certainly has cast a new light on the importance of sheer thought, its contiguity and communicativeness, the way notions spread from head to head, intertwining society by invisible links; but it is a hard, cold light. Human beings seem to be eddying in rather pitiful circles under this intangible influence. Romains does not yet seem to have visualised any higher or more fruitful co-ordination. He is too near the mean streets just as Haldane is too near the stars. So even if they were to hold out hands it is probable that neither could reach the other.

If we can trust the evidence of the last hundred years, this dichotomy is a vice of modern civilisation, the result of over-education and under-culture. The idealist feels strong in the abstract world, but weak among the claims of manhood and womanhood. Like Baudelaire's albatross

Ses ailes de géant l'empêchent de marcher,

and he would rather haunt the skies than crawl on the earth; so strong is the Victorian tradition, reinforced by post-Victorian discontent. The old masters did not suffer in that way. The heroic age of the Achaeans was a period of cruelty, baseness and unendurable egoisms; a life of rapine and futile conflicts; hordes of men crowding on to their enemies with yells of defiance and then breaking into flight. Yet the outstanding feature of the *Iliad* and the *Odyssey* is human grandeur. Or take the Athenian drama. Its themes originated in odious and orgiastic crimes, cannibalism, incest, matricide, and treachery. Yet who have created nobler figures than Aeschylus and Sophocles? Modern travelling agencies enable almost everybody to wander at will among the enchantments of medieval culture. The tourist admires the unity of effect— a thousand emotions blend in a single aspiration which is certainly not the renunciation of the world. The architectural outlines, like "frozen music", the stained glass, the filigree tracery, and especially the pictures, breathe the sensations of life and recreate the wonders of medieval existence. It comes almost as a shock that all this concerted creativeness has evolved out of the doctrine of Original

Sin, and the contemplation of human perversity, and that the same desolating conviction underlies *La Divina Commedia* and *Paradise Lost*. The more modern developments of literature become too complicated to be summarised allusively, but it might be remembered that the Elizabethan drama throve on the influences which the Renaissance most feared, the dominance of the baser passions; and in the eighteenth century, when life seemed to have lost its zest for adventure and discovery, the literary imagination found scope in recognising the charm of town life (including the Stock Exchange, coffee-house and theatre-gallery) or in celebrating what man could accomplish by sheer force of intellect. But examples need not be multiplied. It will surely not be disputed that the virtue and value of literature consist not so much in the rectification or reconstruction of life, still less in its idealisation, as in the discovery of human worth, a residuum hidden somewhere and somehow among the uses and pursuits of every civilisation.

If, then, we may trust the history of culture, contemporary authors are too fond of the reverse of the medal when seeking their inspiration or their material. They seem to be haunted by the injustice, vulgarity, materialism and self-indulgence of the twentieth century, whether they turn away from the spectacle in disgust, or dwell lovingly on the more repulsive features. Yet our age, like every other, offers its special prize, or rather, its two special prizes, one genuine and the other counterfeit. The true prize is power, and the false prize is wealth, not the wealth which creates power, but which often takes its place and acts as if it were the more genuine. The grandeur of possessions passes for the grandeur of the possessor, even in his own estimation. But power, as offered by this century, is no longer, as in Victorian times, the control of other people, but the control and direction of oneself. It is personal freedom. It is our privilege to be free from prejudice, class-sentiment, false-delicacy, superstition, sectarianism; to be free from the persuasion that slum-poverty and industrial serfdom are necessary vices of modern society; or that disease is a destiny to which everybody must submit; free, again, to argue ourselves out of the unhappiness and self-depreciation which we now know to be self-inflicted; and free to realise our dreams of self-expression, at any rate, by proxy. And not only by proxy. The very poor, like the very weak, are still excluded from achievement, but the rest of us need not always be content with imagining the adventures of explorers, athletes, antiquarians and naturalists. Even quite modest citizens can now and then rake among the dead bones of antiquity or climb into the perilous solitudes of the Alps, or watch (if not imitate) the grace and ease of accomplished ski-runners who have surely surpassed the Greek ideal, even as imagined by Grecians, or, finally, can enjoy those appliances for personal cleanliness and domestic refinement, which Milton and Louis XIV never knew. It is the virtue of our age to free the mind by freeing the body.

This outlook is clouded, but not darkened, by the world-crisis through which we are passing, and which almost compels the optimist to believe that backward races may trust in the League of Nations but progressives must trust in poison-gas. The complicated exigencies of nationalism, political administration, and financial redistribution do not prove that the spirit is only breath nor that the individual is a fool to believe in individual worth. The danger which threatens our moral freedom is moral licence. Now that man has acquired so much knowledge about himself, and his environment, he may be hypnotised by the prospect of his own opportunities, may lose "the good-humoured resignation in the daily imperfections of human well-being which formed the discipline of earlier generations",[1] may develop an insatiable hunger for the unknown, and may set his heart on the accumulation of impressions which efface each other, till he is left with only a craving for inexperienced sensations, just as the vulgar classes imagine that an orgy of noise is the only expression of cheerfulness. We may also lose sight of human limitations. Now that the powers above us appear to be falling within our reach, soon to submit to the powers within us, we shall never again worship God as a man, but we may begin to worship Man as a god. Solitude and contemplation will always be necessary to correct this latest and basest anthropomorphism. But in this age it is the humanist's special concern to see that philosophic and religious meditation lead us to accept the responsibilities of our civilisation—not as regards the destructiveness of warfare or of industrial unrest—but as regards the problem of self-realisation. Will authors succeed in rediscovering the prime and primeval virtues in a twentieth-century guise or disguise, will they demonstrate that self-expenditure amid the distractions of civilisation can quicken the intellect and enlarge the sympathies as of old? Can they trace a spiritual community

[1] J. Huizinga, *In the Shadow of Tomorrow*, 1935. Transl. J. H. Huizinga, 1936, chap. XI.

beneath the flashy, jazz-jigging hurry of modern existence, with its crowded railway stations, its congested streets, and its mania for gambling with the resources of society?

The literature of the immediate future must reveal how human worth should and could illumine these slippery complicated ways which do not all lead downwards. Such is the example set by the great works of the past; and such seems to be the direction which present-day thought is taking. Some of our novelists, poets and dramatic writers are beginning to portray new aptitudes and susceptibilities, new senses of contact, more intimate understandings and affinities which are bred out of the business of life. Perhaps the most remarkable exponent of this incipient tendency is not an Englishman but Germany's most eminent novelist, Thomas Mann. He seems to have explored the romantic cult of nature in the depths of his being, even the mysteries of sleep and death, and to have sought for a sense of reality in solitary self-contemplation and the self-surrender induced by music. So it was not without having tested solipsism, that he turned away from the dreams and aspirations of the temperamental artist, away from all the intensive culture which stakes its salvation on the inward life, and that he became a disciple of Nietzsche and studied the love of life and the will to power.[1] Under his influence Mann has produced one widely read novel, *Buddenbrooks* (1900), and many even more significant short stories, to show how men could make as well as mar their souls in the pursuit of this world. But because nature and spirit are not always to be adapted to Nietzsche's dream of power, he was quick to revise without revoking his theories. It is noteworthy that in order to adjust the inner to the outer life he has reverted to Goethe, the nineteenth century's most practical counsellor (as we have seen) whenever the spirit has come to grips with its earthly environment.

So Thomas Mann's literary development is some sort of evidence that culture may be moving in the direction which this chapter suggests. Possibly the reader may agree up to this point but may object that the prospect does not end in a goal worthy of our spiritual history. It discloses no divine far-off event, no reunion with the superhuman; it reveals science insisting that nature has no other object than her own survival, and that our best hope is to be merged in the continuity of life. Such a conclusion distressed the idealists of the nineteenth century, but need not distress their

[1] *Ante*, pp. 357-9.

successors in the twentieth, because our present discontents impose a concerted spiritual effort, a creative anti-materialism, which quickens the imagination and unites the well-wishers in their aspiration towards a freer, more intelligent future. The culture of the future need not falsify facts but must transfigure them. Self-devotion, often involving self-sacrifice, involves so many enthusiasms and visions that for the present it may take the place of a less worldly religion. Instead of teleology, it implies entelechy. The creed which Newman, Tennyson and Carlyle rejected was good enough for Prometheus who taught men to conquer life which would otherwise conquer them. By the time that this problem has been solved, our descendants will have passed into another phase of civilisation which concerns neither the readers nor the writer of this book.

EPILOGUE

In the course of this long inquiry we have watched three persuasions pass through educated opinion. First, the belief in a creative Intelligence permeating the Universe and reaching its consummation in the human mind which can divine the supernatural scheme and sketch its purpose in art and philosophy. This tendency may best be associated with Goethe, who still had the power to hold such beliefs and to live them and clothe them in human shapes. English literature failed to substantiate this reasoned supernaturalism among the developments of Victorian industry and science. But the science which discarded Goethe's *Hinterland* established in the mid-century the idea of man as a being who condemns mysticism for mystification, but relies on the sheer power of his intellect, and expects by dint of observation and logic to find his own best human way among the phenomena which he can never hope to understand. This religion of intellectual confidence and clear-headed discussion may be associated with J. S. Mill.

Out of that principle there has arisen a third system such as Mill never visualised—or, at least one feels that some such emergence will be the fruit of post-Darwinian culture—a scheme infinite yet definite, a body of ordered theories which stagger the imagination and yet conform to the control of human calculations. Such is the new scientific humanism in which Physics, after a century's controversy and research has displaced Metaphysics in the quest for ultimate reality. This principle enables thought to wander among insoluble mysteries with the confidence of Theseus, holding fast to his clue; and to wander among human contingencies with the confidence of Prometheus who knows enough of social and physiological causes to begin controlling the effects.

This is the world of humanistic insight and scientific imagination, which poets, moralists, and novel writers also must capture.

INDEX